The Chinese Way

As business becomes increasingly globalized and China establishes its growing role in the international business environment, developing an understanding of the complex culture is important to anyone acting in the global arena. This book offers readers a thorough and nuanced resource to that end, describing the ever-evolving Chinese way of life circa 2014, based on extensive primary and secondary data.

Taking an anthropological approach to achieve a well-rounded representation, the book covers 51 topics that would have been studied if China were a newly discovered civilization. It explores the culture through its examination of the nine core concepts that best represent the Chinese way of life. While the book is a rigorous treatment of the Chinese way of life, it is also filled with personal stories and perspectives from close to 1000 successful Chinese from academia, business, and government.

The Chinese Way equips international business students, scholars, and practitioners with a deep understanding of a society that is a major player in global business today and offers a foundation for successful business interactions with Chinese companies, organizations, and people.

Min Ding is the Smeal Professor of Marketing and Innovation at Pennsylvania State University, USA and Advisory Professor of Marketing and Director of Institute for Sustainable Innovation and Growth (iSIG) at Fudan University, China.

Jie Xu is a Research Associate at Institute for Sustainable Innovation and Growth (iSIG), Fudan University, China.

The Chinese Way

Min Ding & Jie Xu

NEW YORK AND LONDON

First published 2015
by Routledge
711 Third Avenue, New York, NY 10017

and by Routledge
2 Park Square, Milton Park, Abingdon, Oxon OX14 4RN

Routledge is an imprint of the Taylor & Francis Group, an informa business

© 2015 Min Ding

The right of Min Ding & Jie Xu to be identified as authors of this work has been asserted in accordance with sections 77 and 78 of the Copyright, Designs and Patents Act 1988.

All rights reserved. No part of this book may be reprinted or reproduced or utilised in any form or by any electronic, mechanical, or other means, now known or hereafter invented, including photocopying and recording, or in any information storage or retrieval system, without permission in writing from the publishers.

Trademark notice: Product or corporate names may be trademarks or registered trademarks, and are used only for identification and explanation without intent to infringe.

Library of Congress Cataloging-in-Publication Data
Ding, Min, 1967-
The Chinese way / Min Ding & Jie Xu.
    pages cm
Includes bibliographical references and index.
1. China—Social life and customs—21st century. 2. National characteristics, Chinese. I. Xu, Jie, 1988- II. Title.
DS779.43.D56 2015
951.06′12—dc23   2014007395

ISBN: 978-0-415-53496-3 (hbk)
ISBN: 978-0-415-53497-0 (pbk)
ISBN: 978-1-317-81830-4 (ebk)

Typeset in 10/12 Minion Pro
by codeMantra

Printed and bound in the United States of America by
Edwards Brothers Malloy on sustainably sourced paper

Contents

Preface		ix
1	The Chinese Way of Life, Version 2014	1

PART I
Customs and Traditions

9

2	Face: The Three-Tiered Chinese Version of Honor	11
3	From a Nation of Etiquette to a Society of Gifting	15
4	Presumption of Untrustworthiness (Guilt)	21
5	Unwritten Rules	25
6	Promises	31
7	Pursuit of Quick Success and Instant Benefits (PQSIB)	37
8	Drinking Culture	41

PART II
Social Structure

49

9	Harmonious Society	51
10	Subcultures	57
11	Social Circles	63

vi   *Table of Contents*

12	Employment Equality	69
13	The Status of Women	77
14	Migrant Workers	83

PART III
Marriage and Family

89

15	Families	91
16	Ideal Spouse and Child	97
17	Extramarital Relationships	101
18	Divorce and Divorcees	107
19	Leftover Women	113

PART IV
Needs, Values, and Aspirations

121

20	Life Objectives and the Chinese Dream	123
21	Role Models	129
22	The Generations	133
23	The Nouveau Riche	139
24	Environmentalism	143

PART V
World View

149

25	Attitude towards Foreign Nations	151
26	Cultural Identity	157
27	Faux Emigrants	163

Table of Contents   *vii*

PART VI
Religion and Belief

169

28   Religions and Faith

171

29   Superstition

179

PART VII
Arts and Entertainment

185

30   Nine Traditional Skills of the Cultured Chinese

187

31   Duanzi

193

32   Cuisines and Restaurants

199

33   Nightlife

207

PART VIII
Governing System

215

34   Political System: Governing as Partners

217

35   The Legislative System: People's Congresses

225

36   Administrative System

231

37   The Legal System

237

38   Corruption

243

39   Social Thoughts

251

PART IX
Economic System

257

40   The Three Types of Chinese Companies

259

41   Business to Business

267

viii Table of Contents

42	The Business to Consumer Market	273
43	Brands	279
44	Pursuit of Expensive Products	285

PART X
Education System   291

45	K–12 and Beyond	293
46	Studying Abroad	299
47	Executive Master of Business Administration (EMBA)	305
48	Professors and Scholarship	311

PART XI
Communication System   317

49	Unidirectional Communication	319
50	Bidirectional Communication	325
51	Open Circle Communication	331
52	Closed Circle Communication	337

Index   343

Preface

English writer Alexander Pope once wrote, "A little learning is a dangerous thing." This quote was exactly what came to mind when a senior VP from a large, privately-owned Chinese chemical company told us the following story. He and two of his colleagues traveled to North Carolina recently to negotiate a deal with a chemical company to establish a possible joint venture in Shanghai. The discussion went well, and they signed the agreement. On the eve before their return trip, they each received a nicely wrapped present from their American partners after dinner. Upon returning to their hotel rooms and opening their presents, to their astonishment and bewilderment (and probably outrage although he didn't tell us explicitly), they each found a nicely made small coffin. Why on earth would anyone give a coffin as a gesture of good will? (One must remember that the Chinese generally see things as omens, and they do not even give each other clocks as presents since the phrase "song zhong" [give someone a clock] is pronounced the same as "be at one's side until he/she dies.") But coffins? After throwing the coffins in the hotel's trashcan and returning to China, they told their associates about this experience and eventually discovered that in one part of Guangxi province, there is indeed a custom of giving someone a toy coffin as a gesture of good will based on pronunciations. "Coffin" is pronounced "guan cai" in Chinese; guan is pronounced the same as the character for "government official" and cai is pronounced the same as the character for "wealth." So in that particular part of China, giving someone a coffin symbolizes wishing someone well because acquiring a position in government and/or gaining more wealth are both desirable outcomes in China. The only problem, of course, is that the majority of the Chinese population has no idea this custom exists and would be greatly offended to receive a coffin as a gift.

However, we cannot blame the students alone. This led us to paraphrase Pope's famous statement as: "Dumbing down a complex subject is a dangerous thing." Teachers must bear responsibility when they simplify a complicated topic to the extent that superficial and distorted interpretations are all but guaranteed. On a topic as important and as complex as China, one cannot afford to be the wrong type of teacher or student.

Today, one needs no justification for wanting to understand China. The best recipe for helping someone understand China has two ingredients: comprehensiveness and descriptiveness. Comprehensiveness is required in the presence of complexity. China is a country with a very long and uninterrupted culture. One cannot possibly understand the Chinese until she has at least some understanding of all things that are important to them, as everything they do and think are intricately related in that background. For example, it would be folly to try to

x Preface

understand how the Chinese do business only by observing how they do business. The second ingredient is descriptiveness. As human beings, we have the urge to simplify our tasks so that we can do things more efficiently or at least with less effort. People often ask us what they should or should not do when visiting China or how to do business with or against the Chinese. A Chinese person may not even know what he would do in a given situation. (We discuss being flexible as a key Chinese characteristic later in the book.) Thus, the answers to these seemingly simple questions are actually quite complex.

The best way to learn about China is not by studying heuristics, theories, or anything that has been abstracted away from real Chinese life (i.e., a prescriptive approach). Rather, one must get to know how the Chinese think and live in real life in order to make appropriate judgments in specific situations as to how a Chinese person might think or act (i.e., a descriptive approach). The challenge to this descriptive approach is that real data are hard to come by in China. The Chinese will not tell you anything that you cannot read from public sources unless they trust you completely, and they are very good at telling you politically correct stories (or the stories you want to hear). Books based on Western style interviews and focus groups with Chinese participants, or those based on the personal experiences of expatriates in China, for example, are often ridiculed. Many have asked us, "Do Westerners really believe that?"

The book you are reading now was written to pass a face validity check by the Chinese, with large doses of both comprehensiveness and descriptiveness. One thing should be made clear, however. This is not intended to be a timeless book on China. One of the major characteristics of China is that it is evolving, and quickly. This book is an attempt to describe, in a comprehensive and candid manner, *the Chinese way of life circa 2014.*

This book contains 52 short chapters. Chapter 1 presents an overview of the Chinese way of life in 2014. Chapters 2–52 are organized into 11 sections based on content. The subjects of the sections and chapters follow anthropological standards based on topics that would be studied in a newly identified culture. This ensures that our descriptions of Chinese society to outsiders are as comprehensive as possible. While we have ensured comprehensive coverage at the topic level, it is not possible to comprehensively describe each topic, given the inherent limitations of a book. Instead, for each topic, we drill down on a few key details to reveal its depth and richness, just as prospectors will drill a few wells in an oil field to prove oil reserves to potential investors.

This book is meant to be descriptive; as storytellers, we have striven to synthesize material into a coherent story without contaminating the plot with our personal perspective. There are two exceptions to this descriptive rule. First, we have included a segment at the end of each chapter (except Chapter 1) called "Road Ahead," where we do often share our perspective on the topic covered in that chapter. The second exception is Chapter 1. In attempting to provide an overview of Chinese way of life in 2014, we must weave into the chapter our own judgment in the process of abstraction and conceptualization.

We adopted a two-pronged approach to data collection for each topic. First, we collected secondary data. We surveyed all types of public sources for information related to each topic, including books, newspapers, magazines, blogs, and social media. (We discuss the importance of such unofficial writings in the communication section in the book.) All such data were collected from material written in Chinese, although English language websites also were consulted on some topics. Second, we collected primary data from Chinese citizens from all walks of life. These data informed the core of the majority of chapters where publicly available information tends to be superficial, biased, or uninformative. As we mentioned earlier, the Chinese will only tell you their true thoughts if they trust you. So, all of our primary data were collected from people we know, who felt comfortable telling us the truth (or felt uncomfortable giving us "official" responses, knowing that it would be disrespectful to us). The primary data were collected from approximately 1,000 individuals. The largest group was comprised of EMBA students Min taught from 2010–2013 at Fudan University. Data were collected in various forms while he was teaching them and afterwards. The second largest group was intellectuals in China. The third group included Chinese students and faculty with whom we interacted outside of China. The fourth group included personal friends who have occupied various positions in China. To ensure data quality, we only asked them to describe their personal experiences and perspectives, or the experiences and perspectives of people they knew. In other words, there was a maximum of two degrees of separation for each account. Some data were collected in classrooms using a question and answer format. Most data, however, were collected during conversations at dinner parties (see our discussion in the relevant chapters on the importance of dinner parties) and some over lunch. Conservatively speaking, we probably attended 60 to 80 dinner gatherings of various sizes in China, substantial information from which found its way into this book. Data from individual meetings also were used, but often for supplemental purposes to balance the "official" atmosphere of the inquiries.

While the fact that we were writing a book about China was never explicitly concealed, we did not announce it every time we talked to people or attended a dinner party. Truth be told, data included in the book are only the tip of the iceberg of information we received, and we plan to embark on other intellectual endeavors based on some of it. When we talked to people, we simply engaged in casual, friendly, and candid conversations, with the exception that sometimes we intentionally guided the conversations to topics of interest to us for the book. We typically sought relevant information from people who were likely to be more knowledgeable about a particular topic (e.g., a professor on an education topic, a business owner on a business topic). In collecting the primary data, we followed the doctrine of grounded theory research, and we stopped seeking information on a topic when additional conversations no longer yielded new concepts and ideas and/or qualitatively different findings. Frankly, we learned a lot during the data collection process. The data we collected constitute a true treasure trove that would otherwise never be accessible to an outsider.

During the writing, we excluded any examples or perspectives that we believe our informants heard from others. Although they would have had no reason to lie or exaggerate, there was, of course, a slight chance that some stories may not have happened as they described. All stories included in this book, however, pass the face validity check. If a story sounded outlandish, we sought confirmation of probability from other Chinese people with similar backgrounds (e.g., business owners for a story from a business owner, professors for a story from a professor, etc.). When in doubt, we erred on the side of being too conservative.

xii   Preface

The sources of all secondary data are cited in the book, while the sources of all primary data have been made anonymous. In some cases, we have even made an effort to disguise the data if substantive information could not be changed. For example, we may have changed "he" to "she." The decision to preserve the anonymity of our information sources was mostly to make our Chinese colleagues, students, and friends feel comfortable in telling us their stories and also to ensure that we do not accidently cause any negative impact to a source by associating his or her name with a story in the book.

We are, of course, forever indebted to the people who have provided the personal stories, observations, and perspectives that have made this book possible. We cannot name names, but you know who you are. To you, we are grateful! We also want to thank the two great universities that we are associated with for their support: the Smeal College of Business at the Pennsylvania State University, home of the Nittany Lions and THON; and the School of Business at Fudan University, the alma mater of both authors. As always, any errors or oversights are ours alone.

In this book, the word "we" is used to refer to the authors in all cases, and could mean (1) Min, (2) Jie, or (3) Min and Jie. So a story that Min heard would be described in the book as a story we heard, and so on. We use the word "informant" to refer to primary data sources, and where further characterization is helpful to readers, we add a brief description. For example, we may say, "One of our informants, a business owner, ..." Since all original data were collected in Chinese, in the process of writing this book, we have tried to identify and use the prevailing English translation for a given term, but we sometimes also provide an alternate translation if we feel the prevailing English translation does not accurately capture the essence of the Chinese term or if there is no prevailing translation. For example, we use the same translation for the names of the books that constitute the canon of Confucianism: *The Four Books and Five Classics*. However, we did provide a revised translation for certain quotations from these books. In addition, all currencies are stated in their original form, USD, RMB, etc. in the book unless specifically stated otherwise. (Note, the rate USD/CNY was 6.11/1, January 16, 2014.)

This book is intended to be the first book someone should read if she is interested in understanding China, regardless of purpose (e.g., business, politics, travel). It can also help someone develop a full perspective if he previously had a limited view of China (either through personal experience or from reading other books). This book is not meant to be a treatise on the 51 topics it covers, and readers who are interested in a particular topic are urged to seek out more in-depth information. We will be happy to point you to such material. We also hope readers keep in mind that this book is meant to capture the Chinese way of life in 2014. After reading this book, we are confident that you will agree with us when we predict that the Chinese way of life in 2020 will be much different from that in 2014. Until then ...

Min Ding
Jie Xu
February 16, 2014

1   The Chinese Way of Life, Version 2014

We have identified nine concepts that form the foundation of the Chinese way of life around the year 2014 (CWOL v2014). The most important thing to remember is that the Chinese way of life is evolving. Although this chapter accurately describes fundamental aspects of current Chinese society, this does not mean that the Chinese are content with the way things are. In fact, many are quite dissatisfied with some current societal norms. The desire to create a better CWOL is palpable among the entire populace, and we have no doubt that they will succeed.

Doctrine of Mean

A concept translated as "Doctrine of Mean" is fundamental to the Chinese way of life and is based on one of the *Four Books* that form the canon of Confucianism. Confucius originally taught people to be inclusive and consider all opinions; he advocated using a decision heuristic that takes everything and everyone into consideration. In essence, he was referring to an equilibrium concept. Achieving equilibrium typically involves creating a solution that draws on everyone's perspectives, but not necessarily equally. However, this concept is so nuanced that even members of the general Chinese public have misinterpreted its meaning as being something closer to the misleading English translation, Doctrine of Mean— that people should not go to extremes and should instead strive to be in the middle. Finding equilibrium is not the same as finding the mean, and most certainly, finding the mean should not be the objective.

While this is not the meaning conveyed in the original text, the Chinese have adopted "striving for the middle" as a guiding life principle nonetheless. Thus, we will use this (mis)interpretation of the Doctrine of Mean (DoM) to frame our discussion of CWOL v2014. The current interpretation of DoM, which is arguably much easier for an ordinary person to follow and much more practical to implement, substantially impacts both individual and collective decisions.

Based on DoM, a Chinese person typically does not want to stand out. A common Chinese saying reflects this sentiment: "A pig is afraid to be strong and a man is afraid to be known." Just as the strong pig will be slaughtered first, someone who is well known is an easy target. Most members of Chinese society do not like to express radical ideas or be noticed for being different. However, once someone starts something, others will readily follow.

2   *The Chinese Way of Life, Version 2014*

On social issues, DoM is reflected in a collective desire to seek a middle ground solution when there is a difference of opinion on a particular topic. Organizational supervisors use this as a guiding principle when both managing their teams and dealing with their peers. It also means that radical ideas that lack consensus typically are not adopted, regardless of their inherent merits. As a result, the Chinese see everything as shades of grey, not as black and white.

Tribalism

Westerners classify the Chinese as collectivistic and Americans as individualistic. However, this Western characterization of the Chinese could not be further from the truth. We believe the most appropriate label for this dimension is tribalism. The Chinese behave very differently when they are in their "tribes" than when they are outside of them.

A tribe can be blood-based or non-blood-based. A blood-based tribe is built around the grandparents-parents-children family unit. This is the core unit of relationship in China, and typically, a member is willing to do anything for any of the other members. The perfect family in Chinese culture is one in which several generations live under the same roof; people's lives revolve around family. Typically, Chinese parents will literally do anything for their children. Beyond raising them and paying for major expenses such as educations and weddings, many purchase homes and cars for their adult children and help raise their grandchildren. Likewise, adult children feel obligated to take care of their parents in their old age. The blood-based tribe concept also extends beyond the core unit. Whenever possible, family members are expected to assume responsibility for caring for more distant relatives. At the extreme, a young person from a poor village who becomes successful may feel responsible for helping his entire village.

Non-blood-based tribes are called "circles" in Chinese culture. Circles represent more than typical friendships or social connections and can take different forms. The strongest form in traditional China was blood (sworn) brothers. Many legendary stories are told about blood brothers who fought together and died for each other. The traditional oath taken by blood brothers includes the sentence: "Do not wish to be born on the same day, but to die on the same day."

As discussed later in this book, people behave differently when they are within a circle than when they are outside a circle. Within a tribe (circle), one exhibits dedication, loyalty, and sacrifice, but the opposite is likely true towards people outside the tribe. One trusts people within the same tribe, but not outsiders. Within the tribe, collectivism reigns supreme; but outside the tribe, the Chinese are quite individualistic—even more so than their American counterparts. Since one belongs to different tribes at the same time and each tribe has a different level of closeness, it is conceivable that a casual observer may misunderstand a Chinese person's behavior.

At the core of tribalism is the "us versus them" mentality. As long as one's own tribe can survive, another tribe's fortune or misery is inconsequential. Taking this perspective, it is easier to understand why some Chinese can be extremely clean and organized within their tribal boundaries (e.g., inside their homes) while completely disregarding public spaces. Another ramification of this mentality is that one's own survival becomes the most important criterion in any situation.

Tribalism also impacts how the Chinese view other countries. The guiding principle of Chinese foreign policy—non-interference—can be traced back to tribalism, where one is not supposed to interfere with other tribes' internal affairs and vice versa. Extrapolated to the country level, tribalism in China can assume the form of nationalism.

This also leads to a strong desire among the Chinese to belong to tribes, as it is difficult to survive alone in a tribal society. All members must establish their positions in the tribe. Once a tribe's internal order is established, it is important for it to establish a reputation among competing tribes. Perhaps this is why the Chinese are constantly comparing themselves and their children to others; in tribes, and thus in Chinese society, relative position is important.

Hierarchicalism

While there is no official noble class in China, the Chinese accept and practice hierarchicalism. Some even lament that China does not have noblemen, so they invented two new higher classes, the Red Second Generation (i.e., the children of the founders of the PRC) and the Rich Second Generation (i.e., the children of the founders of successful businesses), whom they envy yet resent at the same time. This behavior probably stems from China's long history under a feudal system characterized by a strict hierarchy of authority, both outside the family (from the Emperor down) and inside the family (from father to son). According to traditional teachings, one must find his position in such a system and behave accordingly.

When hierarchicalism is the dominant ideology, people tend to defer to their superiors, whether in business, government, family or other social contexts, and expect those who are lower in the hierarchy to do the same. For instance, in the business world, it is quite typical for even a very senior person to do chores for his superior (e.g., a VP will carry a CEO's luggage when they travel together). These expectations also translate to other parts of social life. For example, the Chinese are typically not polite to servers in restaurants, and even in other contexts they like to be served by others whenever possible. Another implication of hierarchicalism is a general lack of personal responsibility or accountability, because all actions are done for someone else.

Hierarchicalism also typically results in unequal status in romantic relationships. Chinese young women often act like children with their boyfriends and husbands, as if they need attention and protection. Chinese men, of course, generally like and encourage this behavior, as it makes them feel that they are more powerful. Although many educated Chinese women are already financially independent, happiness is still largely defined as "marrying well."

4 *The Chinese Way of Life, Version 2014*

Polymorphism

Polymorphism in China takes two forms: across individuals and within an individual. Polymorphism across individuals is essentially the heterogeneity that exists among the Chinese. As we describe later in the book, different geographic locations in China have very different cultures. It would be pure folly to interact with all Chinese people using the same heuristics.

Polymorphism within an individual is more complex, yet integral to the Chinese way of life. In essence, the Chinese are taught and expected to behave differently in different situations, and they do not consistently follow the same principles in all contexts. For example, they will behave differently in front of subordinates versus superiors, in public versus private, when confronting one issue versus another. The important thing to remember is that such incongruences do not reflect poorly on a Chinese person's character; this behavior is expected. The Chinese say, "Principles are dead [fixed], but people are alive [changeable]." Thus, people are supposed to find ways to circumvent principles when they are preventing a goal from being accomplished.

In extreme cases of intra-person polymorphism, people will reverse their positions and sacrifice everything they stand for just to survive. In a story that every Chinese school child is taught, around 500 BC, the defeated king of the Yue Kingdom pretended to be a loyal servant and endured daily humiliation for years from the king of the Wu Kingdom before finally gaining his trust. He then trained a strong army, returned to defeat his former master, and forced him to commit suicide. Stories like this are meant to teach the Chinese to do whatever is needed to survive while waiting for a future opportunity.

Usefulism

Our informants often described the Chinese (especially those who grew up after the 1978 reforms) as utilitarian (if the word is translated into English directly). But what they actually meant differs somewhat from the English definition of the word. Our informants were referring to a societal norm dictating that one only does something if there is a personal benefit. The usefulism in China does overlap somewhat with pragmatism and utilitarianism; however, a main difference is that usefulism focuses on personal gain, even at the expense of breaking moral or ethical rules. To some extent, one can think of usefulism as the opposite of idealism.

Usefulism has contributed substantially to corruption and a general degradation of morals and ethics in China. It has permeated society so much that it is typically assumed that a person will not help someone else unless there is personal benefit to him or her. Another ramification is that for some Chinese, relationships now have expiration dates. If a person thinks a relationship is no longer useful, regardless of what that person may have done for him or her in the past, there is no reason to maintain the relationship. This often happens after a person retires from an important position; suddenly, many so-called friends disappear.

Notably, usefulism stands in direct opposition to the traditional teachings of Confucianism that people are to prioritize benevolence to others and discount personal benefit in their actions. Many cherished virtues in the traditional value system, some as simple as always keeping promises, have been thrown out the window under the dominant usefulism ideology. In the words of an informant, "Benevolence is for fools these days."

Emotionalism

Emotion plays a central role in personal interactions in China. One senior Chinese academic commented to us: "A fundamental guideline in how the Chinese deal with others is 'satisfy emotion, satisfy reason.' Someone who understands both emotion and reason will find it easy to fit in." The phrase "satisfy emotion, satisfy reason" essentially means that when confronting a particular issue and evaluating possible solutions, one must first examine whether a solution satisfies emotional needs of the self, all parties involved, and the general populace before examining whether a solution satisfies the standards of reason (i.e., rationality, science) and maybe even the law.

To the Chinese, emotion is not just an individual affair; it is an integral part of how society operates. A common justification used by the courts in China when determining capital sentences is, "Any sentence short of execution will not mitigate mass rage."

Scientific research has shown emotion as a useful tool for individuals, in that it helps them make advantageous decisions in certain situations. Although emotion plays an important role in all human cultures, prioritizing emotion as such an important decision-making heuristic by the entire society is uniquely Chinese.

Emotionalism has been a fundamental part of Chinese culture for thousands of years. While we believe it will continue to play an important role in personal interactions, its equal status with rules and laws in social decisions may gradually diminish.

Wealthism

Although the Chinese desire material possessions, Chinese culture differs somewhat from a typical materialistic culture like that of the United States. Whereas a typical American may save money to buy something special, a Chinese person wants to accumulate money because wealth is the dominant (if not only) metric for success in life now. Another dimension of wealthism is the envy or even resentment many people feel towards those who are wealthy.

To some extent, many contemporary Chinese people share some characteristics with the fictitious species Ferengi in the *Star Trek* television series. Profit is paramount, and wealth accumulation is a goal in life for many. Interestingly, wealthism is a relatively recent phenomenon in China and represents the antithesis of traditional Confucian values.

6 *The Chinese Way of Life, Version 2014*

Effortlessism

Effortlessism means one should ideally get things without expending any effort. Mark Twain's quote "Work is a necessary evil to be avoided" most appropriately describes how the Chinese view work. Historically, the kind of work that was not valued was manual labor, but now this perspective has expanded to include any kind of work that involves effort. Rewards are all that matter and effortlessism prevails. The ideal scenario for most Chinese would be to receive rewards for doing as little work as possible, or even no work. Many Chinese are generally perfectly content to do nothing; if they do not have to work, they will not.

Effortlessism has led to the pursuit of all kinds of shortcuts in life and in business. A common belief is that a one-step-at-a-time work ethic is for those who are not smart enough to skip steps. They seek opportunities that give them huge rewards with minimum investment (in capital and/or effort) in the shortest possible amount of time. It is not surprising, therefore, that the Chinese love to receive freebies if they perceive that they do not have to do any work to get them.

In general, the Chinese also like talking and debating about strategies and solutions more than actually executing them. In *The Art of War*,[1] generals are taught that the optimal strategy is to subdue enemy forces without fighting. This strategy has been applied to many aspects of Chinese society. Many of the Chinese see life as a military campaign, and most military strategies (including *The Art of War* and others) focus on how to win the most with the least amount of resources and effort; deception is not only acceptable, but encouraged.

As we describe later in this book, many role models selected by the Chinese in recent years were highly dedicated to their work. Their stories, which were "impressive" to the Chinese, would be considered normal by most Americans. Americans salute people who dare to say, "The difficult we do immediately; the impossible takes a little longer." The Chinese, on the other hand, puzzle over why they do not go and find something easier to do instead.

Cynicism

Cynicism is not a traditional characteristic of Chinese society, but it is quite pervasive today. Many Chinese people are cynical; they do not believe what the government tells them, are suspicious of everything, and do not have an optimistic view of the future. Based on our research, it seems that the average Chinese person is more pessimistic about China than the average American.

One possible factor has contributed to this cynicism. Since the feudal system was overthrown in 1911, the Chinese have still not reached consensus on what constitutes the new China. The changes that opened China to a market economy after 1978 further confused many Chinese citizens about the nation's future direction.

Due to this cynicism, the Chinese tend to focus more on the present and near term, for they feel uncertain about what the future will bring. They also tend to focus on the things and people in their immediate surroundings. In general, the Chinese appear to have substantial anxiety about life, especially the future.

Cynicism also leads to fatalism, at least to some degree. The Chinese will try to get ahead, but if things do not work out, they attribute their failures to fate. They also believe, right or wrong, that society has constrained them from achieving many possible goals, including social mobility.

Summary

Clearly, CWOL v2014 is a complex, evolving phenomenon. Our goal in this chapter was to provide our readers with a contextual framework that will facilitate a better understanding of why the Chinese behave in certain ways and to some extent, why things are the way they are. This understanding can lead to insights that bridge the cultural gaps between us, not only as nations, but also as members of the human race. In this spirit, we encourage you to read on and learn *The Chinese Way*.

Note

1 Sun Tzu (1963), *The Art of War*, translated by Samuel Griffith, Oxford: Clarendon Press.

Part I
Customs and Traditions

2 Face
The Three-Tiered Chinese Version of Honor

In Chinese culture, "face" is a concept similar to honor. An example from the television show *Star Trek* may help Westerners understand the importance of face to the Chinese. A Klingon values honor above everything else. In fact, the guiding principles for the Klingon species are documented in a tome entitled *The Book of Honor*. Klingons cherish honor so much that they are willing to die in order to preserve it. Likewise, sometimes there are disagreements about what constitutes an honorable action in a given situation. In China, face is quite analogous to the Klingons' honor.

There has been extensive discourse on the concept of face both within and outside China, and often with negative connotations, as if face were a superficial reflection of vanity. After extensive research based on interviews and focus groups, we think face is a topic that should be treated with great respect as a dominant folk philosophy in China. Granted, some people may attempt to achieve face through not-so-honorable actions, but one should not dismiss the important and positive role it plays in Chinese society. In fact, we conclude that face will always be part of the Chinese culture in the Road Ahead section. In the rest of this chapter, we first provide our own definition of face as a three-tiered concept analogous to the concept of honor and discuss some of its characteristics. We then discuss how one achieves face and how one can offer face to others, two very important aspects of social interaction in China.

Face as Three-Tiered Honor

Face is a fundamental concept that explicitly and implicitly determines many decisions Chinese people make in life, from purchasing decisions to social interactions to business deals to diplomatic negotiations. Based on our extensive research, we believe the concept of face should be given its proper role in society as a concept closer to honor than vanity. Careful analysis of the concept of face revealed a three-tiered structure comprised of dignity, respectability, and superiority.

The tier of dignity refers to the fact that one must maintain honor so that his self-respect is preserved. Note, however, that different people have different definitions of dignity, and even the same person may have different definitions of dignity in different contexts and stages of life. The tier of dignity can be interpreted as the baseline one wants to achieve in honor, making it the most important tier of face. Losing face at this level may lead to strong reactions from a person in order

12 Customs and Traditions

to compensate for lost honor. Consider, for example, the 2012 case of a senior police officer who sought asylum at the U.S. consulate and then became a government witness who took down Bo Xilai, a prominent member of the Politburo of the Communist Party of China (CPC) and a candidate for the Politburo Standing Committee. It was rumored that the incident was partially triggered because Bo slapped the police officer on the face, a terrible insult in China that evidently hurt the police officer's dignity.

The tier of respectability refers to the fact that one does things that others consider proper or expected based on his or her social and family status. Respectability has less heterogeneity, is more socially defined, and is specific to certain segments of people. For instance, a business owner who allowed others to pick up the dinner tab would lose honor related to respectability, but people in other professions would not be held to this same expectation.

The last tier of face, which we call superiority, is honor that surpasses social norms. When this type of honor is achieved, a person is perceived as being better than his peers. For example, if one can get an important person (e.g., a celebrity, a government official) to accept a dinner invitation that normally would be accepted only rarely, then the superiority aspect of face would be achieved, since one would have demonstrated that he has more power and influence than others.

Across all three tiers, it is important to remember a few characteristics. First, different people have different definitions of face (honor) that sometimes conform to social conventions (e.g., are based on profession, family status, social status, etc.) but other times are personal and nonobvious. It is important to understand another person's definition of honor so as to avoid accidently causing others to lose face, or even better, to help others achieve face when appropriate. Second, if we define face as honor, then clearly certain actions bring dishonor. The boundary between honor and dishonor should be carefully observed, as well as the grey area in between. Third, like Klingons, honor (face) is a very important goal (and asset) that Chinese people pursue. The Chinese are willing to go to great expense, both literally and figuratively, to gain and maintain face, and are grateful for anyone who can help them achieve it. Thus, one who understands the complex nature of face in China can benefit substantially.

Achieving Face for Self

One of the key aspects of achieving face, especially face associated with the respectability tier, is associating oneself with products and services that are deemed appropriate and even necessary. Since what is expected for a given class of people changes drastically based on what most people in that segment do, this can create an unhealthy "keeping up with the Joneses" mentality, where everybody ends up spending beyond their means to save face, even to the extent of "biting off more than they can chew."

The luxury industry, which has benefited from the high value placed on the concept of face, has experienced rapid growth in China in recent years. Brand-name outfits, watches, cars, and luxurious handbags with prominent, famous logos all support the superiority tier of face. Some white collar workers spend several months' salary on designer dresses; likewise, some freshmen ask their parents to buy them a suite of Apple products (i.e., MacBook Pro, iPad, and iPhone). In these cases, what they buy is not necessarily what they really need or want, but rather a tool to achieve face.

Some take achieving face so seriously that they are willing to put themselves in financial peril. For example, an undergraduate in Wuhan (the provincial capital of Hubei Province) bought an iPhone 5 for his girlfriend on a payment plan: the down payment was the equivalent of USD 333.30 and he had to pay USD 66.50 per month for 12 months. He was supposed to make the payments by saving money from his monthly support allowance equal to USD 133.30 from his parents, but he failed to control his expenditures and defaulted on his debts. Home Credit, the largest supplier of small consumer loans in Wuhan, has published rough statistics showing that from January 2012 to the end of February 2013, more than 20,000 undergraduates applied for secured loans in amounts totaling more than the equivalent of USD 26.7 million. The purpose for most of these loans was to buy new iPhones, iPads, and other 3G smartphones.

Pursuing face beyond one's means sometimes results not only in financial problems, but personal disaster. In Fujian, a man in his sixties committed suicide because he could not afford betrothal gifts of about USD 10,000 for his son and suffered severe depression.[2] This story exemplifies an old Chinese saying: "Puff oneself up at one's own cost."

Help Others Achieve Face and Do No Harm

Since achieving face is critical in Chinese society, anyone who can help others maintain or gain face will be greatly valued. To some extent, face can be exchanged like goods in a market. The Chinese expression "courtesy demands reciprocity" means that achieving face comes at a price, in the form of helping others achieve face. One must first maintain and increase others' face in order for them to be willing to help you achieve face when you are in need, and vice versa. Two simple actions that help others achieve face include paying compliments in front of others (especially important people) and never denying any request that is made in front of others (even if you cannot deliver on it in the future) because denying a request would cause the other person to lose face and experience great embarrassment. Later in the book, we describe the case of a chief justice of a district court who never tells his friends that he cannot provide help on a particular case, even though both parties understand that nothing will be done. This is a perfect example of allowing a friend to achieve face in front of other people.

At a minimum, one should do no harm; in other words, do not cause other people to lose face. In a story widely told in Shanghai, after an American boss publicly demanded an explanation from a Chinese manager for his team's underperformance and failure to meet sales goals for the previous month, the manager left the conference without saying a word and never returned.[3] In the case above, public blame from the foreign employer hurt the Chinese employee's self-esteem

14 Customs and Traditions

and he felt that he could not recover from losing face so badly. It is normal to feel embarrassed when deficiencies or mistakes are made public, but Chinese people are especially sensitive to this. Therefore, he resigned. Similarly, it has been reported that nearly 30% of people who quit their jobs in China resign because they lose face.[4]

Furthermore, giving face within couples may seem trivial but actually matters quite a lot in Chinese families. In public, if a wife does not give her husband face, their family will be very likely to be affected. For instance, one story serves as a lesson for wives. During a dinner party, one lady blurted to her friend, "Your husband earns much more than the monthly salary of my husband!" Upon hearing this, her husband felt extremely embarrassed; to save face, he made up an excuse and left.

Road Ahead

Face is the Chinese version of honor. It is an important and positive aspect of Chinese culture that must be cherished, respected, and learned. We believe this social phenomenon will withstand the test of time and will continue to be an integral part of the culture for the foreseeable future. However, two shifts are on the horizon. First, perceptions of the role of face in Chinese culture will evolve; instead of thinking of face as a form of vanity and ego, people will understand face as a guiding principle of proper behavior in China. Second, the definition of face (i.e., honorable actions) may evolve in various contexts and for various people. It is highly likely that face based on pure vanity will no longer be expected or accepted. Instead face will be more closely tied to morality and ethics, and Chinese values in general.

Notes

1　Song Dandan, Zuo Yang, Sun Yue, & Zhao Huike (2013, March 18), "More than 20,000 Wuhan undergraduates got into debt for iPhones," *Wuhan Evening News*, retrieved January 2014 from http://edu.cnhan.com/content/2013-03/18/content_2060924.htm

2　Wu Shuibao & Lin Guilong (2013, June 23), "A man committed suicide for betrothal gifts," *Quanzhou Evening News*, retrieved January 2014 from http://szb.qzwb.com/dnzb/html/2013-06/23/content_540620.htm

3　Vorhauser-Smith, Sylvia (2012, May 29), "When your Chinese employees lose face, you lose them," *Forbes*, retrieved January 2014 from http://www.forbes.com/sites/sylviavorhausersmith/2012/05/29/when-your-chinese-employees-lose-face-you-lose-them-2/

4　Zhang Yue'e (2010, March 12), "Nearly 30% of job hoppers resigned due to face," *Workers' Daily*, retrieved January 2014 from http://www.hi.chinanews.com/pdcontent/2010-03-12/4640.html

3 From a Nation of Etiquette to a Society of Gifting

Gifting is an integral part of current Chinese society. The saying "You can never go visit people empty handed" is taken more literally in China than perhaps anywhere else in the world. As a matter of fact, even if one does not visit people in person, one is still expected to send gifts to both friends and business associates on important occasions such as major holidays and birthdays. A report published in 2012 estimated demand for gifts at RMB 768.4 billion per year (with individual annual demand totaling RMB 505.5 billion and organizational annual demand totaling RMB 262.9 billion).[1] China is most certainly a society of gifting, in terms of both scope and scale.

How did this custom of ubiquitous gifting evolve? Based on our research, we believe its roots lie in China's original reputation as the "Nation of Etiquette," a point of pride for many in Chinese society over the last 2,000 years. In fact, it was such a point of pride that many lament the shift away from etiquette in recent years.

In this chapter, we discuss the historical custom of observing a well-developed and institutionalized etiquette in China over two millennia. We then discuss how the current custom of gifting is related to the custom of following etiquette, which we follow with a description of the current practice of gifting in terms of when and what one should gift. We finally conclude in the Road Ahead section with an outlook for the societal custom of gifting and predict that some aspects of the original Nation of Etiquette will be restored.

Nation of Etiquette: Historical Context

Throughout history, China has been recognized by the rest of the world as the Nation of Etiquette. This is an important point of pride that unites all Chinese people, past and present, on par with China's cultural, scientific, and economic achievements. In China, etiquette is more than superficial politeness; rooted in the foundation of Confucianism, it is treated as an important aspect of societal behavior that all individuals must learn and observe.

The canon of Confucianism is recorded in *The Four Books and Five Classics* (Chinese: 四书五经, Pinyin: Sìshū Wǔjīng) written before 300 BC. These nine books (each book is a compilation of many essays and stories) became required reading for any educated Chinese person. *The Four Books* record what Confucius (551 BC–479 BC) and his disciples said and did, and the *Five Classics* are

16 *Customs and Traditions*

five pre-Qin (before 221 BC) Chinese books that Confucius himself had compiled or edited and used in his teaching. One of the *Five Classics*, the *Book of Rites*, describes the rites, social protocols, and ceremonies that have formed the foundation of Chinese etiquette over the last two millennia. More importantly, it justifies practicing etiquette from philosophical, ethical, and social perspectives. Confucius believed that rite-focused education served as the foundation of national politics and enabled the construction of ethical and moral orders.

Etiquette is classified into five types: rules for festivities, rituals for funerals or disasters, military rituals, protocols for receiving guests, and rules for interpersonal communication. Rules for festivities stipulate how one should worship the gods and spirits of the heavens, the sun, the moon and stars, the Five Mountains,[2] the forests and rivers, etc. Rituals for funerals or disasters are rules for proper behavior related to mourning the dead or interacting with people who are suffering from great loss. Military rituals dictate protocols for military strategy, going to war, dividing the spoils of war, hostage treatment, building fortresses, hunting, etc. Protocols for receiving guests are the basic manners practiced in Chinese culture. Rules for interpersonal communication are followed in work and personal contexts, such as wedding ceremonies. Each protocol may involve several elaborate processes with moral or social connotations. Due to the influence of Confucianism, etiquette is inherently intertwined with the Chinese political system, moral code, and folk culture.

Several key concepts define the Nation of Etiquette. First, proper etiquette is extremely important in Chinese society. It is taught in Confucianism that one has nothing to stand on if he does not learn proper etiquette. It is the foundation of a harmonious society. The rules of etiquette are not simply practices to be used on special occasions or by a particular social class; rather, they are the social fabric that weaves everyone together in all aspects of life. The core tenets of Chinese etiquette are self-control and respect, regardless of social status. The rich and powerful can avoid extravagance and complacence if they practice proper etiquette. Likewise, the poor and those with lower social status can foster a strong will and prevent feelings of despair by practicing proper etiquette.

Second, etiquette is pervasive. It is present in every aspect of social life, and has been institutionalized and continuously practiced for more than 2,000 years. One must be aware of the specific etiquettes associated with any given occasion in life.

Third, etiquette has two components: protocols and offerings. In the old form Chinese character for etiquette used in the *Book of Rites*, the right half is "豊" (Pinyin: lǐ), and the oracle bone inscription consists of two parts. The upper part is "丰丰" symbolizing two strings of jade, and the bottom part is a pictograph of a drum (Chinese: 鼓, Pinyin: gǔ). Drumming is a behavior (i.e., a protocol) that brings pleasure to others in the form of music; giving jade is a sacrifice (i.e., an offering), which characterizes the most paramount and genuine rites. Later, "豊" was added to "示" (Pinyin: shì, literally, offering sacrifice) on the left to emphasize the role of sacrifice and worship in rites.[3] These offerings later evolved into gifts.

Fourth, it is absolutely necessary to return favors and equally important to expect others to return favors. Thus, doing favors for others without being rewarded and asking for rewards without doing favors are both discordant with the principles of etiquette.

From Etiquette to Gifting

If Confucius saw how etiquette is practiced in contemporary China, he would be quite disappointed. We discuss here the elements from his teaching that have been forgotten and those that have been retained, as well as new elements that have been incorporated into the society of gifting that China has become.

The original purpose of etiquette, to build a morally strong and harmonious society, has been all but forgotten. People are practicing certain forms of gift giving without knowing or asking why. Furthermore, nonmaterial aspects of etiquette have been cast aside, and etiquette has become solely about material gifting. Without a spiritual and moral component, the value of a gift has become more important than the proper rules one must follow on specific occasions. Specificity of practice, and with it the rich meaning of each type of etiquette, has been lost. Instead, etiquette has been oversimplified into a generic practice of giving gifts. The one original aspect of etiquette that has been preserved, however, is returning favors, which is very much a social norm in the Chinese society.

In addition, many other purposes have been co-opted into the idea of etiquette and gift giving that were not originally intended or practiced. For example, gift giving has become a way of providing mutual financial support. In rural areas to this day, the people who host banquets to celebrate life events such as marriage or moving into a new house receive cash gifts from guests to be put towards the expenses of the celebration. Cash gifts in the same amounts (or even a bit more) will be given in return when the host attends future events hosted by their guests. In essence, this is a way of borrowing and returning money, disguised as gift giving.

Gift giving also is used as a way to build up credit one has with another person. Because the idea that a favor must be returned is so ingrained, the more credit one has with another person (i.e., by giving more gifts than one has accepted from the other party), the easier it is to later request a (possibly bigger) favor in return. In the age of information overload, gift giving also becomes a way to ensure that other people remember you favorably, even when there is no particular favor you might ask of them in the future. The most prevalent permutation of this traditional practice is bribing. The otherwise noble and proper act of giving a gift as part of etiquette provides a perfect cover for offering and accepting a bribe.

Gifting: When and What

One may give gifts because everybody else is doing it, but one may also give gifts to maintain good relationships (and build up credits, as discussed in the previous section). The key thing to remember in terms of timing, as revealed to us by many of our informants, is to refrain from giving gifts only when you need someone to do something for you. Instead, gifting should be a continuous process over a long

18 Customs and Traditions

period of time with an emphasis on building relationships so that one can easily call in a favor when there is a need. Continuous gifting also reduces the perception of a direct exchange of gifts for favors.

For example, one informant told us that if a business owner wants a government official's help, the business owner begins the gifting process at least a year beforehand. No favors are asked during this period even though many gifts are being provided, just to build the relationship. A year later, when the person asks for a favor, perhaps by pretending to vent frustration in front of the government official, the official may choose to help his friend—not because his friend gave him gifts but because he values the relationship.

During holidays, especially Chinese New Year, those who hold important positions will receive a nonstop flow of gift-bearing guests. One informant told us about one of her neighbors who served as the head of a bureau in one district in Shanghai: "Starting from a month before the New Year until the end of Spring Festival, a continuous queue of visitors, gifts in hand, would flock to his home each evening. What a scene! The doorbell kept ringing and things wouldn't quiet down until the festival came to an end. In addition, gift giving sprees were not uncommon during other festivals. His wife said that the house is overflowing with so many gifts of all kinds, which is actually annoying, for they take up all the space and she cannot just throw them away."

What to gift is also very important.[4] One informant, a business owner, described how his company handles gifting. A few days before festivals, they will send clients cases of daily necessities, such as tissues and shampoo. This approach is a subtle and creative way to tighten the bond of friendship. Expensive gifts are not uncommon, but are sent less frequently. In some cases, luxury goods will be combined with daily necessities and sent all throughout the year so as to facilitate communication. Using this strategy helps keep the overall cost of gifts reasonable.

As discussed in Chapter 2, the concept of face is deeply ingrained in Chinese culture. In the context of face, more expensive gifts are thought to convey more sincerity. As a result, many people will spend a fortune on gifts, straining their budgets to do so. It is said that those who drink Maotai (a very expensive and highly sought-after liquor in China) do not buy it for themselves. Driven by this tremendous demand for expensive gifts, many foreign luxury items also sell extremely well in China.

In other situations, a thoughtful gift may be more valued, especially by the wealthy. For example, some of our informants (who are worth more than USD 100 million) hand delivered their home-grown vegetables to provincial government officials. Another informant told us a clever solution he came up with when struggling to figure out what to buy for a potential business partner. He wanted the gift to be impactful, but he was unfamiliar with the recipient's tastes; although everyone can use cash, it seems a bit tacky in a business context. Thus, he purchased jewels from a store close to the recipient's home, which could easily be returned for cash if the client wished to do so.

Road Ahead

A derivative of the etiquette that has guided China for 2,000 years, gifting has become the social norm in contemporary China. Unfortunately, the current gifting culture is devoid of the spiritual and moral components emphasized by Confucius and some traditional etiquette practices have been co-opted to disguise immoral activities, especially bribing.

That said, we believe that members of Chinese society will rediscover some of the lost art and philosophy of etiquette, and gradually shift away from focusing solely on the material and utilitarian aspects of gifting. None of our informants (or secondary data sources) indicated a specific aversion to the current gifting phenomenon; however, all were very proud of the historical reputation of China as the Nation of Etiquette. Because of this deep pride, we predict that China will slowly shift away from being a society of gifting back toward a society that more closely resembles a Nation of Etiquette (though not in its original form), facilitated specifically by the current government crackdown on bribing.

Notes

1 Yao Dongqin (2012, January 30), "Gifting in China," *China Economic Weekly*, retrieved January 2014 from http://www.ceweekly.cn/html/Article/201201304079618002.html
2 The Five Mountains in China refer to Taishan Mountain in Shandong, Hengshan Mountain in Hunan, Huashan Mountain in Shanxi, Hengshan Mountain in Shanxi, and Songshan Mountain in Henan.
3 Tang Han (2001), *The Codes of Chinese Characters,* Shanghai: Academia Press, p. 893.
4 What not to give on specific occasions is also important. For example, watches or clocks are taboos on the gift list, for the phrase "sending a clock" (Chinese: 送钟, Pinyin: sòng zhōng) sounds like "saying goodbye to a relative at a funeral" (Chinese: 送终) in Chinese. In addition, pears cannot be taken as gift to a hospital patient, for the Chinese character for pear, 梨 (Pinyin: lí), is a homophone for 离, meaning "to depart or pass away."

4 Presumption of Untrustworthiness (Guilt)

It is said that one of the worst problems in China today is a lack of trust between people, and between people and various entities (government agencies, firms, and even the Red Cross). We discussed this problem with our informants on various occasions, and everyone agreed that trust is a major problem in Chinese society. A society built on the presumption of untrustworthiness (POU) is very different from a society built on trust. In this chapter, we discuss the historical and cultural origins of POU in China, how it affects the legal system, people's attitudes toward other individuals, and its ramifications on attitudes toward firms and government. We conclude in the Road Ahead section with a prognosis that this social phenomenon will persist for the foreseeable future.

Origins of POU

Contemporary POU has two origins: the presumption of guilt underlying the legal system during many Chinese dynasties, and the still fresh and painful lessons learned during the Mao Zedong era (from the 1960s through the 1970s). Another moderating factor is the fact that Chinese society historically has been comprised of diverse and isolated subcultures. Until fairly recently, people did not know others outside their hometowns well and thus tended to be suspicious of outsiders due to a lack of mutual understanding.

Unlike the "innocent until proven guilty" precept ingrained in Western cultures, the presumption of guilt was the foundational principle of the Chinese legal system for hundreds of years beginning during the Tang Dynasty (618–907). The Tang penal code included a category called probable crime. That is, if a person was accused, the judicial authorities would assume guilt until the person was able to gather enough evidence to prove his innocence. Based on the presumption of guilt, a suspect arrested for a probable crime could be convicted without sufficient evidence but be given a lighter sentence. The basic underlying philosophy is that it is better for the legal system to wrongly convict a person than to let a real criminal go free due to insufficient evidence. The same probable crime code was adopted during the Song Dynasty (960–1279) as well. Although this particular classification of crime was eliminated during the Ming (1368–1644) and Qing Dynasties (1644–1911), the presumption of guilt was still very much ingrained in Chinese society.

22 *Customs and Traditions*

During the Mao Zedong era, especially from the 1960s through the 1970s, brothers were pitted against brothers, wives against husbands, and children against parents, not to mention friends against friends and colleagues against colleagues. It has been said that during that period, a husband sometimes was afraid to even talk in his sleep because he might say something that his wife would hear and she would report him to the authorities. During this era, leaders often tricked people into revealing their true opinions in the spirit of democracy and constructive criticism, and then would turn around in a few months and imprison and torture those who had done so. Those who hid their true opinions survived these purges. These compounding effects led to the societal heuristic of not taking what other people say at face value and not disclosing honest opinions. Chinese people who are 60 years old or older vividly remember this painful era, and the heuristic of mistrust is still very much passed on from generation to generation.

Last but not least, China historically was a large kingdom with many unique and local subcultures, and minimal communication occurred with people outside one's local area due to difficulties associated with traveling and understanding different local dialects. This lack of understanding contributed to suspicion of outsiders because it is quite normal for people only to trust others whom they know.

Legal System

The presumption of guilt was a precept of the Chinese penal code until very recently, in March 1996. Article 12 of the first revised version of the *Criminal Procedure Law of the People's Republic of China* clearly states: "No person shall be found guilty without being judged as such by a People's Court according to law." Previously, the judicial authority operated based on the presumption of guilt and judged probable crimes leniently or with delayed sentences. When cases were delayed, suspects were imprisoned for long periods of time without definite end dates.

A recent case motivated these changes in the legal system in China. She Xianglin from Hubei province was suspected of killing his wife by his relatives after his wife disappeared on January 20, 1994. On April 11 of that same year, a female corpse was found in a pool in their village whose characteristics were consistent with those of the missing wife according to relatives. The police put it on record and began to investigate. Due to a lack of sufficient evidence, sentencing for the "murder case" was delayed for a long time. Finally, in 1998, he was sentenced to imprisonment for 15 years for intentionally murdering his wife. After spending 11 years in prison, his wife suddenly was discovered alive in March 2005, at which point he was proven innocent and released without charge.[1] For this reason, on November 21, 2013, the Supreme Court released a document entitled "Opinions on perfecting the working mechanism to prevent miscarriages of criminal justice" in which the justices officially abandoned the presumption of guilt in favor of the presumption of innocence. However, it will take some time for this dramatic doctrinal transformation to be truly adopted by the legal profession.

Interpersonal Attitudes

POU in personal interactions is best illustrated by a guiding principle that is taught to children: "You should not have a heart intended to hurt other people, but you must have a heart that is always alert to potential harm other people will do to you." With early education like this, it's no wonder POU is so well ingrained in Chinese society.

One informant made an interesting comparison for us. He said, "The Americans and the Chinese are opposites when it comes to trusting others. Americans will trust you until you do something bad, then they will not trust you anymore. The Chinese are opposite. They do not trust you initially. Only after many interactions and experiences will they start to trust you." POU has led to some cases that are unlikely to be observed elsewhere, or even in the future in China. We describe three such cases here for illustrative purposes.

Just before the Chinese New Year in 2013, a migrant worker lost the hard-earned money his family had made during the previous year while he was on the way to the bank. While many Chinese people who saw the story on the internet sympathized with him and even chipped in to make up for the loss, many also made negative comments on Weibo (a microblogging site similar to Twitter) questioning whether the migrant worker simply created a sad story to get donations and/or attention.[2] In a second case, a junior college student accidently drowned while swimming. When the student's classmates tried to contact his family (who were out of town) none of the family members believed the story. They all thought it was a hoax to cheat them out of money, even after 56 phone calls.[3] In a final example, a woman in Henan province was pinned down by a truck in a traffic accident. She begged the driver not to drive the truck over her again, assuming he would try to kill her in order to silence her. In reality, the driver had only intended to move the truck off of the woman so that she could be rescued.[4]

Attitudes toward Companies and Government

Another unfortunate ramification of POU is that many people do not trust government agencies even if they are working for the good of China's citizens. Some of our informants who are government officials vented their frustrations to us. No matter how hard they work and how selfless they are, their constituents assume that they have ulterior motives for everything that they do. Attitudes toward businesses are no better. Most of the Chinese think firms are evil—trying to make a buck, cutting corners, and providing exaggerated, if not downright false, claims.

Unfortunately, bad apples can almost always be found in any government agency or firm. However, in China, any evidence that validates POU only serves to perpetuate and strengthen behaviors based on it and causes POU to be applied to all entities.

Road Ahead

POU is a Chinese phenomenon that is both rooted in history (i.e., the presumption of guilt in the legal system) and personal experiences during the Mao Zedong

24 *Customs and Traditions*

era. It is fundamentally opposite to the social code of Western cultures, where a person is assumed to be innocent and/or trustworthy until proven otherwise. It is critical for an outsider to understand the ramifications of POU as it is fundamental to how Chinese society operates.

It is hard to predict whether POU will persist in Chinese society or whether people will gradually adopt Western presumptions of trustworthiness. There is a saying in China, "Once bitten by a snake, one will be scared by the sight of a rope for 10 years." Given recent memories from the Mao era, we predict a future in which POU is still the dominant guiding principle in personal relationships.

Notes

1 Tang Weibing & Li Changzheng (2005, April 7), "'Murder' case of She Xianglin in Hubei: What caused injustice?" retrieved January 2014 from http://news.xinhuanet.com/legal/2005-04/07/content_2800483.htm
2 Shen Yanbin & Yan Ying (2013, March 4), "The case of Qin Xiaoliang," *Morning News*, retrieved January 2014 from http://newspaper.jfdaily.com/xwcb/html/2013-03/04/content_982741.htm
3 Shang Weizhi & Huang Lu (2013, July 2), "The son drowned, and the parents took 56 emergency phones calls for fraud," *Wuhan Evening News*, retrieved January 2014 from http://whwb.cjn.cn/page/21/2013-07-02/14/61441372701476468.pdf
4 Xinhuanet.com (2013, July 3), "A woman, hit by a truck, begged the driver not to kill her," retrieved January 2014 from http://news.xinhuanet.com/photo/2013-07/03/c_124946846.htm

5   Unwritten Rules

In today's China, one would be at a loss without knowing the unwritten rules related to all aspects of life. Unwritten rules exist everywhere in the world, but they exist in such a pervasive manner in China that one must know them to fully understand the inner workings of society, for anything from seeing a doctor to making a business deal.

The existence of unwritten rules in China has a long history. Compared to the sometimes neutral nature of unwritten rules outside China (where the term may literally refer to rules that are not written down), the Chinese use this concept to refer to rules that allow one to benefit by specifically countering openly stated regulations. Such unwritten rules are thus typically unethical.

In this chapter, we first provide a short discussion about the origins of unwritten rules to shed some light on why so many exist in China today. We then provide some examples of unwritten rules in the public sector, private sector, and personal life. We conclude with a very optimistic view on how these rules might change in the near future.

Origins of Chinese Unwritten Rules

While many unwritten rules are now considered to be unethical, their origins can be traced to three different sources: customs from the past that have become part of Chinese culture; painful lessons learned from recent history; and self-interest in an environment characterized by weak enforcement of rules.[1]

Red envelopes are a good example of an unwritten rule based on customs from the past. In China, it is customary to give someone a red envelope containing cash as a gift. Grandparents give their grandchildren red envelopes on holidays and birthdays; friends and relatives give couples red envelopes as wedding gifts. It is a very innocent and respected custom that dates back over thousands of years.

However, this practice has gradually become part of the unwritten rules for asking a government official to do something. During the Qing Dynasty (1636–1912), citizens gave red envelopes to government officials during the three festivals (i.e., the Spring Festival, the Dragon Boat Festival, and the Mid-Autumn Festival) and two birthdays (i.e., the birthdays of the official and his wife). There were even specific names for the various types of red envelopes given on different occasions during the Qing Dynasty. The red envelopes given to cadres during official

26 Customs and Traditions

trips were called "routine honoraria" (Chinese: 程仪, Pinyin: chéng yí); the red envelopes given to officials when seeking help were called "errand commissions" (Chinese: 使费, Pinyin: shǐ fèi); and the red envelopes given to the central bureaus to ensure approval of certain affairs were called "bureau dues" (Chinese: 部费, Pinyin: bù fèi).

We also identified how some of the unethical unwritten rules in China originated from painful experiences, some in the recent past. For example, there are two unwritten rules in government: do not tell the truth in public, and deliver fake good news (typically to impress more senior government officials higher up the ranks). During the 1959 Lushan Conference (the 8th Plenum of the 8th CPC Central Committee), the Chinese Great Leap Forward Movement (1958–1961) had already led to an extensive nationwide famine. Although everybody knew the truth, only Peng Dehuai, Huang Kecheng, Zhang Wentian, & Zhou Xiaozhou had the courage to proclaim it in public. At the end of the meeting, however, the four of them were accused of being counter revolutionaries, fell subject to abuses and insults, and finally endured miserable deaths.

Examples like this have served as lessons for all in China since then. Tell the truth, and you will be digging your own grave. It is also historically and culturally ingrained that one should broadcast good news and hide bad news. This practice can be very innocent in some cases (e.g., a parent may not tell her child that she is sick for fear of worrying her), but it has contributed to the habit of inventing good news to share with others. During the Chinese Great Leap Forward Movement, the newspapers and the radio were filled with fake positive news to please superiors; for instance the per-acre productivity was inflated ten- or even a hundred-fold above de facto gains, from several hundred Jin (a unit of weight, equal to 500 grams) per acre to tens or hundreds of thousands of Jin. Today, government officials at various levels continue to create false statistics concerning GDP, finance and taxation, the employment rate, foreign investment, and so on because pleasant news will lead to promotion and other personal benefits. One informant, an economics professor at one of the best universities in China, told us, "There are three sets of data government has for everything: those collected by its statistics agency, those reported by the statistics agency to the government, and those released by the government to the public."

The third source of unwritten rules is plain old self-interest. When a monitoring and punishment system is either not in place or well executed, some people will attempt to circumvent stated rules in order to benefit personally. This, of course, is human nature and not unique to China. Many of the examples provided in the rest of this chapter reflect this motivation. In China, there is a popular saying, "Where there is an official policy, there will always be a countermeasure against it." This is used to both describe various phenomena and teach people how to circumvent rules. Back door deals best illustrate this phenomenon. Countermeasures are so widely practiced and even predominant in certain circles that they have become unwritten yet common rules contradicting official ones.

Examples in the Public Sector

Money is required to get almost anything done in China, and bribery is very much the social norm, especially in the public sector. In some cases, government agencies even have budgets specifically designated for this purpose. Bribery has a long historical tradition in China, and some current practices can be traced back hundreds of years, if not longer. During the Qing Dynasty, when a provincial official came to Beijing to get something done, he would follow the unwritten rules and visit the art dealers on Glass Street who served as the middlemen for bribes.[2] An art dealer would first ascertain how much money the provincial official intended to offer the senior official. Later the art dealer would buy a specific painting from the official for that amount of money and deliver the painting to the briber after taking a commission. The briber would simply bring the painting as a gift when he visited the senior official, thereby completing an elegant and tasteful transaction with no trace of money involved. Everything was legal on the surface without the direct exchange of a bribe (providing plausible deniability for the senior official) and with ambiguity surrounding the painting's price.

We have heard from several informants that such practices have been revived recently in China, with new twists. One such scheme was described in a report published in 2012: "A curio of an antique dealer's, actually a counterfeit worth no more than several thousand dollars, was bought by a businessman and given to an official. When buying this curio, the businessman made a deal with the antique dealer that when a man having the characteristics the businessman described came several days later to sell the curio, the antique dealer should buy it at the price as if it was the true curio instead of a counterfeit. The price difference would be paid by the businessman himself. This very curio was bought and sold to different officials and came back to the antique dealer five times, providing huge commissions for the art dealer."[3]

Another example is public bidding on government projects. While the original intention was to make the process transparent and remove backdoor dealing, public bidding has made it even easier for some government officials and firms to collude. Take land auctions, for instance. A land seeker bribes the officials concerned in advance, and the officials then fix the situation in the briber's favor. The easiest way to do this is to raise the funding threshold, for example, by stipulating that within five days, land bidders should each bring a fund of RMB 40 million to the auction. Having known this information in advance, the briber has his money ready before the bidding begins, while most firms are not able to collect such a large sum within such a short time period. Manipulations such as this effectively exclude other potential bidders from an auction, and a briber is then able to acquire land for a very low price.

Examples in the Private Sector

The most common example in the private sector is illegal kickbacks. We discuss the medical profession as a case in point. Doctors' commissions are generally set

28 Customs and Traditions

at 10 to 30% of the price of medicines purchased. For antibiotics, the commissions are even higher, from 30 to 50%. However, the commissions are not necessarily paid to the doctors who write the prescriptions. Different hospitals and departments have different regulations. In some cases, the money goes to the department head, who further allocates the commissions. "We are the 'walking RMB [the official currency of PRC and used as a synonym of the currency]' in our hospital," remarked one sales representative.[4]

Even major international pharmaceutical firms have fallen into the trap of such dealings and participated in providing kickbacks. In 2013, public security organizations discovered that in recent years GlaxoSmithKline (GSK) Investment Co. Ltd. (China) had wantonly bribed government officials, pharmaceutical industry associations and foundations, hospitals, doctors, and others. The company had bribed both directly (i.e., cash) and indirectly (e.g., through travel agencies) in order to market and increase the prices of their products. For instance, employees submitted travel expenses for fake conferences organized by travel agencies. All the receipts were reimbursed by GSK, and money was then transferred to the travel agencies, doctors, and government.[5]

An informant who is the co-owner and SVP (Senior Vice President) of a B2B company told us that his company has a budget for such kickbacks. He said people convey their desire for kickbacks in a variety of ways, ranging from explicit demands (e.g., asking for a percentage of the sale), to subtle cues (e.g., being too busy for dinner and suggesting tea instead), to seemingly innocent suggestions about how to get a deal done.

Despite the fact that many leaders of government projects in China claim they use randomly selected external experts to evaluate different bids, we were told that the process is not necessarily random. For example, one can keep picking names from a pool of potential judges until the one they want is selected. Furthermore, a firm may use all of its power to identify anonymous judges and pay visits to each of them to ensure they win the bid (through red envelopes or other types of benefits).

Another example of an unwritten rule applies to the food sector; specifically, one does not eat the products one makes himself. A person often will justify using inferior or even harmful ingredients and processes in food production, saying "I am not going to eat this." There is a popular saying in China: "Milk powder dealers never drink their milk powder; butchers never eat their meat; and greengrocers only eat the non-poisonous vegetables they produce exclusively for themselves." Everyone fancies themselves as clever, while in effect they all fall victim to each other's evil deeds.

In 2008, many infants who consumed Sanlu infant milk powder were diagnosed with lithiasis of the urinary system. It turned out that some dairy enterprises had been exploiting testing loopholes by adding melamine (a chemical material) to increase the tested protein concentration, a "trade practice" at that time. Innocent infants experienced serious bodily harm just so the milk powder companies could falsely increase protein content data. As discussed in detail later in this book, we heard stories about firms reprocessing and selling unsanitary gutter oil to restaurants, selling mouse meat as lamb, injecting red dye into watermelon, injecting water into beef (to increase weight), etc. The examples are so numerous in the food sector that one of our informants started a chain of stores that sells only imported food. His selling point: It's safe!

Examples in Personal Life

No matter how comprehensive regulations are, loopholes are inevitable. Moreover, so many people are skilled in petty shrewdness that slick opportunism and speculation in China are by no means rare.

In recent years, a marriage boom has been partially triggered by housing issues. In 2013, "Five policies and measures to regulate real estate market" ("the fives") were issued by the Chinese government.[6] The most significant and controversial point is that "an individual income tax of 20 percent will be levied on capital gains made by those home sellers whose families own more than one apartment." However, this new policy has by no means hindered the "brilliant" masses. Master plans to avoid transfer taxes in real estate transactions have emerged. In one particularly conniving scheme, the buyers and the sellers both agree to get divorced and the husband of the selling couple gets the real estate. The husband of the selling couple marries the wife of the buying couple and they share the real estate that had previously belonged to the selling couple. This newly married "couple" gets divorced, and the selling couple's real estate goes to the "wife," who was originally the wife of the buying couple. The two couples then remarry their own spouses, and the real estate has changed hands without incurring a transaction tax. People from the marriage registration center of the Shanghai Minhang District Civil Affairs Bureau said that previously only a few couples applied for divorce each day; however, since "the fives" were issued, divorce applications have soared to a steady rate of 30 per day.[7]

The most common type of unwritten rule in personal life is that one should be prepared to give red envelopes, literally or figuratively, to anyone. People think if they have power—any power—then they should exchange that power for money. It has been reported that even driving school instructors expect red envelopes. One informant told us this has become such a prevalent practice that if a patient needs to undergo an operation and the operating surgeon refuses to accept a red envelope, the patient will be really nervous that the surgeon will not do his best. The informant commented: "There is no mutual trust. Therefore, the only things that can be used are previous fellowship (whether the two were classmates before) or money."

Road Ahead

While these descriptions of (often unethical) unwritten rules may be quite depressing, we see the prognosis as quite positive. As shown by all of these examples, unwritten rules make it more costly to operate in all aspects of life (public sector, private sector, and personal life). There is no inherent reason why China will hold on to most of these unwritten rules. As described elsewhere in the book, China is moving toward a society governed by law instead of interpersonal relationships,

30 Customs and Traditions

and this will make some of the unwritten rules either obsolete or too costly for those who bribe and accept bribes. We also feel that transparency, both voluntary and involuntary (facilitated in large part by the internet), will further accelerate the demise of these unwritten rules.

It should be noted, however, that in China, where the culture dates back thousands of years, it will remain important to follow certain customs. One informant, a successful entrepreneur, told us that some current government officials do not take bribes, but a citizen must still show unconditional respect or he may not have their support. Thus, a new set of unwritten rules is emerging that is qualitatively different from what we described here.

Notes

1 For historical review, refer to: Wu Si, *Unwritten Rules: The Real Game in Chinese History*, Fudan University Press, reprinted in February 2009.
2 Glass Street is a very famous street that represents Chinese traditional culture. It is situated outside the Gate of Peace and dates back to Qing Dynasty. At that time, most of the intellectuals who came to the capital to partake in the national exam lived along this street. As a result, a strong cultural atmosphere was formed here. There are a lot of antique shops that sell ancient calligraphy and paintings. It is also a place of interest for foreign visitors.
3 Zheng He (2010, April 22), "Unwritten rules according to an antique dealer," *Qi Lu Evening News*, retrieved January 2014 from http://yun.qlwb.com.cn/paperNews/504000.html
4 Hu Xinxin (2011, November 11), "A medical representative revealed the unwritten principles," *21st Century Business Herald*, retrieved January 2014 from http://www.21cbh.com/HTML/2011-11-11/1OMDY5XzM3ODc1OA.html
5 Wang Weijia (2013, July 12), "GlaxoSmithKline top executives bribing doctors," *First Financial Daily*, retrieved September 2013 from http://www.yicai.com/news/2013/07/2853024.html
6 For more information on "the fives," see "Five policies and measures to regulate real estate market (English version)," retrieved January 2014 from http://www.china.org.cn/chinese/2013-04/19/content_28596123.htm
7 Zhang Wei (2013, June 3), "The rising divorce rate caused by the fives," *Legal Daily*, retrieved January 2014 from http://www.legaldaily.com.cn/Community/content/2013-06/03/content_4525281.htm

6   Promises

During a conversation with an informant during an early stage of research for this book, we mentioned an admiration for the famous Chinese idiom, "Once a promise is made, even a wagon drawn by the four fastest horses cannot catch up to it and take it back." In other words, a person cannot take back what he has promised. Upon hearing this, the informant burst into uncontrollable laughter and told us that we had been away from China for too long. She explained that today, a promise does not mean much and can be taken back at any time. In other words, now "even a dead horse can catch up to a promise made." She advised that one should not take what other people say too seriously; otherwise, it will cause awkwardness and misunderstanding on both sides. In fact, it is highly likely that a person who makes a promise never expects the other party to take him seriously. We relayed this story to many informants in many contexts (interviews, focus groups, lectures, etc.), and never once did anyone object to the perspective of the first informant.

Evidently, cultural norms about promises have changed drastically over the last 30 years in China. One recent story about a widely celebrated person chosen as one of the Most Inspiring Chinese of 2010 perfectly illustrates this cultural shift. For 20 years, a small time contractor named Sun Shuilin had never failed to pay his migrant workers before the start of the Chinese New Year, when they would go home to enjoy what often was the only trip they took each year to be united with their families. He paid his workers every year, even if it required borrowing money. Unfortunately, on his way to distribute the money to the workers, he and his entire family perished in a car accident. Despite this tremendous loss, his younger brother, Sun Donglin, rushed to pay the 60 migrant workers just before the eve of Chinese New Year, fulfilling Sun Shuilin's wish. Since the accounting ledger was destroyed during the accident, Donglin told the workers that he would pay whatever amount they said his brother owed them. Even their 70-year-old mother chipped in her own savings and said, "I can't let my son die with a reputation that he still owes people money."[1]

While the Sun family was admired and celebrated for upholding their promises, their story revealed two things about promises in China. First, the fact that a contractor kept his promise to pay his workers on time (and note that it was at the very last minute, before they took their annual trip home) is seen as something worth admiring, which speaks volumes about what other business owners are doing (or not doing). Something that should be considered normal (paying

32 *Customs and Traditions*

your workers on time, even if you have to borrow money) has become a virtue; this is very indicative of the current state of commitment and promises in China. Second, the fact that Sun's brother and mother felt obligated to pay their deceased relative's debt shows that the traditional Chinese value system is still very much alive in some people. Of course, it also shows that people do not necessarily follow laws in China to the letter (a topic covered elsewhere). Sun's relatives had no legal obligation to pay his debts; nevertheless, they felt social pressure to do so, in order to preserve his good reputation.

In the rest of this chapter, we discuss traditional Chinese teachings on making and keeping promises. We then dissect broken promises: who is making them, why people are making them, and the types of promises that cannot be taken seriously. We follow this with some simple guidelines on how to tell a real promise from a not-so-serious promise. In our Road Ahead section, we predict that current cultural norms around promises will revert back to the traditional value system.

Traditional Teaching on Trustworthiness

One of the core traditional Chinese virtues is trustworthiness (Chines: 信, Pinyin: xìn). Trustworthy people keep their promises, do not make commitments lightly, and are faithful and devoted to friends. Confucian scholars regard trustworthiness as one of the Five Constants of Confucianism, along with humaneness, righteousness (or justice), propriety (or etiquette), and knowledge. ZengZi, a famous Chinese philosopher and student of Confucius, once said: "I reflect on myself three times a day: first, did I spare no efforts when helping others? Second, was I honest and trustworthy to friends? Third, did I review what I have learned?" Trustworthiness has been one of the guiding principles for generations of Chinese people over the last 2,000 years. Many Chinese teachings speak to the value of keeping promises: "One's word is as weighty as nine tripod cauldrons [an ancient metal Chinese ritual device with three legs];" "one promise is worth a thousand gold pieces;" and "a man has no place to stand if he breaks word."

Many stories, both nonfictional and fictional, have been told to instill trustworthiness (and the importance of keeping promises) in Chinese young people throughout history. One such story in *Han Feizi* (a work of Legalist school of thought) is about ZengZi slaughtering his pig (which once was a valuable possession).[2] One day, ZengZi's wife was planning to go to the market and their child was crying because he wanted to go with her. She told the child, "Don't cry. Stay at home, and when I come back, we will slaughter the pig and cook meat for you." Upon her return, ZengZi prepared to slaughter the pig. His wife stopped him and said, "I was kidding with the child. Don't take it seriously." But ZengZi replied, "You cannot joke with children when they have no ability to discriminate between right and wrong. They need parental instruction and personal examples. If you lied to him today, it would be tantamount to teaching him how to lie. And he will never trust you even you deceive him only once." So the pig was slaughtered and meat was served.

Broken Promises: Who and What

Given that for thousands of years people have been taught to keep their promises, what has changed recently? We discuss who breaks promises and what aspects of promises are broken in this section. In the next section, we will discuss why promises are broken.

In our discussion on promises, many informants asked some form of the question: "In a society in which we cannot even trust the government officials, how can we trust other people?" According to our informants, broken promises are made by all three entities in society: governments, businesses, and private citizens.

Results of our research reveal that governmental promises are generally broken because of either ineffective policies or untrustworthy individuals. Some of our informants from the legal profession revealed that the Chinese government tends to legislate without performing careful groundwork. As a result, many laws, although well-intentioned, tend to be difficult or even impossible to implement. Similarly, policies created by the central government are often resisted or even distorted at the local level. Aside from these policy-level issues, government officials also break promises. One example that has been well-circulated in social media relates to a party secretary from a city in Shandong province who visited a farmer's home. The farmer had gone to the provincial government to complain about the forcible seizure of his 18 acres of land and was deemed to have a valid case. During his visit, the party secretary promised to solve the problem within three to five days. However, three years later, the problem remains unresolved.[3] We have no statistics on how widespread this phenomenon is in government, but sometimes perception is the reality.

Promises broken by businesses are quite well documented and widespread. As a matter of fact, one is often advised not to believe anything a business claims. The clearest example is false advertising. For instance, KongYi Gold Education, an afterschool education agency, advertised, "We guarantee that, starting from the day a student enters our school, the student will improve a minimum of one exam point per day, and by the time a student takes the College Entrance Exam, she should have improved by at least 100 points. If a student does not obtain such improvement, we will refund RMB 100 for each point below the promised level." They further promised, "All our students will score higher than what second tier colleges require." When one of their customers scored 53 points lower than promised and asked for a refund of RMB 5,300, the agency manager refused and stated, "The promise made by the company is an advertisement, and if it's an advertisement, of course we are allowed to exaggerate. It was not part of the contract. You cannot take it too seriously."[4]

With such cavalier attitudes about promises, it is no wonder that Chinese consumers do not trust what businesses say. Customer policies that are taken for granted in the United States cannot be treated as such in China. Many Chinese stores make price guarantees just like the American stores, but most have no intention of fulfilling them. If you bring a product back for a price match, they often will find a reason to justify why they cannot do it (e.g., you misread the guarantee, the product is not the same, the competing store cannot be trusted, etc.). In the

34 *Customs and Traditions*

worst cases, one cannot even trust whether a product is real. In a recent case, businesses made fake lamb from mouse meat and sold it to some of the most popular restaurant chains in China. Fake Maotai, the most sought after liquor in China, is also produced in large quantities. It is so prevalent that people sometimes impress their guests by stating that their Maotai was delivered via military trucks (and is, therefore, real)!

At a personal level, examples are abundant, and we discuss some in other chapters. One curious phenomenon worth noting is that, in some cases, people are asking other parties to put their promises in writing. These promises typically do not hold up in the legal system, but nevertheless, such documentation is used quite often in the court of public opinion. The former deputy director of the Department of Agriculture in Shandong, for example, wrote down his promise to his mistress that he would divorce his wife and marry her within one month. When he did not follow through, his angry mistress publicized the written promise later on the internet.[5]

Broken Promises: Why

There are many reasons why promises are broken or never intended to be fulfilled, ranging from innocent social convention to sinister self-serving purpose. First, the social norms around "promises" or commitments have changed. It is now assumed that promises are things someone says but never intends to fulfill. For example, if you meet someone for the first time or run into an acquaintance you have not seen for a long time, it is traditionally appropriate and expected for you to invite that person to visit you in your hometown. This stems from the traditional Chinese teaching that one should warmly receive guests. Although such invitations are still extended, nobody takes them literally.

In addition, a person may agree to a request (promise) because he wants to help the other party save face. In some cases, it would be considered extremely rude to refuse outright, even though one has no intention to fulfill the request; sometimes the other party fully understands that as well. The chief justice of a mid-sized city near Shanghai commented on this behavior: "Sometimes a close friend will call me over the phone and ask me to pay special attention to a particular case going through my court. I always say yes. In reality, I will not do anything about it. The friend who called me also knows I will not do anything about it. But I know the person whose case is going through my court is most likely standing next to my friend during the call, so I have to help him save face by agreeing to the request."

The second reason is less innocent and pertains to saving one's own face. If a person is incapable or unwilling to do something for another person, he may lose face if he states it outright, and saving face is supremely important in China. In some cases, the ability to make a commitment is seen as a reflection of one's power and social status in circles. So one would rather agree to a commitment and find a way out of it later than decline a commitment outright.

The third one is more sinister and self-serving. In a world where circles of friends determine one's power and people operate under the Pursuit of Quick Success and Instant Benefits (PQSIB) syndrome (discussed in a separate chapter), making a grandiose promise will instantly increase one's value in other people's eyes. The more one promises, the more attention one will receive. We have heard stories where business owners go to less developed cities in China and make pie-in-the-sky types of promises of transformation, when in reality they have no such capability. Often they are able to gain favorable policies and large tracts of land from these city governments, which they then monetize to great personal gain. Because there is such a strong focus on material wealth in China, stories like this encourage people to over-promise and worry about delivering later.

Contrary to traditional Chinese teachings, there is generally a less serious attitude toward promises today than in prior eras. We once heard someone justify not following through on a promise by saying, "Of course, you understand, I cannot do it simply for the sake of keeping a promise." If everybody understood that as she presumed, the very definition of "promise" would need to be rewritten.

To Trust, or Not

Since one cannot take others' promises at face value in China, being able to discern whether a promise made by another person (or entity) can be taken seriously is an important skill. Clearly, this takes a lot of practice and depends on the people one deals with, but some general heuristics can be followed.

First, it is important to learn how to discern the original intention of the promising party. As discussed earlier, if a promise is simply a form of social norm, one should learn to recognize it as such in order to avoid causing embarrassment to both parties. For other types of promises, one should learn to recognize whether the promising party has no intention to fulfill them, or will try, but may not have the ability to deliver.

One way to do this is to recognize the tactics Chinese typically use if they do not plan to follow through on their promises. Typically they choose to delay by saying that they are working on it or that some external events have prevented them from completing the task (e.g., someone is out of town). The idea is that if they keep dragging their feet, the problem will either become irrelevant (e.g., helping a child get into a good high school is no longer relevant after the new school year starts) or resolved (e.g., a different person solved the problem). In both cases, the promising party can still claim credit by saying she tried.

It is also important to understand that even similar promises must be treated differently based on who makes them and in what context. In general, promises made between people in the same circle (characterized by stable, complex interactions, and members who command respect) will likely be fulfilled. An unfulfilled promise in this context would likely give the promising party a severely bruised reputation within the circle, which would have severe social consequences. Interestingly, that same circle may accept the same person not keeping a promise made to someone outside the circle.

The context in which a promise is made is also important. A promise made in front of other people may or may not be more likely to be fulfilled, depending on who is present and what they are doing. For example, promises should not be trusted during dinner parties and after a lot of alcohol has been consumed.

36 *Customs and Traditions*

However, a promise made in front of others that is repeated later in private (over the phone or in person) can be more readily trusted.

Last but not least, one needs to recognize differences in how people see promises across subcultures. Very generally, people from northern China tend to make more promises than people from southern China; but of course, this is a vast simplification. The point is that subcultures have different norms about promises, and an outsider must pay close attention.

Road Ahead

Our research points to a future in which the Chinese will again follow their traditional teachings on promises based on the desires of the people. There are no fundamental reasons preventing the people from reverting to the old ways, especially since "keeping one's word" is consistent with the rule of law and Western culture.

As stated by our informants, this change must be initiated and led by the government. The government can set an example, and then encourage (and if necessary, force) businesses to follow. Once this is achieved, it is only a question of time until individuals behave accordingly in their personal lives.

More than 2,000 years ago, the famous statesman of the State of Qin, Shang Yang, encountered a similar lack of trust in government, according to the *Records of the Grand Historian*.[6] To reestablish trust, he erected a large wooden stick at the South City Gate and posted a notice that whoever took it to the North City Gate would receive a cash reward that would make him instantly wealthy. Nobody believed him until someone decided to give it try, and indeed received the prize from Shang Yang. After that, everybody believed in Shang Yang & Qin. Restoring trust may certainly prove to be a more difficult task this time, but drastic measures might need to be taken if the government wants to change these norms quickly, to the benefit of every stakeholder. After all, a society where promises cannot be trusted is very costly to live in for everyone.

Notes

1 Story about Sun, based on the CNTV (China Network Television) program *The Most Inspiring Chinese of 2010*, retrieved January 2014 from http://www.cntv.cn/

2 Han Feizi (1964), *Han Feizi*, translated by Burton Watson, New York: Columbia University Press.

3 Li Xiaoqing (2011, October 20), "Not-so-serious promise by a Secretary Municipal Committee," *People's Daily*, retrieved January 2014 from http://leaders.people.com.cn/GB/15960312.html

4 Wang Yong (2013, September 10), "Manager of the KongYi Gold Education didn't take the promise seriously," *Dahe Daily*, retrieved January 2014 from http://henan.sina.com.cn/news/2010-09-10/092137248.html

5 Wang Shiyu, & Zhang Weiwei (2012, December 1), "A former deputy director wrote down his promise to his mistress," *Southern Metropolis Daily*, retrieved January 2014 from http://news.nandu.com/html/201212/01/5848.html

6 Sima Qian (1961), *Records of the Grand Historian*, translated by Burton Watson, New York: Columbia University Press.

7 Pursuit of Quick Success and Instant Benefits (PQSIB)

It was Dong Zhongshu[1] of the Han Dynasty (202 BC–220 AD) who first warned enlightened men against the pursuit of quick success and instant benefits (PQSIB). More than 2,000 years later, this is one of the most common phrases used to describe the current generation of Chinese people. Many informants, professors, and executives alike lament the fact that the Chinese people currently tend to approach life with a PQSIB mindset, an unfortunate syndrome that most in society would like to eliminate. If you encounter a Chinese person and want to make an insightful, yet inoffensive critique of the Chinese, just empathize with him about PQSIB syndrome; it will make an instant impression and he will likely be ready to engage in a deep conversation with you.

In this chapter, we discuss the key effects of this syndrome, which we follow with an analysis of factors that have led to its existence. We then briefly provide a few illustrative examples of this syndrome in various facets of society—personal, work, business, and government. We conclude with the Road Ahead section, where we predict that this syndrome will continue (albeit in a modified form) in the near future.

Effects

On the positive side, PQSIB syndrome has served its intended purpose; everything is accelerated in Chinese society compared to other societies. The energy of Chinese entrepreneurs, for example, is unsurpassed worldwide. Such energy emanating from a population of 1.4 billion people has driven and will continue to accelerate economic development. In an elementary school we visited, the principal told us that most students in his school want to be "bosses" (i.e., business owners) when they grow up. This positive effect, however, comes at great cost.

First, people tend to think and act favoring short term goals over long term priorities. An important ramification of this is that people see events in life as transactional. Second, quality suffers. Instead of doing things in the best possible way, most who suffer from this syndrome tend to do the bare minimum amount of work required to complete a task. Last, people often attempt to cut corners and circumvent rules to speed up the process, in some cases going as far as breaking laws. A common saying used by many to justify these types of behaviors is "rules are dead, but people are alive." In other words, rules are fixed, but people are flexible; thus, one should always strive to find ways to get around rules. We illustrate these effects in the examples we provide later in this chapter.

Causes

While many factors have contributed to PQSIB syndrome, some are more permanent while others are more transient and unique to this stage of social development in China. First, there is an almost exclusive emphasis on material wealth now across all social strata. Since wealth is the primary criterion used to judge success, people strive to achieve it, and as quickly as possible.

The second factor is the speed of change of the macro environment. China has undergone unprecedented growth over the last 30 years. The Chinese people have grown accustomed to seeing their environment change quickly and substantially. For example, as we describe elsewhere, Shenzhen grew from a fishing village into a thriving metropolis with 10 million people that rivals Hong Kong in just 30 years. Apartment prices in Shanghai have increased 10-fold within the last 10 years. The speed of such change makes people feel that they must change at the same or even a faster rate in order to have any chance of succeeding.

The third factor is uncertainty about the future. Almost all of our informants, regardless of whether they worked in the public or private sector, had accumulated much wealth or very little, were old or young, wondered about China's future. Therefore, they are trying to get what they can now, before it is too late.

Fourth, the herd effect is at work. "Do what others are doing" is a well observed decision heuristic in China. Since PQSIB syndrome is so pervasive, one must embrace it or be left behind—or worse, be laughed at for not fitting in.

Finally, the scarcity of resources has also played a role. Although China is a big country, considering its 1.4 billion people, resources and opportunities are very limited. Thus limited resources must be snatched up quickly under such huge competitive pressure.

Examples in Personal Life

The shortest distance between two points is a straight line. Therefore, many Chinese people feel that if you can find a line between the start and the finish (i.e., a shortcut), why take the long route? This logic sometimes can be observed literally; people jump the queue if possible, and pedestrians cross busy streets where it is prohibited, with some even climbing fences to do so.

One excellent example is the widespread goal to find a rich spouse in order to avoid 20 years of hard work. The idea has become so acceptable that, in 2011, the first domestic high-end marriage training school was launched in Beijing to teach women how to find a wealthy spouse. When a wealthy man puts out an advertisement to search for a potential wife, hundreds or even thousands of young women will respond, literally, as if they were applying for a job.

Examples in Work

A story from one of our informants best illustrates PQSIB at work. A Chinese company bought a large piece of equipment from a European company. As part of the agreement, three engineers from the European company were sent to China to supervise the installation. After following their instructions for three days, the Chinese engineers were frustrated with the slow progress. So on the fourth day, the Chinese engineers decided to do it their own way. They finished putting the entire machine together in two hours while the foreign engineers were on their lunch break. However, when the foreign engineers came back, they were very angry and insisted that they take the machine apart and reassemble it following the procedure, step by step. The entire episode caused substantial embarrassment on both sides.

Another informant who runs a shipbuilding business told us: "Americans are not as flexible or pragmatic as Chinese people are. So I think Americans' minds are square, while Chinese heads are round. Americans do not want to do things that will shorten time and increase efficiency, if such modifications are against procedures or contracts, even if a contract is unreasonable." In his view, the Chinese care more about results and are willing to be very flexible as long as the results are achieved. In other words, to the Chinese, the ends justify the means. However, from his perspective, Americans not only want results, but also to follow processes to the letter; how something is done matters a great deal.

Examples in Business

Businesses are focused on how to make money now, while and wherever they still can. This attitude reflects the prime business model many firms have adopted in China: copycatting. Copycatting is the fastest way to generate money, and because commerce was lacking in China until 30 years ago, many firms have done pretty well by practicing this model. A lack of willingness or capability to innovate will likely inhibit the further development of many Chinese firms as the domestic market becomes mature and China loses its competitive strength as the world's manufacturing base.

In the worst cases, firms are even willing to engage in behaviors that are either in the legal "gray area" or outright illegal, all in the pursuit of quick money. We give two well-known examples here. The first example is the fully developed and large scale production of gutter oil. Gutter oil is cooking oil produced from waste oil typically collected from restaurant sewer drains, grease traps, etc. There are many players in this supply chain who collect, recycle, reprocess, and resell this oil (typically to restaurants). All participants in the value chain know it is illegal. We asked several restaurant owners why restaurants buy gutter oil and whether they know what it is. Their rationale was simple: it is much cheaper than regular cooking oil. They are fully aware that they are buying gutter oil because of the price and the fact that it is typically not labeled.

The second example was reported on the *Weekly Quality Report* program on CCTV (China Central Television) on April 15, 2012. Some companies in Hebei produced gelatin for drug capsules using leather scraps. Since leather production involves using chromium, a heavy metal unsuitable for the human body, capsules made from this reprocessed gelatin caused severe harm to patients.

There are countless examples of Chinese firms using inferior or illegal materials and processes to produce products that will yield quick profits. One of us

40   *Customs and Traditions*

once asked a group of 60 executives about developing a new product to address food safety concerns of the Chinese people, a portable device that could detect the heavy metal concentration in food before it is bought. Nobody doubted the value of such product, except one remarked, only half-jokingly, that one may end up buying nothing because most of the food is contaminated.

Examples in Government

Governments at all levels suffer from the same syndrome. Many local governments have rushed to invest in grandiose projects, regardless of actual demand, in order to create major achievements (i.e., transform their cities) in a short time period. Many urban development projects, unfortunately, have become nothing more than ghost towns and deserted malls. One example is the industrial park in Ordos, a new business district in Henan, a city located in central China. The government built a business park covering more than 10,000 acres planning to attract 1,500 firms. In the end, 50 firms moved in, and 90% of the area was deserted.[2]

Road Ahead

Despite associated negative ramifications and a general distaste for PQSIB among the Chinese, we predict a continued presence of this syndrome, albeit in a modified form, in the near future. If properly channeled, PQSIB can morph into high energy in entrepreneurship and innovation, as well as personal development.

Notes

1 Dong Zhongshu (179 BC–104 BC) was a Han Dynasty Chinese scholar, philosopher, and politician. He also promoted Confucianism as the official ideology during the Han Dynasty.
2 Zhang Jiazhen (2013, January 21), "Wuhan Industrial Park in 'ghost town crisis,'" *China Business Journal,* retrieved January 2014 from http://www.cb.com.cn/index.php?m=content&c=index&a=show&catid=6457&id=442222

8 Drinking Culture

The Chinese drinking culture goes back thousands of years. To the Chinese people, alcohol is part of the culture, part of the identity. It is an activity engaged in not only by the brawny, but also by the brainy. During the last few years, demand for expensive hard liquor has gone through the roof; for example, the price of the most popular variations of a famous liquor, Maotai (a highly sought-after Chinese liquor by Kweichow Moutai Company Limited), increased from about RMB 300 per bottle to RMB 1,900 over a 5-year period. Corporate revenue for the producer of Maotai was RMB 51.4 billion in 2011. Another dominant player, Wuliangye (Wuliangye Yibin Company Limited), reported revenue of RMB 60 billion in 2012. This huge demand for liquor is driven by a unique drinking culture in China. In this chapter, we discuss why the Chinese drink (a lot), rules one should observe when drinking at dinner parties, drinking as a job skill, drinking interactions among Westerners and the Chinese, and finally, our predictions about how this drinking culture will evolve in the coming years.

Figure 8.1 A dinner party

42 *Customs and Traditions*

Why the Chinese Drink (A Lot)

There are many reasons why the Chinese drink alcohol. In this section, we discuss several factors that support the strong drinking culture in China. Specifically we explain how alcohol plays a role in evaluating a person's character, building trust, maintaining relationships, building credit, facilitating business interactions, and evaluating employees.

Two types of toasts are made in China. The first one is identical to what Westerners are used to, in the sense of "proposing a toast" or "toasting someone." The person making the toast normally describes an accomplishment or makes a wish for the future and says, "Let's drink to that!" In China, there is also a second type of toast that is more similar to the meaning of the Chinese phrase jìng jiǔ (敬酒). The first Chinese character loosely means "to respectfully provide" and the second character refers to liquor. In other words, alcohol often is used to show appreciation and respect. The difference between the two types of toasts is critical, as it determines whom one should toast, how one should toast, how often one should toast, how one should behave when another toasts him, etc.

First, business owners often determine employees' roles in their companies based on their drinking behaviors. There is a common saying that "the way one drinks reflects the way one works." If a person exhibits unacceptable behavior (e.g., not manly enough, honest enough, devoted enough) while drinking, others will expect similar behaviors in a professional setting, and trust will be broken. One informant who is a successful and experienced business owner told us: "I can use the alcohol drunk at dinner tables to judge each person's personality and character, and decide how I will use him or her in the future. Those who always fight to make the first toast before their colleagues have a chance to do so are most suited for the public relations department. Those who insist on not drinking show that they adhere to principles, and are suited for accounting and financial work. Those who are willing to show their loyalty by drinking a lot, even at the expense of hurting their bodies are those I can count on. Those who always find excuses not to drink when they in fact can drink (and quite a bit), I will not give them important responsibilities, as they will find excuses to retreat during a critical stage of the business. Those who drink more than they should and 'tell the truth' also cannot be relied on for important things, as they do not have good self-control and may likely leak important information during business negotiations. Bosses will always use people with different personalities and characteristics for different positions, so drinking more does not always curry favor with your boss. It's important to be yourself when liquor is served during dinners, and never drink more than you can handle."

Drinking can energize the atmosphere during dinners because alcohol is the lubricant of personal relationships. One informant told us: "Liquor is the conduit. When there is not a whole lot to say, toasting each other can change the atmosphere from dull to exciting, and creates an interface for people to communicate. Liquor is a stimulant, which lets people go back to their true selves. So we can see a person's true personality when drinking, a time when people have no masks and do not pretend."

How much one drinks is a metric for mutual trust. During our interviews, we asked why people drink so much—sometimes even to the point of being drunk—especially in business contexts when they are with people they do not know very well. The answer is to build trust and shorten the distances among strangers/acquaintances quickly. One of the most important problems in China is a general lack of trust in society. However, when someone is drunk, he is unlikely to keep any secret from you. So the fact that someone is willing to drink to the point of being drunk shows that he has nothing to hide. At an even higher level, the fact that another person is willing to drink so much at the expense of his own health shows how much that person values the relationship. This is a critically important point. People host dinners and provide ample quantities of alcohol not only to evaluate their guests, but also to allow their guests to evaluate them.

Often, how much one drinks during dinner is used as an indicator of a person's sincerity in a relationship. This is a way to reaffirm friendships and business relationships. There is a common saying in China: "If it's a superficial relationship, you sip; if it's a solid relationship, you drink until you need to go to the hospital for intravenous treatment; and if you are buddies, you drink until your stomach bleeds." A more refined statement that is often quoted among the Chinese is: "When drinking with someone who understands you, a thousand glasses are not enough." When a host says something like this to a guest, how could a guest say no to the next drink?

Some business owners we interviewed told us that 90% of business in China is discussed over dinner and liquor. When exploring potential collaborations or sales opportunities, some basic information may be presented during formal business meetings. However, what happens during business dinners often is more important. Because alcohol facilitates a more relaxed atmosphere, it is easier for both parties to open up and talk about things that are not appropriate for discussion in the office. When discussions happen in the office, they are official events. Dinners, however, are semi-official and semi-private. As a result, many things can be said in a restaurant that would not be said in an office setting. Sometimes, nothing needs to be said directly. Just drink enough, make sure everybody has a good time, be honest, and give a lot of face to the other party, and everything else (including the business deal discussed in the office) will happen in due course. Many people noted that although on the surface these dinners seem to be about drinking, in reality they are about doing business. Sometimes people even refuse to talk about business issues during dinners because it is considered to be impolite. One informant told us that a real estate professional would need to attend four to five dinners each week with people from banks, tax offices, and other government agencies. Although these dinners all take place after official business hours, the Chinese do not clearly separate work and private lives, and everybody recognizes that going to business dinners is a basic job requirement. Although business dinners (and the alcohol consumed at them) are important business tools, unfortunately, they are also sometimes tools of corruption.

As discussed elsewhere in this book, in China personal relationships and circles are among the most important things in life. Many Chinese people believe

44 *Customs and Traditions*

that going to dinner parties and drinking a lot is the requisite way to develop both personal and business relationships. Therefore, the number of such events that one must attend is amazing. If one person hosts a dinner party for 12 people, the other people will likely reciprocate, so it quickly turns into 12 dinner parties that one must attend. It is quite common for people to attend such dinner parties multiple times per week; even an ordinary (non-business) person is expected to attend at least one dinner party per week. Many senior people even attend more than one party per night, similar to American politicians during the campaign season. These behaviors span all occupations. CEOs and owners of billion dollar companies follow drinking patterns that are quite similar to very high level public servants such as provincial governors or minsters of the central government.

Rules of Drinking

While some events might seem more like fraternity parties than gatherings of mature adults (who are very accomplished in terms of both career and wealth), there are still many rules that must be carefully followed. It is important to remember that people are always watching. Even those who were too drunk to remember will be reminded by their associates later about how someone else behaved during the rounds of toasts. Many inferences are made based on those behaviors.

During a dinner, the most important guest always sits at the head of the table, which can be confusing, since round tables are used for almost all dinners. In general, the seat facing the door is the most important seat. Sometimes the most important visiting party sits in this seat, and sometimes the host who is paying for the dinner sits in it (in which case, the host tends to have equal or higher status than the most important visitor, who then sits next to the host). In some restaurants, the napkin for the head seat is folded differently than the others. Often, the server will put a dish on the Lazy Susan at the end of the table (close to the door) and then turn the Lazy Susan so that the most important person can taste it first. In some places that we visited, such as Henan province, other guests are not supposed to eat a dish until the person sitting at the head of the table tries it (especially something presented whole, like a fish).

At the beginning of the dinner, everyone will sit around the table, and the most important person will make one or more toasts. After that, the real drinking begins. Everyone around the table will propose toasts to each other, sometimes to the entire table, sometimes to specific individuals. To show respect, a guest often will leave his seat (especially when there are more than eight people around the table), walk around the table to a specific person, and carry out a personal toast. Once a person leaves the table, she will normally start by toasting the most important person, and then walk around the table, making toasts (in order) to almost every person seated at the table. When clinking glasses, the person with lower or junior status should always keep his glass slightly lower than the other person's glass. The sequence of toasts is also very important. A junior person must allow more senior people to toast first; stealing the boss's thunder would be frowned upon.

When a toast is made, it is perfectly acceptable not to finish all of the liquor in one's glass, but it is not acceptable to drink nothing. (If a person does not drink alcohol for religious or health reasons, a non-alcoholic beverage may be substituted.) One of our informants was a Christian who did not drink at all. We never once saw anyone force him to drink at three large dinner parties we attended with him, including one he hosted and paid for. Another informant did not drink anything at a dinner because he said he was in the hospital twice recently for drinking too much; again, nobody insisted on him drinking even a sip. Although it is perfectly fine not to drink alcohol, a person (especially a junior person) is still expected to toast other guests around the table. Both of our non-drinking informants were very active participants at the dinner parties we attended and toasted people with orange juice. If a person does not drink alcohol, it is fine as long as she never touches any liquor in any situation. However, once a person drinks on one occasion, she will be expected to drink in other contexts. Otherwise, it will be taken as a personal insult by other guests who will assume that they are not as important as previous drinking partners.

One business owner who has attended countless dinner parties remarked: "Drinking is taken even more seriously when government officials are involved. If one is in government and your supervisor asks you to drink, you must drink, even if you are going to die by drinking more. If you don't, government officials will think you don't respect them. Dinner parties are all about keeping the government officials happy and giving them face. The best thing you can do is drink until you pass out, to show your sincerity."

Note that there are substantial regional differences associated with the Chinese drinking culture, reflecting cultural differences in general. The northerners are like the old time cowboys in the United States. They can hold their liquor and they enjoy drinking a lot. The westerners have much in common with the northerners in China. They like to drink until they can drink no more. During a trip to Xinjiang, we were told by the host that it is customary there for a guest to finish all the liquor in his glass if he agrees to a toast—never a sip! The southerners, however, are more subtle (or in the eyes of the northerners, girlish) and often just drink moderately.

There is also a difference between large metropolitan and rural areas, and between developed and less developed regions. Heavy drinking is said to play an especially important role in business in less developed regions and rural areas. In Beijing and Shanghai, business can be conducted without the presence of alcohol on the dinner table. In Shanghai in particular, the notion that one should not drink too much is now widely accepted. The chairwoman of a boutique investment company in Shanghai specializing in entertainment told us: "If one agreed to something during state of drunkenness, and then retracted the commitment the next day on the excuse of being drunk the previous night, what am I supposed to do?"

China Interacts with the West

As the number of interactions with Westerners has increased, we have heard some interesting examples of conflict and reconciliation related to the consumption of

46   *Customs and Traditions*

alcohol. We were told by a senior executive that he once took a team of 10 people from his company in China to attend an executive training program in Frankfurt, Germany. In the evening, the host, a German, treated them to a nice dinner at the Marriott and bought an expensive bottle of wine. One of his Chinese colleagues poured a full glass of wine and raised his glass to make a toast and said, "Bottoms up!" The host, however, stopped him immediately and told them that good wine must be enjoyed slowly. The host then turned around and ordered a few bottles of cheaper wine for the toast. This was a major faux pas in the eyes of the visiting Chinese executives. One even remarked that Germans are misers. (How easy it is to stereotype an entire nation!) In China, regardless how expensive the liquor is, you always let your guests drink it however they want. Interestingly, the host's point is quite rational. The differences in wines are subtle, and one will unlikely be able to tell the difference between an average wine and a really good wine if one simply dumps glass after glass into his stomach. This anecdote highlights an interesting difference between the drinking cultures of the West and China.

That said, we also have heard many stories of how Westerners (even titans of industry) have adjusted their drinking behavior when they interact with the Chinese. We were told by the number-two person at one of the largest airlines in China that his company had formed a joint venture with a leading airline in the United States. Over the course of many years, he noticed that the behavior of his American counterparts shifted from perfunctory drinking at business dinners to energetic drinking equaling his own, even with strong liquor like Maotai.

Drinking as a Job Requirement

Because of the strong drinking culture, many people are forced to adopt this lifestyle even if they do not want to. In a recent survey[1] jointly conducted by a newspaper (*Life Times*) and online portals (Sina & Sohu's Health Channel), out of the 8,433 respondents, 75.8% reported drinking because of social and work requirements, while just 4.4% reported that they enjoy drinking a little during regular dinners. They said they were "forced" to drink for several reasons, including: wanting face (42.5%), being asked by a boss during business events or company gatherings (19.9%), and dining with potential customers or asking someone for a favor (10.5%). Interestingly, 8.3% also reported that they had to drink at dinner parties on behalf of their bosses. (Please note this is proper only if the one who toasts is of lower status than the boss.) Similar to cultures in other Asian countries like Japan, those who refuse invitations or requests from their bosses to drink have slim chance of being promoted or being given important responsibilities in the future.

Thus, a person becomes more employable if she can drink. Many college students even begin practicing their drinking skills by building up their tolerance to alcohol and fitting into the drinking culture. (Imagine telling American undergraduates that this is an important job skill!) An ability to drink heavily may not only help a young person find a job but also may put him on the fast track to promotion within a company. In extreme cases, some companies even hire people whose sole job is to drink with their clients until they are satisfied. One informant told us that a company specifically hired two people for this purpose; they can drink 750 ml of liquor with 53% alcohol and still carry on a lucid and energetic conversation around the dinner table.

Those who can drink more have a distinct competitive advantage. A vice president responsible for client management described his experience to us. He spends more than 80% of his time making sure his clients, both old and new, feel they are well treated. He also must maintain relationships with various government agencies via dinner parties. If he does not carefully orchestrate these parties, they will think he is not friendly enough or not giving them face, and such grievances would become ticking time bombs leading to dissolution of the relationships. He lives under a tremendous amount of pressure, and he said he feels exhausted after each dinner, both physically and mentally.

Road Ahead

While the drinking culture in China has deep roots over thousands of years, we do see it evolving substantially in the near future. Most importantly, we believe the culture of "drink until you drop" will gradually disappear, at least in official settings. Several factors contribute to this prediction.

First, the Xi government takes drinking very seriously, as alcohol is seen as facilitating corruption. Spending on liquor (and dinners in general) is now restricted among all public branches of government, military, and government-owned enterprises. While many people are adopting a wait and see attitude, nobody wants to risk being made an example by central government.

The second reason is that people are beginning to care more about their health. Very senior business people told us that it is no longer worth it to exchange health for money. This attitude is trickling down the ranks. If the owner of a private company publicly says that he would not drink to win business, his employees will no longer feel pressured to drink. After all, most people drink because they have to, not because they want to.

In addition, China is transitioning from a relationship society to a rule-based society. When transactions are based on rules, one does not need to call in personal favors. Thus, the need for so many drinking occasions specifically to cultivate such relationships will decrease.

Finally, the Chinese like to learn from the best, however that is defined. Many business owners have made the transition from drinking heavily to drinking moderately and from drinking hard liquor to drinking wines. Wine imports in China totaled USD 2.6 billion in 2012, up 8.9% from 2011, and the trend is continuing. The Chinese view Western drinking patterns as being more cultured and sophisticated, so they want to mimic those behaviors just as they buy Western luxury goods, whether automobiles or handbags.

Note

1 Wang Yue (2011, September 30), "Online survey on drinking," *Life Times*, retrieved January 2014 from http://paper.people.com.cn/smsb/html/2011-09/30/content_934496.htm

Part II
Social Structure

9   Harmonious Society

One of the fundamental concepts of Confucianism is that harmony is precious. In other words, people should get along and refrain from activities that disrupt unity. In fact, achieving harmony should be one of the most important objectives of both leaders and followers when any decision is made, whether it affects a single family or society at large. This philosophy, which has become ingrained in Chinese society over the last 2,000 years, has recently been thrust into the spotlight due to its official adoption by the government. We discuss the historical origins of societal harmony as a concept, the government's stance toward it, and three major behavioral patterns related to conflict that have emerged as a result of the government's stance. In the Road Ahead section, we question whether the Chinese will continue to emphasize societal harmony as an important goal.

Historical Context

According to the teachings of Confucius, harmony requires coordination, mediation, and conflict avoidance. Harmony is believed to be the highest state one may achieve in life. In his Doctrine of the Mean, Confucius said that a superior man pursues equilibrium; this is commonly known in the West as "finding the happy medium." (Note that Confucius did not explicitly discuss the concept of fairness in this context; rather, the focus rests solely on finding common ground.) Under this doctrine, people expect and practice a strategy of making bigger conflicts smaller, and making smaller conflicts disappear. Even to this day, this doctrine influences interpersonal and managerial relationships.

There are four different types of harmony: personal, interpersonal, between a person and society, and between society and nature. In most cases, however, when the Chinese refer to "harmony," they mean interpersonal harmony.

Harmonious Society as a Governing Doctrine

During the 4th Plenary Session of the 16th CPC Central Committee in 2004, "harmonious society" was formally adopted as the governing doctrine by the Hu leadership (in power from 2004 to 2013), and it is still very much a guiding principle in many aspects of Chinese society. Specifically, the government wants to build a harmonious society based on "democracy, rule of law, fairness, trust, love, energetic life, stability, and coexistence between man and nature."

52 *Social Structure*

The government officially adopted the harmonious society concept mainly in response to the many non-harmonious phenomena that occurred as a result of rapid economic development. A plethora of problems exist related to corruption, employment, safety, and the distribution of income, resources, and opportunities (i.e., urban versus rural, rich versus poor). Relationships between people of different social strata are strained; medical and education costs are skyrocketing and accessibility is limited; existing residences are being demolished for development without sufficient compensation or consultation; environmental pollution is out of control; and decisions are based primarily on a short-term perspective. These are but a few of the present-day challenges to societal harmony.

Our research, based on both primary and secondary data, revealed that members of Chinese society are very concerned about a bleak future if something is not done to address issues that are negatively impacting societal harmony. Xi, who took over the leadership in 2013, sounded an even bigger alarm, stating that "the Chinese Communist Party and China will dissolve if we don't eliminate corruption." Thus, the objective of building a harmonious society is to resolve existing conflicts (i.e., complaints, concerns) so that a stable society can be maintained in perpetuity—not to create a better society, per se. Building a harmonious society is seen as a solution that will prevent a potential governmental crisis.

Since China has a top-down style of government and the government's primary focus is on building a harmonious society, all government officials' evaluations are partly based on how harmonious their regions are. As a result, it is no surprise that local government officials will do whatever they can to maintain perceptions of harmony. Unfortunately, this has led to three major unintended behavioral patterns related to conflict: firefighting, concession-seeking, and timidity and disrespectfulness in law enforcement contexts.

Firefighting

Firefighting refers to the practice of treating symptoms quickly so as to preserve harmony instead of investing the time and effort necessary to address a problem's underlying cause. One informant told us that in China, if there is a headache, the head is treated and if there is foot ache, the foot is treated; rarely will someone try to identify the actual cause of the headache or foot ache. Another informant recounted a joke from ancient times that he thinks captures the current state of affairs in China. In that joke, a soldier who was hit by an arrow went to see a surgeon. The surgeon took out a pair of scissors, cut off the end of the arrow, and said, "Done! I am a surgeon who treats only external problems."

Since government officials at all levels hold their positions for just a few years, one of their primary objectives is to maintain harmony during their tenure; what happens after they leave is of no importance to them. We have been told that the worst thing that could happen at any level of government would be for a group of citizens to interrupt governmental operations and create an impression of an unharmonious society. Officials are equally afraid that constituents will complain to their governmental superiors (especially to Beijing). So government officials often either cave in to demands or suppress them. They solve problems quickly without attempting to address their root causes because doing so would likely take longer and not be perceived as harmonious.

Concession-Seeking

Another unintended behavioral outcome of placing such great emphasis on societal harmony is concession-seeking. Since "the squeaky wheel gets the grease," some Chinese people strategically behave in ways that may cause unharmonious perceptions or outcomes so they can extract concessions from another party that wants to maintain harmony. Many citizens understand that it is important for the local government to maintain a harmonious image. Therefore, they feel that if they can turn a small thing into a big thing, then the other party (whether a government agency, government-owned firm, or even a private firm with governmental stakeholders) will be willing to compromise and give up more in order to assuage the situation.

According to a news report,[1] in August 2013, a dozen people dressed in traditional funeral clothes brought a dead body to the City Urban Administrative and Law Enforcement Bureau (CUALEB) in Wuhan (the provincial capital of Hubei). They claimed the dead person was a street vendor whom the officers of CUALEB (known as Cheng guan) had beaten to death while removing him from a street corner where he had unlawfully set up his stall. During the ensuing three hours, many citizens gathered in support of the vendor; traffic was disrupted, and the police were called to maintain order. To everyone's surprise, the dead person came back to life after a few hours! It turned out that the street vendor had not died at all. Due to the hot weather, the person who was pretending to be dead could no longer lie still. The whole event was just a ruse used by the vendor and his family to escalate their fight with the CUALEB in order to exact more concessions.

In another example,[2] a woman in her sixties claimed she was hit by a security guard in the Forbidden City and suffered a broken bone. As it turned out, she had insisted on going into a section that was closed to the public and hit the security guard with an umbrella. The security guard simply acted in self-defense. Nevertheless, in the spirit of maintaining a harmonious society, a senior manager of the Forbidden City not only took the elderly woman to the hospital to be evaluated (nothing was broken), but also paid an undisclosed amount for police mediation. The senior manager even apologized, saying: "We have not done a good job in educating our employees. Our rule is that our employees cannot have any conflict with visitors under any circumstances."

Many patients have also resorted to disrupting hospital operations when they think there is a chance to extract concessions from the hospital for real or perceived medical malpractice. In order to make incidents bigger, patients may get dozens of their relatives and friends to join them when they go to complain. Often these mobs resort to physically damaging the hospital facilities or even hurting medical staff. The logic is, the more people you bring, the more likely the hospital is to make a quicker and bigger concession in order to maintain a harmonious environment.

54 Social Structure

Timidity and Disrespectfulness in Law Enforcement Contexts

Many stories have circulated regarding the poor treatment of detainees by law enforcement agencies in China. Less reported is the fact that many Chinese citizens also are disrespectful and confrontational toward law enforcement officers—something that would be unthinkable in the United States. Because they are trained not to escalate conflict, many police officers are very timid about enforcing the law. We were told by a vice chief justice of a district court in Shanghai that police officers are explicitly told not to hit or yell back when others hit them or yell at them. He saw many cases where police officers had been hit, pushed, or otherwise physically intimidated by angry citizens who were confronted for violating laws.

Because people know police officers have orders not to hit back, many feel they are entitled to engage in confrontation with them, especially when they are stopped for traffic violations. In June 2013 in Nanjing, the provincial capital of Jiangsu, a woman who ran a red light called her boyfriend on the phone; he rushed to the scene and punched the police officer in the face.[3] The fact that someone could even contemplate doing such a thing is quite unthinkable in the West. However, police have been trained to not make a small thing bigger and to try to make bigger things smaller in order to prevent escalation and preserve some semblance of harmony.

One informant, a senior executive at a major airline in China, relayed another story that illustrates this point. A few months ago, there was heavy fog in Kunming and all flights were delayed or canceled. Travelers were extremely unhappy and began to argue and disrupt the work of airline employees. When the police were called, they arrived but did nothing. They did not separate the two parties, nor did they inquire about the reason for the argument; instead, they just stood in the general area, facing the opposite direction. Some of the airline's equipment and facilities were damaged by the travelers, who did so with impunity. Our informant was extremely disappointed by the failure of the police in Kunming to take action and wished they would have responded more like the police in Hong Kong, who would have stopped the fight immediately.

Another informant provided another telling example. One of his friends was walking his dog one day and the dog bit a child. After the police officer came and listened to the arguments from both parties, the police officer told them, "I don't know who is right, so just pretend I never came."

The fact that current Chinese citizens do not fear or respect police was a curious finding for us. One informant described it this way: "When I was young, we respected and even were afraid of the police. If he told me to do something, I would do it. This is respect for authority. This is not the case anymore. I think society should have respect for authority."

Road Ahead

The pursuit of a harmonious society will continue to be a focus of the Chinese government in the coming years. Although different terms may be used, the underlying concept will be the same. As illustrated by the examples we provided in this chapter, current behavior patterns associated with conflict are destructive and must change. Interestingly, not everyone even agrees that achieving a harmonious society is the right objective. One informant said: "If we treat harmony as the end goal, many things will be done wrong. There are things that can be resolved within the legal framework, but they will all be covered up if one pursues harmony."

Our outlook on this fundamental social phenomenon is that given the long history of Confucianism and deeply ingrained personal practices based on Confucian teachings, harmony will continue to be part of the governing doctrine—at least until governmental leaders feel that the looming crisis has been averted. On the other hand, we foresee a gradual integration of law into the implementation of harmony, or even harmony becoming conditional on laws.

Notes

1 Dai Wei, Wang Yuesheng, & Gao Xing (2013, August 5), "Exposure of photos on fake death of the street vendor in Wuhan," *Wuhan Evening News*, retrieved January 2014 from http://whwb.cjn.cn/images/2013-08-05/7/34811375637359500.pdf
2 Bai Ying & Liao Yi (2013, July 5), "The Forbidden City's response to the incident," Xinhuanet.com, retrieved January 2014 from http://news.xinhuanet.com/2013-07/05/c_116425318.htm
3 Ren Guoyong & Lu Gongxuan (2013, July 1), "A police officer was punched in the face," *Yangtse Evening News*, retrieved January 2014 from http://epaper.yzwb.net/html_t/2013-07/01/content_84741.htm?div=-1

10 Subcultures

There is a common misconception that the Chinese people are relatively homogenous in terms of how they think and act, but in reality, this notion could not be further from the truth. In order to truly understand China, one must first appreciate the differences among its people. In the English speaking world, there are many variations of a popular joke that starts with "An Englishman, an Irishman, and a Scotsman walk into a bar ..." The actual content varies based on who is telling the joke, but it invariably plays on cultural stereotypes. In China, there is a similar joke that also contrasts stereotypical differences among people from different provinces. Here is a version that might be told by someone from the Shandong province:

> One day, seven passengers, all from different places (the Northeast Provinces, Guangdong, Henan, Shanghai, Beijing, Zhejiang, and Shandong), boarded the same plane. During the flight, the captain informed them, "We are in trouble. I'm afraid that somebody must jump off the plane to lighten the load so we can continue to fly safely."

> Upon hearing this, the Cantonese took out his checkbook and said, "Not a problem. I'll write a check to the one who is willing to jump."

> The Beijinger replied indignantly: "How can you buy life with money? Though death befalls all men alike, it could be weightier than Mount Tai or lighter than a feather. It's just a life, what's the big deal!" While others looked at the Beijinger admirably, he continued, "Unfortunately, I have a meeting with the envoy of the UN Secretary General Ban Ki-moon to discuss peacekeeping issues today. This meeting concerns the well-being of mankind. I can't die, so I'll leave this glorious opportunity to you."

> The Shanghainese said, "The one who jumps off should be the one who has the least value to the society. One from a city should be more highly valued than one from a rural area, and one from Shanghai, the biggest city, should have more value than one from other cities. I'm Shanghainese and my valuable life should be devoted to the economic development of Shanghai." Then he turned his eyes toward the Henanese who dressed like a peasant.

58 *Social Structure*

On hearing this, the Henanese burst into tears and cried, "I'm a poor peasant and my value for the society is the smallest among us. It should be me who jumps off, but I have to support my 84-year-old mother. I can't die!"

Growing impatient, the Northeasterner waved his iron fist and said, "Shut up! Let's settle this with our fists."

Then everyone turned to the tiny Zhejiangese. Unflustered, he took out a scale calmly and stood on it, "Well, I weigh only 45 kilograms. If I jump off, you're still overloaded."

The Shandongese, who had been silent during the entire process, stood up and opened the cabin door. Just when he was about to jump, another Shandongese suddenly came out of the cockpit and said proudly, "Only we Shandongese can be counted on at critical moments. My brother, I'll jump with you!" And so they jumped.

As the rest started to cheer for their heroic deed, the plane abruptly began to nosedive. As it turned out, the second Shandongese who came out of the cabin was the pilot.

While somewhat stereotypical, this joke does capture some of the major differences that exist among these groups of people. It should be noted, however, there are many more regions and subcultures in China. This joke only scratches the surface of the rich heterogeneity that exists in the country. In the rest of this chapter, we will discuss a few examples of the traditional division of subcultures, as well as the "melting pot" trend that has escalated over the last two decades or so. We conclude with a short discussion about future cultural trends in the Road Ahead section.

Historical Subcultures in China

With a vast territory covering 9.6 million square kilometers, China is a land that includes all types of geographical features and climates, which have bred a variety of distinct regional cultures over the last 5,000 years. China also has a rich history of integrating multiple nationalities and cultures. Thus, like the United States, China is referred to as a "melting pot" with several distinct regional cultures. Yunnan province alone has 52 of the 56 formally recognized ethnic groups. Among those, 25 are minorities each with a population of more than 5,000 people. In addition to various ethnic distinctions, people within the dominant Han ethnicity speak different dialects, wear various folk costumes, have their own cuisines based on local foods, live in houses built on different topographies, and adhere to diversified folk customs and beliefs.

Culturally, the simplest way to divide China would be into the north and the south. Although China can be divided geographically along the Qinling Mountains–Huaihe River line, the cultural differences that distinguish "northerners" from "southerners" are more complex and do not necessarily correspond to this geographic division. In general, northerners are perceived to be kind, and southerners are thought to be wise. Northerners are also typically bigger and taller than southerners. Northerners tend to speak a dialect closer to the standard Mandarin, while the southerners use so many different dialects that it can be difficult for a person from a different region to understand them.

As the earlier joke conveyed, almost every province has unique characteristics, and sometimes even within a province there are several distinct subcultures. We briefly elaborate on three subcultures here for illustrative purposes.

Beijing is a military center and transportation hub first built by the State of Yan during the Western Zhou Dynasty (1046 BC–771 BC). It was chosen as the capital of the State of Yan, the Jin Dynasty (1115–1243), the Yuan Dynasty (1271–1368), the Ming Dynasty (1368–1644), and the Qing Dynasty (1644–1912). Today, Beijing is the political center of China, so many aspects of everyday life are closely connected to politics. From civil servants to street vendors, most people have views on all sorts of political and social issues and can speak eloquently about them. The taxi drivers in Beijing are just as well informed about international and domestic issues as students majoring in international politics.

By contrast, Guangdong (Canton) is located in the Pearl River Delta. Located far from the political center, the Cantonese focus their efforts on business. Guangdong is a transportation hub of the maritime silk routes. Since the late Qin Dynasty and early Han Dynasty, businessmen have been sailing across the sea to explore new markets. People around the world have come to know China through Cantonese restaurants. The number of Cantonese emigrants is more than 30 million, constituting two-thirds of all Chinese people living abroad. They have settled in more than 160 nations and districts in Asia, North America, South America, Europe, Oceania, and Africa.[1] People who have lived abroad promote cultural exchange between China and Western countries. As a result, the Cantonese culture is a combination of local culture and the culture of Chinese citizens who have returned from far flung locales.

Unlike Beijing and Guangdong, Wenzhou is a small region within Zhejiang province, but the people there play such an important role in contemporary Chinese commerce that it deserves its own description. Just like the Cantonese, Wenzhounese people are hard-working and enjoy an excellent business culture. Nothing is too small for a Wenzhounese person to sell; many wealthy and successful entrepreneurs from Wenzhou started out selling shoestrings, buttons, and simple hardware. According to recent statistics,[2] 1.7 million Wenzhounese have left their hometowns to run businesses nationwide, and approximately 170 Wenzhou Chambers of Commerce have been established all over China. Additionally, 600,000 Wenzhounese people reside outside China and are engaged in business in 93 nations and districts all over the world. The Wenzhounese are also famous for their willingness to help each other in business. A business owner originally from Wenzhou told us, "Wenzhou is surrounded by mountains and resources are limited. Under these circumstances, people must learn to cooperate in order to survive, just like hunting."

60 *Social Structure*

Merging of Subcultures

Like every society, China is changing, and changing quickly. In the past, people were required to reside in a particular place, and moving to a different city (especially a larger city or a more developed region) involved challenges such as registered residence, identity recognition, expensive real estate, and so forth, that few people could overcome. This has substantially changed over the last 30 years. First, the need to migrate has increased due to economic development and job opportunities, in both blue- and white-collar sectors. Second, any benefits associated with remaining in one's hometown have decreased significantly; in almost all cases, people can buy anything, anywhere as long as they have enough money. As a result of this migration, we have seen the emergence of new fusing subcultures in China. Here, we discuss subcultures that are developing in Shanghai (when local residents meet newcomers) and Shenzhen (when newcomers meet newcomers).

Although Shanghai is a southern city, the Shanghainese have distinct characteristics that can best be described as more Westernized, business-oriented, and perhaps even more refined. During his 2013 visit to Shanghai, French President Hollande called Shanghai the "Paris of the East." Unlike people from Beijing, Shanghainese typically do not concern themselves with politics; instead, they focus more on commerce and life. Compared to other places in China, the Shanghainese (as well as the government agencies there) tend to follow rules and require less personal connection. The Shanghainese used to be overly proud of their culture, so much so that many considered them to be arrogant. Before the 1980s, the Shanghainese looked down on anyone who could not speak the authentic Shanghai dialect. As a matter of fact, they did not even think people from the suburbs of Shanghai had equal status.

However, all of this has changed over the last 30 years. As Shanghai has developed and people from all over China have moved there, bought properties, and become "real" Shanghainese (at least according to official records), the overall culture of the city has also changed. Residents have not only become more tolerant of outside culture, but many have embraced it—perhaps even a bit too much. The younger generation in Shanghai no longer speaks the local dialect (which used to be a point of pride), and their parents are forced to speak Mandarin with them. For this reason, as of May 2013, more than 100 primary schools now offer Shanghai Dialect Programs. People working in service industries all readily speak Mandarin. Like the residents of New York City, the degree to which you are considered a Shanghainese is judged by how long you have lived there and what experiences you have had, not whether you were born there and whether your family is originally from Shanghai. Out of the ashes of the old Shanghai style, a new all-inclusive culture (called Hai style) is gradually forming that assimilates not only other regional cultures but also Western cultures.

Any dialogue about the merging of traditional subcultures in China would be incomplete without discussing Shenzhen. The Shenzhen Special Economic Zone was founded in August 1980 in a small fishing village neighboring Hong Kong. Over the last 30 years, due to a large influx of talents, capital, and opportunities,

Shenzhen has been transformed from a village into a prosperous and inclusive international metropolis that rivals Hong Kong, with a population of 10 million.

Unbounded by traditional culture, it is a new city receptive to anything, and the spirit of reform and innovation is the essence of its culture. On the thirtieth anniversary of the establishment of Shenzhen Special Economic Zone, citizens and experts jointly selected the "Top 10 Shenzhen Concepts:"[3]

1 Time is money, efficiency is life.
2 Empty talk will lead the country astray, and hard work can rejuvenate the nation.
3 Dare to be the pioneer.
4 Reform and innovation are the root and soul of Shenzhen.
5 Let the city be respected for its love of reading.
6 Encourage innovation and tolerate failure.
7 Achieve cultural rights of its citizens.
8 The fragrance always stays in the hand that offered the rose.
9 Shenzhen embraces the world.
10 You are a Shenzhener the moment you arrive.

Road Ahead

Three major factors are influencing the evolution of Chinese subcultures: mass migration associated with economic and social development, easy access to information, and ease of travel. Although it may sound cliché, China has quickly become a truly connected country, and with such connections, we expect that subcultures will continue to evolve. We believe, however, that changes will be gradual unless there is a major reversal in flow from coastal areas to inland areas, from large metropolises to small cities (or even rural areas), and from north to south and vice versa.

Our first prediction is that the dialects will gradually fade away throughout China, except for ethnic languages. Even in those cases, we expect that minorities will become fluent Mandarin speakers as well. This will be facilitated by education at all levels and by migrants who have traveled, especially to the coastal areas, and then returned to their hometowns. The second prediction is that cultural differences will persist for a much longer time. As a result, anyone who will be working with a Chinese person must be mindful of his or her subculture. Geographic variations in cuisine will always be preserved, as the Chinese people take eating very seriously and maintaining variation has tremendous commercial value, if nothing else.

One tremendous concern is that many medium and small sized cities are quickly losing their identities by mimicking the development styles of larger cities. Overall, regions in China are rushing to modernize and, in the process, are showing no consideration for preserving the past. Old buildings and districts are being bulldozed to make way for new business districts, office buildings, shopping malls, and residential complexes. Such strategies may affect many aspects of culture with unintended consequences.

Notes

1 People's Government of Guangdong Province (2013, March 12), "Guangdong is a famous hometown of overseas Chinese," *Guangdong Yearbook*, retrieved January 2014 from http://www.gd.gov.cn/gdgk/sqgm/qxqq/201303/t20130312_176017.htm
2 Li Jianping (2010, February 11), "About 600,000 Wenzhounese explore the world," *China Youth Daily*, retrieved January 2014 from http://www.cyol.net/zqb/content/2010-02/11/content_3088131.htm
3 For more information, see Report (2010) on "Top 10 Shenzhen Concepts," retrieved January 2014 from http://www.chinadaily.com.cn/dfpd/2012szsdgl/

11 Social Circles

In his influential treatise *From the Soil* written in 1947, the famous sociologist Fei Xiaotong (1910–2005, Ph.D. in anthology from the London School of Economics) defined China as a society of acquaintances, where one thrives in complex social networks based on personal relationships. In this society of acquaintances, backgrounds and relationships (or Guanxi) are foundational. More than six decades later, the Chinese people continue to cultivate and thrive on such personal relationships, although for different reasons. Such social networks are now commonly known as circles, although they have unique characteristics compared to social circles elsewhere in the world. In this chapter, we discuss the reason why Chinese circles exist, their types, rules, structures, and maintenance. We conclude in the Road Ahead section by making predictions about the future utility (or lack thereof) of Chinese circles.

Raison d'Être

Social circles are not limited to the Chinese culture; they can be found throughout history, among people from various social strata and civilizations. Even Google now uses "circles" to help people categorize their contacts. However, a key difference between Chinese social circles and others is that, in China, they are a necessity, not a luxury.

This necessity comes from the perception (which accurately reflects reality, for the most part) that one needs to know someone in order to get anything done in China—at least if it is to be done right. If a person needs to have an operation, for example, the first question she will ask herself is whether she knows someone at a good hospital, and if not, whether she knows someone in her circle who knows someone at a good hospital. Without a good inside contact, one generally has to wait a long time for service that usually yields subpar results. When a Chinese person casually mentions a need to a friend, the most often heard response is, "Oh, not a problem. I know someone there!" This is how things are accomplished in general, from important issues such as finding the right surgeon or getting a child into a good school, to trivial issues such as finding a restaurant in a new town. People have told us that a person would not even consider lying on the operating table unless (a) someone in the hospital knows him, and/or (b) the surgeon has received a cash gift from him (which normally requires an introduction).

64 *Social Structure*

The necessity of strong circles goes beyond one's personal life. It is also a must for business and career success. In most cases, people form friendships first and do business later. For example, an informant who is a senior executive in the auto industry said, "No company will buy my products if I go through the official channels. Almost all business associates are first introduced through my friends. Then, I will need to develop the relationship step by step until they become my new friends, and only then we can do business."

Because of this real or perceived necessity, Chinese people spend an astonishing amount of time building and maintaining their circles. As described elsewhere in the book, people work diligently to create a currency of goodwill that can be exchanged for favors with others. Thus, it is desirable for a person to also conduct affairs with those who are in her circle, which further increases the demand for the circles in the first place, creating a self-fulfilling cycle.

There is also an emotional aspect to circles: a sense of belonging. One netizen described this phenomenon: "Having no one to play with is worse and more frightening than unemployment, break-ups, and blindness because it means that you become a social outcast, someone outside the circle."

Types

Circles can be classified based on why they are formed (purpose) or how they are formed (external factors). One informant told us that there are three types of circles based on purpose: interaction, transaction, and friendship. Circles built for interaction provide a platform for socialization, perhaps among people who share a common interest. Circles built for transaction provide a platform for mutual assistance, in either the family or business context. In circles built for friendship, relationships are much deeper, but they may also serve interaction and transaction purposes. In some circles of friendship, however, transaction activities are explicitly frowned upon for fear that the value of the circle might be degraded, especially if something goes wrong.

Circles that are formed due to external factors tend to be more valuable and perceived as less utilitarian. Many circles of friendships are built this way. External factors that bring people into the same circle include education (people who went to the same elementary school, middle school, high school, college, MBA, or EMBA program), work (people who worked at the same place in the past or present, whether civilian or military, or people of the same occupation), and residential situation (people from the same hometown, people from former places of residence).

Out of all these types of circles in China, the general consensus is that the two most valuable circles to a person are those comprised of classmates or fellow military servicemen. This is likely because such circles are formed during key developmental years; the people in these circles grew up together, so to speak, so there are no pretenses. As a result, the distance between members in such circles is much smaller and trust is much higher. Based on our research and interactions, the third most valuable circle is related to hometown. This is reinforced by the fact that people from each province speak a distinct dialect with slight variations within a province. This linguistic characteristic can instantly connect people at a deeper level when they are not in their hometowns, making it harder for other people to join a circle.

Rules

Rules within circles are never explicitly stated but are implicitly practiced and enforced. Different circles may have different rules, but the two most important rules are: (a) behave in a trustworthy way and (b) help others in the same circle. It is interesting that these two rules are so highly valued in contemporary Chinese circles because this ethos is clearly lacking in general society. Our informants told us many times that in business deals, you always assume the other party wants to cheat you unless he proves otherwise. Clearly, different types of circles expect and enjoy different levels of trust and mutual help. In very close-knit circles, even if a person does something distasteful (e.g., does not return borrowed money), there is a reluctance to seek legal action for fear of breaking the unspoken rule of helping others and tarnishing the image of the circle.

Mutual support from members of a social circle can be extremely beneficial, and these benefits extend among people living abroad. A businessman who now works in Paris said, "In France, although many Chinese restaurant owners feel that it is hard to survive, the restaurants run by Wenzhou businessmen perform quite well, thanks to their united circle. We will support, for example, whoever opens up a new restaurant in many ways; we provide financial support if he is short of money, and if we are in the restaurant business as well, we even introduce our own customers to him."

A recent case, however, has caused people to question whether they should blindly trust people within their circles. In January 2014, an obstetrician in Shanxi province was given a suspended death sentence for selling the newborns of some of her relatives, neighbors, and classmates after falsely telling the mothers that their children had serious congenital diseases.[1]

Structure

While no formal structure or hierarchy exists in circles, many circles do have a few people who command the respect of the others. These "old brothers" normally are people who have both the will and the resources to help others in the circle. The value of a circle, even the survival of the circle, depends on how these old brothers behave. They do not necessarily have the power of a mafia boss, but their words count nevertheless. If they say something negative about a person, most likely that person will not be able to stay in the circle. There are even sayings that one may mislead a government official, but he would not dare to mislead an old brother.

The structure of the rest of a circle tends to be flat, but everyone is expected to follow the culture of that particular circle and behave accordingly. Regardless, one may elevate her status in a circle by doing more than her share to help other

66   *Social Structure*

members. The closer the members of a circle are, the more exclusive the circle is towards the outside.

Maintenance

A striking phenomenon of Chinese circles is the effort people expend to maintain them. One of us once attended a dinner while visiting Hangzhou. A few hours before the dinner, the host called up a few friends in Shanghai (180 km away), and asked them to come to Hangzhou to attend the dinner, and they did! Embarking on a 4-hour round trip to attend a dinner with an old friend on such short notice would be quite an unusual occurrence in American society. However, such gestures are quite common in China.

Our informants and research revealed that people put forth a tremendous amount of effort to cultivate their social circles and maintain good standing within them. Like flowers, they explained to us, relationships will dry out if they are not watered regularly. But not all circles are created equal. For the most important circles, one must attend dinners and other activities regularly. For less important circles, the minimum expectation is to call people from time to time; in-person visits can be less frequent. For the least important circles, maintaining a virtual presence through various social network platforms is all that is required. Before the age of smartphones and WeChat (a social media platform discussed in Chapter 52), people spent hours in front of their computers chatting online with members of various circles. Now they spend hours each day communicating through the WeChat platform via smartphone.

One of our informants said: "Friends should meet in person at least every two months to eat, drink, and chat. SMS and phone calls do not count because those are just ways to ensure that others remember you. I have about 10 core friends with whom I can talk and share anything. For instance, once we went to Xiamen; the four of us flew there from four different cities (Beijing, Changsha, Shanghai, and Hangzhou) just for a meal."

The contrast between how Americans and the Chinese prioritize their personal and work lives is quite dramatic. It is perfectly acceptable for Americans to excuse themselves from work-related social engagements for family reasons, but such behavior is unacceptable in China. We attended a high level meeting in the United States during which a Pepsi vice president received a phone call. Before taking the call, he explained, "Sorry, it is my wife." The other attendees laughed knowingly. This type of behavior would be unthinkable in China. Using family as an excuse for skipping social events in various circles is considered odd. A person who uses family as a regular excuse may soon find that invitations are extended less and less frequently. This essentially has the effect of removing him from the circle.

Road Ahead

Despite the role social circles play in current Chinese society, we believe China is on the brink of shifting from a society of acquaintances to a society of rules.

When in need, one will turn to relevant rules, regulations, and laws, rather than acquaintances for help. In other words, we expect China to more closely mimic Western societies in this regard, and quickly. As the rule of law becomes more standardized in China, the raison d'être for circles will diminish. As a result, one will no longer be able to justify expending the tremendous amount of effort required to maintain these circles at the expense of her family and personal life. Social circles will always exist but will become less utilitarian, require less maintenance, and will become optional instead of necessary for successful functioning in everyday life.

Note

1 See the verdict (2014, January 14) from Weinan Intermediate People's Court, retrieved January 2014, http://wnzy.chinacourt.org/public/detail.php?id=5490

12 Employment Equality

Employment equality in China is an evolving landscape. One informant, a senior executive, told us, "Business is about maximizing profit. It is logical for a firm to find the best possible employees, which possibly means hiring those who are taller, stronger, prettier, and more capable." His sentiments were echoed by another senior executive, who said, "In a hospital, patients of course want to see prettier nurses. Patients are already in a bad physical and mental state, and they want to see someone whose appearance can make them more comfortable. On the other hand, there is no need to screen the appearance of applicants for positions that do not interact with patients, such as those working in the back room of the hospital pharmacy. But it's not acceptable to put those whose appearance is not pleasant in positions that directly interact with patients because patients will not accept these people."

We can make several observations from comments such as these. First, biases appear to be customer driven. Businesses may selectively hire people because they feel certain characteristics are desired by their customers and such hiring practices may give them a competitive advantage (or at least not put them at a disadvantage). Second, there is still confusion among executives about what constitutes employment equality, as the first informant seemed to believe that "pretty" equates to "capable". Third, it points to the important role that government must play in ensuring employment equality as is done in other countries, including the United States.

In fact, the Chinese government has already come a long way in terms of ensuring employment equality. In this chapter, we first discuss the government's formal stance toward employment equality in China and highlights of the policy. This is followed by three particular criteria (some institutionalized and others implicit) that are still used in some parts of society that would be considered employment discrimination elsewhere. We conclude with a very positive outlook in the Road Ahead section.

State of Employment Equality

Several major national laws are in place to ensure employment equality in China. According to the *Law of the People's Republic of China on Promotion of Employment (Law on Promotion of Employment)* that came into effect in January 2008, "In seeking employment, workers shall not be subject to discrimination because of their ethnic backgrounds, races, gender, religious beliefs, etc." Employment discrimination was further addressed in *Decisions*[1] made during the 3rd Plenary Session of

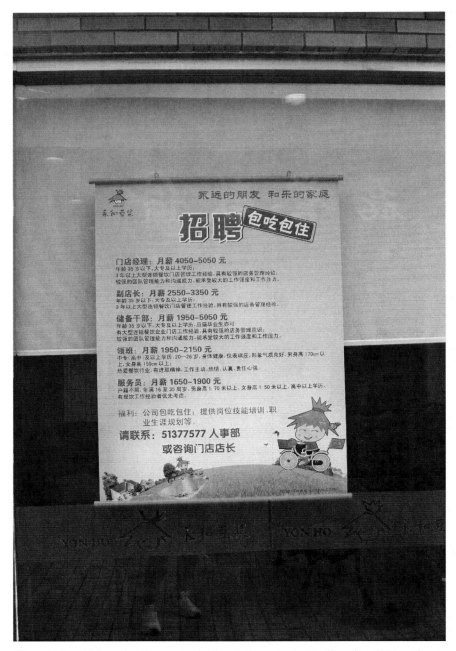

Figure 12.1 A hiring advertisement outside a chain restaurant in Shanghai, 2012, with relevant criteria translated below.
Store Manager: younger than 35 years. Assistant Manager: younger than 35 years. Shift Supervisor: 20–26 years, healthy, appearance must be presentable, male taller than 170 cm, female taller than 150 cm. Server: 16–35 years, male taller than 170 cm, female taller than 150 cm.

Employment Equality   71

18th CPC Central Committee: "We will regulate human resource management by removing all institutional barriers and employment discrimination practices that affect equal employment, such as the birthplace of a person (cities or countryside), industry, social status and gender."

China has done an especially good job at ensuring opportunities for minority ethnic groups. Article 28 of the *Law on Promotion of Employment* stipulates: "The peoples of all ethnic groups enjoy equal rights to work. When an employing unit recruits persons, it shall give appropriate considerations to persons of ethnic minorities in accordance with law."[2] The rate of employment for ethnic minority undergraduates in 2011, for example, was higher than the average rate of undergraduates nationwide.[3] We have observed this throughout our research. Universities and government agencies have either a quota system for employing and promoting ethnic minorities or a point system in which ethnic minorities receive extra points. This favorable treatment is not restricted to employment; for example, ethnic minorities are exempt from the rigid one-child policy (i.e., a couple can have two children if one of them belongs to an ethnic minority). This is very similar to the equal opportunity actions taken by universities and government agencies in the United States. Interestingly, none of the Han majority informants we interviewed or interacted with in China complained about the favorable treatment of ethnic minorities.

Another area in which China has made great strides is in its treatment of disabled citizens. One informant even told us that his company has a quota for hiring disabled employees. Unlike the United States, however, many disability-friendly infrastructures (e.g., ramps instead of steps) have yet to be built.

After a careful review, we identified three areas in which employment equality has yet to be fully realized. They are: gender equality (something codified in Chinese law, but not implemented sufficiently), age equality (not codified in Chinese law, but relevant laws exist in other countries), and appearance equality (e.g., height, weight, facial attractiveness) (not codified in Chinese law or in other countries). We include a picture (Figure 12.1) of a hiring advertisement posted outside a chain restaurant in Shanghai here for illustration purposes.

Gender Equality

Gender equality in Chinese society, including in employment contexts, has been enshrined in laws. According to Article 27 in *Law on Promotion of Employment*, "The State guarantees that women enjoy the same rights to work as men."[4] When an employer recruits new workers, it may not refuse to employ women, nor raise recruitment standards for females by using gender as an excuse, except where the types of work or posts are not suitable for women as prescribed by the State. Likewise, employers may not restrict female workers from getting married or bearing a child in the labor contract. Further requirements to eliminate gender based discrimination were published in recent decisions by the CPC.

Despite this legal protection, females have experienced many forms of employment discrimination. Curiously, we never encountered any informants who said they believed women were less capable than men even though they practice gender

72   Social Structure

discrimination implicitly or explicitly for many other reasons. According to an online survey,[5] out of 1,845 respondents, more than 90% believed they or their friends had suffered gender discrimination in the job market, and 85.3% believed the discrimination was against women. By education level, graduate students encountered the most discrimination (93.3%). The reasons contributing to gender discrimination included "having a child" (43.3%), followed by "women don't fit in to the lifestyle associated with some types of work, such as frequent dinner parties and business trips" (35.2%), "women tend to focus on family after marriage" (12.6%), and "ingrained traditional culture of discrimination against women" (8.9%). Another reason provided by our informants is the legal amount of time off a company must offer to its female employees after childbirth. As per the *Special Rules on the Labor Protection of Female Employees*, women can enjoy 98 days of maternity leave, during which time employers must hire replacement workers. Because of this extra cost, many companies are reluctant to hire married women who have not yet had children or female employees who are about to get married.

The same survey revealed that after experiencing gender discrimination, 81.4% of females choose to "tolerate it in silence, try harder, and look for the next job opportunity." One often cited reason for this behavior is that gender based discrimination is ubiquitous, so everybody thinks it is normal and just accepts it. But this is changing now. The first ever lawsuit based on gender discrimination in employment was filed in July 2012, but it took the court more than a year to finally accept the case (in August 2013), as it is unprecedented and counters societal norms. The case was filed by a female job applicant in Beijing whose job application was rejected because the firm said it would only hire a male.

Age Equality

Age discrimination was a somewhat surprising finding in a society in which elders are to be respected. Reflecting on this, we attribute age discrimination in China to an overcorrection to the lifetime appointment practices of the Mao era. To open doors to younger people, the government under Deng (Deng Xiaoping, core of the second generation leadership) and those who followed (1978 onwards) adopted a series of regulations introducing mandatory retirement ages and maximum promotion ages (both explicit and implicit) for all government positions. These practices have propagated down to the local level and out to businesses and other social structures.

We were shocked during a conversation with a senior executive who was in his mid-thirties. He had just been promoted to the position of group senior VP over a few people who were more experienced and held more senior positions prior to this promotion. When asked why these other people were not promoted, he said, "Oh, they are in their mid-forties now, too old for the next phase of our company's expansion."

Age discrimination currently occurs in three contexts in China: hiring, promotion, and retirement. In general, only applicants who are younger than 35 may apply for open positions in government, as explicitly stated in recruitment announcements. With the consent of the hiring agency, those who just graduated with a Master's degree or who are studying for a Ph.D. may be hired if they are younger than 40. In private business, this practice is very common. As shown in the restaurant job advertisement earlier in this chapter, managers were required to be younger than 35, shift supervisors had to be between the ages of 20 and 26, and servers had to be between the ages of 16 and 35. In another restaurant, a posted job advertisement required the hostesses to be between 18 and 26 years old, servers needed to be between the ages of 18 and 28, and even the cleaning staff had to be younger than 45. In general, the implicit (sometimes explicit, in government positions) rule is that anyone older than 40 will have a hard time getting a new job.

It is also very typical, both in the public and in the private sector, for promotions to be based on age. Age is either used as a cutoff (i.e., no one older than a certain age will be promoted to a certain level) or in a points system (i.e., a person who is a certain age or older receives negative points during an evaluation). We found out later that the experience of the group SVP that we described above is not atypical. In the public sector, there are written rules that prohibit promotion of public officials to the next level if they are older than a certain age. Such rules even exist in the highest decision-making body in China, the Politburo Standing Committee, which we discuss in Chapter 34.

Finally, there is the issue of mandatory retirement. In the public sector, interestingly, the mandatory retirement age is also related to one's rank and gender. For example, in government, once a man reaches 55 and a woman reaches 50, he or she will not be assigned a frontline position lower than provincial governor. At the vice governor level, the retirement age is 60 regardless of gender, and at the governor level and above, it is 65 regardless of gender. In the university system, those at the rank of lecturer must retire at 60 (male) or 55 (female). Those at the associate professor level retire at 60 regardless of gender, and full professors may delay retirement until 65. The official retirement age for people in the public sector (including government owned enterprises) is 60 (male) and 55 (female). As a result, according to the *Human Resource Development Report (2011–2012)*[6], the average retirement age for Chinese citizens is 56.1 years old; average male and female retirement ages are 58.3 and 52.4, respectively. Many senior people in the public sector remarked to us that they do not want to retire, but they must when they hit that age. Many feel it is a pity to sideline someone who still has many years of productive life ahead. Reflecting this general sentiment, in late 2013, the central government committed to reevaluating the mandatory retirement age.

As of now, China does not have formal legislation like other developed countries prohibiting age discrimination, such as the *The Age Discrimination in Employment Act (ADEA)* in the United States that forbids "age discrimination against people who are age 40 or older when it comes to any aspect of employment, including hiring, firing, pay, job assignments, promotions, layoffs, training, fringe benefits, and any other terms or conditions of employment."[7]

Appearance Equality

Employment discrimination based on appearance is widespread in China. No legislation on this issue exists in China or in other countries. While we cannot comment on why other countries do not have such legal protection, our extensive

74 *Social Structure*

research revealed that the Chinese people think it is perfectly acceptable to use appearance as a criterion in hiring decisions, as shown in the quotes from some of our informants at the beginning of this chapter. To most of the Chinese, appearance requirements are customer-driven and nothing personal. For the purposes of this discussion, we are not interested in whether or not service providers with prettier faces actually make customers happier. Instead, we focus on describing the various forms of appearance discrimination that exist in China.

The first thing a potential employer will evaluate is an applicant's face. This practice has become so commonplace that a professional resume in China will almost always include a passport style color photo of the individual. If a resume is submitted without a photo, most employers will assume the individual has something to hide. To ensure one will pass the initial screen, most people will find a studio to take an almost artistic headshot, complete with post-shot Photoshop modifications. As with many things in life, however, overdoing it can have negative effects. One of our informants recalled an interview where the actual person who showed up looked so different from the photo that he was completely speechless and lost interest at once despite the applicant's other merits.

Unsurprisingly, the aesthetics industry is thriving in China (and in South Korea, as they have a reputation for doing an excellent job at very reasonable cost). In one clinic, out of more than 1,000 procedures conducted in 2011, less than 20% were to correct congenital conditions or flaws caused by accidents, 50% were for those who already had regular or above average appearance, and the remaining 30% were those who were already very attractive but had even higher standards for some part of their appearance. Out of these 1,000-plus cases, 30% were college students (most of them juniors or seniors) who underwent procedures with a very clear objective: to be considered for better employment opportunities.[8]

This may come as a big surprise to many foreigners, but the height of an individual is very important in China. Just as many people will only date and marry someone who is taller than a certain height, many firms will only hire someone who is taller than a certain height. It is quite typical for firms to only hire men who are taller than 170 cm and women who are taller than 160 cm. A graduate of a top-tier university in China with an M.S. in finance was rejected for a job by a bank because he was only 160 cm, and according to the person who interviewed him, the bank wanted male employees to be at least 170 cm.[9] Even the restaurant example we described earlier in this chapter had a minimum height requirement for its employees.

Although there is no explicit form of discrimination based on weight, some implicit discrimination exists. Of course, this may be because very few Chinese people are obese.

Road Ahead

Looking into the future, we are quite optimistic about how employment equality will evolve in China. We believe the three forms of inequality described above will gradually recede. However, we believe the public sector must lead the change. The government should change internal hiring practices, create appropriate legislation, and last but not least, aim to change public perceptions about what is normal and acceptable behavior.

The government will need to change social perceptions about what constitutes a competitive advantage. One informant remarked, "Humans are like animals; the best wins. If someone has advantage in terms of height and face, and if we force society to treat them as the same as those who do not have an advantage, wouldn't it be unfair to those who have a better appearance? Of course, we should not look down upon them as human beings, but jobs sometimes can require certain appearance." Another one remarked, "In Australia, you see many obese people working as cashiers. But their labor force is small (so employers do not have much choice). In Europe, many airline flight attendants are middle aged women [in China, it's almost always young ladies in their twenties]. But China's situation is different [with a much bigger labor force, and a much larger applicant pool]." Chinese citizens must understand that such views are simply not acceptable in fair societies. We are convinced that appearance discrimination can be eradicated quickly in China if the government decides to make it a focus.

Notes

1 *Decisions of the Central Committee of the Communist Party of China on Some Major Issues Concerning Comprehensively Deepening the Reform* (2013), retrieved January 2014 from http://www.china.org.cn/china/third_plenary_session/2014-01/16/content_31212602_12.htm

2 *Law of the People's Republic of China on Promotion of Employment (English Version)*, retrieved January 2014, http://www.npc.gov.cn/englishnpc/Law/2009-02/20/content_1471590.htm, Chinese version retrieved January 2014 from http://www.molss.gov.cn/gb/zt/2007-08/30/content_197492.htm

3 Lin Xiaojie (2011, October 19), "Ethnic minority undergraduates enjoy a bright future," retrieved January 2014 from http://www.clssn.com/html/Home/report/46167-1.htm

4 *Law of the People's Republic of China on Promotion of Employment (English Version)*, retrieved January 2014, http://www.npc.gov.cn/englishnpc/Law/2009-02/20/content_1471590.htm, Chinese version retrieved January 2014 from http://www.molss.gov.cn/gb/zt/2007-08/30/content_197492.htm

5 Hu Yating (2013, December 9), "Childbirth becomes the first factor of gender discrimination," *People's Daily*, retrieved January 2014 from http://gx.people.com.cn/n/2013/1209/c179482-20099835.html

6 Chinese Academy of Social Sciences (2012), "Human resource development report (2011–2012)," retrieved January 2014, http://www.china.com.cn/guoqing/node_7174898.htm

7 U.S. Equal Employment Opportunity Commission. "Age discrimination," retrieved January 2014 from http://www.eeoc.gov/laws/types/age.cfm

8 Zhan Wen, Shen Xiaoli, Wang Hui, and Hu Jing (2008, March 31), "Beauty equals competence?" *Strait Herald*, retrieved January 2014 from http://epaper.taihainet.com/html/20080331/hxdb78305.html

9 Ma Duosi and Zhao Wangyue (2007, January 5), "Appearance discrimination," *Beijing Morning Post*, retrieved January 2014 from http://news.sina.com.cn/c/2007-01-05/023011954922.shtml

13 The Status of Women

The ancient Chinese character for "woman" inscribed on bones or tortoise shells from the Shang Dynasty (1600 BC–1046 BC) takes the form of a woman who is on her knees with a broom in hand. Tidying, cleaning, nursing, weaving, and silk-worm-breeding all were basic domestic responsibilities of women. Thus, the form of the character itself provides a true and vivid portrayal of Chinese women's social standing for the 2,000 years prior to the abolishment of the feudal system in 1911. However, like many things in China, the status of women has changed substantially over the last century.

In this chapter, we first describe the traditional view of the role of women during the feudal age when females were considered to be second-class citizens. We then discuss the gradual elevation of women's status, mostly due to the influence of Western values between 1911 and 1976, culminating in a shift towards absolute equality in the 1960s and 1970s. Finally, we discuss the status of contemporary women in China since the open-door policy was enacted after Mao's death in 1976, which reflects a mixture of traditional and Western values and societal realities.

Role of Women Under the Feudal System

Women had inferior social status in ancient China. From times dating to the Western Zhou Dynasty (1046 BC–771 BC), women were confined to household chores and excluded from political and military affairs. At that time, submission and industriousness were regarded as the most important female virtues. During this period, the "Three Obediences and Four Virtues" became an institutionalized doctrine that dictated how women should conduct themselves; it also became the common standard among Chinese men for choosing wives. The three obediences required of a woman were to obey her father before marriage, her husband in married life, and her sons in widowhood; the four virtues were fidelity, physical charm, propriety in conversation, and ability to manage a household. The three obediences and four virtues helped lay a solid foundation for the gender-based division of duties in China's patriarchal society, namely that men focus on the outside (career) and women focus on the inside (household).

During the Han Dynasty (202 BC–220), Dong Zhongshu identified "The Three Cardinal Guides and the Five Constant Virtues." The three cardinal guides (i.e., ruler guides subject, father guides son, and husband guides wife) and five constant virtues (i.e., humaneness, righteousness (or justice), propriety (or etiquette),

78 Social Structure

and knowledge and trustworthiness) further shifted the balance of power towards husbands by reinforcing the idea that a wife must obey her husband absolutely and deepened the ideology that men are superior to women.

During the Song Dynasty (960–1279), the ethical teachings of Cheng & Zhu furthered the oppression of women. The practice of binding women's feet became popular at this time. Small feet were regarded as beautiful among all members of Chinese society, poor and rich alike. Smaller was always better, and the goal was to create feet just 3 inches long, called "golden lotuses." Such tiny feet could only be created by wrapping cloth tightly around a young girl's feet from a very young age until her body stopped growing. The process was excruciatingly painful and rendered women anguished, disfigured, and literally trapped inside their own homes for years. In addition, upon her husband's death, only a woman who obeyed her son and refused to remarry was deemed loyal and chaste. Monuments to chastity and virginity were created to commend women who did not remarry. Some even committed sacrificial suicide after their husbands died. At the same time, men were free to be polygamous and take not only wives but also many concubines.

Throughout the long history of China, there was only one female emperor, Wu Zetian, who ruled for just 15 years, from 690 to 705, during the Tang Dynasty (618–907). During this period, feudalistic China was in its prime and the country was economically prosperous, socially liberal, and culturally advanced. During her reign, women enjoyed a relatively high social status. Female officials, including her daughter, Princess Taiping, took an active part in political affairs. Women received education through many different channels and thus contributed significantly to culture. They had high self-confidence, distinct individuality, and strong independence. Although the influence of matchmakers still dominated, they enjoyed some freedoms in relationships and marriage. Women could wear jackets and shirts, men's clothing, and Hu clothing and shoes accessorized with various decorations. Economically, they became relatively more independent and even gained certain rights of inheritance, while during other dynasties, more often than not, inheritances belonged to males only.

Unfortunately, the Wu era was but a short reprieve from the oppression of women in ancient China. Confucius once said, "Only women and unenlightened men are hard to deal with. They are disrespectful if you let them too close, resentful if you keep them afar." To some extent, many Chinese men still hold these beliefs.

1911 to 1976

Once the feudal system was overthrown in 1911, women finally took their place as full members of society. The emancipation of women started with education. Colleges for female students rapidly emerged, which endowed women with more educational and personal development opportunities. After the Revolution of 1911, women no longer accepted the practice of foot binding and no longer catered to such morbid aesthetic standards. Women rapidly began asserting their independence. One such example is Lin Huiyin, the first female architect in China, a professor, writer, and poet. (One of her most famous poems is entitled "You Are the Heavenly April on Earth.") She traveled all over Europe and received a degree from the University of Pennsylvania in 1927. Her life represents the aspirations of many women during the post-feudal era in China, which centered on rejecting traditional female stereotypes, pursuing education, traveling abroad, and achieving lofty career goals.

Since the People's Republic of China was established in 1949, the movement for female liberation has continued to develop. In 1958, Mao affirmed that "women can prop up half the sky;" his support helped women obtain a more equal social status and genuinely become "half the sky" in social affairs, signaling the dawn of a new age in China.

Women were no longer seen as delicate and obedient beings in need of male protection. In fact, some women were encouraged to take hard labor jobs previously performed only by men, such as mining, steel manufacturing, and moving. The term "iron woman" was coined during the Cultural Revolution and became quite popular. More often than not, women were (correctly) depicted as being dark-skinned from exposure to elements, with broad shoulders and large waists, in stark contrast to former depictions of women with slim and fragile bodies. The heroines of that time were those who could hold jobs traditionally held by men and perform them even better.

This stance of absolute equality has only recently changed. In the 1990s, the Ministry of Personnel prohibited women from participating in specific jobs such as lumberjacking or mining so as to guarantee their safety and health. But it was during the Cultural Revolution when women first enjoyed and expected to have the same status as men, even if just as ordinary citizens. One notable exception was in government. As noted earlier in this chapter, no females held positions at the highest levels of government in China, with the exception of Mao's wife.

Current Status

Currently, contradictions abound in China on the role of women, both in society and in families. On one hand, Chinese firms have the highest percentage of female senior executives; on the other hand, people are taught (and many accept) that women should focus on their families while men should focus on their careers.

In 2013, Grant Thornton International, a leading accounting firm, released its "Report of Global Commerce."[1] According to this report, among the 200 Chinese mainland companies surveyed, up to 94% have female senior executives. This is the highest percentage in the world, much higher than both the global average of 21% and the average in developed countries such as those in Europe. According to this report, among the companies surveyed, 81% of Chief Human Resource Officers and 61% of Chief Financial Officers are women, illustrating women's unique strength in positions requiring detailed management and communication skills.

Orthogonal to this observation, however, is society's re-adoption of the perception that men should focus on the outside (i.e., career) and women should focus on the inside (i.e., family). Even some highly educated women believe that

80 *Social Structure*

marrying the right husband is more important than having a good career. In the Third Survey of the Social Status of Chinese Women conducted in 2011 by the All-China Women's Federation and The National Bureau of Statistics,[2] although 83.5% of interviewees agreed that "women do not have inferior abilities than men" and 88.6% agreed that "men should also undertake domestic chores," both male (61.6%) and female (54.8%) respondents agreed that "men should focus on social and public affairs while women should focus on family," representing increases of 7.7% and 4.4%, respectively compared to responses in 2000. One informant told us, "Just look at all the alcohol we have to drink every day, all the social engagements we must maintain, all the travel to places few people want to go. How can you ask a woman to do this?"

Such beliefs likely contribute to the gender bias observed in many companies, where hiring managers are less willing to employ females who are married but have not yet given birth or who are to be married soon (and thus are expected to have children soon), which we discuss elsewhere in the book. We know of recent college graduates who postponed their marriages until they found an ideal job due to such concerns.

While no formal statistics exist, women with young children are also likely at a disadvantage in terms of career advancement. Many women consider their main responsibility to be raising their children; thus their careers become just jobs to them, sometimes jobs they would rather quit, if possible. Experiences with previous employees have likely caused managers to have second thoughts about promoting women at that stage of life. Because managers are unwilling to give women with children promotion opportunities, many young women at this stage decide to focus more on children and family, creating a self-fulfilling cycle. Interestingly, males are not the only managers who take this stance. We encountered many female senior executives who voiced precisely the same concerns without considering themselves to be promoting gender bias.

How should one reconcile these seemingly conflicting phenomena? It would be too simplistic to cast these hiring and promotion practices as discrimination against women in general. It is more appropriate to characterize that women at certain life stages and in certain types of jobs are at a disadvantage. To be fair, senior executives are much more willing to hire and promote women instead of men for other types of jobs, such as accounting and human resources, as evidenced by the survey data described earlier. One informant (a business owner) even said that he did not want to hire men for office jobs because they have little job loyalty and will leave at the first sign of a better option.

Road Ahead

Based on our research, we feel the most important perception that constrains the potential of women is the idea that men should focus on the outside and women should focus on the inside. Many have argued that this simple division of labor in a family is based on the natural strengths of men and women. However, there are major problems with this argument. First, stereotyping unfairly diminishes opportunities for some women who would be happier focusing on the outside (career). Second, in China, one's status is still judged by how much money one makes. Since someone who focuses on the inside (family) will never generate tangible financial income, this unfairly diminishes women's status, both within families and in society at large.

We believe this perception will be exposed as the root of gender discrimination and will be criticized and eliminated from mainstream culture. In general, what strikes us is the lack of a true feminist movement in China that counters any such perceptions and decision rules. Many publicly held views about women are considered biased or politically incorrect but often are rationalized as emerging out of concern for women (as the physically weaker sex that requires male protection). Plenty of women disregard such stereotypes in China and continue to balance careers with raising their families, and have done so very well. We see this trend continuing.

Before we conclude this chapter, we would be remiss if we did not address regional differences associated with the status of women across China. For instance, husbands from Shanghai are a popular target for jokes, as they tend to do a lot more household chores than their counterparts in the northern part of the country. Some even suggest that a husband from Shanghai will go to his in-laws' apartment over the weekend to help with their household chores! Thus, the views represented in this chapter reflect a more general ethos in China and do not necessarily reflect the experiences of all women.

Notes

1 Grant Thornton International (2013), "Women in senior management," *Grant Thornton International Business Report 2013*, retrieved January 2014 from http://www.grantthornton.cn/upload/Women_in_business_20130307_CN.pdf http://www.internationalbusinessreport.com/files/ibr2013_wib_report_final.pdf
2 All-China Women's Federation and National Bureau of Statistics of China (2011, October 21), "Report on major results of the third wave survey on the social status of women in China," retrieved January 2014 from http://www.china.com.cn/zhibo/zhuanti/ch-xinwen/2011-10/21/content_23687810.htm

14 Migrant Workers

Migrant workers, also called peasant workers, are people who officially reside in rural areas but are working in cities temporarily; often, they leave their families behind. According to the *2012 Migrant Workers Report*[1] published by the State Bureau of Statistics, there were 262.61 million migrant workers in China, up 16.5% from 225.42 million in 2008. The overwhelming Spring Festival travel rush is a testament to the huge number of migrant workers in China. According to statistics, during the 2014 travel rush (lasting 40 days, from January 16 to February 24), flow was expected to reach 3.62 billion passengers, an increase of more than 200 million passengers over 2013. As the existence of migrant workers has grown into a major and unique social phenomenon, it receives much public attention and piques the interest of many in Chinese society.

We first provide a history and overview of migrant workers in China and then discuss several key challenges they face in their social and family lives. We highlight the importance of resolving the challenges faced by migrant workers and their families in the Road Ahead section.

History and Overview

In the early 1980s, China implemented the household-responsibility system in rural areas. Under this system, farmers are held responsible for their own profits and losses of production, unlike the previous practice of egalitarian distribution. This change motivated farmers and boosted the rural economy, which freed much of the labor force from farming. Meanwhile, the establishment of special economic zones buoyed the development of coastal cities. As a result, the surplus rural labor force (China's earliest group of migrant workers) flowed into urban areas to work in the new factories.

According to the *2012 Migrant Workers Report*,[2] 111.91 million migrant workers (42.6%) were from the east, 82.56 million (31.4%) were from central China, and 68.14 million (26.0%) were from the west. In terms of employment location, 169.8 million worked in eastern China (64.7%), 47.06 million worked in central China (17.9%), and 44.79 million worked in the west (17.1%). Provinces such as Anhui, Henan, Hubei, & Sichuan are major sources of labor outflows, while Zhejiang, Jiangsu, & Guangdong are among the provinces with labor inflows.

Most migrant workers hold jobs in construction, manufacturing, or service industries. By the end of 2012, the average monthly income of migrant workers stood at about USD 400, with few significant regional differences. What is noteworthy is

84   *Social Structure*

that average income for migrant workers is gradually increasing; blue-collar workers with desirable skills now may earn even more than their white-collar peers.

The New Generation

Migrant workers are now at the threshold of transition. Most migrant workers are in their prime working years; 54.4% are between 21 and 50 years old. However, the National Bureau of Statistics has called those born in the 1980s or later the "new generation" of migrant workers. This new generation has become the main source (58.4%) of labor outflow according to recent statistics. The ratio of females in the migrant labor force has also increased to 40.8%.[3]

Obvious distinctions exist between the two generations of migrant workers. Most older migrant workers specifically plan to return to their hometowns eventually. Because they are expert farmers, it is easy for them to make a living when they return to rural areas. Many in the older generation find it harder to adjust to urban life, and their return rate is therefore much higher than the younger generation.

However, the younger generation of migrant workers is more undecided about returning to their hometowns. They generally do not have farming skills, which makes it more difficult for them to return and be employable. Many have done a better job of assimilating into urban culture (e.g., by dressing in a more urban style). Unlike the previous generation, they generally prefer to live in cities; however, the material resources required to achieve a decent quality of life can quickly shatter their urban dreams. Therefore, many are faced with a difficult dilemma. According to one survey, *Number, Structure and Features of the New Generation of Migrant Workers 2012*,[4] 8.1% of migrant workers had decided that they would never return to their hometowns and 37% had decided to try to stay in the cities if they could. Generally speaking, about 45% of migrant workers from the new generation are more likely to stay than to leave.

Social Challenges

Migrant workers face tremendous social challenges while living in urban areas. The current household registration system (the hukou system) poses a discriminatory threat to migrant workers. The household registration system, which identifies a person as a resident of a certain area, came into being in 1958 in order to control the movement of people between rural and urban areas. As of now, when migrant workers do not have registered urban residences, they are marginalized from urban public services, including healthcare, education, and so forth. In addition, some urban residents have exclusive attitudes. Differences in lifestyle and education often are readily apparent, and it is not uncommon for migrant workers to be treated as inferior residents, often with overt hostility. Urban residents also resent labor inflows from rural areas because migrant workers compete for limited local resources such as jobs and social welfare. As if these challenges were not enough, one informant said, "The label 'migrant workers' exudes nothing but the unbearable odor of insult and injustice," because migrant workers are often suspects in criminal cases.

Figure 14.1 Migrant workers playing poker outside a bank branch in Shanghai

As a result, migrant workers may not have any sense of belonging to the cities where they work. What is worse, their social networks are quite limited, for they seldom use advanced technology. Often, their only social interactions are face to face, with people in their rural networks and fellow workers. Because they return home very rarely and their work is highly mobile, social bonds are easily weakened or lost. Generally speaking, migrant workers live in social isolation.

Family Challenges

Permanently reuniting their families seems to be an unattainable dream for most migrant workers, largely due to skyrocketing housing prices in urban areas. According to the *2012 Migrant Workers Report*,[5] 41.3% of migrant workers do not receive any housing subsidies from their employers. In fact, housing is so expensive that some construction workers have no choice but to live in temporary sheds at construction sites. In addition, the percentage of migrant workers who receive employment benefits is quite low, making it even more difficult for them to take care of their families. The *2012 Migrant Workers Report* also revealed that just 14.3% received pension insurance, 24% received work-related injury insurance, 16.9% received medical insurance, 8.4% received life insurance from employers or employing units, and 6.1% received maternity insurance.

It is not uncommon for the marriages of migrant workers to become quite strained. In fact, NPC delegate Liu Li identified a unique phenomenon among migrant workers: temporary couples. A significant number of migrant workers start new families when they move to a new location. For example, a young couple left their 2-year-old son with his grandmother in their hometown and went to work in two different cities. However, the husband then entered into a relationship with a woman at work, and the couple got divorced.[6]

The children of migrant workers are at a distinct disadvantage. Some children of migrant workers in China relocate with their parents to urban areas (i.e., migrant children), while others stay in the workers' hometowns with their grandparents due to the high cost of living (i.e., left-behind children). According to a report[7] by the All-China Women's Federation, there are 61.03 million left-behind children in rural areas, concentrated primarily in the provinces of Sichuan, Henan, & Anhui, which are major sources of labor outflow. The number of migrant children in China totals 35.81 million, and most live in top-tier cities; as of 2013, 4 out of 10 children in Shanghai were migrant children.

Children of migrant workers have long been plagued with a lack of educational resources, family care, and so on. In many cases, rural villages are left with only old people and children, while young adults join the labor force far away from home. Loneliness haunts these left-behind children every day, for most see their parents just once a year during the Spring Festival; some do not see their parents for several years. Without parental care and guidance, many of these children lack direction, have emotional and social problems, and/or drop out of school.

Migrant children who follow their parents to the cities also face severe challenges. First, because of the current household registration system, many children do not have access to the same educational resources as their urban counterparts. They, too, are more likely to drop out of school because they are constantly moving. Frequently changing cities, schools, and classes makes it hard for the children to keep up with coursework. In addition, migrant children are very prone to accidental injury when both parents leave home for work and they are left alone.

Figure 14.2 Migrant children in an elementary school in Shanghai.

Although many challenges still exist, the situation for migrant children has improved greatly in recent years. For example, we visited an elementary school (Figure 14.2) in Shanghai for the children of migrant workers; the education quality was better than we expected, and now these children have the same opportunity to attend middle school and high school as their urban counterparts.

Road Ahead

There are now over 260 million migrant workers in China, plus 100 million migrant children and left-behind children; together, they comprise a significant segment of society whose needs must be addressed and handled appropriately in the coming years. Otherwise, the challenges faced by migrant workers will pose a tremendous threat to the harmonious society that China seeks. Treating migrant workers as they were treated a decade ago would be a major mistake. Current migrant workers are more educated, connected, informed, and ambitious, and it is only a matter of time until they demand treatment equaling that of urban residents, such as education, healthcare, and other social welfare benefits. This will cause a seismic shift in the social fabric in China.

Notes

1 National Bureau of Statistics (2013, May 27), "2012 migrant workers report," retrieved January 2014 from http://www.gov.cn/gzdt/2013-05/27/content_2411923.htm
2 Ibid.
3 Institute of Population and Labor Economics, The Chinese Academy of Social Science (2012, April 20), "Number, structure and features of the new generation of migrant workers," retrieved January 2014 from http://iple.cass.cn/news/479487.htm
4 Ibid.
5 National Bureau of Statistics (2013, May 27).
6 Wu Di (2013, March 17), "Temporary couples," *Xiamen Evening News*, retrieved January 2014 from http://www.fjsen.com/d/2013-03/11/content_10833954.htm
7 All-China Women's Federation (2013, May 10), "Report on China's migrant children and left-over children," retrieved January 2014 from http://acwf.people.com.cn/n/2013/0510/c99013-21437965.html

Part III
Marriage and Family

15 Families

While the physical transformation of China in recent decades has been mind-boggling and almost surreal with city skylines nationwide changing seemingly overnight, other gradual changes are happening beneath the surface that will have a more enduring impact on Chinese society overall. One such change relates to family structures and the roles of family members. In this chapter, we describe the historical Chinese family structure, which we follow with a description of family structures in contemporary China. We then present a detailed discussion on the core family unit (i.e., grandparents, parents, child) and the distinct challenges faced by each member. In the Road Ahead section, we predict how the Chinese family structure and the roles of each member may change in the years ahead.

Historical Family Structure

A traditional Chinese family had two major characteristics. First, it had a patriarchal structure; older males in the family had power over other family members. Daughters were considered to be members of other families, which is what they would become later in life when they married. Likewise, a married woman was considered to be a member of her husband's family. Second, in a traditional Chinese family, multiple generations often lived together. In fact, according to traditional teachings, the best possible outcome is to have four generations of a family living under the same roof; when this occurs today, it is still considered a point of pride. These multigenerational families not only lived under the same roof but also operated as a unit in which each person had his or her own responsibilities and made specific contributions to the family.

This traditional family structure has changed drastically over the last 100 years. Except for pockets of underdeveloped regions in China, it is now rare for the eldest male to have absolute authority over a family. Multigenerational family structures, however, remain quite common and family members still play distinct roles.

Contemporary Family Structure: 4-2-1 and 2-1-1

China began to enforce the one-child policy in 1980; now, the first generation of only children has reached childbearing age. As a result, the traditional big family structure has evolved into the 4-2-1 family structure, with a young couple (2) who are in their twenties or early thirties at the core, together with their respective parents (4) and their child (1).

92 *Marriage and Family*

Figure 15.1 A couple selling popcorn in Shanghai to support their only child who is studying in Nanjing.

According to the *Sixth National Population Census* (2010), among 31 provinces, autonomous regions, and municipalities in mainland China, there are 401.5 million households, with a total population of 1.24 billion people. So the average population per household is 3.10 people, a reduction of 0.34 compared to the 3.44 average reported in the 2000 population census.[1] With shrinking household sizes, the inverted triangle family structure has gradually become predominant. To a large extent, this is due to the one-child policy. Even with the one-child policy in place, based on a report from 2005, it is estimated that in 2014 the total number of children under the age of 18 will be 111.53 million; of these, 66.66 million will be living in rural areas and 44.87 million will be living in urban areas.[2]

Another type of family structure is 2-1-1, comprised of a single parent (usually a single mother) (1), her parents (2), and her child (1). We discuss the plight of single mothers in detail in Chapter 18. While the number of single mothers is still relatively small, it has reached an unprecedented level in China and is a major societal challenge that must be addressed.

While the main reason for these new family structures is the one-child policy that has been in place since 1980, a more permanent shift is also driving this phenomenon: changes associated with the costs and benefits of having a child, especially more than one. There is no doubt that raising a child is expensive, but in China today, such expenses have increased substantially. Child-rearing costs are not even restricted to the period before a child turns 18. Parents normally must support their child whenever and however they can throughout their lifetimes, including paying or substantially helping to pay for an apartment so that their child can marry.

Meanwhile, the benefits of having more children have decreased substantially. Historically, children (specifically sons) were the parents' retirement plan. In rural areas, sons were employees who could work in the fields for free. Families with multiple sons were considered powerful in a village because when a dispute arose or a fight broke out, a family with more sons would likely win. This has obviously changed or is changing rapidly. As a result of these economic considerations, more and more younger Chinese couples are deliberately choosing to have just one child, even though the one-child policy has now been eased for couples comprised of at least one only child.

Relationships Among Grandparents, Parents, and Children

While a typical three-generation family may or may not live under the same roof (without a patriarchal structure, it is almost impossible for two sets of grandparents to live harmoniously with a young couple and their child anyway), traditional family roles still very much exist, even if virtually.

Many members of the younger generation long for the independence enjoyed by their Western counterparts who establish their own nuclear families after they grow up. Typically, Western parents neither interfere with their grown children's decisions nor expect their children to take care of them in old age. However, the younger generation in China cannot afford, monetarily and emotionally, to be independent. The younger generation needs their parents to help pay for the apartments and cars that are required in order to get married. Grandparents often help pay for the costs of raising their grandchildren as well. In Shanghai, for example, a young man has little chance of finding a wife if he does not have an apartment, but an average apartment usually costs a few million yuan while the starting salary of a college graduate is typically the equivalent of RMB 6,000 per month or less. So young adults must listen to their parents even though they may not want to because the parents may cut off financial support if their children do not defer to them. In addition, the younger generation grew up receiving the full attention of their parents because they were only children, and their parents made many sacrifices for them. Faced with this kind of emotional and financial debt, children find it very difficult to stand up to their parents when they have different opinions.

Unlike in Western cultures, Chinese parents always see their children as children, regardless of how old they are. This is the legacy of a society where the opinions and authority of the oldest person in the family are accepted without question. Some parents of adult children have thus continued to interfere in their children's lives. They feel this is both their right (a common expression is, "I raised you, so of course I can tell you what to do") and their responsibility.

It is in this context that we discuss distinct challenges faced by the three generations in a typical Chinese family.

The Grandparents

The major challenge faced by grandparents centers on who will take care of them when they can no longer take care of themselves. China is now an aging society. In 2012, the proportion of the population over the age of 60 reached 14.3 percent.[3] At the end of 2013, the total elderly population was estimated to be 200 million. It is further estimated that by 2050, China will have 400 million people over the age of 60. Members of the one-child generation who enjoyed the full attention and devotion of their parents will be forced in the very near future to assume the responsibility of caring for their parents. While a survey shows that more than

94   *Marriage and Family*

68.4% of people care for several elderly people, 50.1% of children live apart from their parents. If a child lives in a different city, it will prove very difficult for her to assume responsibility for the daily care of her parents.[4]

In the past, children and their spouses, as well as other relatives, would help elderly family members when needed. Although this cultural tradition still exists, the pool of people who can potentially chip in is much smaller. If only one older parent is sick, a young couple can try to help, but if two parents are sick (especially one from each family, who therefore live in separate households), it is nearly impossible for a young couple to manage caring for both.

In Chinese society, the idea of children taking care of their parents is so ingrained that it is assumed in many settings. Hospitals, for example, expect a patient's family members to stay in the hospital and take care of the patient; nurses only address medical needs (e.g., provide medication, take vital measurements, etc.). If a patient is bedridden (permanently or temporarily), family members (or someone they hire) must be in the patient's room 24 hours a day.

The Parents

The young parents in the middle of the Chinese family structure benefit greatly from grandparent involvement both in terms of childrearing and financial support. However, in this type of family structure, any marital decisions involve six people, not two. As in any decision making process, the greater the number of people involved, the lesser the chance of agreement. In addition, parents and grandparents are not just six individuals; the Chinese family is a complex structure in which two families often are pitted against each other. A husband and wife not only feel affection for each other, but they also feel strong loyalty to their own parents. When these two loyalties come into conflict, loyalty to parents often wins out, creating more conflict and even divorce.

Based on statistics from a district court for the first half of 2012, among the 60 divorce cases involving those born after 1980, 90% were accompanied by their parents in court.[5] Sometimes, because of resentment between their respective families, a young couple may not be able to reconcile even if they want to.

The Child

The challenge associated with the youngest generation of a Chinese family centers on who should raise and educate the child, and how. Many young couples rely on their parents to raise their child, something unthinkable in many other cultures. In most cases, the grandparents will live with the young couple; sometimes, however, a young couple will leave their child at the grandparents' home in another city and only visit the child on weekends (or holidays if work schedules do not allow).

While grandparent involvement may make the lives of young parents much easier, problems arise when the parents and grandparents have different opinions about how to raise the child. Grandparents often insist on having it their way and say things like, "This is how I raised you, and see, you turned out okay!" Needless to say, this constitutes another source of stress in the family that is further complicated when the child's mother and father do not agree with each other.

Due to constant lavish attention from six adults, only children tend to grow up feeling that they are, and should be, the center of the universe. Based on feedback from our informants, this is especially problematic when the grandparents are the main caregivers. Grandparents in China tend to indulge their only grandchild, give them whatever they want, and do anything they can to satisfy their desires.

Road Ahead

At the end of 2013, China made a major change to the population control policy. A couple can now have two children if the husband or wife is an only child. In the coming years, we will likely see more 4-2-2 families in China. Nevertheless, the main generational challenges discussed here are unlikely to change anytime soon.

We do see two major changes that are more subtle but more likely to have a lasting impact. The first is how the Chinese see the future family structure and the roles of each generation. Many informants in their forties already told us that they do not expect their children to take care of them when they are old, and they have made such expectations (or lack thereof) explicitly known to their children. However, few informants stated that they would not help their children after they become adults or that they would not interfere in the affairs of their children or grandchildren. It will likely take more time for such a huge shift in norms to occur, if ever.

The second major change that will happen is a shift in assumptions about close family support across multiple generations. The hospital example described earlier is based on the assumption that family members are obligated to help out regardless of their own life circumstances. Given these changes in both the Chinese family structure and the roles of different family members, society will have to accommodate by building non-family based support infrastructure such as more retirement facilities.

Notes

1　National Bureau of Statistics of China (2011, April 28), "Communiqué of the National Bureau of Statistics of People's Republic of China on major figures of the 2010 population census (no. 1)," retrieved January 2014 from http://www.stats.gov.cn/english/Statistical-Communiqu/201104/t20110428_61452.html

2　Wang Guangzhou (2009), "The structure and the trend of Chinese single children, Chinese one-child structure and amount of estimated future trends," *Population Research*, 1, retrieved January 2014 from http://www.usc.cuhk.edu.hk/PaperCollection/Details.aspx?id=7019

3　Ministry of Civil Affairs of the PRC (2013, June 19), "Data from statistical communiqué on the 2012 social service development," retrieved January 2014 from http://cws.mca.gov.cn/article/tjbg/201306/20130600474746.shtml

4　Wang Congcong (2011, May 26), "Can backbones of the 4-2-1 family withstand the responsibilities and challenges?" *China Youth Daily*, retrieved January 2014 from http://zqb.cyol.com/html/2012-11/13/nw.D110000zgqnb_20121113_2-07.htm

5　Shan Xiaotong & Sun Haiyinying (2013, July 26), "The 80s accompanied by parents in divorce court in 90% of divorce cases," *Life Daily* retrieved January 2014 from http://society.hljnews.cn/system/2012/07/26/002409061.shtml

16   Ideal Spouse and Child

We have mentioned in Chapter 2 that the Chinese value "face" and care deeply about how others judge them. People generally conform to societal expectations and seek others' acceptance and respect. At the extreme, this has become a competition to see who can best meet social expectations. One young informant commented, "It seems that one's life path has been chosen and paved at the very beginning, in line with expectations from family, friends, and society." Choosing another path can be quite difficult and create a life filled with burdens and pressures.

To a great extent, these expectations explain how the Chinese seek out their ideal spouses and raise their children. In this chapter, we describe the criteria for an ideal husband, wife, and child. We discuss how this might evolve in the near future in the Road Ahead section.

The Ideal Husband

The three criteria used these days in selecting a husband are tall, rich, and handsome. Rich is basically an oversimplified version of the traditional criterion of talent sought in a husband. Based on traditional spouse selection heuristics, a talented man and a beautiful woman make an ideal couple. Furthermore, interpretations of "talent" have varied over the years. In the 1980s, talent was interpreted as being able to provide the "big three" betrothal gifts: a refrigerator, a color TV, and a clothes washer. In the 1990s, the big three were a color TV, a clothes washer, and a DVD player (VCR); now they are a house, a car, and cash. When looking for the ideal husband, many Chinese women firmly believe the saying, "For a man, the worst thing is entering the wrong career, while for a woman, it is marrying the wrong man." Often women try to "marry up" (i.e., marry men whose circumstances are better than their own) or at least marry men who are richer than their friends' husbands.

Tall means a man should be taller than a minimum height (typically 170 cm); someone who is taller than 180 cm gets bonus points. Handsome is more icing on the cake, and it is the most subjective criterion among the three.

In addition, women use some rather unexpected criteria to select a husband in China. We conducted a survey of about 200 Chinese university students on the heuristics they use in constructing a consideration set of potential husbands. Many used elimination heuristics such as whether the other party would agree to live with her parents and whether the other party had certain diseases.

98 *Marriage and Family*

Apart from young women's expectations, parents do not want their daughters to suffer misery and poverty either, so they expect their daughters to marry someone who can provide the "big three" mentioned above. In a common plot on many TV programs these days, the son-in-law goes to visit his mother-in-law who first inquires about his house, then his job, and then his financial situation. These ideas are thus ingrained into the younger generations. A 26-year-old woman once said, "If my husband has a fairly good financial status, I could save myself years of effort. So financial status will be the principal criterion. Unless he has an apartment or a house, I won't go on a date with him."

From spouse selection to marriage maintenance, great expectations and consequent pressures push husbands to work hard and struggle for money. On the other hand, the Chinese do not place high expectations on the role a husband plays inside the household. Following the principle that males focus outside, while females focus inside, husbands live busy lives and spend their days on business trips, at dinner parties and working overtime.

This was well articulated in a newspaper article in which the author wrote: "We, or most of the mothers in China, are faced with the same reality. Western men are better at striking a balance between family and work than their counterparts in China. I think that is because of the traditional culture and special economic environment here. 'Promising' men are those who can grasp every opportunity to strive for their careers, rather than those who focus inside the household."[1]

The Ideal Wife

While women expect their spouses to be "tall, rich, and handsome," men hope their wives will be "fair-skinned, rich, and attractive." "Fair-skinned" refers to a specific preference for white skin. A woman who is fair-skinned, attractive, and from a decent family will become quite popular. As discussed in other chapters, a Chinese man also typically wants a wife who is slightly less educated and younger.

Rich refers to the resourcefulness of a young woman (or her family). One informant told us the following story. A very popular young man from her university broke up with his girlfriend upon graduation. However, within one month, he married a lady whose father turned out to be a senior official in the Beijing Police Office. The official helped the man find a job and obtain a registered residence (Hukou) in Beijing. (A Hukou is rather desirable and difficult to obtain in top tier cites in China.) In making his decision, the young man reasoned, "Marrying this girl could save me three decades of effort."

Compared to traditional roles played by women in China, many people expect modern women to multi-task and balance family and work. A text message that was widely circulated among the Chinese in 2010 has since been quoted widely as the "new standards for females;" that is, "they can have a decent career as well as a happy family; they can solve problems such as IT problems by themselves; they can afford expensive cars and good houses; and last but not least, they can fight against concubines and rascals as well!"

The Ideal Child

When China implemented the one-child policy in 1980, only children (more than 100 million of them) become the central focus of the new 4-2-1 family structure. Therefore, they have always been given copious amounts of attention and been saddled with high expectations for every aspect of their lives. Talk about pressure! If one has to summarize parental expectations, an ideal child should attain excellent academic achievement in school, land a decent job after graduation, and create a happy family life as an adult. In some cases, an ideal child is also someone who can help her parents and relatives achieve things they never could themselves in terms of status and/or wealth.

The key criterion used to judge whether one's child succeeds or not is to compare him or her to their peers. The performance of children from other families is frequently used as a manipulation tool by Chinese parents. They praise other children in front of their own and raise expectations by proclaiming how well others have done. "Do not fall behind others from the starting line" has become the guiding principle. One informant told us, "It can be said that 99% of people place too much pressure on children, hoping their children will stand out among others. Although sometimes they complain about that pressure, which has made children less happy and even led children to commit suicide, they immediately forget about that after 10 minutes and focus again on how to push their children to work harder instead."

A majority of Chinese families are willing to devote plenty of money to their children's education, fearing that their children will fall behind at the starting line, although ironically, nobody knows exactly where the starting line is. So, these efforts begin in the form of antenatal training and classes for newborns (e.g., swimming, foreign languages). Parents will buy a house in a specific school district, select prestigious schools and teachers, and then help their child enter a top tier university or study abroad. However, this massive investment is tied to tremendous expectations. According to the latest statistics released by Mintel, 75% of middle-class families hope their children will obtain a master's degree or above.[2] This is largely driven by comparison as well. There are two reasons why Chinese people compare their children to other people's children: the face culture that dominates Chinese society and fierce competition in contemporary China for everything (education, jobs, and even future spouses).

The second factor that drives parents to push their children is their own unfulfilled aspirations. We have often heard people who are still in their thirties or forties say, "As we can hardly move a leap forward, the child is my only hope." In extreme cases, children from rural areas who study outside of their counties are regarded as heroes who can change the fate of their families; sometimes they are even obliged to help their entire home villages.

Under such expectations, parents invest a lot in their children and ask their children to do a lot in return. According to results of the 2013 PISA test given to 15-year-old students worldwide, among 65 countries and areas, Shanghai students rank first in math (613; average 494), reading (570; average 496), and science (580; average 501). The report also revealed that students in Shanghai spend 13.8 hours

100   *Marriage and Family*

on homework every week, 5.3 hours more than the average (United States: 6.1 hours; France: 5.1 hours).[3]

Almost without exception, mothers are in charge of their children's education and are responsible for turning their children into model citizens. By contrast, fathers are typically uninvolved in their children's education. It is quite common for a mom to spend most of her evenings and weekends accompanying her young child to all types of extracurricular activities related to typical school subjects (e.g., mathematics), foreign languages (e.g., English), and enrichment (e.g., music and sports). A more recent trend is for a mother to accompany her child while studying abroad. For example, a mother may move to the United States with her teenage child and take care of the child while she attends a local high school. The husband usually stays behind in China, and the entire family may unite only on holidays. In many cases, families will even purchase property in a specific school district. A house near the Pennsylvania State University was recently purchased, allegedly with cash, by a Chinese mom whose daughter was 16 and was attending the local high school. In a more dramatic example, in early 2012 a Chinese mother bought a USD 6.5 million house for her 2-year-old daughter in preparation for her future college life.[4]

Road Ahead

We do not expect spouse selection criteria to change substantially in the near future. Through our research, however, we have heard a lot of younger parents who want to change how they educate their children and modify their expectations for them. A successful business owner in Shanghai who is in her forties said that she told her daughter, "Physical and mental health is a prerequisite. Then you can do whatever you want to do as long as you can survive, either for a company or start up a business yourself. It's quite simple to decide based on your happiness." Such sentiments are quite representative of parents who were born during and after the 1960s.

Notes

1 Morningpost.com (2010, April 19), "When will Chinese men return to family?" retrieved January 2014 from http://www.morningpost.com.cn/fukan/qgyz/2010-04-19/49110.shtml http://health.ifeng.com/psychology/romantic/detail_2010_04/20/536231_0.shtml

2 Sina.com (2012, December 7), "75% of middle-class families hope their children obtain Master's degrees," retrieved January 2014 from http://edu.sina.com.cn/l/2012-12-07/1509222887.html

3 OECD (2012), "PISA 2012 results: What makes schools successful? Resources, policies and practices (volume IV)," retrieved January 2014, http://www.oecd.org/pisa/keyfindings/pisa-2012-results-volume-iv.htm

4 CCTV (2013, March 26), "Chinese mom bought grand house for 2-year-old daughter," retrieved January 2014 from http://news.xinhuanet.com/world/2013-03/26/c_124504875.htm

17 Extramarital Relationships

Extramarital relationships are a fact of life in most societies, and China is no exception. As the following story illustrates, certain aspects of Chinese extramarital relationships are culturally unique. A senior executive told us that he once attended a dinner party in Nanchang, the provincial capital of Jiangxi. During the dinner, he noticed a female undergraduate student go out of her way to flirt with a middle-aged businessman whom she had just met for the first time. When our informant saw her again a few years later, he discovered that this young college student had agreed to be the businessman's mistress for three years in exchange for an apartment and a car, thus achieving her objective for attending the dinner party.

Some might suppose that she wanted to get ahead of her fellow college students early in life. Others may characterize her behavior as a rational exchange of assets. Sadly, this is not a unique story. Throughout our research, we have found that many people (typically females) willingly exchange youth and beauty for money or influence (typically from males). Most surprisingly, such trades are rationalized and accepted in many circles (including among highly educated people). These trades tend to take two forms, loosely translated as concubines (Pinyin: er'nai) and mistresses.

Infidelity in marriage happens in all cultures and across the political spectrum; countless examples have been well documented in the United States involving governors, senators, and presidents. However, three aspects of Chinese affairs are somewhat unique: first, youth and beauty are considered to be tradable and depreciable assets that can be exchanged for power and money; second, affairs are nearly ubiquitous; and third, a considerable number of people in Chinese society accept the phenomenon. We discuss concubines and mistresses separately below and highlight the first two aspects where relevant. We then discuss the third aspect of social acceptance. While married Chinese women also have affairs, it happens on a much smaller scale and the behavior is not accepted by close relations, or by society at large. Therefore, we focus our discussion here on extramarital affairs conducted by married men.

Concubines

Concubines have a long history in China that extends over millennia. Until 1911, China had been governed by a feudal system. It took until 1930 for monogamy to be formally endorsed by the state in the Civil Code of the Republic of China, and

102 *Marriage and Family*

concubines were not officially outlawed by the "Marriage Law" until 1950, just one year after the establishment of the People's Republic of China (PRC).

While concubines have completely disappeared from public life in mainland China, some people still remember when concubines lived openly, often with the families of their lovers; these relationships remain a subject of intrigue in modern literature and films. In Hong Kong, public relationships with concubines still exist, albeit only in a few wealthy families. One mainland executive said she had been invited to a dinner in Hong Kong where the host had four "wives" who all attended the so-called family dinner. Evidently they live openly as a big family, in an arrangement that echoes historical norms.

When China opened its borders in the 1980s, businessmen from Hong Kong and Taiwan flocked to the Pearl River Delta area in the southeastern part of the mainland. Many businessmen decided to have concubines where they set up their businesses, as their relative wealth compared to mainland Chinese at the time made it possible for them to attract and support them. It is estimated that during this early period, about 100,000 citizens of Hong Kong and Taiwan had concubines in Shenzhen. In fact, some new residential developments that were dominated by concubines of these visiting businessmen became known as the "Villages of Concubines."

As the economy has developed, some mainland Chinese citizens who are becoming wealthy also have adopted the practice of having concubines. However, since China officially outlaws polygamy, concubines usually do not live with the family and are often kept secret. In other words, they enjoy even less status than their historical counterparts. A concubine is normally involved in a long term relationship with a man; the couple may even have a child together. A concubine family normally lives separately in an apartment paid for by the man, who also normally pays for all living expenses. Concubines exchange years of life for material income, such as an apartment, a car, cash, or a job; such relationships typically are not driven by love.

In examining why these exchanges happen, we have come to identify two current perceptions in China. First, women and men (with their endowed possessions such as appearance and age, and acquired possessions such as wealth and power) possess tradable assets. Second, women are mostly judged by their endowed possessions, which unfortunately depreciate quickly over time, while men are mostly judged by their acquired possessions, which typically appreciate over time. Voicing the predominant social opinion, one informant told us, "Historically, men can usually have three or four more wives or concubines. Women bear a very low status and depend on men. In reality, these days it's very difficult for divorced women to find a husband as good as their ex-husband. Women's assets are beauty and youth, while men's are power and career. A woman is worth little when she becomes old, but a man can potentially become even more valuable as he becomes old."

Based on these two social perceptions, many men and women believe that a potential concubine relationship can be evaluated like any other trade of assets; hence, it is rational to trade if, after a careful cost benefit analysis, the exchange is beneficial to both parties. Absent from such a calculation, of course, is the value of one's dignity and morality. In addition, many Chinese like to take shortcuts (Chapter 7, an entire chapter of this book is devoted to the topic), and do not value the process one must undertake to achieve a goal. Referring to concubines, another informant observed, "Some young women think this is the shortcut to a comfortable life, so if there is such a shortcut, why not take it?" Essentially, the relationships are exclusive exchanges of youth (and beauty) for wealth, and such exchanges have become socially acceptable, even among some of the highly educated. At one of the top business schools in China, we were told a story about an MBA student who was interning in the dean's office. She met a successful businessman who came to visit, and soon after, she became his concubine and bore a child for him, with the full approval of her mother.

Although formal statistics on concubines are hard to obtain, having one or more concubines has become a popular practice among corrupt officials. In 2008, the party secretary of Zhejiang Commission for Discipline Inspection stated that among government officials who had serious criminal cases brought against them, more than 50% had concubines or long term extramarital sex partners. According to the Chinese People's University Crisis Management Research Center's *Public Official Image Crisis Report—2012*, 95% of officials who embezzle or bribe also have lovers; in fact 60% of embezzlement and/or bribery cases involve concubines.[1] In 2011, Yan Yongxi, the Deputy Head of Mentougou District, Beijing, was accused of bribery and embezzlement totaling RMB 42 million, 36 million of which related to his lover.

Mistresses

One of us asked a group of senior executives what the differences are between concubines and mistresses in present-day China. There appear to be at least two major differences, although clearly one can move from one category to another over time. First, a concubine does not expect to have official status as a wife and is usually content to lead a life that (more often than not) is secret, while a mistress's goal typically is to break up her lover's marriage so that she can become the wife one day. Second, unlike concubine relationships, mistress relationships may involve love, and the exchange of youth and beauty for material goods is more subtle. In addition, concubine relationships are usually long term (if not lifelong) and exclusive (at least on the woman's side), but mistress relationships are shorter in duration and may not be exclusive on either side.

Within the category of mistresses, there are two subtypes that represent the extremes. At one extreme are those who are having "traditional" affairs motivated by excitement and love as is typical in the United States. At the other extreme are those who are in relationships purely for material exchange, as in the example we provided at the beginning of this chapter. Unlike a concubine, this second subtype of mistress only intends to engage in an affair for a short time period and typically will not bear a child while in the relationship.

Why are there a large number of young women who want to break up someone else's marriage with the goal of assuming the role of wife? We observe three factors

104   *Marriage and Family*

that contribute to this phenomenon. First, this group of young women prefers their husbands to be mature and successful. Unfortunately, most such men are married; faced with a dwindling pool of potential suitable husbands, they feel they must try to break up someone else's marriage. Second, these young women believe that if they marry someone of similar age, it will take a long time and a tremendous amount of effort for them to become successful. Even worse, when their husbands finally do become successful, even younger women will come and steal their husbands away! So, what's the point? Finally, in the eyes of these young women, breaking up other people's marriages carries little moral guilt. They rationalize it as being the wife's fault; otherwise, why would a man choose to have a mistress?

In the eyes of wives, mistresses are members of a selfish "peach-picking gang." They come to pick the peaches when they are ripe and disregard the people who have put in all of the effort to actually grow the peach. They break the marriages of older and mature men and take away everything a wife has: her husband, her property, her family, and the precious youth the wife sacrificed for her family. This phenomenon is so pervasive that certain consulting companies actually provide classes for wives on defending their marriages against mistresses.

We also have observed that many men take advantage of potential mistresses' aspirations. They seduce young women by falsely promising that they will eventually divorce their wives and marry them. The duration and complexity of such deceptions can be mindboggling. For instance, a graduate of one of the best universities in China who became the mistress of a businessman from Singapore believed such promises for more than 10 years before he finally admitted that he does not intend to divorce his wife. Interestingly, many corruption cases have come to light in recent years after mistresses turned against lovers who broke similar promises.

From the male perspective, the motivation to have a concubine or a mistress also differs slightly. One may choose to have a concubine because he wants a big family, more children, etc. However, the motivation for taking a mistress often can be attributed to what many would call a "mid-life crisis."

Social Acceptance

There is a saying in China that is quite telling about social perception: "Keep the red flag flying high at home, but keep many colorful flags outside." The red flag (the color of the national flag) is a metaphor for one's wife, and the colorful flags represent concubines and/or mistresses. In other words, it is acceptable for a man to have many concubines/mistresses as long as the marriage is maintained. This phenomenon has not only become accepted by many people but also has become some men's objective.

Our informants revealed that in some circles, extramarital relationships signal status. In fact, in certain social settings, it is quite normal to bring a mistress to gatherings. If a man frequently changes his mistress, his friends and business associates will consider him to be a powerful/successful man. There is even a belief that a man's success can be measured by how many lovers he has. We were told that even some EMBA students/alumni from top programs who are highly regarded in the business world will bring their mistresses to gatherings, much to the dismay of their fellow classmates. What is more telling is that classmates rarely voice their objections, even though they typically also know the wives of the men involved.

In the *2010 Survey on the Attitudes and Behaviors of China's Urbanites on Dating and Marriage* (released by China's Marriage and Family Research Council with respondents from more than 30,000 families across China), many respondents took a neutral stand on affairs. In fact, about 40% of respondents agreed to at least one of the following statements about affairs: "[they are] a normal social phenomenon after opening up to the West, beyond reproach," "an emotional supplement, though immoral, is understandable," and "[an affair is] acceptable as long as it does not affect the marriage."[2]

More surprisingly, social acceptance even extends to wives. Many wives accept the presence of concubines and/or mistresses as long as their husbands do not seek divorce and maintain a façade of normal family. One successful businesswoman (who eventually divorced her husband after multiple episodes of infidelity) told us: "Wives are forced to accept the presence of concubines and/or mistresses, largely due to their inability to change it. Maybe it's also because the wives have too many concerns. When my ex-husband had his first affair, I forgave him. I was really hurt because I had invested a lot in the relationship. In the past, I didn't even allow him to go to KTV [karaoke] with other people, as I would be jealous. I married him despite opposition from my parents. The reason I forgave him the first time is because I couldn't leave the marriage, couldn't give up on many things, simply couldn't do it. I was concerned about my family and parents, and I had to accept that because I didn't want to cause them pain. I suppose women are typically soft hearted. When I talked to my female friends on this topic, maybe three out of five had forgiven their husbands in the past, and that set the tone for the conversation and my own decision in the future."

Not only do many accept affairs, but some have figured out how to profit from it. In a story fit for Hollywood, the son of Zhao Zhanqi, the former director of Zhejiang Provincial Transportation Department, discovered that his father had a mistress. After conducting a secret investigation, he told his mother that the young woman was meek and submissive. Instead of confronting the husband and his mistress, the mother and son decided to be "nice" to the mistress by putting her in charge of project planning and business development for the Transportation Department. Zhao Zhanqi selectively approved projects brought in by the mistress, and bribes from the companies whose projects were approved were then deposited into the son's company account.[3]

Road Ahead

Affairs have always been a part of human society and will likely continue to exist, both in China and elsewhere. The question is whether some of the unique behaviors described above will continue. We make several predictions.

First, the social perception of what is acceptable and what is not acceptable will continue to change as the Chinese people gain a deeper understanding of Western

106 *Marriage and Family*

culture. Many Chinese are not even aware that Americans are generally much more conservative on such matters. In addition, the younger, more independent generation of women will take the lead and denounce the practice as unacceptable, through both the media and daily participation in politics, commerce, and other aspects of life. While a true feminist movement does not yet exist in China, it is just a matter of time until such ideas take root and women become a true social force.

Second, concubines will eventually disappear over time because the practice counters all of the progress that has been made in modern developed cultures. Social opinions will change, and the benefits of having concubines will disappear. This social shift has already begun. An informant who is in the investment business clearly stated, "Before we invest in a company, we will investigate whether that owner has concubines, especially whether that person has kids out of wedlock." Although his motivations may be self-serving because he is trying to protect his investment, his statement reflects a shift towards viewing the practice of having concubines as a liability. Furthermore, as more Chinese citizens achieve middle-class income status, they will recognize that achieving material wealth is not worth sacrificing one's dignity and morality.

Third, relationships with mistresses will persist, but they will likely become secret. Such relationships will be conducted behind closed doors, not flaunted in public. We also believe that the number of mistresses (especially the type who explicitly seek to break a marriage and believe that such behavior is perfectly justified) will diminish in response to shifting social opinion.

In short, when the dust of pursuing material wealth settles and the Chinese people achieve a comfortable living standard, we believe the state of extramarital relationships will gradually evolve towards a more conservative style similar to what is common in the United States, rather than the more open-marriage style prevalent in some European countries. This is due to the fundamental Chinese value of loyalty and devotion to one's family. In time, the Chinese people will look back on this period of trading youth and beauty for material wealth as an unfortunate side-effect of fast economic development, a blemish on its proud and conservative culture.

Notes

1 Zhao Xibin & Xi Nan (2013, January 28), "95% of the corrupted officials have concubines," *Beijing Evening Paper*, retrieved January 2014 from http://bjwb.bjd.com.cn/html/2013-01/28/content_44258.htm

2 Marriage and Family Research Council (2011, November 29), "2010 survey on the attitudes and behaviors of China's urbanites on dating and marriage," retrieved January 2014 from http://news.xinhuanet.com/fashion/2011-11/29/c_122351860.htm

3 Shi Zhanqi (2007, September 4), "Corrupted official's wife and mistress become 'sisters,'" *Procuratorial Daily*, retrieved January 2014 from http://www.jcrb.com/n1/jcrb1407/ca633840.htm

18 Divorce and Divorcees

In 1986, 8.82 million Chinese couples registered marriages, and about 214,000 were granted divorces after failed mediations. In 2011, 13.02 million couples registered marriages, and 2.87 million couples became legally divorced.[2] During the past 25 years, the marriage rate in China has increased only slightly, to 1.48 times the rate reported in 1986, compared to a divorce rate that has skyrocketed to 13.43 times the rate reported that same year. This rapid increase in the divorce rate reflects a major societal transformation in China. In this chapter, we describe the historical equivalent of divorce and discuss several factors that have led to the current astronomical divorce rate. We then focus on the post-divorce lives of women, as their lives tend to be altered substantially more than those of divorced men. In the Road Ahead section, we predict how the lives of divorced women will continue to evolve.

Historical Equivalent of Divorce

Historically in China, females almost never initiated divorce. A so-called divorce was a decision imposed upon a woman in the form of a letter from her husband announcing that he no longer regarded her as his wife. (These types of letters were not abolished until 1930.)

Although it sounds relatively simple, a husband could not divorce his wife on a whim; men were required to follow traditional rules, which were called the "seven cans" and "three can'ts." Only when the wife met a condition of the "seven cans" could the husband and his family ask for divorce. However, if the wife met a condition of the "three can'ts," her husband could not seek a divorce, even if she fulfilled one of the "seven cans." As a result, marriage was a relatively steady state for most people in feudal China. While no quantitative data are available, divorce was quite rare by today's standard.

The "seven cans" were seven circumstances under which a husband could justifiably divorce his wife in feudal China. These seven circumstances were (1) failing to obey her parents-in-law, (2) failing to give birth to a son, (3) committing adultery with other men, (4) being extremely jealous, (5) becoming ill with severe diseases, (6) gossiping too much, and (7) committing theft. The "seven cans" first emerged during the Han Dynasty and were formalized during the Tang Dynasty in the Tang Code. Women who met any of these conditions were considered to lack womanly virtues or to have failed to fulfill their marital obligations. The second "can," failing

108 *Marriage and Family*

to produce a son, was considered a dereliction of responsibility to continue the family bloodline, which is one's most important duty to the family. Since many men had multiple wives and concubines, however, very few wives were actually divorced because of this.

To ensure the stability of family and society, a counterbalance was established against a husband's power. The "three can'ts" describe three conditions under which a husband could not divorce his wife under any circumstances: (1) the woman had no place to go (e.g., her parents had passed away); (2) the woman had served the 3-year mourning rites with her husband after his parent(s) had died; and (3) the husband was poor when he married the wife and had become wealthy. Two exceptions could be made in rare cases, even if one of the "three can'ts" conditions was met: severe disease and adultery.

A Skyrocketing Divorce Rate

According to the Ministry of Civil Affairs, except for a brief reduction of 8.16% in 2002, a continuous upward trend has been observed in the Chinese divorce rate from 2000 to 2011, with an average annual growth of 7.5% (see Chart 18.1).

Several factors have contributed to this steady increase in the divorce rate. First, attitudes towards marriage have changed. The traditional "till death do us part" view has disappeared, and divorce for emotional reasons is now accepted (and sometimes even encouraged). In some cases, a wife will choose to leave her husband if he fails to provide material comforts. The bond that keeps modern Chinese families together is not commitment but rather enduring affection between a husband and wife.

In addition, there is much less external pressure to remain married. Traditional Chinese morals and ethics have weakened with the influence of Western values. Western behaviors (e.g., extramarital affairs) are not only engaged in but also

Chart 18.1 Statistics on Chinese Marriage Rate, Divorce Rate, and Divorce Growth.[3]

Year	Marriage Rate	Divorce Rate	Divorce Growth
2000	6.70	0.96	
2001	6.30	0.98	2.08%
2002	6.10	0.90	-8.16%
2003	6.30	1.05	16.67%
2004	6.65	1.28	21.90%
2005	6.30	1.37	7.03%
2006	7.19	1.46	6.57%
2007	7.50	1.59	8.90%
2008	8.27	1.71	7.55%
2009	9.10	1.85	8.19%
2010	9.30	2.00	8.11%
2011	9.67	2.13	6.50%

Divorce and Divorcees   109

accepted by society. In the past, if a professor married a farmer, they would spare no effort to maintain their marriage despite the wide gap between their educational backgrounds. Back then, divorce was humiliating and associated with great social stigma and public condemnation. There was a popular saying in China: "Decent people never divorce, and he or she who divorces must be indecent."

Attitudes have changed substantially since then. A young female (born in 1988) who divorced her husband after a year said, "After getting married, his defects showed and I could hardly stand them. It is better to have short, sharp pains than long, dull pains. Plus people are not as conservative as they used to be, so it is nothing to be ashamed of to get a divorce. So we just called it off."

Second, more women are willing to get divorced now, even though it is difficult. As attitudes towards marriage have evolved, many Chinese females have begun to stick to their principles and determinedly oppose any behaviors that cross moral boundaries, such as love affairs, domestic violence, etc. This requires great courage, as current society is not friendly to divorced women, an issue that we discuss in the next subsection. Dramatically different from traditional females, modern Chinese women are typically unwilling to remain passive. In fact, according to statistics, women initiate divorce proceedings more often than men. After investigating more than 800 divorce cases, the local court in Shunyi, Beijing, found that around 70% of cases were initiated by the wife, and the reasons for most of those cases were the husband's extramarital affairs or domestic violence.[4]

Finally, legal changes have made it easier to get divorced. Before 2003, a divorce request required a letter of introduction from the couple's respective employers or a representative of their local district office. As such, divorce was very much a public affair, and countless people would attempt to persuade the couple to reconcile. At that time, many people also chose not to go through with the divorce due to potential career ramifications. For instance, the letter of introduction made the divorce public to the employer, which might result in decreasing the chances of the concerned person to be promoted. After 2003, however, divorce procedures have become simplified, private affairs, and an introduction letter is no longer required.

Post-Divorce Life: Flying Solo

Divorce is never easy for either spouse, but in China, the woman is typically the one whose life is altered completely after a marriage ends. A divorcee's quality of life typically decreases substantially, as she may need to raise a child on her own, be subjected to all kinds of social pressure and discrimination, and perhaps even be deprived of a chance to marry again. A popular saying in China captures the general attitude towards divorcees: "Divorced women are like second-hand cars, while divorced men are like second-hand apartments. Cars depreciate once used, while apartments hold their value all the same." Compared to divorced men, divorced women (particularly single mothers) are vulnerable to much more social pressure and public prejudice. A 38-year-old divorced man told us, "Although I have experienced a divorce and have a child, I am still unwilling to marry a single

110 Marriage and Family

mom who shares a similar experience with me. The reason is simple. It is too hard and too complicated to hold the two families together. Blood is thicker than water. I don't want to raise someone else's kids."

The divorce rate increases each year, and with it the number of underprivileged single mothers. According to a survey by the All-China Women's Federation, 67% of divorces affect families with children, and only 1/6 of these children are raised directly by the fathers. In other words, divorced females more often play the role of single parent. Based on this ratio, the number of single mothers increased by an estimated 1.61 million in 2011. Even single mothers who are still young more often than not dismiss the thought of a second marriage out of concern for their children's feelings, the hustle and bustle of the life after divorce, and gloomy memories of the first marriage. So, raising their children becomes their most important activity. In one interview with a 30-year-old single mother, we learned that she decided to bring up the child on her own because she was worried that a second marriage would create additional trauma; she gave up the idea of remarrying in order to provide her child a stronger sense of security.

In Beijing, a follow-up survey was conducted with 100 divorced couples who, on average, were older than 35. Most of these families had one or two children. When they divorced, the wives assumed guardianship for 85% of the children. After 5 years, most of the men had remarried, while less than 15% of the women had married again.[5] In contrast, according to statistics published by the U.S. Office of Population Censuses and Surveys, within the 5 years following a divorce (1985–1989), 50% of men and 45% of women had remarried.[6]

Why is there such a difference in the rate of remarriage between American and Chinese women? Most Chinese men feel that single mothers are not ideal partners because they tend to be older and have a track record of failed marriage. If divorced men harbor biases against single moms, it is even worse among those who have never been married before. As a result, the pool of potential mates becomes quite small for single mothers, who all but give up on the idea of remarrying.

Furthermore, most single moms face financial hardship. According to a 2012 survey by the Yangpu district of Shanghai, most single moms do not have a high monthly income; 51.6% earn RMB 1,281–3,000 and 31.0% earn RMB 1,280 or less. Main income sources include salary or retirement pensions (54.2%), social security payments (at the lowest level) from the government (12.2%), alimony (10.4%), the salary or retirement pension of a temporary partner who lives with them (8.7%), and financial aid from relatives or friends (6.7%). Such meager income must cover the cost of daily living expenses (40.2%), children's education (34.7%), medical services (17.3%), and housing (7.5%), as well as all other expenses.[7]

Not all single moms are poor, of course. We interviewed several divorced informants who are very successful career women or have their own businesses. They do not lack financial resources in their lives and are attractive, both physically and intellectually. Nonetheless, they confessed to us that it would be extremely unlikely that they would find the right person and marry again.

Road Ahead

There is no doubt in our minds that the divorce rate in China will level off in the foreseeable future. Despite the importance of family in Chinese society, we do not feel the current divorce rate will have much substantial impact on the lives of the Chinese people in general. What will be critical in the coming years is how society will treat divorced women. The Chinese people have now accepted the Western notion that marriage should be based on love and mutual respect, and increasingly are adopting Western cultural justifications for divorce. However, one fundamental difference is the treatment of divorced women, especially in terms of being given a second chance at marriage. Until the majority of Chinese men judge a potential wife's attractiveness regardless of her prior marriage record and feel comfortable raising a child from a previous marriage, divorcees in China face a long road ahead. Such changes cannot be legislated, and we are not optimistic that rapid changes are on the horizon. Thus, we believe women who choose to divorce their husbands are brave pioneers.

Notes

1 Ministry of Civil Affairs of the PRC (1986–2012), "Social service development statistics bulletins," retrieved January 2014 from http://cws.mca.gov.cn/article/tjbg/
2 Ibid.
3 Ibid.
4 Qiu Wei & Xiu Zhi (2011, March, 2), "Around seventy percent of divorce cases initiated by the wife's side," *Beijing Morning Post,* retrieved January 2014 from http://www.morningpost.com.cn/xwzx/bjxw/2011-03-02/128314.shtml
5 Li Xiaohong (2011, June 2), "Faced with the shock wave of divorce: Why are Chinese people's marriages becoming more and more fragile?" *People's Daily,* retrieved January 2014 from http://news.xinhuanet.com/politics/2011-06/02/c_121486065_3.htm?prolongation=1
6 Rose M. Kreider, *Remarriage in the United States,* presented at the annual meeting of the American Sociological Association, August 10–14, 2006, retrieved January 2014 from http://www.census.gov/hhes/socdemo/marriage/data/sipp/us-remarriage-poster.pdf
7 The Women's Federation of Yangpu District (2012, December 3), "A survey report of the needs of single mothers in Yangpu," *Shanghai Women,* retrieved January 2014 from http://www.shwomen.org/renda/08women/llyj/fnyj/u1a1805325.html

19   Leftover Women

Although its exact origins are unknown, the term "leftover women" was adopted in 2007 as a new Chinese word of the year by the Ministry of Education of China; since then it has become a popular part of the Chinese vernacular. The term is defined as women who could be married but are not, are typically 27 years old or older, generally well educated, earn a high income, and have relatively high standards when it comes to choosing a spouse. Originally used to refer to those born in the 1970s, the word is now used to refer to those born in the 1980s as well. In the focus groups we facilitated for this book, most people did not feel that the term "leftover women" was offensive.

There is no demographic reason for this phenomenon; on the contrary, there are more single men than single women in China. According to a study published by the Training and Communication Center of National Health and Family Planning Commission and jiayuan.com, there are 249 million unmarried people over the age of 18 in China, and there are 23 million more unmarried males than females.[1]

In this chapter, we discuss two fundamental factors that have contributed to the presence of this segment of women, specifically the materialization of marriage and unequal spouse selection heuristics. We then discuss three factors—cultural expectations about marital age, media hoopla, and pressure from family and friends—which have turned an otherwise minor private issue into a major social challenge.

Materialization of Marriage

It is said that in small towns and big cities alike, a single man will never be able to find a wife unless he owns an apartment and a car. According to one matchmaking agency, most of their male clients either own a home or are financially prepared to buy one; it is one of the most important criteria Chinese women and their parents consider when looking for a spouse. While the minimum price for an apartment in Shanghai is around RMB 3 million, a new medical school graduate makes just RMB 6,000 per month. Thus, even the most successful, highly educated young person could not come close to achieving the goal of buying a home unless his family provided it. On one of the most popular TV dating programs, a young woman famously declared that she would rather be weeping in a BMW (i.e., wealthy, but in an unhappy marriage) than laughing while riding on the back of a bicycle (i.e., happy, but in a marriage with little material wealth). This

114   *Marriage and Family*

expression has quickly become a popular phrase in China, providing justification for the choices of many other young women.

Much of the focus on the material wealth of a potential husband is not initiated by the young women themselves. Rather, it comes in the form of pressure from parents and peers. The parents of the younger generation lived through great hardship in the 1960s and 1970s, and they do not want their (often only) children to live materially deficient lives. This overcompensation probably contributes to the strong emphasis on material wealth in marriage. The glorification of material wealth in contemporary China has undoubtedly contributed to this as well since a person's success is now often judged by his or her bank balance. In addition, in a society where one's happiness is frequently determined by how one compares to his or her peers, the desire for material wealth that is at least as good as (or better than) that of friends or colleagues is palpable and ubiquitous.

Unequal Spouse Searching Heuristics

Foreigners often are puzzled as to why young, attractive, and successful Chinese women face challenges in finding spouses. Often, such women do not even use material wealth as a selection criterion since many of them already own apartments and cars. This is a unique phenomenon in China, where men prefer to marry down and women prefer to marry up, in terms of age, education, and income. It is said that in China, class A men seek class B women, class B men seek class C women, and class C men seek class D women; those left are class A women and class D men. In addition, while women are expected to marry in their mid-twenties, men enjoy no social stigma even they remain single well into their thirties. In fact, single males in their thirties enjoy advantages over their twenty-something competitors due to their financial strength. It is even said that any successful and single man under the age of 45 can find an attractive wife in her twenties. Such unequal spouse searching heuristics thus artificially create a large number of single men and women.

Likewise, there is a substantial difference in gender ratios between urban and rural areas. There are more single women in urbanized areas, particularly in large cities like Beijing and Shanghai. A city girl will almost never marry someone living in a rural area, while women living in rural areas generally want to move to cities (or from a small city to a large city) in search of a better life. Men from rural areas also come to cities to find better jobs, but most of them eventually return to their hometowns.

Cultural Expectations about Marital Age

In traditional Chinese culture, couples tended to marry young. Historically, the government enacted policies to encourage early marriage in order to expand the population. This practice extends back as far as the Spring and Autumn Period (770 BC–476 BC). During that time, King Huan of Qi ordered that "men marry at the age of 20 and women at 15." Similarly, King Goujian of Yue declared: "Guilty are the parents if their daughter isn't married before 17 or their son isn't married before 20."

Of course, much has changed since then, but Chinese men and women still marry at a much earlier age than citizens of other countries. In 1980, the Chinese government enacted a policy meant to help control population growth that provided incentives for people to marry later in life. However, according to its definition, a "late" marriage involves a man older than 25 or a woman older than 23. Although unintended, the general public has now accepted the idea that young women who have not married by the time they are 23 years old are marrying "late." This means a college graduate would be considered to be marrying late within 1 or 2 years. According to the Sixth National Population Census (2010), on average, Chinese women marry at the age of 24.9;[2] by comparison, in 2011 the average marital age of French women was 30.1,[3] and the average marital age of Japanese women was 29.[4] According to a 2010 survey conducted by the All-China Women's Federation, however, 92% of male respondents still believe that women should be married by the time they turn 27.

Such cultural expectations have artificially accelerated the crisis by making women who should be enjoying their single lives think that they are already late in the spouse searching game. As a matter of fact, in popular culture, "leftover women" are classified into age groups and labeled with progressively pessimistic and derogatory terms (or one could classify them as dark humor). Single women between the ages of 28 and 32 are "Leftover Fighters" who still have a chance to find a happy marriage. Those between 32 and 35 years old are labeled with the unflattering title of "Leftover Forever." A "Queen of Leftover" is an unmarried woman between the ages of 35 and 38, while any single woman over the age of 38 is called a "Leftover Goddess."

Media Hoopla

The Chinese media have played a major role in popularizing this "crisis." News and popular culture outlets alike use the derogatory term "leftover women" to attract readers and viewers, making the concept even more prominent in the public consciousness. To boost readership, popular micro bloggers vastly exaggerate the experiences of leftover women, saying things like they "are either blind dating or on the way to blind dates." Some media outlets even promote the idea that women who go too long without marrying reach an "expiration date" and become "leftover," something that would clearly be labeled derogatory and might even induce legal action in the United States. Unfortunately, there are no such watchdog groups in China that attempt to turn the tide of media coverage.

On the contrary, even official media outlets participate in this hoopla. One article that was widely reported and mocked outside China was "How Many Leftover Women Deserve Our Sympathy?" It was posted on one of the most popular online news outlets in China[5] and reposted on the website of the official All-China Federation of Women in March 2011.[6] It put forth the assertion that girls hope to

116 *Marriage and Family*

further their educations in order to increase their competitiveness in seeking a husband. However, according to the article, the tragedy is that these women do not realize that they are worth less as they age. So by the time they get their Master's or Ph.D. degrees, they are like yellowed pearls with little value. With such "theories" being circulated by the mouthpiece of the official women's rights organization of the country, one can only imagine how the general media treat this subject! Such media coverage has a substantial negative impact on young women's confidence, and many of them resort to calling themselves "leftover women" in front of others as a coping mechanism.

As a result of all of this negative attention in the mass media, many women who should be enjoying their single lives like their equally well educated contemporaries in other countries are forced to rush into the process of seeking spouses, thereby artificially fulfilling the perception that many young women are seeking husbands. According to a popular dating site, the ratio of single women to single men registered in Shanghai is 4:1. This statistic only amplifies the popular (and likely false) belief that there are a lot more women "left" than men.

In addition, the labeling of leftover women substantially decreases their value when they do eventually seek spouses. Most men feel that they should not marry a leftover woman (or at least that they deserve a better position in the dating hierarchy). In extreme cases, women older than a certain age are excluded from consideration altogether due to popular beliefs that such women are supposed to be leftover forever.

Parents, Relatives, and Friends

In 2013, China introduced the Elderly Rights Law that adult children may be held criminally liable if they do not visit their aging parents regularly. Reporting on people's reaction to this law, one journalist decided to interview an old Chinese man. To his surprise, upon hearing the question, the old man suddenly lost his temper and responded: "Why should not coming back to visit us be against law? Those who remain unmarried by 30 are the ones breaking law; they should be sentenced to prison!"

While extreme, such sentiments are well grounded in the societal expectation that getting married and producing a child is the most important responsibility a person has to one's parents. Chinese parents traditionally pour all of their resources and hope into their children—especially now, since many young women are the only children in their families. It is very typical to hear parents tell their child, "We don't expect anything from you. Just give us a grandchild!"

To make things worse, the current hysteria about "leftover women" has placed even more pressure on susceptible parents to seek marriages for their daughters as soon as possible. Unfortunately, they inadvertently transfer that pressure onto their daughters, who might have perfectly valid reasons for marrying later in life. Parents may even take matters into their own hands and actively participate in their children's dating lives. Thus, matchmaking corners like the one in People's Park in Shanghai have emerged.

Leftover Women 117

Figure 19.1 The matchmaking corner in People's Park in Shanghai.

Figure 19.2 The information wall: Matchmaking agencies charge RMB 10/month to place an eligible individual's information on these walls, much like newspaper classifieds.

118 *Marriage and Family*

Such pressure can be unbearable. In addition, relatives and friends all pitch in to "help." When single women gather with friends and family, they are often bombarded with questions and advice, such as: "Do you have a boyfriend?" "You should hurry up and meet someone!" and "I know a single guy I could introduce you to!" It is so bad that some 30-year-old single women feel the need to hire fake boyfriends to bring home for Chinese New Year or other family gatherings.

Road Ahead

In most countries in the modern world, whom and when to marry are personal choices that are not subjected to the scrutiny of the public, the media, or even one's parents. It is even more surprising, from an outsider's perspective, that a derogatory phrase such as "leftover women" is widely used in society and by official sources. Looking ahead, it is conceivable that this phrase may itself receive negative publicity and will eventually become a historical artifact in Chinese language.

While other factors discussed here might also slowly evolve with development, the one thing we believe will remain relatively unchanged in the near future is the unequal spouse searching heuristic. This is something more fundamental to the Chinese culture, and it will take a lot more than shifting attitudes about marriage to facilitate such a change.

Out of the ashes of the "leftover women" label, we are already seeing the rise of a new generation of single women, whom we label as "3U Bachelorettes." The 3Us are *unmarried* in status, *unfettered* in their spiritual and material lives, and *unhurried* in their pursuit of a traditional family. They differ vastly from their parents and society in their perceptions of themselves and the institution of marriage. They are confident, independent, and level-headed and are unconstrained by the moral concept of celibacy, but are rather unwilling to tolerate a life partner with whom they are not completely compatible.

Several factors contribute to these women's carefree attitudes about their bachelorette status, most importantly higher education levels, exposure to Western culture (through travel and study abroad), and access to information online. Unlike traditional Chinese females, these women believe that when and whom they marry is a personal, autonomous choice. They no longer see themselves as products on a marriage assembly line, to be packaged and shipped out to the recipients once their parents think they are ready. Today, Chinese women have full, colorful lives filled with their own circles of friends, varied interests and passions, and successful careers for which they are well compensated. They no longer need to enter practical, loveless marriages to cultivate lives for themselves. While not opposed to the idea of marriage, many are unafraid or even willing to remain single. Furthermore, since more women are attaining advanced degrees, longer periods of education postpone the age of marriage.

Parents who had their children in the 1980s also tend to support these shifts. One informant, a business owner, even declared to us, "I feel that my daughter does not need to marry. She does not need to depend on a man."

Notes

1 Training and Communication Center of National Health and Family Planning Commission, and jiayuan.com (2012, December 12), "Report on Chinese attitudes towards marriage (2012–2013)," retrieved January 2014 from http://yn.people.com.cn/news/domestic/n/2012/1226/c228494-17920785-1.html

2 National Bureau of Statistics (2010), "The 6th national population census," retrieved January 2014 from http://www.stats.gov.cn/english/Statisticaldata/CensusData/rkpc2010/indexch.htm

3 Insee, Statistiques de l'État Civil et Estimations de Population (2012), "Average age of women at first marriage," retrieved January 2014 from http://www.insee.fr/fr/themes/detail.asp?ref_id=bilan-demo&page=donnees-detaillees/bilan-demo/pop_age3b.htm

4 Government of Japan (2013), "Mean age of first marriage," *Statistical Handbook of Japan 2013*, retrieved January 2014, http://www.stat.go.jp/english/data/handbook/c0117.htm#c02

5 Xinhuanet.com (2011, March), "How many leftover women deserve our sympathy?" retrieved January 2014 from http://news.xinhuanet.com/lady/2011-03/10/c_121170425.htm

6 We can no longer find the original article on the ACWF's website except various commentaries and reposts online, but the BBC has cited the same article and commented on this: http://www.bbc.co.uk/news/magazine-21320560

Part IV
Needs, Values, and Aspirations

20 Life Objectives and the Chinese Dream

What a person should pursue in his or her short life and what will make him or her truly happy are eternal questions. Some people spend a lot of time and energy trying to figure this out for themselves; others simply do what others do. Individual pursuits and standards of success, and collective societal goals are the key driving forces of a nation. In China, the dominant life objective now is the accumulation of wealth, and the dominant social pursuit is the Chinese Dream. In this chapter, we will discuss the pursuit of wealth, the reasons behind this single-minded pursuit, the gradual shift to diversified objectives, and finally, the Chinese Dream.

Wealth Accumulation as the Dominant Life Objective

According to a survey of 3,000 entrepreneurs and senior executives from 10 countries on "success"[1] conducted by the ESSEC Business School in France, a decent career and the accumulation of wealth fail to provide people with happiness and a sense of achievement; instead, respondents said that a happy family (96%), true friends (95%), free time (93%), and a life led according to ethical principles (91%) were key determinants of their own happiness. The survey also revealed that 51% of American entrepreneurs and top executives thought that successful people "create and know how to *distribute* wealth;" entrepreneurs from Great Britain (50%), France (59%), Germany (51%), Brazil (79%), Morocco (83%), India (42%), and Russia (79%) agreed. In contrast, 79% of Chinese entrepreneurs and top executives responded that successful people "create and *accumulate* wealth." For those who truly understand current Chinese societal norms, this comes as no surprise.

Dong Pan, a professor at Beijing Normal University, told his graduate students on Weibo, "If you fail to possess a wealth of RMB 40 million, when you are 40, do not come visit me or reveal that you are my student." He went on to claim, "For a well-educated person, to be poor is equal to disgrace and failure."[2] These sentiments from a college professor are quite indicative of how citizens in China are judged.

An extensive social tendency towards money worship in China is worth noting. According to a survey by *Global Times*, 60.9% of interviewees admitted to money-worshipping, and 95.1% think that mammonism is flourishing in China.[3] Mammonism, or devotion to the pursuit of wealth, has gradually become a mainstream attitude in society. People are becoming more utilitarian and materialistic. As it was written in the *Records of the Grand Historian*,[4] "In such a teeming world, everyone is simply profit-oriented."

124 *Needs, Values, and Aspirations*

In our research, we grew accustomed to hearing people making comments such as, "If you really think you are smart, why don't you go and make some more money?" These types of comments are made quite often to children, spouses, friends, and even strangers. In today's China, success means wealth and vice versa, and power can be exchanged for wealth.

Factors Contributing to the Dominant Role of Wealth Accumulation

In Chinese society, business owners used to comprise the lowest social tier. In China, traditionally people are divided into nine classes. The order from superior to inferior is: the monarch, intellectuals, officials, physicians and witches, monks and Taoist priests, soldiers, farmers, craftsmen, and merchants. During the Han Dynasty (202 BC–220 AD), merchants were not allowed to wear silk clothes or to be officials. During the Tang (618 AD–907 AD) and Ming (1368 AD–1644 AD) Dynasties, even the farmers were allowed to wear fine clothes; however, the merchants were forbidden to wear silk clothing and the colors red and purple. Thus, merchants historically had a very inferior status among the nine social classes. Exactly the opposite is true today. So what happened?

Based on our research, several factors seem to have contributed to this. First, material goods have a strong allure after their long absence from China. Before China opened up to the outside world in the early 1980s, almost no one in China owned a private car, few had televisions, and almost everyone dressed in the same dull style. It was a world of 1 billion people that had been cut off from modern civilization. Imagine someone who has been starved for a long time suddenly being given an opportunity to accumulate food. It is understandable that he will start to stock all kinds of food in his apartment simply because he has never seen so many varieties and he wants to try all of them.

Second, as one informant said, "At present, many things can only be realized with money. China is now on a fast track of development, so wealth becomes a most important measurement index, which is simple, and can be quantified." For example, mothers-in-law typically require their future sons-in-law to own cars and houses. Most men (whose intended age of marriage is about 28 to 30), however, will not have been able to save enough money to buy an apartment and a car just six or seven years after entering the job market. So if a young man does not have sufficient financial assets, he may not even be able to find a woman who will be willing to marry him. A huge income gap exacerbates the wealth accumulation frenzy. According to the *Chinese Cities' Development Report No.4 on People's Livelihood 2011,*[5] the current urban-rural income gap in China is 3.23:1, the most dramatic urban-rural income gap in the world.

Third, there are few social norms related to other life objectives, and the government has endorsed current norms around wealth accumulation. After the disastrous years of the Cultural Revolution, the Chinese lost their faith in many things that they had traditionally treasured. In the 1980s, the Chinese government encouraged wealth accumulation with campaigns promoting attitudes such as "being rich is glorious." The original intention was to motivate more Chinese citizens to become entrepreneurs after a long hiatus when China was a socialist society. However, that original goal has morphed into something else altogether. As a result, money has become the golden standard by which a person's social status is judged.

Fourth, a "keeping up with the Joneses" mentality is pervasive in Chinese society. In the face of intense peer pressure, people have made a contest out of money and material well-being. In other words, when a person's friends are financially better off and have both houses and cars, it elicits feelings of disgrace and even puts a person with less material wealth at a disadvantage when it comes to choosing a marriage partner. The people who have accumulated more wealth, on the other hand, spend money on luxury goods so as to flaunt their social status and wealth (see the chapter devoted to the issue of face in this book).

Last but not least, wealth accumulation is motivated by minimizing uncertainty and providing more stability and security for oneself and one's family. Specifically, a sense of security is based on one's ability to afford a house, access medical care, raise a child, and have a decent quality of life, even after retirement. Comparing the living conditions of the professors from different departments of a college, one informant remarked: "The professors from the department of architecture drive Audi Q7s at worst, while the professors from the department of mathematics are still riding bicycles. There lies such a sharp difference. It is quite hard for the professors from the department of mathematics to look at their counterparts who are comfortably driving fine cars, as it is not merely the difference in transportation, but rather the lifestyle. More things can be reflected upon with this insecurity in wealth accumulation. What if you get sick? For instance, if you require a kidney transplant, first if you fail to have Guanxi [circles], then you cannot find a kidney source, so you have to wait for the matching process; second, a kidney transplant is not covered by medical insurance, and the price was RMB 400,000 a few years ago, and now it is RMB 600,000."

From Wealth Accumulation to Diversified Life Objectives

Life objectives are changing, however, especially among members of the younger generation. A survey conducted by the research center of the *China Youth Daily* in December 2012[6] confirmed that young people's career values are transforming. Among those surveyed, 51.5% held the view that their ideal job is not necessarily one that pays better but rather one that is well-suited to them; 48.8% were concerned more about their own feelings and interests; and 36.0% regarded themselves as mature and mentally independent.

One of our informants, a college student, said, "One of my high schoolmates has a rather special life objective. He wants to be a poet and writer and has persevered with writing poems for years. Now he has graduated, but he gave up job hunting, as his first choice is to complete his literary works; he intends to be a professor of Chinese language and literature. His friends and fellow students do not understand this, nor has his family from the beginning. But now that it has already been five years, his family has stopped complaining and discouraging. His current financial source mainly depends on his family."

126   *Needs, Values, and Aspirations*

Furthermore, according to a survey of adolescents about individual values in 2012,[7] many more respondents said that an individual's values lie in good morality (67%), contributions to society (58.2%), and talents (56.9%) than in wealth (12.2%) and power (10.1%). When asked what kind of person they want to be, the majority of respondents said that they want to achieve some career accomplishments (58.4%); other popular responses included wanting to make contributions to the nation that are useful to society (26.9%) and wanting to command respect (20.3%). Relatively few respondents wanted to achieve great wealth (11.5%) or have great power and a high position (7.9%). Clearly, attitudes are changing. The younger generation wants others to encourage and respect their diverse values and life choices.

The Chinese Dream

The Chinese Dream is a concept that has been adopted by the current generation of Chinese leaders and is used as a rallying cry for the Chinese people. President Xi defines the Chinese Dream as the great revival of China as a nation; specifically the goal is to develop a country that is prosperous, powerful, and revitalized and to make the people happy. This has undoubtedly become the primary objective that will be pursued collectively by members of Chinese society in the coming years and decades.

We asked several groups of informants to share their thoughts about the Chinese Dream. Almost everyone was in favor of this objective, believing it is beyond politics, acceptable to every Chinese citizen, and inspiring. However, most of our informants could not agree on how the Chinese Dream should be defined. One informant's comment is quite representative: "Right now, we don't have time for daydreaming. We are too busy with our own accumulation of material wealth. What dream could we have yet? Perhaps we dream of leading such a high-quality life as the middle class in Europe and the United States. For me, I hope that I can live life as I like, have spiritual and economic freedom, and then do something beneficial for society."

Road Ahead

A society is defined by the life objectives citizens choose to pursue. Like the Americans who pursue the dream of "life, liberty, and the pursuit of happiness," the Chinese are now searching for their own version of a dream—a dream that involves more than just the accumulation of wealth. Looking ahead, we are quite optimistic that Chinese society will gradually come to accept, and celebrate, that one does not need to be rich to be successful in life.

Notes

1 Sophie Péters (2011, December 3), "La réussite, c'est quoi pour vous?" *La Tribune*, retrieved January 2014 from http://www.latribune.fr/carrieres/carrieres-salaires/20110310trib000607182/la-reussite-c-est-quoi-pour-vous-.html

Life Objectives and the Chinese Dream 127

2 Dong Pan (2011, April 4), Post on Weibo.com, retrieved January 2014 from http://weibo.com/1149665262/3f4DddweFD

3 Gao Youbin (2010, February 26), "Six-tenths of interviewed netizens admit to being 'money-worshippers,'" *Global Times*, retrieved January 2014 from http://china.huanqiu.com/roll/2010-02/727100.html

4 Sima Qian (1961), *Records of the Grand Historian*, translated by Burton Watson, New York: Columbia University Press.

5 Institute for Urban and Environmental Studies, The Chinese Academy of Social Sciences (2011), "Chinese cities' development report no.4 on people's livelihood 2011," retrieved January 2014 from http://iue.cass.cn/

6 China Youth Daily Research Center (2013, January), "Survey on young people's career values," *China Youth Daily*, retrieved January 2014 from http://zqb.cyol.com/html/2013-01/31/nw.D110000zgqnb_20130131_1-07.htm

7 Qiu Pengzhen (2012), "A survey and analysis of contemporary adolescents' values," *Science of Social Psychology*, 5.
The interviewees consisted of students and new entrants in the job market from five cities in Hubei province, including Wuhan, Xiangfan, Jingzhou, Yichang, & Huangshi. The age range of participants was between 14 and 28 years. Of the 3,000 questionnaires sent out, 2,612 responses were returned.

21 Role Models[1]

One way to understand the state of a society is to study its norms, which we have done extensively in this book. However, it can also be useful to study societal aspirations. In this chapter, we discuss role models in Chinese society and the kinds of people and stories that the Chinese find inspirational.

The Most Inspiring Chinese, a national television program that has aired on China Central TV (CCTV, the official television station of China) each year since 2002, helped us identify current role models in China. Each year, 10 individuals or groups who touch the hearts of the Chinese public are selected from across the nation. The program has now become quite popular and is referred to as "a spiritual epic of the contemporary Chinese" by various media.

To understand more about Chinese role models, we analyzed the 30 individuals who were selected as the Most Inspiring Chinese from 2010 to 2012. We then created categories based on why they were selected. The categories are: being dedicated to work (14 people), helping those in need (10 people), behaving as Good Samaritans even at the cost of their own lives (3 people), showing devotion to parents (2 people), and displaying positive attitudes towards life (1 person). We use these five categories as a basis for discussing five types of role models that current members of Chinese society value. In the Road Ahead section, we discuss how this set of role models will evolve in the coming years.

Type 1: Dedicated to Work

Nearly 50% of all winners (14 out of 30) from 2010 to 2012 can be categorized as being dedicated to work. They include scientists, government officials, academicians, as well as soldiers and doctors. We highlight one such winner here to illustrate why people in this category are chosen as the Most Inspiring Chinese.

Lin Junde (2012 winner) was a Fellow of the Chinese Academy of Engineering and a Research Professor who worked for the General Armament Department of the Chinese military. The announcement recognizing his achievement described Lin as a substantial contributor to the development of nuclear technology in China over a 40-plus year career. He was diagnosed with bile duct carcinoma in May 2012. He refused surgery and chemotherapy so that he would not delay his research project. After his condition deteriorated and he was sent into the ICU, he urged the medical staff to send him back to the general ward. He said, "I do nuclear tests. I am not afraid of hard work, and I am not afraid of death. All I need

130   *Needs, Values, and Aspirations*

now is time." Even on the morning of the day he passed away, he begged his family and doctors nine times to let him go back to work.

During our research, we were somewhat taken aback by the existence of this category, especially the fact it comprised almost 50% of the winners. In the view of many Americans, for example, a person who is highly dedicated to her career and works until her death is certainly laudable, yet the behavior is too common to be considered worthy of national hero status. In addition, dedication to one's work is a personal choice and does not seem worthy of being called inspirational. We expressed our puzzlement to our focus groups, and they said that dedication to work is included and featured so prominently because a lack of dedication is so prevalent. One informant commented, "Dedication to work is a good characteristic, but it has nothing to do with inspiring China." So a general lack of dedication to work in current Chinese society makes it necessary to draw attention to those who have it and build them up as the most important role models. Although being dedicated to work is not something Chinese people would typically find inspiring, it is a societal aspiration.

Type 2: Help Those in Need

Comprising 10 out of 30 cases, those who help others in need is the second-most prevalent category. Based on the descriptions of winners in this category, the actions and sacrifices made by each individual vary widely. Among the Most Inspiring Chinese were a 12-year-old girl who donated an organ after she died, a person who has donated blood continuously for the last 20 years, and a foot masseuse who had funded the educations of 37 poor students in her hometown on her meager salary since 2006. We describe one winner in this category that is more in line with what Americans would consider inspirational.

Gao Shuzhen (2012 winner) is an ordinary 56-year-old rural woman whose son suffers from rheumatoid arthritis. He was rendered disabled at a young age and therefore could not attend school. After hearing of other cases where kids could not go to school due to disabilities, she transformed her home into a small school and educated hundreds of disabled children free of charge for 14 years, providing food, education, and even accommodations. The food for the children came from her family's 20-acre rice paddy, and supplemental items were bought with a meager income earned from selling items at a market almost 60 miles away. Interestingly, while some of our informants were inspired and moved by this woman, they wondered why the local government did not do anything to help the disabled kids.

Type 3: Behave Like Good Samaritans

A total of three winners were in this category. Upon closer examination, however, it seems the criteria over the years have become less stringent for some reason. The 2010 winner was a 27-year-old man who sacrificed his own life while working with his father-in-law to save five children from a fire. The 2011 winner was a 28-year-old teacher who, in order to save the lives of students, was crushed by a van and had both legs amputated. The 2012 winner was a young woman who, after seeing a 2-year-old girl about to fall from her tenth-floor apartment, rushed over and caught her, suffering a broken arm that would take 6 months to heal in the process. By comparison, if these events had occurred in the United States, the 2010 winner likely would have been hailed as a national hero, but the 2012 winner likely would have received praise only in a local newspaper. From an observer's perspective, it is a bit perplexing as to why the 2012 winner was honored, as there were people who made bigger sacrifices that year (e.g., those who died trying to save others in danger of drowning). Regardless, the fact that these people were chosen clearly reflects a desire in current Chinese society for more Good Samaritan-like behavior.

Type 4: Devoted to Parents

Judging by recent legislation that criminalizes any children who do not visit their parents regularly (discussed in Chapter 19), the Chinese must believe that not enough people are fulfilling their duties as children. So it is no surprise that two of the Most Inspiring Chinese were devoted children who take great effort to look after their mothers. One of the winners was a college student who has taken care of her disabled mother since she was 8 years old after her father abandoned the family. Again, it would be highly unlikely that such an individual would be honored in the United States because relationships between parents and children are considered to be private matters.

Type 5: Maintain a Positive Attitude

Only one winner belonged to this category over the three-year period, even though the selection process actively sought examples of people who maintained a positive attitude. Liu Wei (2011 winner) lost both of his arms at age 10 due to an electric shock, which killed his dream of becoming a soccer player. When he was 12, he joined a swim team for the disabled in Beijing; after two years of training, he won two gold medals and one silver medal at the National Swimming Championship for the Disabled. Unfortunately, his immune system deteriorated quickly due to the exhausting physical training. At his doctor's recommendation, he quit swimming and turned his focus to music, a field in which he succeeded in later life. "There are only two ways to go through my life: die quickly, or live brilliantly." He won the "China's Got Talent" competition in 2010 by playing *Marriage d'Amour* with his toes on the piano. Based on discussions with informants on various occasions, almost everyone is impressed with what he has done and many admire his attitude towards life.

Road Ahead

To obtain firsthand information about Chinese role models, we asked members of several focus groups, including senior executives, partners in law firms, and business owners to evaluate our five categories based on the Most Inspiring Chinese. They did not find dedication to work and devotion to parents particularly

132 *Needs, Values, and Aspirations*

inspirational, although they all agreed that China currently needs more people to exhibit those behaviors. An informant who owns a chain of healthy product stores remarked that his employees must be trained on the importance of dedication to work and treating customers with genuine politeness and warmth. Another remarked that this is especially the case in government-owned companies; one of his friends works for the environmental protection agency, and his daily routine involves killing time with newspapers and tea. However, almost all agreed that China needs more role models who have positive attitudes towards life, help those in need, and behave like Good Samaritans. These three seem to be the consensus aspirations of the Chinese.

Note

1 Based on the CNTV (China Network Television) program *The Most Inspiring Chinese*, retrieved January 2014 from http://www.cntv.cn/

22 The Generations

In China, people characterize themselves and discuss generational differences based on the decade in which they were born. The five most important generations in Chinese society currently are: post-50 (i.e., born between 1950 and 1959), post-60, post-70, post-80, and post-90. In this chapter, we describe these generations briefly, and contrast their needs, values, and aspirations. We then discuss the post-80 generation in detail, as it includes people who are in their early twenties to early thirties, a critical stage of life. In addition, it is the first generation to have been born after the one-child policy was implemented in China. We firmly believe that one must understand each generation, and the relationships between them, to understand China. We expand on this in the Road Ahead section.

The Five Generations of Chinese

In this section, we briefly describe four of the five key generations in China: post-50, post-60, post-70, and post-90. We follow this with an entire section devoted to the post-80 generation.

The post-50 generation is the most powerful generation in China now. The most senior positions at all levels of government are occupied by members of this generation, including President Xi Jinping and other top leaders. This generation also has produced the first generation of Chinese to have acquired substantial wealth since 1949 (the establishment of the PRC). Several characteristics unite this generation. First, they share much in common with those who grew up during the Great Depression in the United States. The post-50 generation grew up during the Three Years of Great Chinese Famine (1959–1961) when food was scarce everywhere and many people starved to death (especially in rural areas). In addition, they were deprived of the opportunity to obtain an education, and many were sent far away from home to work on farms during the Cultural Revolution in the 1960s. These childhood experiences have left a lifelong impression on them and largely dictate how they live their lives today. In addition, they were the first generation to return to universities after they were reinstated in 1978. (The entire university system essentially had been abolished in the preceding decades.) Being the first generation equipped with modern education at the highest levels, they entered a society that welcomed them with limitless opportunities, and many of them advanced quickly in their careers.

134 *Needs, Values, and Aspirations*

At home, the post-50 generation was the first child-bearing generation to be subject to the one-child policy in China. Over-compensating for their difficult childhoods, many used their newfound material wealth to provide as much as they possibly could for their children (the post-80 generation). Many continue to link their aspirations and satisfaction to their children's (or even grandchildren's) achievements. Although members of the post-50 generation want to provide unconditional support for their adult children, they are often frustrated by the fact that the post-80 generation holds a value system that differs substantially from their own. They also feel responsible for sharing their children's burdens, whether related to buying an apartment or finding the right spouse.

The post-60 generation, in general, did not experience the same hardships as the post-50 generation, and they grew up in a much more normal environment. Education has always been a primary focus for this generation. The goal during their formative years was to do better on tests in order to get into the best middle school, high school, and university. Although material wealth was not common, this generation grew up in an era of hope, as China was gradually opening up to the outside world and everything seemed possible. This was also the first generation to be exposed to Western value systems during their college years. The first business schools were established at elite Chinese universities while members of the post-60 generation were in college. Generally idealistic, they eagerly supported seismic change in China in pursuit of wealth. Many of the best college graduates across all disciplines decided to pursue graduate degrees outside China, with most going to the United States. The majority did not return.

The post-70 generation could probably be defined as the last generation to have experienced what China used to be, an egalitarian society. When they were growing up, the phrase "ten thousand yuan family" was an encouraging term used by the government and media to promote successful entrepreneurship among peasants, the lowest societal tier at the time, in order to facilitate social acceptance of private business. This was an era when money was not a universal aspiration, and the rich were not necessarily envied. After graduating from universities, the post-70 generation joined the work force before property prices began their astronomic ascent in 2003. They were able to get married and afford houses and cars shortly after graduation. Their transformation from university students to contributing members of society coincided with the rapid development of the 1990s.

The post-90 generation is often characterized as the "alternative" or non-mainstream generation. As a subculture, post-90s tend to be rebellious, but in a subtle way. We will not go as far as to compare this generation to young Americans in the 1960s during the Vietnam War, but they share the same lack of hope and anti-establishment mentality. We list a few characteristics here, but note this only represents some post-90s; not every post-90 can be identified by each characteristic.

First, post-90s often use the so-called Martian language online and on mobile platforms. Martian language emerged during the internet era and is based on homophones (words that sound similar), special symbols, and translations for words in other languages (English, Japanese, and Korean being the most commonly incorporated), among others. A Chinese person who is not well-versed in Martian language will often be at a loss when such expressions are used. Second, they focus more on themselves and care very little about other people's opinions. Third, they like to post "selfies" (self-portraits) on various social networks, normally taken from a slightly high angle (e.g., 45°). Fourth, although some of them do not have much hope for society, they still seek to be accepted. Having stated these characteristics, one must keep in mind that this is a young generation; some of these characteristics could describe teenagers and young adults from any culture. As a generation, they are likely to evolve and acquire new defining characteristics in the future.

The Post-80 Generation

The post-80 generation is the watershed generation of China and will define its near future. This is the first generation to have entered a society in which they cannot possibly live a respectful and independent life on their own salaries. If we had to use just one word to describe post-80 generation, it would be anxiety—over changing roles, unfamiliar environments, and an uncertain future.

As the first generation of only children (the one-child policy came into effect in 1980), they grew up as China began to open up to the world, so they were materially better off than their parents were as children. However, owing to a peak in birth rate during the 1980s, intense competition accompanied them from an early age.

When the first post-80s began to enter college in 1999, the Ministry of Education increased university enrollments, leading to a continuous increase of college students. At first glance, the post-80 generation seemed to have more educational opportunities and in turn, more life choices. But more people going to college meant fiercer competition, which inevitably led to the depreciation of bachelor's degrees. Students had to fight their way into a highly competitive job market after graduation, especially once the government eliminated the policy of job-assignment for university graduates. This current environment is quite different from the one encountered by post-60 college students, who had limitless opportunities because of their educational backgrounds.

Fresh graduates experience great employment pressure. In 2013, a total of 6.99 million students graduated across the country, while in 2003 there were only 1.88 million fresh graduates. For example, in 2013, there were nearly 300,000 college graduates job-hunting in Guangzhou, a 20% increase over the previous year. Among all age groups, the new labor force (aged between 16 and 25) had the highest unemployment rate (7.03%).[1]

In addition to employment, there is immense pressure related to housing, marriage, and the wealth gap. In 1997, the Chinese government ceased engaging in welfare-oriented public housing distribution practices. Still in college, members of the post-80 generation missed their chance to buy real estate before prices skyrocketed, as the post-70s did. In China, marriage is usually a requirement for housing loans to be approved; however, a residence is a traditional betrothal gift. Driven by this high demand, housing prices continue to climb, especially in first and second tier cities. For example, real estate prices in Shanghai have approximately

136 *Needs, Values, and Aspirations*

quintupled over the last 10 years. Many young people, therefore, choose to marry those who are wealthy or have residences instead of the people they love.

To date, most members of the post-80 generation have entered society, and housing has become their biggest problem. According to a survey, 48% of post-80s have their own residences, yet most of them were born before 1984. Thus, many in this generation are still fretting over buying an apartment. When asked, "How much of your monthly salary do you use to pay for housing," 30% of those surveyed said 30–50% and 8% said more than 50%.[2] A netizen who was born in 1982 in Hunan province complained online that he and his wife paid the down payment for a small 82 m^2 apartment last year when they got married. Although they receive support from their parents, they are practically slaves to it, with a loan of RMB 320,000 over 30 years on a meager monthly income of RMB 5,000. It is therefore unsurprising that many choose to trade youth for wealth (as discussed in Chapter 17).

A popular joke that has circulated widely online summarizes the numerous pressures facing the post-80 generation: "As a member of the post-80 generation, he did not enjoy free compulsory education or job arrangement as a university graduate but had to compete with a large number of peers in order to attain a master or a Ph.D. degree. By the time he graduated, he was already deep in debt. After a decade of endless drudgery, he finally saved some money but was still unable to afford a residence in the face of soaring housing prices. Thus, he invested all of his savings into the stock market instead and unfortunately had very little left the very next year. Suffering this, he got depressed and went to see a doctor for treatment. However, he did not get better. The hospital threw him out, for the medical insurance did not cover 'minor' illnesses like depression. A friend lent him a bag of Sanlu milk powder,[3] which upon drinking, he departed this life."[4]

It is no wonder that the post-80 generation is generally depressed. The harsh reality is that material burdens are gradually chipping away at their independence because they must constantly rely upon, obey, and please their parents in order to receive financial support. They have lost the courage to strive for dreams, romance, or even freedom. Instead, their lives have become an endless struggle for money.

Road Ahead

These five generations define current Chinese society. While sharing certain needs, values, and aspirations, each generation has unique core characteristics that serve as differentiators. We think these generational traits will define society for the foreseeable future. One must understand each generation, and the relationships between them, to understand China. But please keep in mind that each generation is evolving, and their perceptions and life styles will definitely change over time.

Notes

1 Yang Hui and Liang Jiayu (2013, August 3), "Young people aged 16–25 are facing an unemployment rate of over 7%," *Yangcheng Evening News*, retrieved January 2014 from http://www.ycwb.com/ePaper/ycwb/html/2013-08/03/content_219700.htm?div=-1

2 Zhang Ting, Ye Meiying, Chen Yin, and Zhang Yanli (2012, May 24), "Housing loans are wearing away the happiness of the generation 80s," *Foshan Daily*, retrieved January 2014 from http://www.fsonline.com.cn/articles_8212.html
3 Sanlu milk powder became known for containing melamine, a chemical material, which caused irreparable harm to consumers.
4 Chen Yanwei (2010, February 5), "Faced with a multitude of pressures, the Generation 80s can no longer afford to be romantic," *Southern People Weekly Magazine*, retrieved January 2014 from http://news.sina.com.cn/c/sd/2010-02-05/092419635165.shtml

23 The Nouveau Riche

Since wealth accumulation has become the dominant life objective in China, it should come as no surprise that the wealthy have become trendsetters, and a large proportion of society now compares themselves to this reference group. To understand the aspirations of many Chinese people, look no further than the lifestyles of those who are currently wealthy.

In this chapter, we first define levels of wealth in China. We follow with a brief description of the current desires of the wealthy and how each of these desires is being mimicked by other social strata in China. We predict in the Road Ahead section that both the desires of the wealthy and their status as the reference group for most of society will change.

Defining the Nouveau Riche

In China, those who are considered to be wealthy can be divided into four classes based on net worth: RMB 10 billion, RMB 1 billion, RMB 100 million, and RMB 10 million. According to *The GroupM Knowledge–Hurun Wealth Report 2013*,[1] the number of wealthy people with assets of more than RMB 100 million has reached 64,500. While achieving a net worth of RMB 100 million is impressive, those who amass more than a billion are truly revered. Some informants told us that many with RMB 100 million try to surpass the RMB 1 billion threshold but fail. Those who succeed feel that they have achieved true greatness.

The lowest tier of the wealthy includes those who are worth between RMB 10 million and RMB 100 million. According to *The GroupM Knowledge–Hurun Wealth Report 2013*, the number of people on the Chinese mainland with assets totaling more than RMB 10 million has hit 1.05 million; with an average age of 38, more than half are between the ages of 31 and 45, and 70% are male. Unlike people with over RMB 100 million, who typically are entrepreneurs, some who hold regular jobs have joined the RMB 10 million group. Most of them have become wealthy by investing in real estate. In Shanghai, for example, apartments that sold in 2004 for RMB 9,000 per square meter are now worth RMB 50,000 per square meter. So someone who bought a RMB 2 million apartment back in 2004 with a 20% down payment (RMB 400,000) now owns an apartment worth RMB 10 million. In Shanghai alone, we know many middle class residents who entered the real estate market 10 to 15 years ago and bought multiple properties that now are all worth more than RMB 10 million. A colleague of ours who is a professor at a business

140   *Needs, Values, and Aspirations*

school in Shanghai, for example, told us that he sold his apartment for RMB 14 million in 2012.

According to a census report of the super-rich all over the world issued by Wealth-X (the average net assets of people included in the report were more than a billion dollars), China has 157 super-rich people: 89% are self-made; 6% became wealthy through a combination of inheritance and their own efforts; and just 5% inherited all of their wealth. The self-made rate of 89% is much higher than the worldwide average of 60%.[2]

Most of the Chinese in these four classes have acquired their wealth during the last 20 to 30 years. In all of human history, few nations (if any) have had a wealthy class based almost entirely on "new money." Unlike other cultures, the Chinese nouveau riche have no "old money" role models after whom they can pattern their lifestyle. As a result, their desires and aspirations are constantly evolving, and the rest of China tends to follow suit.

Preferences and Behaviors of the Nouveau Riche

It would be wrong to base our discussion of wealthy lifestyles in China purely on stereotypes. Individual differences always exist, and certainly our descriptions below will not apply to every wealthy person in China. As a matter of fact, one of our informants (who is worth between RMB 100 million and RMB 1 billion) remarked to us that he knew people in the RMB 10 billion group who dress like factory workers, and when they talk to you, they are so humble and nice that one could easily mistake them for people who want to borrow money.

Having said that, the nouveau riche do share some common characteristics. Traditionally, the affluent in China engage in conspicuous consumption to an extreme in order to show off their wealth and social status. Expensive watches, jewelry, and limousines are all highly desired goods. Flaunting their wealth is one of their most distinct behaviors. This, to some extent, has influenced the entire society to pursue such luxury products, even if they cannot afford them.

However, as the wealthy class has matured, so have their tastes and consumption habits. The *GroupM Knowledge–Hurun Wealth Report 2013* revealed some interesting statistics about Chinese multimillionaires: 43% possess a Master's degree or higher, or an EMBA; they own three limousines and four luxury watches, on average; they go abroad an average of 2.8 times per year, and travel for business 7.5 days per month; they take an average of 20 vacation days per year; for leisure, they enjoy travel, reading, drinking tea, and playing sports such as swimming and golf; more than 70% have physical examinations regularly, and about 10% have their own private doctors; half are smokers, and 70% drink (half of whom prefer wine made from grapes); 66% collect art, especially watches, ancient calligraphy, and paintings; they access information primarily on the internet; they believe that paying taxes is the best way to engage in social responsibility; they have become more sensitive to environmental issues; and 33% choose to send their children to study abroad during their high school years.

Similarly, people on social media have summarized 10 current trends among the nouveau riche: "1. The accessories they wear have changed from gold chains to Buddha beads; 2. What they pursue has changed from fashion to antiques; 3. What they drink has changed from Chinese white spirits to red wine; 4. What they wear has changed from suits and ties to linen clothes and shoes; 5. What they play has changed from Mahjong to golf; 6. Their transportation tool has changed from Mercedes or BMW to bicycles; 7. Their traveling style has changed from global tours to exploring natural resorts with friends; 8. Their entertainment focus has changed from nightclubs to movies and traditional culture museums; 9. Their social circles have changed from friends in debauchery to EMBA classmates; 10. They have changed from coarse philistines into Buddhism-pursuers."

As one can see from the trends described above, the wealthy are becoming more low-key, healthy, traditional, and cerebral. Unique to China, we have also seen many of the nouveau riche decide to go back to school to get an EMBA, often to fulfill their childhood dreams of attending particular universities. Unlike EMBA classes in the United States and Europe, in China there are typically a few students in each EMBA class whose net worths are above the RMB 100 million mark.

Another hobby that has been adopted by the uber-wealthy is running. Many of our nouveau riche informants got up at 6 am each day to go out and run a few kilometers. Several proudly declared that one of their main objectives in the near future was to finish a half-marathon, and eventually, a marathon.

All of these preferences have now become trends in the rest of society, especially among members of the middle class, which is projected to grow from 230 million people in 2013 to 630 million people in 2033.

Road Ahead

Given the evolving nature of the nouveau riche and the social environment, we believe their desires will continue to change as well. However, it is safe to say the trend towards less conspicuous consumption and healthier lifestyles will continue. More relevant to an observer, we believe in the near future the nouveau riche may no longer be the reference group for the majority of the society. Once society starts to encourage and celebrate achievements other than the accumulation of wealth, reference groups will also change, although the wealthy will always be a reference group for some Chinese.

Notes

1 GroupM Knowledge and Hurun (2013, August 14), "The GroupM Knowledge—Hurun wealth report 2013," retrieved January 2014 from http://img.hurun.net/hmec/2013-08-14/201308141028423282.pdf

2 Wealth-X and UBS (2013), "Wealth-X–UBS billionaire census 2013," retrieved January 2014 from http://www.billionairecensus.com

24 Environmentalism

In the 1960s and 1970s, American citizens launched a large-scale environmental protection movement in response to anxiety over industrial development and fear of environmental pollution. Today, a similar environmental movement is emerging in China. In this chapter, we discuss the state of the environmental movement in China and some general characteristics of citizen environmentalists. We then present cases that exemplify three central concerns of the movement: nuclear technology, chemicals, and metals. In the Road Ahead section, we discuss the future of environmental protection in China.

State of the Environment

The current environmental movement in China is motivated by three factors. The first and most important factor is the severity of pollution. Today, China is facing all kinds of ecological and environmental problems resulting from a growing population, rapid urbanization, and industrialization. Since 1996, the number of environmental incidents has increased by an average of 29% per year, with severe environmental incidents occurring with high frequency. Since 2005, the Ministry of Environmental Protection has formally responded to 927 incidents, including 72 severe cases. The number of severe cases increased 120% in 2011 compared to the same period in 2010, especially incidents involving heavy metals and harmful chemicals.[1]

Figure 24.1 Fog in Shanghai in 2013.

Figure 24.2 Shanghai.

Environmental problems are reaching a crisis point in China. For instance, in 2010, some media outlets disclosed that six mounds of chromium residue in Henan province weighing up to 500,000 tons had encroached on fields and rivers after being washed away by rains over the past 10 years, negatively impacting the lives of several generations. On January 15, 2012, a water test of Longjiang River in Guangxi found that the amount of cadmium in its water had exceeded safe levels by 80 times, gravely threatening the safety of drinking water for residents who live along the river in the city and further downstream. Beijing has now assumed London's nickname of "Fog City" because of severe air pollution. Even southern coastal areas such as Shanghai experienced severe smog in November 2013. Chinese citizens are becoming increasingly aware of the threat pollution poses to enjoying a high quality of life, and they are not willing to simply sit back accepting it.

If the Chinese people are going to create real environmental change, they feel they must take things into their own hands. They do not trust companies to behave in a responsible manner because they believe companies are more interested in pursuing short-term economic profits. In many cases, this suspicion is justified. Firms have generated pollution or even released toxic by-products into the environment with a complete disregard for the people living around the factories. Neither do the Chinese feel that they can trust their local governments on such issues. They believe local governments sometimes compromise on environmental issues in pursuit of increased GDP, and government officials may even accept bribes so that some companies can operate without conforming to environmental standards. Such concerns are not unfounded. One informant told us about a company that produces chemicals that are quite harmful if absorbed into the human body yet has signage posted outside the factory indicating that it is a biotechnology company, all with tacit approval from the local government.

Artificial Factors Contributing to Environmental Concerns

In addition to objective, science-based concerns about the environment, two other artificial factors have contributed to current environmental concerns that often make smaller incidents bigger and safe projects dangerous. The first factor is information asymmetry. While substantially improved over the past decade, local governments still often do not release information about potentially controversial projects to the public until they are already approved and under construction. Residents of a city are not part of the decision-making process in such municipal projects. If any accidents occur, often the mindset of the local government is to play down or even hide the negative impact. As a result, residents do not take what their local governments tell them at face value. They always feel there is something more sinister that has not been disclosed.

The second factor is rumor. Due to the general lack of trust in official communication channels, many Chinese people turn to Weibo (a popular microblogging website) or text messages for information. This opens the door for the spread of exaggerated claims by people who are against a particular project. The longer communication channels are blocked, the more mistrust grows among authorities, companies, and citizens, and the more destructive and powerful rumors become.

Citizens' Environmental Movement

As in early stages of environmental movements elsewhere in the world, the current environmental movement in China is primarily comprised of "not in my backyard" environmentalists. They are concerned about environmental dangers that threaten them personally, in their local neighborhoods. But if the source of danger is relocated elsewhere, then they will be pacified and happy because it becomes someone else's problem. At the national level, of course, such a movement does not solve the root problem.

Because organized demonstrations about environmental issues are not tolerated by the government, the Chinese people have resorted to a different tactic that they call "take a stroll." A text message will be sent around inviting people to take a stroll at a certain hour of a certain day, at a particular place, possibly wearing something that indicates their intention (e.g., a mask, a band, a particular color of clothing). The whole thing appears unorganized but serves the same purpose as an organized protest. Demonstrators are also typically very careful to avoid making any political statements, which would inhibit any possible sympathies from higher ranking government officials. If someone makes a political statement, other people in the demonstration will often tell that person to stop, thereby employing a strategy of self-censoring for self-interest.

In some cases, these "strolls" have gotten out of control; people have gotten into confrontations with police and sometimes even taken over government buildings,

146　Needs, Values, and Aspirations

smashed property, and burned government and police vehicles. In 2012, "strollers" in a city near Shanghai broke into the city government building and roughed up the mayor because they did not want a Japanese paper company to open a factory there. (They believed the wastewater would substantially harm their health.)

To some extent, many citizens are emboldened by how local governments typically react to such resistance. Under the doctrine of maintaining a harmonious society (discussed in detail in Chapter 9), governments are motivated to make bigger issues smaller and small issues disappear as long as an issue is not politically related and does not threaten the existence of government. So as long as a demonstration is about a particular environmental issue, local governments are more willing to strike a quick compromise or even cave in to citizens' demands in order make the resistance disappear than to engage in a serious and detailed discussion based on scientific evidence. Since "the squeaky wheel gets the grease," residents of a city learn that if they make enough noise and create enough negative publicity for the local government, a project will be suspended, canceled, or moved to another area. This, on one hand, is positive in that government officials listen to their constituents, but on the other hand, can be negative, as decisions often are not made on rational grounds.

Case 1: Resisting Nuclear Fuel Production, Jiangmen, Guangdong Province, 2013

On July 4, 2013, an announcement titled "Risk Assessment on Social Stability of China National Nuclear Corporation (CNNC)'s Longwan Industrial Area Project" was published simultaneously on the *Jiangmen Daily* and Jiangmen City Government websites. The aim of the project, with a total investment of 9 billion dollars, was to create a one-stop nuclear fuel (uranium) processing chain and form world-class nuclear fuel processing industrial groups before the year 2020.

It quickly generated huge public uproar. Opposition originated on a few public forums and Weibo, primarily in the form of concerns over safety and hidden dangers. On July 5, the "nuclear anxiety" of the previous day gradually escalated to "nuclear crisis." On July 12, thousands of Jiangmen citizens gathered at the gate of local authorities to appeal the decision, waving signs and banners and chanting slogans. To alleviate citizens' concerns, Jiangmen authorities called in several members of the provincial and municipal media and provided an overview of the project, which they followed with public information sessions on nuclear fuel. The municipal government promised its residents: "The project will not be approved and started until a consensus is reached among all residents." On July 13, the government decided to cancel the CNNC's Longwan Industrial Area Project.[2,3]

Case 2: Resisting Chemical Production (PX), Kunming, Yunnan Province, 2013

Paraxylene (PX) is a chemical used to manufacture plastic bottles and polyester clothing. It is dangerous if inhaled or absorbed through the skin, causing damage to internal organs and the nervous system. Despite the inherent dangers, large factories built to produce PX can create substantial tax income for a local government; as a result, many cities in China seek to build PX factories. Many residents, however, are strongly against establishing such factories in their own backyards. To illustrate, we discuss the 2013 incident in Kunming, Yunnan province in detail.

A refinery project by China National Petroleum Corporation (CNPC) in Kunming was approved by the government in January 2013 and construction was planned for an area 45 miles away from downtown. On May 4, 2013, about 3,000 indignant Kunming citizens walked the streets in protest. Their actions were coordinated through text messages and WeChat, online platforms such as Weibo, and the QQ instant messaging service. In response to the protests, on May 10 the Kunming local government held a news conference that lasted a whopping 2 hours and 40 minutes, during which Mayor Li Wenrong promised to employ a democratic decision-making process and fully respect citizens' wishes. He said, "This refinery project will be stopped if the majority opposes it."[4]

Similar demonstrations had taken place previously in Ningbo, Zhejiang province in 2012 and in Dalian, Liaoning province in 2011, when large-scale PX projects were proposed. In all three incidents, the respective local governments accepted the demands of their residents and either stopped or moved the PX project to a different city.

Case 3: Resisting Metal (Alloy) Production, Shifang, Sichuan Province, 2012

On the evening of July 1, 2012, hundreds of students and citizens gathered separately at the gate of the Shifang Municipal Council and in Hongda Square to protest against the Hongda Mo-Cu (Molybdenum-Copper) Alloy Deep Processing and Comprehensive Utilization Project. Citizens felt the government had kept them in the dark about the project, as few citizens knew about it until construction had already begun. This lack of dialogue between authorities and citizens fostered a sense of mistrust among the general public. As suspicion and fear spread, so did rumors, such as, "The Mo-Cu Alloy factory to be built in Yujiang Village, Shifang will cause severe pollution within 60 kilometers, including in the city of Chengdu. It is far worse than the Fukushima nuclear accident. Authorities bribed residents near the Mo-Cu factory by offering them 20,000 yuan each. Within five years, Shifang will have the highest cancer rate of any county in the entire nation."

On the morning of July 2, some people forced their way into the city government building and hurled flowerpots, water bottles, and sundries at policemen and employees on duty, which resulted in dozers of injuries, 10 damaged government cars, and a broken main gate. To calm the situation, Mayor Xu Guangyong & Deputy Mayor Zhang Daobin made a public promise that the construction would be stopped immediately and would not resume unless approval was received from the majority of residents. In the end, the Shifang Municipal Government decided to stop the project permanently.[5, 6]

Road Ahead

As anger about living in a polluted environment spreads and the government begins to realize the threat a polluted environment poses to the economy and even

148   *Needs, Values, and Aspirations*

societal stability, China will continue down the path towards balancing economic development with environmental protection. However, we believe environmental efforts will be primarily local in scale and short in duration. Both citizens and government officials are now focused on how to remove pollution from their cities and how to ensure a healthy environment in the short term. We hope it will not take too long for people to realize it is important to develop long term solutions at the national level to ensure that the needs of future generations can be met. In the absence of such planning, environmental remediation will shift into firefighting mode, and solutions will not serve the long term interests of the nation.

Notes

1 Data on environmental incidents come from the report published in *The Beijing News* on October 27, 2012, retrieved October 2013 from http://epaper.bjnews.com.cn/html/2012-10/27/content_383829.htm?div=0

2 Liu Jin & Xu Baibo (2013, July 13), "Details of Jiangmen 'nuclear dispute,'" *Southern Daily*, retrieved January 2014 from http://news.southcn.com/d/2013-07/12/content_73340969.htm

3 Jiang Xun (2013, July 13), "Jiangmen Municipal Government: Prolonged publicity of nuclear fuel project intended for deeper and wider public opinions," *Jiangmen Daily*, retrieved January 2014 from http://dzb.jmrb.com:8080/jmrb/html/2013-07/13/content_330662.htm

4 LegalDaily.com (2013, May 22), "Research on public opinion on PX project in Kunming," *Legal Daily*, retrieved January 2014 from http://www.legaldaily.com.cn/The_analysis_of_public_opinion/content/2013-05/22/content_4479996.htm?node=42597

5 Cui Wenguan & Wang Lining (2012, July 7), "Incident of Shifang: Nightmares of Mo-Cu alloy," *China Management Newspaper*, retrieved January 2014 from http://www.cb.com.cn/deep/2012_0707/393581.html

6 Lu Zheng & Su Nan (2012, July 2), "Public notice of Sichuan Shifang Hongda Mo-Cu Alloy Project: No construction without major public understanding," *People's Daily*, retrieved January 2014 from http://society.people.com.cn/n/2012/0702/c1008-18427921.html

Part V
World View

25   Attitudes towards Foreign Nations

In *The Life of Reason*, Spanish American philosopher George Santayana famously wrote, "Those who cannot remember the past are condemned to repeat it." In order to understand the attitudes of the Chinese people towards other nations and China's foreign policy, one must take this well-known quote to heart. The past that the Chinese do not want to repeat is known as the Century of Humiliation, from 1839 (the start of the First Opium War) to 1945 (the end of World War II). China's guiding principle in foreign relationships, quite simply, is to avoid repeating that history at all costs and, if possible, to rectify that humiliation. On this point, all Chinese citizens are united.

In this chapter, we first briefly review the Century of Humiliation and discuss why it plays such an important role in China's foreign policy and how it has affected the attitudes of ordinary Chinese citizens. In this context, we discuss China's complex relationships with the world's largest (the United States) and third-largest (Japan) economies. We conclude in the Road Ahead section by suggesting possible ways for the Chinese and world community to truly put the Century of Humiliation behind them and develop a cooperative relationship based on trust.

The Century of Humiliation in the Long History of China

The events that occurred during the Century of Humiliation are taught and discussed in all schools in China, and Chinese children grow up with a sense of responsibility to never allow such events to happen again. These beliefs comprise the foundation of Chinese nationalism. It is called the Century of Humiliation because China fought many wars against foreign powers during this period and lost them all; in addition, China was forced to sign many unequal treaties.

The Century of Humiliation began in 1839 during the First Opium War (1839–1842) between China and the British Empire. The Treaty of Nanjing, which was signed in 1842, was the first of several unequal treaties against the Chinese. The Treaty of Nanjing includes the cession of islands of Hong Kong, four additional treaty ports, a large amount of reparations, etc. In 1844, the Treaty of Whampoa (1844) was signed between China and France and gave France similar rights as the British. In 1858, the Treaty of Aigun was signed between China and Russia in which China lost a large area of land in the north. The Second Opium War (1856–1860) was between China and the combined force of Britain and France

152   *World View*

over demands similar to those underlying the First Opium War. While China suffered at the hands of European powers during the first half of the Century of Humiliation, Japan was the primary enemy during the second half. The First Sino-Japanese War (1894–1895) was fought primarily over control of Korea. (This is also known as the War of Jiawu in China.) In 1915, China was forced by Japan to sign The Twenty-One Demands that essentially aimed to turn China into a puppet state. Finally, the Second Sino-Japanese War (1937–1945) was fought as Japan tried to dominate China and steal its vast raw material reserves and other economic resources. After Japan attacked Pearl Harbor, the Second Sino-Japanese War became part of the Pacific Front during World War II.

Over thousands of years, China has seen many wars, internal and external. As a matter of fact, China was conquered by foreigners twice in history: the Mongols established the Yuan Dynasty (1271–1368) and the Manchu established the Qing Dynasty (1644–1912). But these are differentiated from the Century of Humiliation in the minds of the Chinese people for three reasons. First, those are distant memories, and the Century of Humiliation is recent. Second, both dynasties eventually adopted the Chinese language and culture, which was a proud validation of China's cultural superiority. In addition, the descendants of the Mongols & Manchu have been assimilated into Chinese society through marriage. By contrast, during the Century of Humiliation, China was defeated by foreign forces that were stronger militarily and at least as sophisticated culturally. Third, both dynasties were eventually brought down by the Han majority (the Ming Dynasty after the Yuan, and the Republic of China after the Qing). Further, China did not bring an end to the Century of Humiliation under its own power. As such, some "old debts" have not been paid in the eyes of some Chinese. In other words, the Chinese have not yet achieved mental closure on this unfortunate chapter in Chinese history.

In our view, outcomes of the Century of Humiliation motivate three dominant attitudes toward foreign powers: (a) a yearning for justice to create a sense of closure on this period of history, (b) fierce independence and suspicions toward foreign intervention of any kind, and (c) a paramount duty to prevent similar humiliation from ever happening again. With this knowledge of historical context, it is easier to understand why many Chinese people say things like, "We need to teach Japan a lesson" and "The United States should leave us alone."

Using this historical background as a starting point, we describe how the Chinese see the United States and Japan to help readers better understand their attitudes towards foreign nations. We selected these two countries for several reasons. First, they are the world's largest and third-largest economies, and China is the second-largest (aspiring to be the largest). Second, both countries are possible military foes: the United States, because it is the world's dominant military superpower and has disputes with China on the Taiwan issue; and Japan because of disputed claims to islands and surrounding water, as well as memories from the second half of the Century of Humiliation. Despite these tensions, both countries are considered to be role models, in different ways, by many Chinese. We cannot, of course, possibly cover even a fraction of the characteristics of the bilateral

Attitudes towards Foreign Nations 153

relationships between these countries. Instead, we will focus on the attitudes of the Chinese people towards the United States and Japan.

Attitudes towards the United States

In order to understand the Sino-American relationship, one must learn about the Flying Tigers. The "Flying Tigers" was the Chinese nickname for the American Volunteer Group (AVG) who helped the Chinese during the Sino-Japanese War beginning in July 1941. They are well-known in almost every Chinese household. In difficult times during the war, the Flying Tigers helped the vulnerable Chinese fight back against the Japanese and regained control of the air space. Their existence boosted the morale of the Chinese and ensured the final victory of the war. The nickname "Flying Tigers" was bestowed by many newspapers at that time as high praise for what they had done. It also marked the very first time since the start of the Century of Humiliation that a foreign nation (even if in this case, volunteers) came to help. One does not easily forget the first person who comes to your side after being bullied by other people for a long time. This is the chip that the United States can forever cash in to obtain goodwill from China.

However, China's attitude towards the United States, both its citizens and its government, is much more complex these days. According to the *Pew Research Global Attitudes Project (2013)*[1] just 40% of respondents had favorable views towards the United States, down from 58% in 2010, representing a decline over three consecutive years. Affection towards Americans dropped from 61% in 2010 to 39%. In the meantime, in a report on Chinese affections towards the United States based on the *BBC Country Ratings Poll*, just 20% of respondents had overall positive views, while 57% had overall negative views.[2] The negative views primarily stemmed from perceptions that the United States likes to play the role of "world's policeman;" on the state level, negativity is linked to disputes over trade, diplomatic strategies, Taiwan, human rights, and so forth.

On the positive side, according to the *Pew Research Global Attitudes Project (2013)*, in 2012, 43% of Chinese interviewees appreciated the popularization of American values and customs in China; 52% welcomed democracy; 43% were fond of American music, films, and TV shows; and 73% admired the United States' advanced science and technologies. In 2010, *China Daily* and *Horizon China* conducted a joint poll on Chinese views towards America. According to this poll, the Chinese think Americans are "independent" (20%), "creative" (13.4%), and "confident" (6.9%); "arrogant" was the main negative impression (22.7%).

According to an article in the *Dong-A Ilbo* newspaper in South Korea on July 19, 2013, a research group studied Chinese people aged 20 to 50 years in Beijing and concluded that Chinese people who watch American television shows are more well-educated and have higher salaries than those who watch South Korean television shows.[3] Chinese youth enjoy watching all types of American television shows, ranging from sitcoms such as *Friends* and *The Big Bang Theory* to dramas such as *Prison Break, House of Cards, Desperate Housewives,* and *Vampire Diaries.*

154 *World View*

These results are consistent with our own research. Two different informants (both are senior executives from different firms) told us how they see the United States and Americans. One informant said, "I do not feel Americans are as friendly as they seem to be; sometimes they are even unreasonable. During my training experience in the United States, they were very polite to me, but when it came to issues involving their core interests, they did not deliver any key information. They are very strong with regard to playing the role of standards setters in many fields. For instance, in the airline industry, 90% of technologies come from the United States as well as 90% of large aircraft accessories. The companies downstream who have no bargaining power must accept their requirements when the United States begins to raise taxes on certain accessories."

The other informant said, "For the moment, it makes no sense for China to compete with the U.S. China should be clear about its own position in the world. The first class now belongs to the United States with high technology, financial power, military power, education system, justice, etc. The second level is Europe, with Germany representing a high value-added manufacturing based economy; France, well-known luxury goods; and the U.K., financial services. Third, Japan and South Korea, with industries noted for low costs. China is the fourth layer. Finally, are the oil states. Therefore, China should get involved in globalization and then compete with the U.S. after it gains advantages over Japan and South Korea."

Attitudes towards Japan

For the Chinese, the defining event that dictates their attitudes towards Japan is the Second Sino-Japanese War. From the Century of Humiliation, this is the war that stands out for several reasons. First, it was a war that threatened the very existence of China. Until the European powers stepped in, Japan was planning to occupy and take over China. This was especially hard to swallow as the Chinese traditionally have looked down on the Japanese, derogatively calling them "the little Japanese" because of the small size of their country and relatively shorter height. Second, the war was especially savage and involved mass killing of civilians, rape, etc. Third, and most relevant today, is that the Chinese still do not feel a sense of closure about the war. When Japan surrendered to the United States at the end of World War II, China really had no say in the terms of surrender. In the eyes of the Chinese, the presence of the Yasukuni shrine in honor of convicted (and escaped) war criminals is equivalent to having Hilter's tomb in modern day Germany and the Chancellor and other politicians paying a regular visit every year. If one understands this analogy, one can then understand the strong emotions people from China (and Korea) have towards Japan, which will flare with even minor instigation.

A joint *Report on Public Opinions between China and Japan (2013)*[4] by Japan's *Genron NPO* and *China Daily* showed that approximately 90.1% of Japanese respondents (up from 84.3% the previous year) and 92.8% of Chinese respondents (up from 64.5% the previous year) had negative or relatively negative feelings towards each other, the highest ratio since 2005. What's more, as revealed by the *BBC Country Rating Poll*, just 5% of Japanese respondents reported affection towards China, while just 17% of Chinese respondents reported affection towards Japan.[5]

The main reason lies in history. Most Chinese people attach great importance to history and consider Japan's denial of history, especially of two key events, unforgivable. One is the territorial dispute over the Diaoyu Islands. The other is their description of World War II in history books. As shown in the *Report on Public Opinions between China and Japan (2013)*, 77.6% of Chinese respondents thought that the Japanese acted arbitrarily on the issue of the Diaoyu Islands and complicated the situation, while 63.8% blamed the Japanese for not sincerely apologizing for their invasion of China. On the contrary, 53.2% of Japanese respondents claimed ownership of the Senkaku Islands (referring to Diaoyu Islands in Japanese) and 48.9% considered the Chinese to be too harsh in their interpretations of certain historical events and to place too much blame. There were no obvious differences between the attitudes of the elites and those of the masses. In addition, according to the poll, the Chinese think the Japanese are "combative" (74.2%), as well as "egocentric," "untrustworthy," and "uncooperative" (all over 60%). In general, the Chinese people believe that Japan has not done enough to atone for its crimes during the Second Sino-Japanese War.

Throughout our research, we also identified a distinctly different attitude towards Japan versus the United States in terms of how forceful China should be. One informant told us, "Japan is an island country with limited resources, thus they tend to follow the strong and bully the weak. They can only be convinced when you have undisputable power to beat them." His comment was echoed by another informant who said, "The Japanese listen to power. The stronger you are, the friendlier they will be to you."

On the positive side, almost all of the Chinese people we have come across who have had the opportunity to visit Japan and/or interact with the Japanese have only good things to say. One informant told us she visited Japan for the first time in August 2013, and her view of the Japanese people changed substantially over the five days when she was there. Her description could almost be interpreted as admiration for Japan and its society. Interestingly, some of our informants who are either business owners or senior executives and have dealt with Japanese companies were especially impressed with how sincere Japanese firms can be. One said, "Japanese companies treasure trust. If everything, either good or bad, is made clear before negotiation and after careful review, they can totally trust and sign the contract." Another said, "From a business perspective, the Japanese are very serious. If they really accept you, they trust you without doubt." These comments stand in stark contrast to their views of American firms described earlier.

Road Ahead

As a world power, how China sees other nations and how it behaves towards them will be critical, both politically and economically. We see the root of many of today's problems as stemming from a general lack of closure on the Century of

156 *World View*

Humiliation, especially when Japan denies its history of aggression towards China and other Asian countries and Japanese politicians visit the Yasukuni Shrine for war criminals. It is important for the Chinese to finally feel that all the wrongs have been righted and that history will never repeat itself, literally or figuratively. Judging by the largely negative opinions towards Japan and the United States (and vice versa), maybe it is time for a dialogue that addresses the root of the problem instead of just the symptoms.

Notes

1 Pew Research (2013), *Pew Research Global Attitudes Project,* retrieved December 2013 from http://www.pewglobal.org/database/indicator/overview/
2 Data from http://www.worldpublicopinion.org, retrieved January 2014.
3 Li Zhenyin (2013, July 19), "Chinese audience: Fans of American TV dramas enjoy a higher income and education background, fans of South Korean TV dramas the opposite," *Dong-A Ilbo.*
4 ChinaDaily.com (2013, August 5), "Report on public opinions between China and Japan," *China Daily,* retrieved January 2014 from http://www.chinadaily.com.cn/hqzx/2013-08/05/content_16872036.htm
5 Data from http://www.worldpublicopinion.org, retrieved January 2014.

26 Cultural Identity

In 1927, Lu Xun, the Chinese thinker and writer whose work has influenced many generations, delivered a speech called *The Silent China* in Hong Kong that was considered a classic description of the Chinese people at that time. He said, "It is the Chinese people's disposition to always prefer reconciliation and compromise. For example, if you say you want to open a window in a dark room to let in some light, everybody will be against you. However, if you suggest that the roof needs to be removed to let in the light, those same people would then want to work with you to reach a compromise. Suddenly, they may be amenable to the idea of opening a window. Unless faced with drastic proposals, the Chinese are not even willing to implement moderate reform."[1]

Over 80 years have passed since then. How do the Chinese see themselves now? In this chapter, we describe the cultural identity of the Chinese people based on secondary data as well as information gathered during private interactions, interviews, and focus groups. Our goal in this chapter is not to be all-inclusive; rather, we present themes mentioned most often by Chinese. In some of the focus groups we conducted for this book, we asked participants to come up with three words that best described the Chinese in 2013. The most common participant responses included negative words, such as insecure, complaining, frustrated, rumor monger, conflicted, anxiety-ridden, and lost, as well as positive words, such as development, dream, hope, anticipation, health, and exercise. In the sections below, we elaborate on prevalent themes in more detail. Other characteristics mentioned often, but not discussed here, include industrious, hardworking, moderate, responsible for taking care of parents, and devoted to children.

The "Center Kingdom"

Historically, the Chinese have taken great pride in their civilization, which dates back 5,000 years. In particular, they are proud of their vast territory, abundant resources, long history, rich culture, and contributions to science and technology. For much of Chinese history, China considered itself to be the center of the world and the shining light of civilizations. The Chinese characters for China, 中国, typically translated as "middle kingdom" in English, is more accurately translated as "center kingdom." The word "center" refers not to China's physical location, but to its status as the epitome of all civilized societies. Chinese civilization is based on a set of rules and systems rooted in imperial power and traditional philosophies (such as the teachings of Confucius). From this internal perspective, all other

158   *World View*

countries were seen as being located on the fringes of China's world, both geographically and societally. These "fringe" countries were considered to be the lands of barbarians. Only after such countries learned and copied the "central kingdom" system could they be recognized and accepted by the Chinese as "tributaries." Historical "tributaries" of China include countries such as Japan, Korea, and Vietnam, among others. Such a long history of not only military but also societal dominance has instilled a sense of immense pride in the Chinese people.

Given this historical context, the humiliations endured by the nation between 1840 (the Opium War) and 1945 (the end of World War II) were almost unbearable. During those 100 years, Western powers waged up to 470 wars against China, including the Opium War, the first Sino-Japanese War of 1894–1895, and the second Sino-Japanese War that was part of World War II (1937–1945). With few exceptions, China lost all of these wars. As a result, China signed 1,145 unequal treaties and was forced to cede territory and pay astronomical indemnities.

This humiliating chapter in China's history not only posed a serious threat to the nation's sovereignty and territory but also severely impacted the Chinese people, whose lives went from bad to worse. Although China had been conquered by other nations in the past, the Chinese took great pride in the fact that their less civilized conquerors all subsequently adopted the traditional Chinese systems for everything from language to values, eventually becoming Chinese themselves. But what happened between 1840 and 1945 was qualitatively different. The Chinese system was treated as inferior, both militarily and culturally. Rulers and common Chinese alike lost more than pride during this period; they lost their common identity, and with it, all confidence.

Fast forward to the current era. Today, the Chinese are undergoing a different type of self-examination. After more than 30 years of explosive economic growth, China has achieved something no country in human history has ever achieved. The generation of people responsible for China's recent success all grew up in economic conditions that were at least 100 years behind the United States; yet, they are now managing the world's second-largest economy. China has leapfrogged many advanced countries, building, for example, more high speed railways than any country in history. In a short 30 years, China transformed the tiny fishing village of Shenzhen near Hong Kong into a thriving metropolis that is already overshadowing its well-known neighbor. In Shanghai, a district that rivals Manhattan was built in just 20 years. But after the long recent history of humiliation and poverty, this development may have happened too fast. The Chinese people are not sure of their current status in the world. Have they been able to erase the humiliation to once again become a shining light of civilization?

The Chinese Dream

The "Chinese Dream" doctrine espoused by the new generation of leaders that took power in early 2013 reflects just such an aspiration. At the 16th National People's Congress, President Xi Jinping set forth the goal of accomplishing a great rejuvenation of Chinese society, the "Chinese Dream," and deemed it as the new guiding principle of governance. By 2049 (the 100th anniversary of the PRC's founding),

Xi wants China's development to match that of medium-level developed countries. According to Xi, the Chinese Dream includes three dimensions: prosperity for the country (rich and strong), renewal of the nation. and happiness for its citizens. He also has stressed that the Chinese Dream applies not only to economic prosperity but also to a comprehensive revival in politics, culture, science and technology, and education, among others.

While personal interpretations of the Chinese Dream may differ, the consensus among Chinese people from all political and economic strata is a desire to erase the humiliation of the 100-year period of war, enjoy lives that reflect the most developed civilization, never again be bullied by a foreign power, and be accepted as one of the leading civilizations of the world.

Never Air Dirty Laundry in Public

The Chinese people believe that problems (whether they affect a family or a nation) should be kept private and not be broadcasted to others. To some extent, this is because the Chinese care greatly about how others view them; as discussed in Chapter 2, this is a form of "preserving face." At the family level, this means that family members are expected to keep family matters private, even those that are morally wrong, such as affairs.

At the national level, the Chinese people are expected not to discuss China's problems with foreigners. As a matter of fact, Chinese citizens are expected to defend China on any matter whenever a foreigner makes a negative comment, even though the person may feel the same way herself. During our interviews, we confirmed that an ordinary Chinese person traveling and living abroad would be extremely offended if a foreigner criticized China for any reason, even if it were true. Jackie Chan, a famous Chinese Kung fu actor, reflected this sentiment: "To tell you the truth, I always tell people, 'We Chinese can criticize our country any way we want behind the closed door. But when we are in a foreign country, we must tell people that China is the best.'" This is considered to be one way of expressing patriotism.

Interestingly, and perhaps precisely because of the desire to maintain as perfect an image as possible in front of others, some major changes in China have occurred in response to foreign criticism, even when the same concerns had been raised continuously and much more forcefully within China already. A good example is the behavior of Chinese tourists. Chinese tourists have a notorious reputation for bad behavior within China; according to the domestic media, many carve their names on historical artifacts, trash tourist attractions, talk loudly, and fail to follow rules. However, it was only after the foreign media reproached Chinese tourists for their uncivilized behaviors abroad that the Chinese people paid attention. The behavior of tourists is now a national issue that is given a level of attention rivaling economic development by national leaders. Large campaigns are now being waged to change the behavior of Chinese tourists, both domestically and abroad.

Contradictory Mind

The Chinese people are full of contradictions. This is due in large part to the inclusiveness of many schools of thought in China, each with a unique theoretical

160 *World View*

foundation and perspective. These diverse ideologies are often referred to as the "three religions and nine schools." The three religions are Confucianism, Taoism, and Buddhism. Instead of strictly adhering to one school of thought, most Chinese people selectively use precepts from all three as guiding principles. As Lu Xun said, "Since the Northern and Southern Dynasties in the 4th century AD, Chinese literati, monks and Taoists have been featured with no specific principles. Starting in the Jin Dynasty (265–420), every celebrity had to possess three small 'trinkets:' first, *The Analects of Confucius* and *The Classic of Filial Piety* (representing Confucianism); second, *Lao-Tzu* (also *Tao Te Ching*), (representing Taoism); and third, *Vimalakirti sutra*, (representing Buddhism). ... Confucians during the Song Dynasty (960–1279) were so sanctimonious that they plagiarized Zen masters' analects. ... Confucians during the Qing Dynasty (1616–1912) believed in *The Book of Rewards and Punishments* and *The Tractate on the Unseen Judgment by the Great Emperor of Literary Thriving* (which are from Taoism), and they also invited monks to their homes and performed repentance."[2] From Lu Xun's perspective, the Chinese are so capricious that they cannot ascribe to any particular beliefs.

In his book, *My Country, My People* (1935), another great Chinese writer Lin Yutang said, "[The] Confucian world outlook is positive while that of Taoism is negative. Those two elements together created the immortal Chinese character where the Chinese act as a Confucian if obtaining success and as a Taoist if facing failure. In other words, Confucians keep establishing ventures and struggling while Taoists comforting themselves when facing failure with tolerance." Similarly, he suggested, "Chinese people are clearly aware of both the necessity of great efforts of human beings and their labor in vain."[3]

Over the course of history, a governing empire will usually endorse and even enforce a particular ideology. In contemporary China, however, such constraints do not exist. As a result, many Chinese people feel even more confused than others when they face difficult situations in life, as so much contradictory advice exists. We list several popular opposing proverbs in Table 1.

Table 26.1 Contradictions in Chinese Proverbs

A real man would rather die than surrender.	A real man is someone who knows when to eat humble pie and when to hold his head high.
Better to die in honor than live in dishonor.	While there's life, there's hope.
Every profession produces its own master.	A scholar is the most desirable profession; everything else is below it.
A good deed has its reward and an evil deed has its punishment.	Lay all loads on the willing horse.
Never attack unless attacked.	He who strikes first gains the advantage.
A good man needs three supporters.	It is better to depend on yourself than on others.

Often in life, these dialectical and diverse philosophical attitudes are used to excuse seemingly hypocritical behaviors. One example is that everyone hates backdoor deals, but if the situation arises, an individual will exploit a backdoor channel without hesitation. Both actions are justified by different Chinese ideologies.

It is often said by the Chinese that the Chinese people do not have faith these days; even if they do, they still do not know what their beliefs truly are. In addition, most people feel that while materially, their lives have improved substantially in recent years, spiritually, their lives remain quite stagnant and barren. We discuss the topic of faith in detail in the chapter entitled "Religions and Faith."

Living in the Fast Lane

Many foreigners find that the Chinese are always in a hurry. They want everything done as soon as possible, ideally and literally today. A Chinese entrepreneur shared the following perspective on this phenomenon with us: "Unlike America, China is going through great changes every day. While there are a lot of traps one should avoid, there exists an equal abundance of opportunities. As a result, many become rich overnight. Seeing how some have achieved great wealth in a short time period, others are unwilling to lag behind and want to become as successful, maybe even within a shorter period (so that they can "catch up"). In other words, rapid development in China has led the Chinese to live in an exciting and yet impetuous mental state." These words reflect how, faced with a widening wealth gap, many Chinese hope to protect their pride and dignity by pursuing power and money. The rapid growth of the Chinese economy has undoubtedly influenced expectations among the Chinese people that they will instantly achieve stratospheric levels of personal success.

One clear implication of all of this is the tremendous energy we have observed among entrepreneurs and potential entrepreneurs. They are always looking for the next opportunity, the next big thing. Without any exaggeration, the entire Chinese nation is in overdrive, not unlike the entrepreneurs of Silicon Valley. This is both an amazing and a scary observation.

Tragedy of the Commons

In his book *The Chinese Way of Life: An Analysis of Chinese Character*, Lin Yutang, the contemporary Chinese writer, stressed: "The Chinese nation is a nation of individualism, since the people care about their respective families while ignoring the whole society. Their psychology of pledging loyalty to family equates to magnified selfishness."[4] This observation aptly describes the Chinese people today. Many people do not take responsibility for public property. For instance, people are apt to neglect, waste, and even damage public resources. Those who are in charge of public toilets have to lock the tissue boxes so they are not stolen; as a matter of fact, most public toilets in China do not provide toilet paper, and a person must buy it or bring his own. Materials in public places (center dividers made of stainless steel, pillars on pedestrian overpasses, manhole covers, etc.) are often stolen.

162 *World View*

People consider such acts to be less evil since they are not taking from private citizens, "just" from the public. It is still quite common for people to spit and litter in crowded public places such as railway stations, parks, streets, and even inside the modern concourse of Shanghai Pudong Airport.

Similarly, a Chinese undergraduate student observed, "A typical residential community is clean and beautiful, but the immediate surrounding area can be very dirty. People spit and litter in public but never do that at home. These all suggest that Chinese people still live with the mentality of caring only about close family and lack the modern concept of the public good." A disheartening ramification of this is the fact many companies break the law and dump toxic waste into rivers. What is worse is that those who possess this knowledge do not feel morally obligated to stop public pollution.

Road Ahead

Realizing the Chinese Dream and never airing dirty laundry in public will likely remain tenets of the Chinese cultural identity in the coming decades as well. This will only be changed if and when China acquires a status in the world similar to the United States. The contradictory mind is much more fundamental to Chinese culture and is unlikely to change anytime soon. Living in the fast lane and the tragedy of the commons, however, are transient, and we expect they will change in the not so distant future.

Notes

1 Lu Xun (2011), *The Complete Works of Lu Xun's Essays,* Beijing: Yanshan Press, p. 531.
2 Ibid., p. 911.
3 Lin Yutang (2010), *My Country and My People,* Jiangsu: Literature and Art Publishing House.
4 Lin Yutang (2007), *The Chinese Way of Life: An Analysis of Chinese Character,* Shanxi: Normal University Press.

27   Faux Emigrants

China is experiencing its third wave of emigration since 1949 and is the largest source of immigrants in the world. The first two waves were the emigration of students overseas in the 1980s and the emigration of technical professionals in the 1990s. Quite unlike the first two waves, however, most current emigrants neither speak English well nor have the ability to assimilate into foreign cultures. In fact, many do not necessarily desire to physically relocate. Rather, foreign permanent residency is seen as a safety net of sorts, an option that can be exercised in the future if their current situations degrade. Many are trying to attain foreign permanent resident status[1] by investing in foreign assets while still living and working in China.[2] Therefore, we feel it is more appropriate to call this third wave "faux emigration."

One-third of Chinese citizens worth RMB 10 million or more possess overseas assets that account for 9% of their total assets. Among the tycoons with no overseas assets, nearly 30% are planning to invest abroad within the next three years.[3] In response to high demand, firms that help people immigrate to other countries have sprung up all over China. In addition to traditional newspaper ads, some firms even pay exorbitant fees to run commercials on the Shanghai Oriental TV channel,[4] which boasts an extremely large audience.

In this chapter, we first provide an overview of the faux emigration that is happening now. We discuss the reasons behind it and why most people in this group do not actually intend to live permanently outside China, at least for now. In the Road Ahead section, we discuss emigration as a continuing trend that will very much depend on the internal state of affairs in China.

State of Emigration

In April 2011, *The Private Wealth Report 2011*, jointly published by China Merchants Bank and Bain Capital, noted that among China's high net worth individuals, nearly 60% of multimillionaires with over RMB 10 million in investable assets had completed or were considering investment emigration; among billionaires with larger investment pools of more than RMB 100 million, this trend was even more obvious, with about 27% of respondents having completed investment emigration, and up to 47% with applications under consideration.[5] *The GroupM Knowledge–Hurun Wealth Report 2012* also showed that 60% of the rich had applied for or were considering emigration. As the trendsetters and primary

164 *World View*

reference group for the rest of China, the desire to emigrate by the wealthy has now become the objective of the middle class as well.

We summarize relevant emigration statistics here for three popular destinations among Chinese citizens: Australia, Canada, and the United States.

The statistics released by the Department of Immigration and Border Protection of the Australian Government showed the number of permanent residence visas issued in the last few years were: 24,768 (2009–2010), 29,547 (2010–2011), 25,509 (2011–2012), and 27,334 (2012–2013). China was the second largest source of permanent immigrants in Australia in 2012–2013. According to the Australian government, 391,060 Chinese-born people were living in the country by the end of June 2011, 51% more than in 2006. They constitute the third largest immigrant population in Australia (after citizens of the United Kingdom and New Zealand), comprising 1.8% of the total population.

In Canada, China overtook the Philippines in 2012 as the largest source of permanent immigrants. According to Citizenship and Immigration Canada, the number of Chinese citizens who were granted permanent residency over the same period were 29,050 (2009), 30,196 (2010), 28,695 (2011), and 33,018 (2012).

Similarly, based on statistics released by the U.S. State Department, the Guangzhou Office (the only office in mainland China that issues immigration visas) issued the following number of immigration visas to Chinese citizens over the same time period: 22,479 (2009), 29,152 (2010), 34,693 (2011), 39,639 (2012), and 31,913 (2013).

Purpose of Emigration

Based on our review of published reports and surveys in China, as well as interactions with our informants, several factors have been driving the third wave of (faux) emigration. A recent survey showed emigration has surged for three major reasons: to facilitate children's education (58%), to ensure wealth security (43%), and to prepare for a better life after retirement (32%). Other reasons include developing an overseas investment (16%), facilitating foreign travel (7%), having more children (6%), and taking advantage of lower tax rates (6%).[6] Here we discuss what we see as the three major drivers of emigration from China: education, wealth security, and quality of life.

First, education has become a primary concern among emigrants in the third wave; 58% cited it as a key motivator. According to another report, *The White Paper on China's High Net Worth Population Consumption Demand*, 85% of multimillionaires planned to send their children to study abroad; that proportion climbed to 90% among billionaires.[7] Since China's students consistently score at or near the top of the world rankings, this may seem surprising. However, many people prefer the foreign education system because they wish to better cultivate their children's interests and provide them with a liberal environment in which to grow. Emigrating enables Chinese children to escape the exam-oriented education structures that create intense competition and constant pressure. In addition, many children want to study abroad in order to broaden their horizons. By emigrating, children are able to study "abroad," but as residents who enjoy the same educational resources as local students. In addition, compared to international students, permanent residents have more advantages when applying to universities, are charged lower tuition fees, and generally have an easier time adapting to college life. Kung fu actor Jet Li, who emigrated from China to Singapore, said, "I just want to find a place for my children during their formative years where they can receive education in both Chinese and English culture, a place where I can go to work without worrying about them. After careful searching, I finally decided on Singapore."

Another reason why people emigrate from China is to ensure wealth security. They see obtaining permanent residence elsewhere as an option that they can always exercise. These faux emigrants are not the first to employ this strategy. Before Hong Kong became part of China once again in 1997, many Hong Kong residents obtained permanent residence in Canada, just in case. Since the economic reform of China in 1978, the whole society has witnessed enormous changes across various strata, and along with these changes comes inevitable uncertainty about the future. Those who have become rich over the last three decades have become anxiety-ridden about risks associated with the current political and economic environment. They lack confidence in the future, so they choose investment emigration as a strategy to ensure their wealth. Why do these people decide against emigrating completely and living abroad permanently? Largely, it is because they do not want to miss opportunities in the emerging economy. At the same time, they are not willing to assume the risks associated with those opportunities. As foreign permanent residents, they have a fall-back option if their situations degrade.

A shadow hangs over the affluent in China, and it is directly related to behaviors of "naked merchants": private entrepreneurs who emigrate after obtaining loans using industry assets as collateral or entrepreneurs who transfer their assets overseas and then declare domestic bankruptcy. An entrepreneur told us: "Many entrepreneurs emigrate just to ensure the value of their assets. Libya & Syria are two examples, with the ongoing wars there. An unstable environment puts assets in danger, no matter how wealthy you are."

Some officials, as representatives of the invisible high net worth population, have intimate knowledge of the risk economic policy adjustments pose to their wealth. So they plan ahead, moving their spouses and children abroad while they remain in China. These so-called naked officials are usually corrupt. They can run away immediately and reunite with their families once their crimes are unveiled. In order to limit these behaviors, in 2009, the Shenzhen government issued *The Interim Provisions on Strengthening the Supervision of Party and Government Officials* and *The Interim Provisions on the Accountability of Party and Government Leading Cadres* prohibiting people whose spouses and children have emigrated to foreign countries or have obtained foreign nationality or permanent residency for non-working reasons from serving as officials in any important positions, either in the communist party or the government.

A third reason people emigrate is to improve their quality of life. As discussed elsewhere in the book, astronomic economic development in China over the last

166   *World View*

three decades has come at great cost in the form of environmental destruction and in some cases, renunciation of basic ethics. The quality of the natural environment has degraded so substantially in China that almost every Chinese person living in an urban area knows the term "PM2.5", which is a measure of air pollution. Air pollution is so severe that residents check the PM2.5 level every day, more regularly than they check the weather forecast. Other minimum health standards also can no longer be taken for granted, such as the safety of the food and water supplies.

It is important to remember that most faux emigrants do not actually emigrate permanently. They do what is needed to maintain permanent residency as a back door option. Often the wife and children will emigrate physically, but the husband will stay behind in China and only visit from time to time. Most do not intend to give up their Chinese citizenships. Unlike previous generations of emigrants, most faux emigrants do not have the ability to assimilate into mostly English-speaking countries. Their circles of friends are in China, and they enjoy many social comforts (e.g., food, entertainment, activities, a sense of belonging) that they could not possibly obtain elsewhere. They also are more traditional and feel that it is better to be "attached to one's native land rather than leave it".

Road Ahead

Although much depends on what happens inside China in the coming years and decades, we believe this wave of emigration will continue. As a matter of fact, we probably are just in the early stages. We predict two major changes moving forward. First, we believe the scale of emigration will increase substantially in the future. The pool of Chinese who want to emigrate is almost unlimited. The only limiting factor is quotas on the number of Chinese immigrants other countries will accept each year. This might change as the Chinese become more affluent and become seen as job creators for local economies, rather than as foreigners who are taking jobs away from domestic populations. Furthermore, family is very important to the Chinese; therefore, it is common for a person who obtains foreign permanent residency (or citizenship) to apply for his relatives (by blood or marriage) to join him. Once his relatives immigrate, they help their own relatives, and so on. Such family-based immigration typically is subject to different quotas (or no quota at all), and the snowball effect can be astonishing.

Second, we predict that Chinese emigrants will likely integrate into their new countries and become an influential force, both economically and politically, in the coming years and decades. Three factors will contribute to this phenomenon. First, the children of faux emigrants will become true immigrants. They will have been educated in these countries, speak fluent English (or the primary language), understand the culture, feel comfortable, and probably prefer living in these countries over living in China. Another reason is the idea of critical mass. Once the Chinese community grows to a certain scale in a given country, they will become an electoral force that politicians will have to cater to in order to get their votes. Of course, this will only happen after Chinese immigrants obtain foreign citizenship. Last but not least, the most popular destinations—Australia, Canada, the United States, and New Zealand—are all countries originally comprised of immigrants. To them, accepting a new wave of immigration from China is simply another stage in their development, not unlike their experiences with immigrants from Ireland, Eastern Europe, and Africa. This receptive attitude towards Chinese immigrants will facilitate such a transition.

Notes

1 A permanent resident is an individual who is permitted to live in a particular country permanently (i.e., without obtaining a visa) but is not a citizen (i.e., does not have the right to vote or a passport from that country). In the United States, identification cards for permanent residents are commonly known as "green cards." For example, a Chinese person who is granted permanent residency status in the United States would still retain Chinese citizenship. China does not allow dual citizenship, so if that person decided to become a U.S. citizen, he or she would be required to give up his or her Chinese citizenship.
2 Many countries, including the United States, will grant permanent residency to "job creators" who are willing to make business investments above a certain threshold and can prove a minimum level of wealth.
3 GroupM Knowledge and Hurun Research Institute (2012, August 2), "The GroupM Knowledge–Hurun wealth report 2013," p. 18, retrieved January 2014 from http://img.hurun.net/hmec/2012-08-02/201208021120412789.pdf
4 Shanghai Oriental TV is China's leading local television news media, program producer, and content platform operator. Currently, Shanghai Oriental TV covers and broadcasts to more than ten countries, serving over 800 million people.
5 China Merchants Bank (2011), "China's Private Wealth Report," retrieved January 2014 from http://www.cmbchina.com/privatebank/PrivateBankInfo.aspx?guid=71402db1-1ce9-463e-a570-2a8f310bb85d
6 Ibid.
7 Industrial Bank and Hurun Research Institute (2012, March 27), "The white paper on China's high net worth population consumption demand," retrieved January 2014 from http://www.hurun.net/zhcn/NewsShow.aspx?nid=187

Part VI
Religion and Belief

28 Religions and Faith

In this chapter, we discuss religious beliefs in China. In the next chapter, we explore another form of beliefs—superstition. Chinese citizens have many options in terms of religion. Religion in China has evolved from the ancient "Three for One," a combination of Confucianism, Taoism, and Buddhism, to a diverse number of religious choices today. However, policies related to the protection and restriction of religious beliefs differ vastly from those of Western countries. In this chapter, we discuss these topics in detail and in the Road Ahead section we predict no major changes related to Chinese religious beliefs in the near term.

Diverse Religious Beliefs

The religious beliefs of the Chinese people have diversified gradually over the course of history as a result of interactions with other cultures. According to statistics released by the Chinese government, there are five major religions in China: Buddhism, Taoism, Islam, Catholicism, and Protestantism. There are more than 100 million followers of various religions, about 139,000 sites designated for religious activities, 360,000 clergies, and over 5,500 religious groups nationwide. In addition, these groups have established roughly 100 religious schools to train clergy.

The history of Buddhism in China dates back about 2,000 years. It is estimated that China now has nearly 33,000 Buddhist temples and 200,000 monks and nuns. Taoism, which originated in China, has a history dating back more than 1,700 years; currently, there are around 9,000 Taoist temples and 50,000 priests and nuns. Islam took root in China in 700 AD, and followers include people from 10 ethnic minorities, including Hui & Uygurs. The total population of these ethnic groups totals roughly 21 million, and there are 35,000 mosques and 45,000 imams nationwide. Catholicism has been introduced into China several times since 700 AD, with significant national expansion occurring after the Opium War of 1840. There are currently about 5.5 million Chinese Catholics, 7,000 clergymen, and 6,000 churches and chambers. Protestantism was first introduced into China during the early 1900s, and also expanded rapidly after the Opium War of 1840. Today, there are about 23.05 million Chinese Protestants, 37,000 clergymen, 25,000 churches, and 30,000 informal places of worship.[1]

Among these five religions, Islam, Catholicism, and Protestantism originated from foreign lands, so we will not explain them in detail here. Our major focus is Buddhism and the Chinese traditions of Taoism and Confucianism.

172 *Religion and Belief*

Figure 28.1 A mosque in Shanghai.

Although Buddhism originated elsewhere, it has a 2,000-year history in China. Closely intertwined with traditional Chinese culture, Chinese Buddhism is unique. Buddhism reached its peak during the Tang Dynasty (618–907), when "Zen" Buddhism emerged.[2] Based on translated Indian Buddhist scriptures, Zen was created by Chinese monks, several of whom wrote treatises explaining their unique Buddhist philosophies. Buddhism has significantly influenced China and Chinese culture. Despite a scarcity of strict Buddhists, the number of disciples or believers in the "Three for One" greatly exceeds that of other religions. "Three for One," a manifestation of Chinese Buddhism, refers to a combination of Confucianism, Taoism, and Buddhism (Sakyamuni). Throughout history, Chinese people's attitudes towards religions were quite open and tolerant, which allowed a variety of spiritual thoughts and practices to flourish. Unlike the incompatibility of some Western religious factions, religious disciples in China are not required to abandon other gods or convert others to their way of thinking. Rather, they are highly motivated to embrace others and coexist within Chinese society.

Central tenets of Taoism include polytheism, the pursuit of longevity, immortalization, and living in harmony with nature. Taoism is based on *Tao Te Ching*, which is a doctrinal classic that documents many Taoist thoughts by a sage Laozi around 600 BC. There are about 9,000 Taoist temples in China,[3] including the renowned City of God Temple in Shanghai. Taoism has significantly influenced Qigong,[4] martial arts, medicine, and customs in China.

Confucianism is the most influential of the three major Chinese religions. Also called "The Holy One," Confucianism has long been regarded as an official and national religion. However, the question of whether Confucianism should be viewed as a religion has been a topic of great dispute over the course of history. In

Figure 28.2 Churchgoers at Mu en Tang, a Methodist Church, located on Tibet Road (near People's Square), Shanghai.

Confucianism, "heaven" is the highest and ultimate belief, and a chief goal is to cultivate a civilization characterized by order, harmony, politeness, and decency.

Figure 28.3 Fashan Nunnery, built during the Qing Dynasty and dating back over 100 years in Shanghai.

Figure 28.4 Pilgrims are burning incense inside.

Ancestral temples and temples of heaven are major sites for religious worship. Nowadays, Confucianism is so embedded in various aspects of life that many are not aware of its deep-rooted influence on their thoughts and behaviors.

Many followers of the traditional religions in China can be quite flexible in their beliefs, as they see religious tenets more as guiding principles in life. This sentiment is well captured in the words of Lin Yutang, a Chinese writer: "Chinese people believe in Confucianism when they are successful; they believe in Taoism and Buddhism when they encounter failure. They hold equivocal polytheism dear to their hearts even if many traditions come and go capriciously."[5]

The Protection and Restriction of Religious Beliefs

There are various sorts of religions and a great number of religious followers in China, and no one may be discriminated against due to their religious beliefs in daily work and life. According to Article 36 of the Constitution of China, "Citizens of the People's Republic of China enjoy freedom of religious beliefs. No state organ, public organization or individual may compel citizens to believe in, or not to believe in, any religion; nor may they discriminate against citizens who believe in, or do not believe in, any religion. The state protects normal religious activities."

However, the fact that diverse religious beliefs exist in China does not mean there are no restrictions at all. The Constitution states: "No one may make use of religion to engage in activities that disrupt public order, impair the health of citizens or interfere with the educational system of the state;" and further stipulates that "religious bodies and religious affairs are not subject to any foreign domination." The Chinese government prohibits religious groups affiliated with other countries' religious organizations from pursuing religious activities in China and encourages each religion to establish its own influence independently. For example, America's Mormonism is prohibited in China, and Chinese Catholic churches are independent from the Roman Catholic Church. This restriction likely has its origins in the Opium War, when Protestant and Catholic preachers participated in activities such as military invasions and helped draft unequal treaties. This policy also reflects the general doctrine in China that nothing within its borders should be subjected to the control of foreign entities.

Another rather peculiar phenomenon is the structural similarity between government and religious organizations. For example, we discovered that monks from different temples hold administrative ranks similar to those held by civil servants in the government. The lead monk at Shaolin Temple holds a rank equivalent to a vice governor of a province and enjoys all the privileges that come with that rank.

Religious Beliefs of Communist Party of China (CPC) Members

As firm believers in communism, CPC members are required to adhere to atheism and refuse any form of religion. According to the CPC Central Ministry of Organization, at the end of 2011, there were a total of 82,602,000 CPC members, while there were just 65,750,000 CPC members at the end of 2001. The total number of party members increased by almost 17 million over 10 years, an average of more than 1 million each year, and this ratio is expected to hold in the future. This means that 6 out of every 100 Chinese citizens are CPC members.

176   *Religion and Belief*

CPC members believe in Marxism and Chinese Marxism, including Deng Xiaoping[6] Theory, the "Three Represents,"[7] and similar doctrines. In fact, communism is not a religion. On the contrary, CPC members are supposed to adhere to atheism and reject all religious beliefs. Thus, paradoxically, CPC members are quite unique. Unlike other countries that separate politics and religion, where people can believe in a religion and maintain a political party affiliation simultaneously, communism and religion are mutually exclusive.

Although party members are required to adhere to atheism, some party members join the CPC for political reasons and thus are not true atheists. Moreover, some people choose to join the CPC solely for potential benefits. For instance, college students who are party members may gain extra points when they are evaluated for scholarships and prizes. Party membership may prove even more advantageous when applying for civil service positions; for instance, for the 2012 National Civil Servant Examination, only CPC members were considered for 1,018 (9.7%) of the 10,486 available positions;[8] in 2013, 1,415 (10.9%) of 12,927 positions required CPC membership. Even if 9.7% and 10.9% do not seem like significant percentages, most people believe that CPC members will gain an edge over their competitors even for non-CPC restricted positions. Thus, a person's motivation for joining the CPC can be quite utilitarian. The logic is that joining the CPC leads to a good civil servant position, and a good civil servant position leads ultimately to fame and fortune. Some civil servants would rather believe in Feng shui[9] and the powers of Temples of Wealth to bring them luck and fortune than in the core values of communism. In fact, these sentiments are so prevalent that those who occupy positions yet barely fulfill their duties are vividly depicted in Chinese society as practicing "communism by day and corruption and/or religion by night."

Road Ahead

According to official statistics, there are approximately 100 million religious followers and 80 million CPC members in China; the remaining 1.15 billion Chinese people officially claim no religious beliefs or do not recognize that they have religious beliefs. Other estimates have put the number of religious believers as high as 300 million. Looking ahead, we feel the status quo will likely be maintained. China, in general, will remain a secular society for the foreseeable future.

Notes

1 Bureau of Religions (2005), "Basic landscape of religions in China," retrieved January 2014 from http://www.gov.cn/test/2005-06/22/content_8406.htm
2 Fang Litian (2007, April), "The foundation of Zen by Hui Neng and domestication of Buddhism in China," *Philosophical Research*, Beijing: Institute of Philosophy, Chinese Academy of Social Sciences.
   Zen, founded by Hui Neng, is a unique type of Buddhism. It can be viewed as a new religion originating from Buddhism. Compared to the Indian version, China's Zen features and emphasizes thoughts such as people-centeredness, popularization, self-reliance,

reality, epiphany, and simplicity. These characteristics represent the domestication of Buddhism in China.

3 Bureau of Religions (2005).

4 Qigong is an exercise of coordinating breath patterns with physical postures and motions, mostly for health maintenance purposes, but also for therapeutic interventions.

5 Lin Yutang (2010), *My Country and My People*, Jiangsu Literature and Art Publishing House.

6 Deng Xiaoping (1904–1997) was a Chinese politician and the core of the second generation of PRC leaders. He led the opening up of China to the West and implemented the economic reform policy that enabled China to become the world's fastest growing economy.

7 A policy developed by Jiang Zemin, previous president of the 16th CPC National Congress: "In a word, the party must always represent the requirements of the development of China's advanced productive forces, the orientation of the development of China's advanced culture, and the fundamental interests of the overwhelming majority of the people in China."

8 Gjgwy.net (2011, October 14), "Overall analysis of positions open for 2012 National Civil Servant Examination," retrieved January 2014 from http://www.gjgwy.net/szrd/zyzx/22152.html

9 Feng shui has its origins in Taoism. The goal is to achieve harmony between humans and the environment.

29   Superstition

Hu Jianxue, the former CPC Party Secretary of Tai'an City in Shandong province, was told by a fortune teller a few years ago that he was predestined to be the vice premier of China, but he needed a "bridge" for this to come true. As a result, he ordered a planned national highway be rerouted to go through a reservoir so that a bridge could be constructed, a decision costing tens of millions of dollars. The bridge is named Dai Lake Bridge, and Dai Lake is pronounced the same as "bring Hu" in Mandarin. So even the meaning of the bridge's name was intended to help Hu achieve great success in his political career. Yet, it was not long before his behavior was exposed and he was fired. This bridge's name is now known for another homophonic meaning: arrest Hu.[1]

This case is just one example of the emphasis on superstition in China. Many people are extremely concerned about their own luck, fate, and fortune; although they believe these are predestined to some extent, they also believe that fate can be changed if certain actions are taken. This is where superstition comes in. Though it has various forms, the purpose of superstition is almost always the same: to achieve personal gain.

While superstition exists in every culture, the most remarkable aspect of superstition in China is its pervasiveness. People from all walks of life, regardless of social status, education level, or age, engage in a variety of superstitious practices to address a wide range of issues. In China, seeking help for illness from those who claim to be able to communicate with heaven and god is not uncommon, especially in remote and undeveloped regions. Even wealthy, educated, and important people engage in superstitious practices to try to increase their fortunes or protect against bad luck. In this chapter, we provide an overview of superstition in China by discussing current popular practices.

Religious Superstition

In the chapter on religion and faith, we discussed the diverse religious beliefs in China, ranging from the Eastern traditions of Buddhism and Taoism to the Western Christian traditions, including Catholicism. Many people who are religious (especially those who adhere to Eastern religions) believe in a supernatural force that determines outcomes in their personal lives, a force that is both omnipresent and omnipotent and can intervene in the daily lives of all people. For such people, following a religion is about believing in a heavenly guardian. By

180 *Religion and Belief*

extrapolation, many believe that monks are able to provide them with accurate and useful guidance.

Most people have no true understanding of the core values of their religion. One informant, a real estate developer, told us a personal story about his life as a Buddhist. He had been a devoted believer until an experience a few years ago. He was on his way to a different city to close a major business deal with a partner. On his way there he stopped at the temple he regularly visited and asked the monks for guidance. The monks told him that everything was great, things one would expect to be said to a successful business man on his way to close another big deal. Unfortunately, as it turned out, this was not the case. When he arrived to close the deal, his partner never showed up. Eventually, he realized that his partner was a fraud. To this day, he is still trying to recover the money he invested in that venture. After that experience, he no longer believed in Buddhism. He reasoned that the religion must not be very good, otherwise the monk would have warned him about the impending disaster that day. This anecdote is a great example of how religion has been co-opted by superstition; many self-proclaimed religious believers have had similar experiences.

Another example is the practice of burning incense at Cheng Huang Temple[2] (or City of God Temple) in Shanghai. During the first month of the lunar year, there is a considerable increase in the number of people who visit the temple to burn incense for good luck. A similar phenomenon occurs at Fahua Temple[3] in Huzhou, Zhejiang province. The time when Fahua Temple has the largest crowds and the most continuous burning of incense is on the fifth day of the first lunar month, which is the day on which people in eastern China welcome the arrival of the god of wealth. Groups of pilgrims rush from all over the country to burn incense and worship this god. Calling these pilgrims pious Buddhists is a bit of a stretch because most participate only minimally and simply pray for financial and occupational prosperity for themselves in the coming year.

What distinguishes people who believe in superstitions from those who believe in religions is that the former usually have utilitarian purposes. For instance, they will say, "If Buddha blesses me by granting my wish, I will donate money in the future to redeem a vow to Buddha." In their eyes, burning incense represents an equivalent exchange: the temple where one prays receives material reward in exchange for the realization of one's wishes.

Another very interesting belief in China is that particular temples have specific powers; not all temples of the same religion are equal in the eyes of the believers. Many temples have now become revenue-generating entities and typically are professionally managed. (For instance, the monk who runs Shaolin Temple took the time to earn an MBA degree.) Truly, "the gate of Buddhism" is no longer "a clean and quiet place."

Inferences about Environmental and Bodily Signals

During early eras of human history, many people inferred that environmental circumstances were actually signals with deeper inherent meaning. People used to believe that thunder meant the gods were not happy with their actions. In China, there is still an expression that "one who does evil things will be killed by thunder." We have come a long way from those early associations; nevertheless, many Chinese people still make inferences about signals from their bodies and nature.

A typical example is the popular saying that one's left eyelid twitches for fortune and one's right eyelid twitches for disaster. An informant working in a foreign company told us the following anecdote. His colleague's right eyelid twitched unceasingly before leaving for a team program in Thailand. Firmly believing in this traditional saying, he lied to his team leader and said that one of his relatives had suddenly fallen ill and had come to Beijing for medical treatment. He said he had to forego the trip to Thailand because he owed the relative a great debt of gratitude and was the only person who could help with his medical treatment. When their eyelids twitch, it is quite common for Chinese people to predict (often aloud) what kind of bad luck or good fortune will come their way.

The attention paid to signs from nature is best exemplified by the meaning attached to dates and numbers. Most Chinese people feel that it is necessary to choose a lucky day for weddings, funerals, business openings, moving into a new house, and so forth. Chinese people like the number 6 because they believe it means everything will go smoothly (possibly from *I Ching*). They also love the number 8 because its homophone alludes to making a fortune. This may be why the Jinmao Tower[4] in Shanghai, the tallest building in China until 2007, was designed to have 88 floors. Likewise, the number 4 is absolutely taboo because its homophone alludes to death.

In general, cash gifts are given in odd-numbered amounts at occasions such as funerals because odd numbers mean no more bad luck will come. In contrast, cash gifts are given in even-numbered amounts on happy occasions because good fortune comes in pairs (i.e., the receivers will receive more good fortune in the future). In any Chinese person's life, anything related to numbers follows these rules, and some people take these rules to a whole new level. A lucky mobile number can often fetch the equivalent of thousands of US dollars, and there are even websites dedicated to helping clients select numbers that meet their needs.

Feng Shui

Dating back to the Warring States Period (476 BC–221 BC), the theory of Feng shui[5] emphasizes the relationship between the physical environment and human beings. Feng shui is used to select sites for palaces, residences, graves, etc. according to wind direction, geology, and hydrology. The culture of Feng shui has been passed down from generation to generation, and believers hold the opinion that human beings are affected by the environment at all times since human beings live between heaven and earth. Feng shui is believed to influence every aspect of a person's life, including fate, fortune, career, and health.

There are two types of Feng shui believers: those who believe in its ethos and those who believe it literally. Those who believe in the essence of Feng shui emphasize its core tenet: humans should live in harmony with their environment.

182   *Religion and Belief*

Ma Yun, the famous Chinese entrepreneur, once said, "I am particular about Feng shui and I believe Feng shui is indispensable for one to do business. 'Feng' is the air and 'shui' is a well in front of your gate. I don't think your employees would be willing to work in a place that has polluted air outside the windows and a chemical plant just next door."[6] Many architects and interior designers now incorporate Feng shui into their work, and its influence has extended to Western culture.

Most often, however, believers take Feng shui literally, and they live their lives based on guidance provided by Feng shui masters. These masters essentially serve as fortune tellers who help clients avoid bad luck, counteract existing bad luck, or attract good luck, health, and/or wealth.

Date of Birth and Eight Characters of a Horoscope

The term "date of birth and eight characters of a horoscope" refers to a calculation that is made about a person's character and destiny based on the year, month, day, and hour of her birth in the traditional Chinese calendar system. In ancient China, Gan-Zhi (or Tian Gan-Di Zhi) was used to form the chronology and calendar. The 10 Heavenly Stems (Tian Gan) were used in combination with the 12 Earthly Branches (Di Zhi) to produce a compound cycle of 60 units. These 60 groups of Gan-Zhi respectively represented specific years, months, days, and hours. Each specific number is represented by two Chinese characters (yielding a total of eight characters).

While the younger, educated, and more Westernized generation may have limited interaction with this traditional Chinese fortune telling technique, they are often introduced to it by their parents. In China, many rationalize, "What harm can be done by checking it out?" One of the most common uses for this information is judging whether a potential marriage will be happy or not. This is somewhat similar to astrological horoscopes in the West but based on a more detailed theoretical system. According to this theory, if the dates of birth and eight characters of a horoscope match each other, then a couple's marriage will be harmonious; otherwise, the marriage will be in danger of breaking up and do harm to both sides. Some of the predictions made can be very specific. We know a young woman in her twenties who was simultaneously proposed to by two young men. To figure out whom she should marry, the girl's father took the date of birth and eight characters of a horoscope for all three to someone who specializes in interpreting them. This person told the father that the woman should marry one but not the other, as the second one would be fickle in love and if the two got married, they would get divorced at the age of 36. Date of birth and eight characters of horoscope predictions have been linked with marriage for centuries.

In a simplified version of the same belief, appropriateness of marriage also is judged based on the animals associated with the years in which two people were born (known as the Chinese zodiac in Western cultures). In the Chinese calendar system, 12 animals are combined with the 12 Earthly Branches (Di Zhi)

Figure 29.1 A Chinese fortune teller on a street corner.

to produce 12 Chinese animal zodiac signs (e.g., 2013 was the year of the horse). There are many popular folk songs about a couple's "fitness" or "unfitness" according to the zodiac. Some lyrics describing "fit" matches are: "Indigo rabbit and yellow dog are from ancient times; red horse and yellow sheep live long; black mouse and yellow ox make prosperity; indigo ox and black pig are radiant with joy; dragon and cock last long …" and "snake coiling itself round rabbit is sure to be rich." Some lyrics describing "unfit" matches are: "Of indigo ox, white horse is afraid; sheep and mouse will break up in one day; snake and tiger are like wrong knives interlaced; dragon and rabbit keep tears-bathed; golden cock fears jade dog; a happy ending is impossible between monkey and pig."

Road Ahead

As China further develops, we believe the pervasiveness of some of these superstitions will diminish. The first to fade away will be date of birth and eight characters of a horoscope predictions, as such predictions are based on natural phenomena that can now be easily debunked by scientific advances. To a large extent, we can now control the date and time of a child's birth. It is unfathomable to think that a child's destiny can be changed simply by scheduling a C-section a few days earlier than a baby's due date.

Regardless, we believe that superstition will exist in some form for a long time. It may gradually evolve into a quaint cultural phenomenon that people engage in but do not take seriously or literally.

Notes

1 Jiang Weiwei, (2007, August 8), "The actual motive behind the superstition of officers," *China Youth Daily,* retrieved January 2014 from http://zqb.cyol.com/content/2007-08/08/content_1852691.htm
2 The City of God Temple in Shanghai is a Taoist temple located by the Yuyuan Gardens. It became a very popular site for citizens who come to pray and ask favors of the city god.
3 Fahua Temple is a famous Buddhist temple with the longest history and the deepest influence located in the Lake Tai region.
4 Jinmao Tower is an 88-story landmark skyscraper in the Lujiazui area of the Pudong district of Shanghai, China. Until 2007, it was the tallest building in China, the fifth-tallest in the world by roof height, and the seventh-tallest by pinnacle height.
5 Feng shui is a Chinese philosophical system of harmonizing the human existence with the surrounding environment. The term Feng shui literally translates as "wind-water" in English.
6 Jrj.com (2011), "How do billionaires see Feng shui?" retrieved January 2014 from http://money.jrj.com.cn/2011/04/2908019855752.shtml

Part VII
Arts and Entertainment

30 Nine Traditional Skills of the Cultured Chinese

In addition to having a long history, Chinese culture is also rich in its scale and scope. Skills in nine traditional cultural areas have been valued consistently throughout the history of Chinese society: guqin (the traditional Chinese musical instrument), Go (a traditional game), Chinese calligraphy, Chinese painting, swordsmanship, poetry, healing, tea, and liquor (Chinese: 琴、棋、书、画、剑、诗、医、茶、酒). A cultured Chinese person is expected to develop expertise in (and appreciation for) each of these nine areas. In order to develop an appreciation for what the Chinese now value in art and entertainment, it is important to gain a better understanding of these nine areas. In this chapter, we first provide a historical overview of each area. We then discuss these areas in the context of contemporary China, including which skills are important or coming back in fashion, which ones are on the way out, and which ones have morphed into newer forms. We conclude in the Road Ahead section by predicting how traditional skills will evolve in the future.

A Historical Review of the Nine Traditional Skill Areas

Out of the nine skill areas, the first four are mentioned most often; collectively, they are called the four arts of a scholar. The four arts originated between 2607 BC and 2110 BC and constitute an indispensable part of Chinese culture and identity. The guqin (Chinese: 古琴) is one of the most ancient Chinese musical instruments, called "the Father of Chinese Music," with a history dating back over 3,000 years. The guqin is a hollow instrument made of platane wood and seven strings made from silk threads. Each string can make multiple sounds, quaint and elegant, succinct yet rich, covering a broad spectrum. The guqin can be used to express many different emotions, but most people associate it with purity and calmness, which facilitates deep reflection.

Go (Chinese: 围棋) is a type of board game invented several thousand years ago. The game is all about strategy; the objective is to build blockades and break through opposing blockades using white and black playing pieces called "stones." Although it is a two-player game with relatively simple rules, Go is played using various complicated strategies. Legend has it that Yao & Shun, two ancient Chinese sages, invented Go to satisfy the political ambitions of other

188   Arts and Entertainment

competitors who were trying to usurp their power. By playing Go, they were able to test-govern a country by applying strategies on the game board instead of in real life. Unlike the guqin which was played almost exclusively by scholars, Go was played (almost obsessively) by a wide range of people, common, cultured, and royal alike. It is said that life is just like playing Go, for one must utilize his intelligence, experience, courage, and perseverance through the game's ups and downs. Playing the game naturally exposes a person's character. If one desires to understand Chinese wisdom more deeply, playing Go makes a good starting point.

In Chinese calligraphy (Chinese: 书法) Chinese characters are expressed as art, for Chinese characters are pictographs by nature. Only by using a writing brush, a piece of art paper, Chinese ink, and an ink stone can the flowing strokes of Chinese characters be transferred smoothly to the paper. In Chinese calligraphy, particular attention is paid to strokes, overall structure, and the pressure one applies to the brush. Calligraphy is a heart-felt image that is thought to reflect a person's character. For instance, a person of integrity and tenacity tends to write the characters with bolder strokes created by increased pressure on the brush. Calligraphy is a unique Chinese art and could even be considered the original abstract art. Historically, calligraphy skills have been highly regarded in Chinese society. In fact, calligraphy was a subject on the imperial examination during some periods in history.

The last of the four arts, Chinese painting (Chinese: 国画), shares some common ground with Chinese calligraphy in terms of techniques, tools, and emotion expression. Usually painted with water colors, Chinese paintings are typically comprised of a picturesque scene and a poem in Chinese calligraphy. Subjects of Chinese paintings include mountains, rivers, flowers, birds, or people. There are two main schools of Chinese painting: meticulous painting, with precise, highly detailed strokes; and free sketch painting, with an emphasis on the ratio of ink to water, and abstract, succinct, and bold strokes. As with poetry, Chinese painting is rooted in context. It is concise in form, yet rich and profound.

Of the five remaining traditional skills of a cultured Chinese person, poetry (Chinese: 诗) is in its own league. Although it is not included in the four arts, its cultural significance equals or even surpasses them. Poems are used to express various emotions, including happiness, delight, sadness, frustration, disappointment, despair. They are often written to commemorate special occasions, such as military victories, deaths, reunions with old friends, etc. The most influential poetry was written during the Tang (618–907) and Song dynasties (960–1279). Poems from the two eras are highly treasured among the works of traditional Chinese literature. The Tang Dynasty is called the era of poetry (Chinese: 诗), while the Song Dynasty is called the era of lyric poetry (Chinese: 词). The Tang Dynasty was an open-minded era characterized by cultural inclusivity. The Chinese people lived full cultural lives during that era, which is often referred to as the golden age. It also marked the heyday of Chinese poetry, and Li Bai (701–762), a famous romantic poet nicknamed the "poet immortal," was its brightest star. Attributed to drunk inspiration, his poems reflect his overwhelming emotions, unfettered imagination, high-flying ambition, and strong desire for freedom. Another genius poet, Du Fu (712–770), also emerged during this period. A realist, he recorded the waxing and waning of a great dynasty. Hence, he earned the title of "poet historian." Compared with poetry, which is more constrained by rhyming patterns and word limits, lyric poetry enables more freedom in terms of sentence patterns, yet follows a well-specified format.

Swordsmanship (Chinese: 劍) was not just learned as a fighting skill but also as an artistic form of self-expression and mental exercise. As an artist, a swordsman is not unlike a musician or a dancer; different movements (either body or hand) are used to convey the inner state of the individual. Just as there are different styles of kung fu, there are different styles of swordsmanship, each characterized by its own sets of movements. And, like jazz, one can also improvise.

The remaining three skills are all related to eating or drinking. Healing (Chinese: 医) refers to the idea of food therapy. The Chinese have recognized and practiced food therapy as a valid way to achieve and maintain a healthy body for the last few thousand years. The Chinese believe that a balanced diet can prevent and cure sickness and prolong a healthy life; they also believe that drug therapy is inferior to food therapy. Tea (Chinese: 茶) is one of the most important components of Chinese life. Like wine, teas are complex and require sophistication to understand and appreciate. Last but not least is liquor (Chinese: 酒). In China, liquor has been consumed on all types of occasions throughout history. It is considered a drink for both the elite and common man alike.

What's In, What's Coming Back, and What's Out

Like many things in China, traditional beliefs about the skills a cultured Chinese person should develop have evolved. Of the nine traditional skills, four remain important and are even more popular, three are coming back in fashion, and two are on their way out.

Three skills that have become even more popular in the modern era relate to eating and drinking: healing, tea, and liquor. As a matter of fact, healing (food therapy) is a major discussion topic on social media. Compared to people from other countries, the Chinese typically pay a lot more attention to what they eat and how they eat, which has its origins in the healing skill. Go also remains extremely popular but exists in multiple forms now. Although the rules for Go are not complicated, it remains hard to master. About a decade ago, a magazine called *The World of Go* estimated that the game had about 20 million fans in China. However, the number of people who play Go has since been on the decline, and more are turning to Chinese chess or other card games, which are much easier to master. Nowadays, it is not uncommon to find groups of people sitting around tables in parks or on sidewalks playing chess and card games.

190 Arts and Entertainment

Figure 30.1 A vendor and an urban management inspector (Cheng guan) are playing Chinese chess along a street.

Three other skills that convey a sense of sophistication are making a comeback, albeit among a smaller proportion of the population: poetry, Chinese calligraphy, and Chinese painting. Many people, especially executives and scholars, are dedicating themselves to learning how to write poems properly. To our pleasant surprise, at the end of a small forum we organized in 2013 in Shanghai, several participants (professors from disciplines as diverse as business and environmental science) spontaneously wrote various poems to commemorate the occasion. "According to the Chinese Poems Association, at least 2 million people are now practicing calligraphy and producing their own works. However, the real figure may far outnumber that, amounting to around 10 million as is estimated by insiders."[1] Calligraphy is also making a comeback. In 2013, calligraphy was incorporated into primary and secondary school curricula by the Ministry of Education. The move aims to popularize Chinese calligraphy among members of the younger generation. One of our informants, a successful entrepreneur, has dedicated an entire room in his home as a space for practicing Chinese calligraphy. Although Chinese painting is harder to learn, the paintings have become sought after as decorations and collectibles.

The final two skills are on the way out. Very few people can play the guqin now. The type of music it can produce is not as rich compared to other traditional Chinese and Western instruments, so many Chinese young people have opted to

Nine Traditional Skills of the Cultured Chinese 191

Figure 30.2 A craftsman is drawing a sugar painting (an edible painting made of sugar) of a rabbit for a girl.

learn those instruments instead. Likewise, swordsmanship has become an esoteric form of exercise and is practiced by a very small group of people.

Road Ahead

One cannot fully understand Chinese society without understanding how the Chinese value and practice these nine skills. Even for those who do not practice a particular skill (e.g., calligraphy), they know how to appreciate the skill and admire anyone who has developed it. For example, we still often hear people compliment others by stating "your handwriting is beautiful." We do not see the trends stated in this chapter changing in the near future. While no one expects a person to excel in all nine skills (or the seven remaining ones) these days, those who can distinguish themselves by mastering even one of these skills will be held in high esteem by their peers.

Note

1 Lu Yanxia (2013, July 18), "Works of traditional Chinese poems flourish among the general public," *Beijing Daily*, retrieved January 2014 from http://bjrb.bjd.com.cn/html/2013-07/18/content_90870.htm

31 Duanzi[1]

Western people are good at expressing humor with solemn expressions, while Chinese people are good at expressing solemn attitudes in a humorous way.
— *Jean Nohain*[2]

The term "duanzi" originally referred to short jokes or anecdotes in Chinese standup comedy that described a social phenomenon or attitude in a humorous way. Nowadays, thanks to the internet, text messages, WeChat, and social media, duanzi have evolved into a standalone category of entertainment that has become part of daily life in China.

Duanzi can be roughly divided into categories based on content. For instance, dirty duanzi have sexual references; red duanzi make fun of positive attitudes; black duanzi feature ghosts or horror; and the most common, grey duanzi, usually describe social phenomena in a humorous way to reveal prevalent problems and attitudes. New duanzi appear almost immediately when hot topics emerge or major news stories break.

Here is an example of grey duanzi, widely circulated in China after Edward Snowden revealed to the world that the United States government had been eavesdropping on pretty much everything and everyone, causing public outrage. The Chinese people saw it as a perfect context in which to mock themselves and a sad social phenomenon, while having a good laugh in the process:

> As disclosed by Edward Snowden, the U.S. has stolen millions of text messages of Chinese mobile phone users. Here is the data analysis presented to President Obama: 35% were to wish others a happy Chinese New Year; 25% were commercial advertisements; 30% were junk messages on fake certificates, mortgages, duplicating SIM cards, eavesdropping on affairs, etc. Hearing this, Obama asked desperately whether the remaining 10% were something important, the Chief of the CIA said: "Mr. President, actually the rest were dirty jokes." Obama asked, "Then how about this popular mobile chat, WeChat, that they use?" "Well," the Chief replied, "35% were Chicken Soup for the Soul; 25% were selfies and other photos they took; 30% were advice on how to be fit and live a long life; and the remaining 10% were contents beginning with a sentence that if you forwarded the messages, good luck would come to you."

194   *Arts and Entertainment*

In this chapter, we focus on grey duanzi, as they are prevalent and typically contain something more than a cheap joke; instead, they cleverly convey information to reflect upon. One informant compared red duanzi to grey duanzi: "A red duanzi is typically consciously written and forwarded to the public. Although it can reach target readers within a short period of time by certain techniques, it can easily get lost due to a lack of public interest, responses, and reposts. On the other hand, a grey duanzi is more culturally attractive, and thus endures. People can even memorize them deep in their minds and then pass them on to others."

As such, we provide a nice set of examples so readers may gain a deeper understanding of Chinese society—not just to highlight duanzi as a prevalent form of entertainment but also to reveal the important topics people care about and the manner in which they express their opinions. The Chinese are typically non-confrontational (see our discussion on face elsewhere in the book), and duanzi allows people to subtly express their opinions on the matters they feel strongly about. We have collected some popular examples of grey duanzi from public sources in China (both internet and mobile platforms) on four topics that the Chinese are deeply concerned about these days: frustrations in daily life, distorted social norms, corrupt public officials, and addiction to mobile phones and social media. In the Road Ahead section, we discuss the future of duanzi, both as an entertainment format and as an outlet for expressing popular sentiment on serious topics.

On Frustrations in Daily Life

There are many frustrations in life, regardless of where one lives. China has some very unique, very serious frustrations, but the Chinese people have found a way to convey them humorously through duanzi. We selected a few of the most popular frustrations in China now and provide one duanzi for each here.

Food safety is the most talked about topic in China. As discussed elsewhere in the book, some companies and restaurants in China are willing to use substandard, fake, or even toxic ingredients in food to create better profit margins for themselves. Here is a duanzi that ridicules this serious problem by referring to the harmful chemicals that are known to be added to these products illegally:

> Here is how Chinese are introduced to science: We learn about paraffin from rice, dichlorvos (DDVP) from ham, sudan red from preserved eggs and spicy sauce, contraceptive pills from eels, formalin from hotpots, sulfur from silver ear fungi and dates, copper sulfate from tree fungi, formaldehyde from beer, and melamine from milk powder.

The next duanzi is a commentary on the stratospheric property prices that make decent housing unattainable for ordinary Chinese citizens:

> A journalist interviews a passerby: "If you win 5 million yuan, how are you going to spend the money?" He says, "Pay my mortgage." The journalist asks, "What about the rest?" The passerby replies, "Well, I will pay the rest bit by bit."

Although the journalist was asking what he would buy with the remaining prize money after paying off the mortgage, the price of property is so high that 5 million yuan could not even possibly cover it. (Note that in China, a fresh college graduate typically earns about 6,000 yuan per month.)

The Chinese high-speed rail system is remarkable in its scale and precision; it leaves on the minute and arrives on the minute as stated on the schedule. A trip one of us took from Shanghai to Beijing via the high-speed train was a pure pleasure and lasted only 5 hours. Air travel in China, on the other hand, ranks among the worst in the world in terms of delays and cancellations. Here is a short duanzi related to air travel:

> China is a large country, and we are really proud of it; even Beijing is huge. Do you how large Beijing is? If you are in Europe and you get on an airplane in London, you will be in Germany in one hour; another hour will take you to Poland. But if you get on an airplane in Beijing, you will still be in Beijing after five hours.

Following is a duanzi on rising living expenses:

> The price of instant noodles has risen. So have prices for eggs, flour, and gasoline. Everything around us has increased, except for salary. Nonetheless, we should do our best to survive because the price of a plot in a cemetery is rising as well.

The Chinese National Soccer Team has failed to be competitive on the world stage over the last three decades, which has frustrated all of the Chinese. This frustration is reflected in the following duanzi:

> A Korean, a Japanese person, and a Chinese person went to see God. They asked God when their national soccer team could win the World Cup. The Korean asked first, "When will South Korea win the World Cup?" God replied, "In 50 years." The Korean cried and said, "Oh, I won't be able to witness it in my lifetime!" Then, the Japanese person asked, "When will Japan win the World Cup?" God answered, "In 100 years." The Japanese person cried, and said, "Oh, even my son won't be able to witness it in his lifetime!" Finally, the Chinese person asked, "When will China win the World Cup?" God cried, and said, "I don't think I will witness it in my lifetime!"

On Distorted Social Norms

The majority of Chinese people dislike certain trends they are currently seeing in society. They believe social norms are being distorted in ways contrary to the traditional Chinese values system and that people are even confusing right with wrong. Here is a duanzi that represents this sentiment:

196   *Arts and Entertainment*

A young person started his teaching career at a new school. During their first meeting, the principal asked him to be kind to every student for the following reasons:

Be nice to those who score 100% because they will become scientists;

Be nice to those who score 80% because they may become your colleagues;

Be nice to those who fail the exams because they may donate money to the school;

Be nice to those who cheat on the exams because they will become government officials;

Be nice to those who get into fights in school because they will become policemen;

Be nice to those who lie because they may become star journalists;

Be nice to those who ramble because they will become government spokespersons.

On Public Officials

Public officials in China now have rather low reputations and are often the subject of ridicule. We have selected several duanzi here to illustrate. Like any humorous material, there is some truth to them; however, we want to be clear that they do not describe all (or even the majority) of public officials.

Leaders' requirements are our aims. Leaders' tempers are our blessing. Leaders' encouragement is our motivation. Leaders' ideas are our action plans. Leaders' lovers are our secret. Leaders' criticism is our aptitude. Leaders' facial expressions are our emotions.

A pig wants to become a human in his next life. God asks, "Do you want to be a worker in a factory?" The pig replies, "Too strenuous." "How about a farmer?" "Too poor." "A businessman?" "Don't know how to calculate." God says, "Okay, then tell me who you want to be." The pig answers, "I'd like to become a government official."

Nice people's faces turn red when telling lies. Unintelligent people tell lies that are full of holes. Scholars have their own system of telling lies. Vendors lie as needed. Leaders' lies are logical and reasonable.

Here is what officials of different ranks do when they make mistakes: Those who admit their mistakes are entry-level staff; those who keep silent are office supervisors; those who find excuses are division heads; those who deny any mistakes were ever made are directors; those who do nothing and to whom everybody else keeps saying, "No mistakes are ever made" are the senior officials.

On Addiction to the Internet, Mobile Phones, and Social Media

It is no exaggeration to say that the Chinese are addicted to various communication formats on the internet, and now, on mobile phones via the WeChat platform. We discuss this in a separate chapter (Chapter 52) later in the book. Here is an interesting duanzi that makes a very fitting analogy between someone reading WeChat in the morning and an emperor.

> When one checks WeChat after he gets up in the morning, he does it as if he were an ancient emperor dealing with urgent reports submitted from all over his empire during the previous evening, as if he were at the top of the decision pyramid. On WeChat, he sees all major national news stories, all requiring him to form judgments, provide suggestions, write comments, and forward to the relevant parties. On WeChat, he also sees all those posts that are worrying the nation and people, posts about ambition, posts with life advice, posts on gourmet cooking, beauty, etc. On WeChat, it is as if one possesses the whole world and the ability to deal with all issues happened in this world. Everybody harbors the secret dream of becoming an emperor, and WeChat is rekindling this dream. When one clicks "like" on WeChat, it is as if he is announcing to the world "Your emperor is now aware of this!"

Road Ahead

Humor has always played a role in people's lives, regardless of cultural background. Duanzi, in particular, play an important role in China. It is not only an entertainment format that fits perfectly with the advent of Weibo and WeChat, it is also a platform that allows people to share views and frustrations that are not possible otherwise, thereby fulfilling a very important human need. As expressed in the quote we used in the beginning of this chapter, the Chinese feel comfortable and are very good at discussing serious topics in a humorous way.

We believe any serious student of China should pay close attention to duanzi and monitor them, as we have done during the course of writing this book. There is a constant flow of new duanzi; they never get boring and can reveal much about the Chinese and China.

Notes

1 All duanzi in this chapter were taken from both internet and mobile platforms (January 2014).
2 Jean Nohain is a French writer who wrote *Histoire du rire*.

32 Cuisines and Restaurants

To understand the important role of food in Chinese culture, look no further than the way references to food are used to describe so many different aspects of the lives of Chinese people. Making a living is called "feeding one's mouth;" a job is called "a rice bowl" or "earning food;" a person who is doing well in life is someone who "eats well everywhere;" a beautiful woman is described as "fit to be eaten;" a popular person is said to have a "mouth-watering aroma;" and someone who is jealous is said to be "drinking vinegar." In fact, instead of asking "How are you?" a Chinese person may ask, "Have you eaten?" In this chapter, we describe historical differences among eight major Chinese cuisine types that have developed over the millennia, the contemporary restaurant industry, and current restaurant trends. We conclude with an outlook for the future in the Road Ahead section.

The Eight Major Cuisine Types

Chinese people attach great importance to food, and dishes are generally judged based on color, aroma, and taste. There are eight major traditional Chinese cuisines, each named after the province where it originated and remains most popular (see figure 32.1): Cantonese, Sichuan, Shandong, Zhejiang, Jiangsu, Fujian,

Figure 32.1 The geographical distribution of China's eight major cuisines.

200   Arts and Entertainment

Hunan, & Anhui. Most Chinese restaurants in the United States serve Cantonese food (e.g., dim sum) and/or spicy Sichuan food; as such, many Americans have tasted just a small sample of Chinese cuisine. The distinct cuisines emerged based on each region's unique climate, natural resources, products, history, and culture. The following map shows the geographical distribution of the eight major cuisines, and in the sections that follow, we provide a brief description of each type. It is important to note that there are also many minor cuisine types in China. However, for the purposes of this book, we limit our discussion to the major cuisines.

Cantonese (Yue) Cuisine

With its subtropical climate, Guangdong (Canton) enjoys ample rain and rich biodiversity, yielding a wide array of ingredients. Cantonese cuisine includes three distinctive local cuisines from Guangzhou, Chaozhou, & Hakka, among which Guangzhou cuisine is dominant. There is a saying, "Food in Guangzhou is second to none." A major goal in Cantonese cuisine is to let the natural flavors of the food shine, so the food tends to be less greasy. People are meant to enjoy the freshness of the ingredients and admire their presentation, and condiments are meant to enhance the food's natural flavor, not cover it up. For instance, in one Cantonese specialty, steamed scallops with ginger and garlic, fresh scallops are steamed and just a small amount of soy sauce, ginger, and garlic are added to ensure the scallops maintain their natural sweetness and tenderness.

It has been estimated that thousands of ingredients have been used in Cantonese cuisine. In addition to typical domestic meats such as pork, beef, fish, and chicken, Cantonese cuisine incorporates almost all edible meats. Even rarely used ingredients such as snake, rat, cat, and dog are considered as prime candidates for a delicious dish. Although many different cooking methods are used, steaming, stir frying, braising, stewing, and smoking are the most common.

The unique characteristics of Cantonese cuisine have been influenced heavily by Cantonese culture. Guangdong was among the first cities to interact with the outside world and to incorporate aspects of Western culture. The combination of Eastern and Western influences, abundant and diverse ingredients, and ceaseless innovation makes Cantonese cuisine truly unique. Because many Chinese immigrants were from Canton, most of the first Chinese restaurants in the United States served Cantonese cuisine.

Sichuan (Chuan) Cuisine

Although it originated in Sichuan province in southwestern China, Sichuan cuisine is favored by a large population and hence has been crowned as being the most popular. Unlike Cantonese cuisine, Sichuan cuisine is characterized by the liberal use of spices, especially three types of peppers (chili peppers, Chinese prickly ash, and Sichuan pepper) and heavy use of chili oil. The cuisine focuses on six basic flavors: numbing, pungent, sweet, salty, sour, and bitter. However, these flavors are combined in different ways and proportions so that each dish has a truly unique taste. There is a saying, "Eat in China, taste in Sichuan."

One notable dish is Kung Pao chicken, in which diced chicken is stir fried with peanuts, Sichuan peppercorns, and scallions. Although this dish is unquestionably hot and numbing, it is less spicy than other Sichuan dishes. Why is Sichuan cuisine so hot and spicy? First, the Sichuan Basin is characterized by a humid climate. Since hot peppers can help reduce water retention, they can help prevent arthritis. The spicy flavor increases salivation and stimulates the appetite, while Sichuan pepper balances out the spice with its numbing effect, enhancing the flavor even more. Another function of the spicy and numbing flavors is that the pungency can offset the sour taste of leftovers, making them more appealing and less likely to be thrown away.

Shandong (Lu) Cuisine

Shandong cuisine, more commonly known in Chinese as Lu cuisine, features delicacies found in northern areas. It is said that back in the Spring and Autumn period 2,000 years ago, a cook named Yi Ya created a dish called mutton-stuffed fish for Duke Huan of Qi. The combination of the two ingredients created an extremely delicious dish. Therefore, the Chinese character for delicious, 鲜 (Pinyin: xiān), is composed of two Chinese characters—fish and sheep.

The salty and savory flavors that characterize Shandong cuisine come from broth that is made of old hens, ducks, pork bones, squab, etc. A particular focus in this cuisine is placed on cutting technique and heat control, which have a direct bearing on the taste and freshness of Shandong dishes. Compared to the other seven cuisine regions, Shandong is closer to Beijing (the capital during many dynasties) and is the hometown of Confucius. As a result, Shandong cuisine is often associated with government and thus typically is served in larger portions.

Zhejiang (Zhe) Cuisine

Zhejiang cuisine, more commonly known as Zhe cuisine, originated from Zhejiang province. Located in the plain of the Yangtze River Delta, Zhejiang province has a temperate climate and fertile land with many rivers. Thanks to many natural advantages, this area boasts abundant resources, including grains, fruits, vegetables, seafood, poultry, etc. It has thus been crowned as "the land of fish and rice." In order to capitalize on the wide variety of flavorful foods, major focuses in Zhejiang cuisine are careful selection of ingredients, detailed preparation processes, and precise cooking techniques. The appearance of a dish is of supreme importance, as is retaining the ingredients' original flavors, echoing the sophisticated culture and gentle disposition of the local people. A great example of Zhejiang cuisine is West Lake fish in vinegar gravy. Before the fish is cooked, it is starved for a couple of days to remove any muddy taste from the flesh. After the fish is boiled for just 3 to 5 minutes, a sauce of vinegar, sugar, rice, wine, and soy sauce is poured over the fish to preserve its tenderness.

Jiangsu (Su) Cuisine

Jiangsu cuisine, known as Su cuisine for short, has much in common with Zhejiang cuisine. While Jiangsu cuisine has a similar emphasis on food selection, seafood is the main ingredient, which creates a lighter taste with a hint of sweet flavor. Like Zhejiang cuisine, Jiangsu cuisine can be thought of as refined, understated, and elegant. Huaiyang cuisine is one of several sub-regional styles within Jiangsu cuisine and was once served at court during the Qing Dynasty. As a result, Huaiyang dishes are typically served at modern state banquets. One example of Jiangsu cuisine is braised pork and crab meatballs, made of pork, crab, and seed shrimp. Not only are they juicy and fragrant, but they also are rich in nutrients.

Fujian (Min) Cuisine

Fujian cuisine originated in Fuzhou, the provincial capital, and is light in flavor. Soup accounts for 40% of Fujian cuisine. The most notable dish is called "Buddha jumps over the wall," a simmered soup made from shark fin, tendons, dried scallops, pig feet, taro, cabbage, red dates, lotus seeds, shallots, ginger, soy sauce, wine, and other high-quality ingredients. The dish gets its unusual name from the legend that the fragrance and taste of the meat-based dish induced a vegetarian monk to jump over the wall of a temple. Fuzhou has a humid climate and abundant resources, with a variety of fruits that can often be found in the dishes. Because of the presence of various fruit ingredients, Fujian cuisine tends to have a sweet and sour taste.

Hunan (Xiang) Cuisine

Hunan cuisine, also known as Xiang cuisine, features hot, salty, and aromatic flavors, with seasonings of chili peppers, shallots, and garlic. Hunan cuisine distinguishes itself from Sichuan cuisine in that it tends to be oiler and spicier. There is a saying, "The Sichuanese are not afraid of spicy food, while the Hunanese are afraid of non-spicy food." In Hunan, local people eat hot peppers to counteract the cold, damp climate. Noted for its pungent taste, steamed fish head in chili sauce epitomizes Hunan cuisine. In fact, the special food culture in Hunan strongly influences the unique local culture. Women from Hunan are nicknamed "spicy sisters" because they eat spicy food beginning in early childhood, which supposedly contributes to their warm, passionate, and hotheaded temperaments.

Anhui (Hui) Cuisine

Anhui province abounds in mountain delicacies; wild game and fowl from the lush and dense forests are unique ingredients characterizing Hui cuisine, which tends to be salty, oily, and rich in color. Braising and stewing are used more often than other cooking techniques such as stir frying. Anhui cuisine became popular when Hui merchants traveled to major cities in China during the Ming & Qing Dynasties. However, it no longer enjoys the fame it once did due to the decline of the Hui mercantile trade. A classic Hui dish is soft shell turtle, which is stewed with ham to enhance the taste.

Each of the eight major cuisines has its merits, just as each human being has unique attributes. It is said that the Jiangsu & Zhejiang cuisines resemble the attractive beauties in southern China, while the Shandong & Anhui cuisines reflect the brawny men in northern China; the Guangdong & Fujian cuisines are like stylish gentlemen, while the Sichuan & Hunan cuisines are like enlightened and talented scholars.

Contemporary Restaurant Industry

Due to the long history of cuisine and the important role of food in China, modern Chinese restaurants have some unique characteristics. Upon visiting China, many are surprised by the sheer number of restaurants and customers. Other notable differences include restaurant size and structure, the cuisines, and the attention to detail in each dish.

Chinese restaurants are unique in terms of scale. One only needs to visit the shopping malls in China to understand the importance of eating in Chinese life. In almost all shopping malls, the top one or two floors house nothing but restaurants, which, amazingly, are always packed. According to the *2013 China Statistical Yearbook*, there were 23,390 restaurant businesses in China in 2012, with revenue totaling RMB 441.98 billion.[1] The restaurant business is booming largely because many urban professionals choose to dine out and do not cook for themselves anymore.

Chinese restaurants are much larger than their Western counterparts; in fact, they are so large that first-time visitors are often shocked. It is not uncommon for

Figure 32.2 A restaurant in Shenzhen specializes in serving bamboo-basket dishes (dim sum).

a restaurant to have a main dining floor that can accommodate 1,000 customers simultaneously (see Figure 32.2). In China, restaurants almost always have private rooms of different sizes that can accommodate 4 to 20 people. Private rooms often are named based on their architectural designs, and some high-end restaurants have become private room-only establishments.

Nowadays, one can almost find any type of traditional cuisine (including the eight major and many other minor cuisines) in the major cities, although the Xiang, Yue, & Chuan cuisines are the most popular across China. In addition, cuisines from surrounding countries such as Korea, Japan, and Thailand have become very popular. Average cost per person at some of the most popular restaurants ranges from RMB 80 to 300. In addition, many fast-food restaurants from the United States have successfully entered the Chinese market, such as Pizza Hut and KFC. Due to fierce competition, Chinese chefs are constantly innovating in the kitchen. Here, we have included a picture (Figure 32.3) of a dish inspired by the so-called four treasures of study: a writing brush, ink stick, ink, and piece of paper.

Recent Changes in the Restaurant Business

Three major changes have occurred in the restaurant business in recent years: reduction in waste, resistance to certain ingredients, and cuts in public spending.

Figure 32.3 A creative dish called the "four treasures of study." In the photo, the writing brush is made of dough, a black glutinous rice cake represents the ink stick, blueberry jam represents the ink, and a flour wrapper represents the paper.

All three have substantially impacted how restaurant businesses are evolving. One informant who recently left his restaurant chain in Shanghai remarked, "It's not easy to make money in restaurants anymore. I used to be able to buy exotic seafood from Thailand and mark it up 100% in my restaurant. Those days are long gone."

The first change we observed happened a few years ago. In the past, the worst thing a dinner host could do was fail to order enough food for her guests at a restaurant. In China, it is customary for the person who is paying to make food selections for all of the people at the table. If most of the plates were empty by the end of the dinner, the host would have inferred that she probably had not ordered enough. At dinner parties we attended in the past, it was typical to have an abundance of food left on each plate.

However, this has gradually changed. The first thing we have noticed is that people now want to take the leftover food home in takeout boxes. This was quite unthinkable just a few years ago, as most people thought such behavior reflected badly on a person's character (i.e., the person was seen as being "cheap"). Now, we have witnessed that even multimillionaires (people who are worth USD 20 million or more) will ask for takeout boxes at the end of the dinner to take extra food home. In addition, over the last year or so, a so-called empty plate movement has taken off where the goal is to order just enough at dinner so that nothing is left. The impact is substantial; at several recent business dinners we attended, hosts announced that they were participating in the empty plate movement and would not order too much food.

The second change is associated with the ingredients restaurants use. Many traditional Chinese cuisines, such as the Yue cuisine discussed earlier, use exotic parts from animals that are hard to obtain, such as shark fins. Since a goal for most dinner parties is to express the value of guests through the value of the food ordered, many restaurants cater to this demand by providing dishes made with exotic animal parts. However, many Chinese people have realized the negative impact this practice has had on delicate ecosystems. Recently, shark fin soup was eliminated from the menus of many high-end restaurants in Hong Kong. We also see this trend developing in mainland China.

Finally, there was a crash (or adjustment) in demand for high-end restaurants in 2013. In the past, civil servants frequently treated each other to extravagant dinners with public funds. Granted, it was customary to conduct business during these dinners, but the amount of public money spent on meals (and liquor) was astronomical. After the new generation of leaders came to power, Chinese President Xi Jinping called for a curb in excessive spending on official receptions, vehicles, and overseas trips. This policy shift sparked a crisis among many in the catering industry, especially those who ran high-end restaurants and clubs frequented by government officials. The central government is so serious about cracking down on any wasteful spending that a small city's mayor, upon being discovered attending a lavish dinner, reportedly knelt down and begged people not to report him. According to China Restaurant Association, the restaurant industry suffered a 20% loss in revenue during the second quarter of 2013, with 60% percent of businesses witnessing a drastic decline in profit. In the scenic city of Hangzhou,

206 *Arts and Entertainment*

the world famous West Lake used to be surrounded by high-end clubs catering to high-end dinner parties. Right now, a club with 15 private rooms that used to rake in several million yuan each year is now struggling to make ends meet.

Road Ahead

It is evident that the Chinese people are changing their consumption patterns. The extravagance and formalism that once dominated the dining context are now fading away. However, what will not change is the role restaurants play in Chinese life. China is a nation that takes eating very seriously, and its people believe that social interactions should involve food. Given the fact that almost no Chinese people have living spaces large enough to entertain large groups of people, and since most people clearly distinguish between their work and personal lives, restaurants will continue to play a huge role in the everyday lives of the Chinese.

Note

1 National Bureau of Statistics (2013), *China Statistical Yearbook 2013*, Beijing: China Statistics Press, retrieved January 2014 from http://www.stats.gov.cn/tjsj/ndsj/2013/indexch.htm

33 Nightlife

Nightlife in China differs greatly from nightlife in Western countries. In the West, nightlife for single people often centers around bars and clubs, and nightlife for married people often centers around family-oriented activities. As one American vice president of a Fortune 10 company joked with us, when he is not working, he serves as the family chauffeur, driving his kids to all types of activities. While most Americans can relate to this lifestyle, few Chinese people can. In China, evenings are to be spent with people outside the family, and this lifestyle applies not just to those who are young and single, but also those with work obligations. In this chapter, we provide a brief discussion of most common evening activities in China, including karaoke (KTV), foot baths and massage, public dancing, and midnight snacks; and those not restricted to evening, such as visiting teahouses and chess and card houses. We share our predictions about Chinese nightlife in the Road Ahead section.

Karaoke (KTV)

In 1991, in the city of Guangzhou, the karaoke machine (KTV) made its debut in China; it quickly became one of the most popular Chinese pastimes and soon nearly every city or county had KTVs. KTV has become one of the three biggest social activities in China, along with going out to dinner and playing sports. In the following table (Chart 33.1), we present the estimated number of KTVs in major Chinese cities as of March 2013 according to dianping.com.[1] (Note that the list is not comprehensive but is provided to give readers a sense of KTV's popularity.)

In China, KTV customers are charged based on the number of singing hours, with extra fees for food and drinks. At a mid-level KTV establishment in Shanghai in July 2013, the cost for a private room for four people was RMB 58 per hour between 6 pm and 8 pm, Monday through Thursday. Since demand is highest between 8 pm and midnight, the cost for a small box increased to RMB 138 per hour. Sound and light effects can be adjusted on the box, and many choices of food and drinks are offered.

Mobile phone KTV has also become quite popular recently. Mobile phone KTV essentially provides the karaoke experience on the mobile platform, where people can sing the lyrics then record the songs and upload them to the web, where anyone can listen. On May 31, 2013, the app "Sing" was launched on Apple's App Store. Just five days later, it was the number one download in China. Although the

208   Arts and Entertainment

Chart 33.1   The estimated number of KTVs in major cities in China in March 2013.

City	Number of KTVs
Shanghai	1044
Beijing	973
Wuhan	851
Chongqing	597
Chengdu	567
Shenyang	530
Guangzhou	385
Changsha	290
Hangzhou	245
Ningbo	229
Ha'erbing	180
Lanzhou	84
Hohhot	82

experience is like a concert with no audience, people use the platform for practice to help them sing better when they participate in real KTV.

In building business relationships, KTV often is the second step after dining, as it is a bonding experience on a more intimate level. In KTV, the level of singing is not supremely important, but singing very well can provide an immediate boost in the atmosphere. Like those who can drink a lot (discussed in Chapter 8), someone who can sing well has an important competitive advantage in the workplace. In a story shared with us by an informant, a junior employee became a small celebrity in her company and was able to participate in major deals after her singing talent was "discovered" by her supervisors. It turns out that she used to lead the chorus on campus. As the result, she is often requested to sing with major clients (often male). Even the public relations department includes her in meetings with government officials. In order to become more competitive in the business world, as well as in social circles, many people have now started to take voice lessons.

KTV is an entertainment format that cuts across all social strata and allows people to open up and express their emotions. We have visited several homes (or private clubs) of successful entrepreneurs, and all have dedicated, well-equipped KTV rooms. Often, our hosts would burst into song without prompting, both good and not so good singers. We did not detect a trace of self-consciousness (which is rather surprising, given the Chinese culture), and they were very into the songs they sang, whether love songs or inspirational songs, judging by their emotional displays. It was interesting to see these people, who are worth RMB 1 billion or more and who made their fortunes by being relentlessly competitive and shrewd in a complex society, bare their weaknesses and true selves in front of others in KTV rooms.

One of our informants, a recent college graduate, told us a story that sheds light on the popularity of KTV from a different angle. He was originally from a small town in one of the less developed provinces in China. During a trip home after being away for some time, he was alarmed to hear that his father, a rather reserved retired low-ranking government official, suggested that the family go to KTV after dinner one night. Once there, he was blown away by the fact that his father not only sang, but actually sang pretty well.

Rest assured, a professional singing voice is not required in order to be an active participant in KTV. It is required, however, that a person be completely into the activity and show his or her true emotions. One informant said, "Many of our colleagues are half-professional singing kings and singing queens. Every time after dinner, they can push the atmosphere to a new climax, even if they are not professional. We have someone in our group who studied engineering in college, who is really smart, but whose music talent is rather limited. Although the notes are often completely out of tune, every time his efforts can effectively boost the atmosphere and people will applaud passionately for him."

Some KTV establishments also have young ladies who will stay in your KTV room and sing along with you at an additional cost. Most are completely innocuous and simply serve as hostesses to ensure that the guests have a good time by helping to create an enjoyable atmosphere. However, sometimes these "hostesses" are actually prostitutes (some are even organized by the establishments) who will leave with guests at the end of the night. Therefore, it is very important to research KTV establishments before visiting them.

Foot Baths and Massage

A uniquely Chinese phenomenon, foot massage (even full body massage, if so desired) has become a social event to be shared with others after dinner. Based on statistics from dianping.com for Shanghai Station, there were 3,320 pieces of information under the category of foot baths and massage. Salons for these purposes often consist of private rooms for 3 or 4 people with designated waiters. Various services are offered, for example, back massage with essential oils, sauna, beauty spa, foot therapy and massage, etc. Participating in these services has become a popular way to develop relationships with business partners. Similar to KTV, there is also a possibility that covert prostitution may be happening in these establishments. Once again, it is important to research establishments before visiting them for the first time.

As with KTV, it is quite interesting to observe how people are willing to be exposed (literally, in their underwear) in front of friends and business associates, and often potential business partners they just met at the dinner table. Some informants surmised that because people have to wear masks so much in their daily lives, it is extremely cathartic to do something unpretentious.

One Chinese business owner who split his time between China and Australia observed, "In Western culture, if someone wants to be healthy and recharge, they go to the gym or for a run outdoors to work out and get sweaty. But in China, the Chinese want somebody else to do the work for them, to help them relax and regenerate, and this is why these places are so popular."

Public Dancing

This Chinese form of entertainment and exercise is almost ubiquitous, and quite surprising! In Shanghai, if a person walks down the most popular commercial street, Nanjing Road, she will see all kinds of groups, males and females, dancing to various rhythms with great confidence. Everywhere in China, at 6 or 7 pm, many middle-aged or senior people will gather to dance in the squares, parks, and living communities; thirty-somethings might join the dancing as well. They perform several kinds of dances, including body jam and ballroom dancing. Except when it is raining or extremely cold, people dance in the streets almost every night. The picture (Figure 33.1) included here was taken around 8 pm in July 2013 on Shanghai's Nanjing Road. Almost 60 people danced on the square.

Two people who were approximately 50 years old led the dance. The other dancers were mostly female, except for three males. The music is usually pop with strong rhythms, and the dance movements are usually easy to follow.

Many Chinese citizens who have emigrated overseas have introduced this type of group dancing in other countries. However, the loud music associated with such activities is not always tolerated in other cultures. On July 27, 2013, New York police arrested a lead dancer for disturbing the peace with loud music during one

Figure 33.1 Public Dancing on Nanjing Road, Shanghai

of these public dances. Interestingly, this act created huge repercussions in China, causing some Chinese citizens to try to ban dances in certain locations at certain hours in their hometowns as well.

Midnight Snacks

The Chinese are famous for their passion about (and dedication to) food. In addition to three meals a day, the Chinese often eat "midnight snacks" after 10 pm. Midnight snack shops are often open from 10 pm to 2 am, sometimes even all night. A wide variety of snacks are available, from small seafood to big crabs, from baked kebabs to dumplings and wontons, from Chuan cuisine to Zhe cuisine. These diverse snacks, together with several bottles of beer, can create quite a nice meal. Many cities have street vendors who serve midnight snacks, costing from RMB 30 to 150 on average. While restaurants specializing in midnight snacks are obviously more expensive, customers enjoy a much better environment. The photo (Figure 33.2) included here was taken near Fudan University in Shanghai; the vendor sells a special type of cold noodles from Shanxi province that is quite popular among the students.

Activities Not Restricted to Evening: Teahouses, Chess and Card Rooms

Other evening activities are also available during the day. Two such examples are visiting teahouses and playing games in chess and card rooms. The first teahouse appeared during the Kaiyuan Era of the Tang Dynasty (713–741). Teahouses typically offer many varieties of tea and serve as popular meeting places for friends.

Figure 33.2 Midnight Snacks

212 Arts and Entertainment

Some teahouses serve various food items, and other teahouses offer various forms of entertainment. According to dianping.com, there were 1,125 pieces of information under the category of teahouses in Shanghai. For example, the average bill at *Breeze Teahouse*, which has 26 locations, is RMB 64 per person. There are seats in the hall and also private rooms provided for groups of people. In a private room, every customer is typically required to order a pot of tea. In the hall, there is a buffet for customers. Cards are sold at the establishment or can be brought in from the outside. Teahouses are popular gathering places for friends from different age groups.

According to dianping.com, there were 332 pieces of information under the category of chess and card room in Shanghai. Games such as Mahjong are played by four people. Games are very popular in China, regardless of age or gender. In towns without KTV, chess and card rooms are requisite. Scattered throughout local neighborhoods, they are great places for people to enjoy convenient entertainment. The cost of going to a chess and card room is similar to going to a teahouse, around RMB 50 per person. Employees at board game studios, which are particularly targeted to young people, help teach game rules. Many Chinese people also play cards and Mahjong in private homes instead of at commercial establishments.

Western Influence: Bars and Clubs

It should come as no surprise that as the influence of Western culture has increased, China has also adopted the concept of bars and nightclubs. In most cities, finding a good bar (usually associated with a restaurant or a hotel) is not difficult. As a

Figure 33.3 Teahouse in Shanghai.

matter of fact, in Shanghai alone, there are several excellent jazz bars and clubs. We visited one club near the Bund twice; the band that played during the first visit was from Boston, and the band that played during the second visit was from Cuba.

Road Ahead

There are several major differences between Chinese and American nightlife. First, a lot more people, across all social strata and age groups, participate in a wide variety of activities outside their homes in the evenings in China. Second, post-dinner activities are seen as ways to unwind from stress and establish and reaffirm friendships. Failing to participate in this aspect of social life can lead to being treated as an outsider in many circles. Third, many business deals are effectively sealed during some of the activities described here (especially KTV and massage); thus their importance cannot be overlooked. Looking ahead, we do not see much change in the near future.

Note

1 Dianping.com is the equivalent of the *Zagat Survey* in the United States. It was established in 2003 and is one of the largest consumer guide websites, with ratings for restaurants, KTV, shopping, etc. based on customer reviews. By June 2013, the website covered 4 million establishments in more than 300 cities with a total of 26 million consumer reviews.

Part VIII
Governing System

34 Political System
Governing as Partners

The structure of the Chinese political system is more like the partnership structure of a law firm, in which people at all levels participate in decisions, than a typical government or corporate structure. This style of governance is called collective leadership. At any given level of government, no one person can make a decision by himself or herself; rather, consensus or at least majority support is needed for major decisions. As in a law firm, each person in the collective leadership can make routine decisions related to his portfolio of responsibilities without consulting his peers. At the same time, every person is asked to participate in discussions and vote on major decisions concerning them, although the process of voting and decision making is typically kept secret.

At the central level, the core leaders are members of the Politburo Standing Committee, who essentially are chosen by the previous generation of leaders. At the next level (ministry of central government and provincial governments), the top branch is essentially determined by the people at the very top of the central government. This structure propagates down through the system; the collective leadership at any given level is always determined by the level above it. While there is a managing partner at each level, the managing partner cannot fire (or hire) a partner at the same level and typically cannot even reassign responsibilities among the same collective without consent from the level above (or the same collective if at the highest level).

Two interesting institutionalized mechanisms also ensure the operation of the collective. There is a strict age limit at each level. For example, for the Politburo Standing Committee, a person who is 67 or younger can be elected to the committee at the party conference (which is held every five years), but anyone who is 68 or older is automatically disqualified. The origin of the rule is unclear, but it was adopted in 2002 during the 16th National Congress of the Communist Party of China and is rumored to be the result of an internal power balance. Governors and party secretaries at the provincial level must step down at age 65. In addition, one is not allowed to serve more than two terms (each term is five years) in the same position, regardless of level. As a result, many people know when they have attained their final positions; like those who cannot run for reelection in the United States, these "lame ducks" are more willing to disagree with their colleagues within the same collective.

China has adopted this partnership system of governance largely because Mao Zedong, who had absolute authority, implemented disastrous economic and social policies, and purged officials at all levels at will. The collective leadership style

218   *Governing System*

implemented during the post-Mao era is meant to prevent, once and for all, a repeat of the same phenomenon. While the Communist Party of China (CPC) is the sole ruling party, the core belief is that a collective leadership structure at each level will ensure some degree of democratic decision making. In addition, a unique dual system of checks and balances exists in China, where every branch of government has both a party apparatus and an administrative apparatus, each headed by a different person.

In the rest of this chapter, we will describe the current generation of leaders who came to power in early 2013 and how the government operates at the provincial level and below. This is followed by a general description of the dual system (party and government) in China.

The Collective Leadership at the Highest Level: The Politburo Standing Committee

The Politburo Standing Committee is the de facto highest level decision-making body in China. Regardless of members' titles or agency affiliations, all important decisions are determined collectively by this committee. The number of committee members has always been odd to prevent voting deadlocks. On the current committee, there are seven members, although the most recent previous committees had nine. Depending on his age, a member knows whether he will serve as a one- or two-term member because once elected, a member is not removed from the committee.

The committee is elected during the CPC National Congress that is held every five years. While it is elected, in reality the list of people who enter the next committee is determined by complex negotiations of various power factions in the party, including various current or past members of the committee.

The incumbent Chinese leadership of the Politburo Standing Committee was elected in November 2012 during the first plenary session of the 18th National Congress of the Communist Party of China. The seven members, all male, are Xi Jinping, Li Keqiang, Zhang Dejiang, Yu Zhengsheng, Liu Yunshan, Wang Qishan, & Zhang Gaoli. Xi is the undisputed leader of this group, but each has his own portfolio of responsibilities. We list their key responsibilities within and outside the party in Table 34.1. Note that China released these names in order of seniority, even though they are technically equal. By default, the person who heads the Politburo Standing Committee during each generation is also the president of the state and head of the military.

Table 34.1 Members of the Politburo Standing Committee and Their Responsibilities

Name	Position within the Party	Position outside the Party	Function
Xi, Jinping	General Secretary of the CPC Central Committee, Chairman of the Central Military Commission	President, Chairman of the Central Military Commission People's Republic of China	Xi is the leader of the three most powerful organizations: party, military, and state.

Political System   219

Name	Position within the Party	Position outside the Party	Function
Li, Keqiang	Party Secretary of the State Council	Premier	Li is responsible for domestic policies, especially economic policies and implementation.
Zhang, Dejiang	Party Secretary of the National People's Congress (NPC) Standing Committee	Chairman of the 12th NPC Standing Committee	Zhang's position is similar to the Speaker of the Parliament in other countries (or the Speaker of the House in the United States Congress).
Yu, Zhengsheng	Party Secretary of the Chinese People's Political Consultative Conference (CPPCC)	Chairman of the CPPCC National Committee	The CPPCC[1] is responsible for facilitating multi-party cooperation under the leadership of the CPC for political consultation, democratic supervision, and participation in the discussion and management of state affairs.
Liu, Yunshan	First Secretary of the CPC Central Secretariat, President of the CPC Party School,[2] Chairman of the CPC Central Guidance Commission for Building Spiritual Civilization[3]		The Secretariat of the Central Committee is responsible for the daily work of CPC Central Committee.
Wang, Qishan	Secretary of the Central Commission for Discipline Inspection		The Central Commission for Discipline Inspection is equivalent to the Inspector General in the United States.
Zhang, Gaoli	Deputy Party Secretary of State Council	First Vice Premier	Supports the work of the Premier.

220 *Governing System*

Collective Leadership at Other Levels of Government

The structure of the Politburo Standing Committee is replicated at all branches and levels in China. The official name is called the Standing Committee of the Party at "X", where "X" can be a province, a city, a municipality, or even a government-owned company.

The chairman of the committee at a given level is the top leader. A governor, for example, is the number-two person and typically also has the title of vice chairman of the standing committee. Unlike the chairman at the highest level (Politburo), the chairmen at the lower levels of government do not have any control over the military, which is organized independent of the provinces.

There are also at least two caveats to this phenomenon. First, the lower the level of government, the more power the administrative leader has (be it a governmental agency or a company). This is obvious even in the universities in China. The president of a university is typically second in command to the party secretary, the deans control college-level affairs, and the party leadership does not get involved at all at the department level. The second caveat is that there is always tension between the party secretary and the number-two leader (i.e., governor, mayor, etc.). Unlike those on the Politburo Standing Committee, the power of the number-one and number-two leaders at lower levels also depend on support from the higher levels. Note there is really no technical difference between them, as one may move from a number-two administrative position to a number-one party position in a different place. Without exception, all people who hold number-two positions at the city level and above are CPC members.

We once asked how a firm should approach the government of a city to propose possible collaboration and investment. We were told that normally it would be the mayor. However, if the potential deal involved acquiring land in that city, the party secretary would be the final decision maker. In state-owned enterprises (SOEs), the CEO is technically the final decision maker. The party secretary of the largest SOE confirmed that this is indeed the case. In some cases, however, a party secretary may also serve as the chairman of the board, which would change the power balance.

During our research for this book, we also found that in autonomous regions (provincial or district), the number-two person in charge of the government is typically a member of a minority ethnic group from that region, but the number-one person (i.e., the party secretary) is always of Han ethnicity. This appears to be an open secret. It is important to note that ethnic minorities can be and are promoted (sometimes over their Han colleagues) to higher levels of government. However, they are not typically given number-one positions at any level.

Given recent progress related to women's rights in China, it is quite surprising to observe that most senior officials are men. Among the five generations of leadership since the founding of the PRC in 1949, not a single female has ever been elected to the Politburo Standing Committee. While none of our informants identified an explicit bias against women, there is also no systematic effort to nurture and promote women. In contrast, promoting younger leaders is an explicit goal at all levels. At a given level, for example, sometimes those with seniority will mandate that the collective leadership must include someone younger than a certain age.

The Ruling Political Party: Communist Party of China

The Communist Party of China (CPC) is the ruling political party in China, and the CPC Central Committee is the highest authority within the party, with about 350 members and alternates who are selected once every five years by the CPC National Congress. Members of the Politburo Standing Committee are elected by the CPC National Congress. Unlike political parties elsewhere, the CPC also has a Central Military Commission (CMC) that is the supreme military policy-making body.

At this point, the Central Commission for Discipline Inspection has substantial power. It plays the role of inspector general within the party and executes a system of discipline outside the legal infrastructure that is specific to party members. Since all leaders of the government are CPC members, this commission has tremendous power within the party. Investigations conducted by this commission are famously (or infamously) known as shuanggui. Literally, "shuanggui" means to ask a CPC member to come clean (confess) about potential wrongdoings at a specific time and location ("shuang" means double, and "gui" means specified). Many people told us that a government official's worst nightmare is to have someone from this commission knock on his door and tell him that he is now under shuanggui.

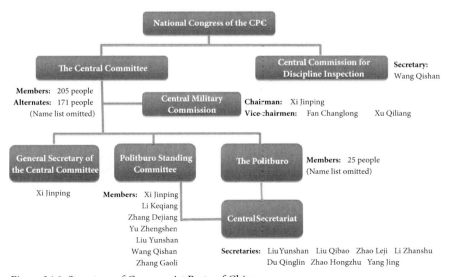

Figure 34.1 Structure of Communist Party of China.

The Government: Legislative, Executive, and Judicial Branches in China

The National People's Congress (NPC) is the highest national legislature in China. Similar to the lower house in a two-chamber parliament, NPC members are elected and are responsible for legislation. As the legislative body of the state, the NPC is empowered to name the President of the People's Republic of China, Premier of the State Council, and President of the Supreme People's Court. Since the judges (including the President of the Supreme People's Court) are not appointed for life, the legislative body essentially controls the judicial branch of government in China. While the premier is also named by the NPC, the premier is the number-two member of the Politburo Standing Committee. Therefore, the premier outranks the president of the NPC (who is also a member of the Politburo Standing Committee).

There is one additional branch of government in China called the Chinese People's Political Consultative Conference (CPPCC). CPPCC members are not elected and the body can be likened to the upper house in a two-chamber parliament. However, in China, the CPPCC is used to accommodate members of other political parties.

While members of the NPC and CPPCC carry very little real power, positions in both governmental bodies carry substantial prestige and are often highly sought after. Many successful business owners who interacted with us take tremendous pride in being members of the NPC and CPPCC, even if only at the city level.

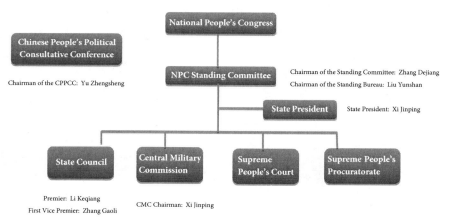

Figure 34.2 Structure of the government.

Road Ahead

It is hard to predict how the governing structure might change. Many signals indicate that Xi is assuming more responsibility and seemingly consolidating his power. Compared to his two predecessors, Xi differs in several ways. First, he represents the core of the Red Second Generation; his father was one of the founding fathers of the PRC. He feels much more comfortable making big decisions without worrying about being criticized by the left or right, or possibly making enemies within the party ranks. Second, as one informant described, as a member of the Red Second Generation, he feels he owns the "property rights to the PRC" and has a responsibility to see the rights held by the CPC forever. He has a much longer perspective and is thinking beyond the 10 years he will be in office. Third, China has reached a critical stage in its development. It has enjoyed astronomic economic growth; however, this growth has come at the expense of the environment and even social discontent. If he does not take drastic measures, he will not be able to sustain development. His immediate predecessor, Hu, governed on the principle of maintaining a harmonious society and often addressed symptoms, not the root problems. Now Xi must solve the underlying problems before progress can continue.

As a result, we believe Xi will gradually assume a much more prominent role in this generation of collective leadership. While we do not believe he will ever achieve the status of Mao or Deng, he is likely to have a much bigger say in how China will operate compared to two of his predecessors, Jiang & Hu.

Notes

1 Chinese People's Political Consultative Conference, retrieved January 2014 from http://www.china.org.cn/english/chuangye/55437.htm
2 The Party School of the CPC Central Committee was established as the CPC Central Committee's Marx School of Communism in Ruijin, Jiangxi, in 1933. It is the higher education institution that specifically trains officials for the Communist Party of China. The current president is Liu Yunshan.
3 The CPC Central Guidance Commission for Building Spiritual Civilization is a commission whose main duty is to supervise and inspect local departments to implement policies concerning the construction of spiritual civilization and help promote best practices.

35 The Legislative System
People's Congresses

It is stipulated in the Constitution of the People's Republic of China that "all power in the People's Republic of China belongs to the people. The mechanisms through which the people exercise state power are the National People's Congress (NPC) and the local People's Congresses." The People's Congresses exercise state power, and the National People's Congress is the supreme state power. Unlike the system in the United States, the NPC is at the apex of the political system, and the executive and judicial branches of government are subordinate to it. As discussed elsewhere, however, the NPC is under the leadership of Communist Party of China (CPC).

There are two layers of relationship between People's Congresses and other governmental organizations, People's Courts, and People's Procuratorates. First, according to the Constitution, "All administrative, judicial and procuratorial entities of the state are created by the People's Congresses to which they are responsible and under whose supervision they operate." People's Courts and People's Procuratorates are required to submit annual work reports to their corresponding People's Congresses. Second, they are relationships of decision and implementation: other state entities execute the laws, decisions, or regulations enacted by the NPC and local People's Congresses.

In China, representatives hold great status. Positions are sought after by many elites because it is a way to elevate status, not necessarily because they want to serve their constituents. Almost no representatives at any level (including the national level) serve full time, making it possible for anyone to potentially be a representative without affecting his or her personal life. Interestingly, many business owners want to be representatives—the higher level the better. The business people we met who were representatives (from county to national levels) all printed the information prominently on their business cards and made sure we knew about it within the first few minutes of being introduced.

In this chapter, we first provide a general description of People's Congresses before discussing challenges associated with selecting representatives for the NPC and executing power. We predict that People's Congresses will play a much more important role, albeit in specific domains, in the Road Ahead section.

Overview of People's Congresses

The election of deputies to a People's Congress is a bottom-up process. According to the principle of democratic centralism, voters can elect deputies at all levels

226   Governing System

through direct and indirect elections. Those deputies form the People's Congresses at all levels and execute state power. According to the third article of *Electoral Law*, "All citizens of the People's Republic of China who have reached the age of 18 have the right to vote and stand for election, regardless of ethnic background, race, sex, occupation, family background, religious belief, education level, property status or length of residence."

Direct election means deputies are elected by constituents at the level of cities (those not divided into districts), municipal districts, counties and autonomous counties, townships, ethnic minority townships, and towns. Here, we describe the process for a county level election to illustrate the basic direct election process.

1   The deputies in a county are elected for a term of 5 years.
2   The base number of deputies is 120, with one additional position for each additional 5,000 citizens in the county population.
3   Eligible voters are determined based on residence location.
4   All citizens of the People's Republic of China who have reached the age of 18 have the right to vote and stand for election.
5   Voter registration must be complete 21 to 25 days prior to the election.
6   Lists of voters are posted in a prominent public area 20 days prior to Election Day and must be displayed for 20 days.
7   Voter registration cards must be mailed to voters 5 days prior to Election Day; alternately, voters may obtain their voter registration cards by showing valid identification cards.[1]

Generally, the list of deputy candidates and their official information must be publicized five days prior to Election Day at the county level. Candidates use the time before Election Day to introduce themselves, deliver public speeches, and answer questions from their constituents. Candidates are allowed to post and distribute flyers, advertise through other media (e.g., TV or internet), and visit families. With prior approval, candidates also can arrange public speeches if they so desire. During their speeches, candidates usually focus on introducing themselves, describing their attitudes, and making promises. All campaign expenses are covered by the candidates personally, and all publicity and canvassing activities must stop on the day of the election.[2] Deputy candidates can be recommended (separately or jointly) by political parties and mass organizations, or by a minimum of 10 voters in a direct election. During a valid election, the number of candidates should exceed the number to be elected by 33% to 100%. The candidates who receive the majority of valid votes by secret ballot are elected.

According *Electoral Law*, indirect election is used to select representatives for the National People's Congress and the People's Congresses for provinces, autonomous regions, and municipalities reporting directly to the central government; cities that are divided into districts; and autonomous prefectures. As in direct elections, political parties and mass organizations may recommend candidates to be deputies, either jointly or separately. Candidates may also be recommended by 10 deputies in an indirect election. The number of candidates should exceed the number to be elected by 20% to 50%. The candidates who receive the majority of valid votes by secret ballot are elected.

Typically, the People's Congresses at each level meet once a year. The NPC traditionally meets during the last two weeks of the first quarter of the year. The Chinese People's Political Consultative Conference (CPPCC) meets almost at the same time; thus they are called the "Lianghui" in Chinese, literally the "two meetings," during which national level decisions are made. During the annual meeting, representatives vote on legislation as well as nominations for major posts in the government, judicial system, and prosecution system. This is also the time when representatives ask questions of various departmental representatives. According to Article 10 of the *Organizational Law of the National People's Congress*, "A delegation or a group of 30 or more deputies may submit to the National People's Congress bills or proposals that fall within the scope of its functions and powers." Deputies usually focus on matters concerning education, employment, medical care, housing, and social security. Article 74 in the Constitution states, "No deputy to the National People's Congress may be arrested or placed on criminal trial without the consent of the Presidium of the current session of the National People's Congress or, when the National People's Congress is not in session, without the consent of its Standing Committee."

Major Challenges Associated with Elections

There are two major challenges associated with elections. First, the government and party often have a large say in who becomes a candidate, either explicitly or implicitly, and thus have large sway in determining who will eventually be in the People's Congresses at all levels. Although the legal threshold for becoming a candidate is quite low (i.e., endorsement from only 10 voters), without the official sanction of the government, it would be rare for a candidate to win any direct election at the county level or above. This is something that is inherent to the system and we believe it is unlikely to change substantially in the near future.

The second challenge is both disheartening and encouraging—namely, buying votes. Based on publicly available data and discussions with our informants, the practice of buying votes is widespread in both direct and indirect elections. Despite the fact that direct elections normally involve many votes and it is hard to influence a substantial number of voters directly, some people have been able to pull it off. Candidates send money and/or cigarettes to constituents, invite voters to dinners, and engage in other illegal activities to bribe voters. In indirect elections, vote buying is taken to a whole new level. One widely reported case serves as an example. During the 1st session of the 14th People's Congress of Hengyang in Hunan province from December 28, 2012, to January 3, 2013, which was attended by a total of 527 deputies, 76 out of 93 candidates were elected as provincial deputies. It was eventually determined that 56 elected deputies had bought votes for a total of RMB 110 million. Bribes were given to 518 deputies at the city level and 68 staff members. All who were involved eventually lost their positions as provincial-level representatives, and the main government leaders at the time also lost their

228   *Governing System*

positions and were prosecuted. The encouraging point of this story is that this proves that votes count now in China and voters have at least some control over who wins elections.

Major Challenges Associated with the Execution of Power

While representatives technically have the power to legislate and monitor the operations of the government, judicial system, and prosecution system, at present, their real power is still limited. However, we have seen signs that government officials are starting to pay much closer attention to what their representatives say, especially those representing their districts in higher-level People's Congresses. If nothing else, they do not want representatives to say negative things about them because their bosses are representatives as well. In one medium-sized city we visited a few years ago, the vice mayor visited a business owner (usually it is the other way around) because the business owner was a representative in the NPC. Interestingly, the most prominent decoration at the entrance of this business owner's establishment was a life-sized photo in which he was one of a group of representatives talking to Hu Jingtao at the NPC. (Hu was the head of the leadership at that time.) In that sense, we have seen more derived power and influence among representatives.

As a legislative body, a People's Congress can examine and approve bills and proposals from representatives or other state entities. Most governmental proposals historically have been passed by the congresses, which, at one time, were ridiculed for rubber stamping such bills. But it seems as though the era of "a unanimous voice" is coming to an end. According to estimates in public reports, from 2000 to 2009, 28 standing committees of People's Congresses had failed to approve 46 proposals, including 17 at the county level, 8 at the city level, and 3 at the provincial level. Proposals and bills from governments, courts, and procuratorates were most likely to be rejected, followed by staff appointments and removals; amendments and modifications to laws and regulations were less likely to be vetoed.[3] On November 28, 2007, the 40th session of Shanghai's 12th People's Congress Standing Committee failed to pass the government's proposal to fix Shanghai's medical insurance system. The bill was rejected because it countered national regulations, the system was too complicated, and there was a lack of government funding.[4]

The quantity and quality of the bills proposed by representatives have increased in recent years. During the 1st session of 12th NPC on March 11, 2013, 40 bills were proposed. Li Bojun, head of the motion committee, said, "The quality of bills this year is the highest in recent years, in particular motions to improve and develop the people's livelihood, such as bills on water, environment, governance, protection of the atmosphere, protection of soil, and other resources." Some bills proposed by representatives have been adopted, such as school bus safety regulations proposed by a university professor.

People's Congresses also have executed their power to approve or remove government officials, although on a small scale. During the 2nd session of the 7th Hunan People's Congress in May 1989, 177 deputies were especially dissatisfied with Vice Governor Yang Huiquan, who refused to provide meaningful responses to their questions. They jointly proposed to recall Yang, who was dismissed with 506 votes in favor, 162 votes against, and 98 abstentions. This was a landmark case in the history of People's Congresses in China. Today, it is no longer rare for People's Congresses at local levels to reject nominations of government officials (but typically only for cabinet positions or below).

Road Ahead

There is no doubt in our minds that People's Congresses will play an increasingly important role in many aspects of life and society in China. Vote buying is usually a phenomenon associated with a democratic system, and with proper control, it will disappear in Chinese society (or at least become a minor issue). We also expect that representatives will become more professional in terms of how they draft and propose their bills, and focus on issues of national importance with actionable suggestions. In that sense, we believe they will become the driving force of at least a few key pieces of legislation in the years ahead, especially those related to economic development, environmental protection, and the lives of ordinary Chinese citizens. We also expect them to acquire substantial real power by exercising the power they already have on paper in terms of monitoring the behavior of government officials. China is closer than most people think to having a system in which any government official will lose sleep over the threat of a single representative filing a motion to remove him or her from office for incompetence or unlawful activities.

Notes

1 Chen Sixi (2003, October), "The procedure of the election of county and township People's Deputies," *China Democracy and Legal System Publication*, pp. 15–44.
2 Ibid., pp. 48–54.
3 Yang Zhanghuai, & Liu Chunrui (2009, October 12), "Change of rubber stamp image of the People's Congress," *Southern Daily*, retrieved January 2014 from http://china.nfdaily.cn/content/2009-10/12/content_5963685.htm
4 Yi Fei (2007, November 30), "We are progress: Shanghai deputy vetoed government's bill," retrieved January 2014 from http://news.xinhuanet.com/comments/2007-11/30/content_7167651.htm

36 Administrative System

The administrative system in China is analogous to the executive branch of the U.S. government but with a few major differences. First, the person at the top of the administrative system hierarchy in China, the Premier, is not the top leader in the country, nor is he the chief executive over all levels below him (e.g., governors, mayors, etc.). All officials in the administrative system are under the leadership of the party. As discussed in Chapter 34, governmental entities are run by a partnership, and the administrative leader is always the number-two person behind the party secretary for each administrative unit (whether a village or the nation). Second, the administrative system is vertically integrated with an organizational structure more similar to a for-profit company than to the executive branch in the United States in that respect.

In this chapter, we discuss the existing organizational structure of the administrative system and some of its origins. We follow with two sections discussing how the system operates from the perspectives of both officials and their constituents. In the Road Ahead section, we provide a brief discussion on what we think will change and what will not.

Organizational Structure

The administrative system in China essentially is organized like a firm. It is vertically integrated, with a strict chain of command that can be traced up all the way to the Premier. Despite variations in how government officials are hired and selected, higher officials in the hierarchy have more power, just as in firms. The government even has position training and rotation systems similar to those in large firms, where junior officials are rotated through different positions to gain experience and be evaluated. Even senior officials (including at the governor level) are rotated (e.g., promoted to head a different province). Unlike a firm, however, at each level, no single person has ultimate authority. As discussed in Chapter 34, in the Chinese government, there is a partnership-like arrangement within each level to ensure that a core group led by the party secretary and administrative head play the ultimate leadership role. All important decisions must be approved by this core group, typically by a majority.

There are 15 classes of civil servants in China, with Class 15 being the lowest and Class 1 being the highest. For example, the Premier is Class 1, a provincial governor or a minister in the central government are Class 3 or 4, and entry

232 Governing System

level staff can have ranks ranging from Class 15 up to Class 10, based on experience. Higher classes typically correspond to positions with more supervisory responsibilities.

Typically, civil servants obtain positions in one of three ways: election, appointment, and exam performance (non-supervisory positions only). In very rare cases, contractors may be hired for highly technical positions, but we will not discuss this selection method here. A small number of civil servants are democratically elected, typically for key positions in the government with substantial supervisory responsibilities (i.e., positions in higher classes). Typically, the core leaders are elected for all governmental entities (i.e., the Communist Party of China [CPC], People's Congress, administrative system, courts, prosecution, Chinese People's Political Consultative Conference [CPPCCC]). However, it should be noted that nominations for such positions are tightly controlled by the government. We are not aware of any candidates who run on their own initiative, at least at the county level or above. Many other government officials are appointed by their direct superiors. Typically, cabinet positions and below are appointed at every government level (from county to national government).

Another way to obtain a governmental position is to sit for a civil service exam. Such exams are open to the public and are based on the principles of equity and transparency; positions are offered based on exam performance. This system is derived from the Imperial Examination system, which was established in 605 during the Sui Dynasty and used as a selection tool until 1905. Those who scored well on the Imperial Exam would receive appointments to various governmental positions, all with substantial status and compensation. The best performers on the exam, which was based on the *Four Books and Five Classics*, the canons of Confucianism, received positions in the central government with the most power. As a result, this exam could instantly change the fortune of a person and his family, regardless of his prior social status or wealth.

One major difference today is that top performers on the civil service exam are only able to obtain non-supervisory positions and cannot instantly acquire

Chart 36.1 Civil Service Exams in the Last Decade

Year	Positions	Examinees	Recruits	Ratio
2013	12,901	11,17,000	20,839	54:1
2012	10,486	9,60,000	17,941	54:1
2011	9,763	9,02,000	15,290	59:1
2010	9,275	9,27,000	15,526	60:1
2009	7,556	7,75,000	13,566	57:1
2008	6,691	6,40,000	13,787	46:1
2007	6,361	5,35,000	12,724	42:1
2006	6,053	5,00,000	10,282	49:1
2005	5,456	2,90,000	8,371	35:1
2004	4,036	1,20,000	7,572	16:1
2003	6,400	87,609	5,475	16:1

Administrative System   233

high-ranking positions within the government. Current exams are also position-specific, unlike generic exams used in the past. Civil service exams have attracted many applicants since they were first introduced in the 1990s. We have included the preceding table with statistics related to civil service exams based on public data from 2003 through 2013.

Internal Operations

We once had a long conversation with a senior executive in the United States who worked for a Fortune 20 company. As we shared information about the internal operations of the Chinese government and American corporations, we couldn't help but laugh at the many similarities. Although it has a firm-like organizational structure, the administrative system in China has several unique characteristics. We discuss two here: efficiency and loyalty.

One of the biggest advantages of a vertically integrated firm-like system is its efficiency. If the CEO of a firm buys into an idea, it will be implemented. The same is true in the Chinese political system. A perfect example is the development of high-speed rail in China. Large-scale construction of high-speed railways began in 1999; today, China has the world's largest and fastest high-speed rail system, with trains traveling as fast as 200 km/h and a network covering 13,000 kilometers as of December 2013. According to current estimates, by the end of 2015, China will be operating 42 high-speed railways for passenger service on four vertical and four horizontal lines constituting the backbone of the national transportation network and covering more than 20,000 kilometers; by 2020, high-speed trains reaching 200 km/h will cover over 30,000 kilometers. This mind-boggling speed of development is probably only possible in China, thanks in large part to its firm-like organizational structure.

However, the long chain of command has disadvantages as well. Lower level governments may not immediately execute less urgent commands from higher levels and may sometimes delay or modify policies to their own advantage. As reported in an article in *China Youth Daily*, Zhang Baoqing, the former vice minister of the Ministry of Education said, "The biggest problem in China is the implementation of policies... Issues like student loans are ignored by the lower level governments. If such policies fail to be carried out, what else can we expect?"[1] This typically happens with policies that are not critical to the performance evaluations of the officials downstream. As in a firm, an executive will not necessarily implement a policy from above if it is not linked to key performance metrics. To be fair, we also heard a lot of government officials at provincial levels and below complain that some of the polices handed down by the central government disregard local contexts and therefore cannot be implemented, even though they may be well intended.

The second characteristic is the loyalty of government officials. In the United States, an appointed cabinet member may say "I serve at the pleasure of the president/governor/mayor," but the president/governor/mayor are all elected, so ultimately, public officials must care about the concerns of their constituents.

234   *Governing System*

In China, however, government officials at all levels mean that statement literally (with the possible exception of the seven members of the Politburo Standing Committee, who are selected by the previous generation of leaders). An official's sense of duty and loyalty, therefore, is always towards the people above him in the hierarchy, not the people below, nor his constituents. Many officials must adulate their superiors in order to ensure their continued employment in government. One self-proclaimed county official confessed on the internet: "We are blamed for our indifference to the people and flattery of superiors. It's true, though, we have to please and flatter our superiors because our whole careers and lives are in their hands. If we offend the people, we get, at most, a few hurting words. However, if we displease our superiors, we push our very careers to the edge." Therefore, a government official cares about the people he governs only to the extent that their satisfaction or dissatisfaction affects how he is evaluated by his superiors.

Like a professor who is evaluated by his students at the end of a course, some local Chinese governmental entities have now realigned incentives so that citizens' opinions will be considered, at least partially. For example, late in 2012, the performance reports of the directors of 27 departments in Wenzhou, Zhejiang province were broadcast on a live television program. After hearing the reports, relevant government members, media, and experts who were present gave feedback that accounted for 10% of the officials' annual appraisals.

The Constituents

In feudal China, the chief executive of a region (the present day equivalent of a province, city, or county) was called the "parent official." One positive connotation of this title was that an official should love his constituents as if they were his children. However, a negative connotation was that constituents should be completely obedient and respectful and exhibit filial piety, one of the Chinese core values. Thus, citizens were not of equal status, and officials certainly were not expected to "serve" their constituencies.

This view still persists today (minus the loving aspect), not only in the minds of officials, but also in the minds of the constituents. Ordinary Chinese citizens still believe that officials are wise and care about their constituents, and they trust officials more than laws. In particular, members of the general public strongly believe that higher level officials are always more competent than lower level officials. This has led to a unique phenomenon that has now been institutionalized in China: complaining to superiors. Complaining to superiors is a political way for people to lodge appeals and resolve problems with the direct help of a higher level government official. There is even a State Bureau for Letters and Calls (SBLC) under the General Office of the State Council that accepts civilian complaints about civil servants' dereliction, malfeasance, misdeeds, or criminal behavior.

Complaining to superiors has a long history in China. Beginning during the Sui Dynasty (581–619), Chinese citizens were granted the right to "petition the emperor." However, they first had to follow the chain of command to try to get their issues resolved. An issue was only escalated to the next rank if no resolution could be found. Problem escalation had to follow a strict order, from county, to prefecture, to province, and finally to the emperor himself, otherwise citizens would be punished. Today, instead of filing lawsuits and resolving disputes through the legal system, Chinese citizens typically complain to superiors in the administrative system to seek out justice. This has now become a major issue in China, and officials at lower levels of government resort to extreme measures to prevent their constituents from doing so, especially from complaining to officials in Beijing.

Road Ahead

The administrative system in China is a unique and critical component of Chinese society. As our informants told us, a business has no chance of succeeding in China unless it knows how to deal with government. (Not necessarily in the sense of bribing but more in terms of understanding how it operates so they may build relationships.) Looking into the future, we do not believe the system will undergo substantial change, as it has thus far served China well. Direct elections for top administrative positions are also highly unlikely

On the other hand, we do see the general public becoming more aware of their rights and status vis-à-vis government officials, and becoming more vocal. This also dovetails well with the current campaign on corruption. We predict that citizens' opinions will become more and more important in determining the career paths of government officials. In that respect, we think the administrative system will become more transparent, and officials will be held responsible by the various constituencies they serve. The evolution of the administrative system will depend on the evolution of the legal system in China. As the legal system becomes more mature and independent, we believe the practice of complaining to superiors will be abolished.

Note

1 Tan Xiongwei (2005, November 17), "Why central government decisions fail to be sent out from the Zhongnanhai Leadership Compound," *China Youth Daily*, retrieved November 2013 from http://zqb.cyol.com/content/2005-11/17/content_1204602.htm

37 The Legal System

During a recent trip to Beijing, we had dinner with some old friends, one of whom is a judge in the Supreme People's Court. When the conversation turned to the role of Supreme Court judges in China, she joked that the title sounds really impressive when she meets foreigners, but in reality, she is burdened with mostly minor cases and does not handle cases that are even remotely as important as those handled by the U.S. Supreme Court. To say the least, the legal system in China is unique and evolving. In this chapter, we first provide an overview of the legal system; then we discuss the court system within the legal system in China. Finally, we highlight key challenges currently facing the legal system and how it is evolving. In the Road Ahead section, we provide our assessment of the future of the legal system in China.

Overview of the Legal System

As discussed in Chapter 35, the Chinese political mechanism is the People's Congress, comprised of the National People's Congress (NPC) and the local People's Congresses, under the leadership of the CPC. Unlike the system in the United States, where the executive, judicial, and legislative branches are independent of each other, the Chinese system is a pyramid structure with the NPC at the top. The NPC controls three branches below it: the executive (or administrative) branch, the court system, and the prosecution system. In addition to the Premier, the NPC appoints the Presidents of the Supreme People's Court and the Supreme People's Procuratorate (the prosecutorial agency). Unlike the system in the United States, the prosecution system is on the same level as the court system and executive system and reports directly to the People's Congress.

In China, the legal system is comprised of three components: the police, the prosecution, and the courts. Some Chinese legal scholars call it an assembly line structure, where these three components are designed to divide responsibilities, collaborate, and monitor each other. In China, the police are considered to be part of the legal system, even though in other parts of the world the police are typically under the executive system at a different level from the prosecution and court systems. In most situations, the police have even more influence than either the courts or prosecutors in China. The main reason is because the police chief at any given level tends to hold a senior position in the executive branch, which outranks the chief justice or chief prosecutor at the same level. This was true for

238   *Governing System*

22 out of 31 provinces in August 2013. Another complication is that there is a Central Politics and Law Commission (CPLC) within the communist party at each level. Within the party structure, the head of the police, court, and prosecution all report to the head of the CPLC, who sometimes also serves as the head of the police. (This has changed since Xi took office; as of late 2013, only four provinces still had this structure.) Since in the Chinese political system, the head of the party is the number-one person at all levels, the CPLC is the de facto governing agency that all three components of the legal system must listen to.

While the three branches of the legal system are designed to work together, the relationship is not necessarily harmonious. One informant, a senior prosecutor in Shanghai, shared stories in which people from these three different branches worked with a somewhat "us versus them" mentality. The fact that court judges are peers with representatives of the other two branches instead being the final authority probably introduces unintended frictions.

The Court System

We discuss the court system first, as this system can be easily compared against foreign judicial systems, such as the one in the United States. According to Articles 123 and 126 of the Constitution, the People's Court is the entity that exercises judicial power independently, free from interference of administrative entities, social organizations, or individuals. The People's Court mainly tries civil cases, criminal cases, and administrative cases. Courts in China include the Supreme Court, local People's Courts at all levels and special People's Courts, in a four-level system with a maximum of two trials for any case. Specifically, the four levels are: primary courts on the district and county level, intermediate courts on the prefectural level, high courts on the provincial or autonomous region level, and the Supreme Court on the ministerial level. Generally speaking, cases of any kind can only be brought up once. Both parties can lodge an appeal against a first sentence, and the second sentence is considered the final judgment.

China's legal system has its roots in the civil law system. Unlike the common law system, the People's Jury[1] mechanism is applicable only in two scenarios: criminal, civil, and administrative cases with extensive social influence; and when defendants of criminal cases, plaintiffs, or defendants of civil cases, or plaintiffs of administrative cases request a people's jury during collegial panel[2] trials.

Those who may serve as people's jurors must: (a) support the Constitution of the PRC; (b) be at least 23 years old; (c) be well-behaved and impartial; and (d) be in good health. Though not explicitly stated, a juror also should have at least a college-level education. People's jurors form at least one-third of a collegial panel, which is subject to majority rule. However, most jurors are not in the legal profession and serve only part-time; therefore they tend to believe in the judge's authority. In this sense, the jury's role is quite limited. More cases have been utilizing jurors in recent years. During the first half of 2013, about 71.7% of first-trial cases included jurors, a 52% increase over 2006, according to the President of the Supreme People's Court.

The court has also become more transparent recently. The recent Bo Xilai case caused a great sensation in China. Bo Xilai, the former party chief of Chong-qing (?) Municipality was charged with accepting bribes, embezzlement, and abuse of power. Notably, the Jinan Intermediate People's Court in Shandong province provided real-time reports on its official Weibo feed, which is followed by hundreds of thousands of Chinese citizens. The transparency and openness of the trial was indeed unprecedented in China's judicial history.

Internal Investigation System for Party Members

In addition to the standard legal system, party members are subject to another system called shuanggui (mentioned in an earlier chapter). Exercised before judicial procedures, shuanggui is an internal measure that restricts personal freedom. It is also used to investigate party members for possible breach of discipline or law. To some extent, it can be likened to the internal affairs division of a police department in the United States. The word "shuanggui" means to ask someone to provide an explanation for his activities at a specified time and location. Shuanggui is proposed after a target group has been confirmed to have violated the rules and is approved by the Central Committee for Discipline Inspection. The officials under shuanggui are secured in a remote place under the 24-hour supervision of eight or nine staff members who work in shifts. In essence, these officials are cut off from the outside world and are suspended from exercising any power.

Another system, reeducation through labor, had been in existence since 1957. The government was empowered to arrest people for minor offenses and keep them in prison without a court decision for up to 4 years. However, the Chinese government decided to abolish the practice in November 2013.

Major Challenges in the Current Legal System

Many discussions in China center on major challenges currently faced by the legal system. All Chinese people, from members of the Politburo Standing Committee to ordinary citizens, want the legal system to serve justice in the best possible way. But there are three major challenges that must be addressed in order to improve this system.

The first challenge is structural. Currently, the courts must report both to superiors and peers in the power hierarchy. Since the president of the court at a given level is a member of the standing committee of the CPC, the party secretary at the same level has direct control over the court president. The governor and the president of the supreme court of a province are technically both appointed by the People's Congress in that province, but the governor is typically the second in command in the party's standing committee in the province and thus has substantial power over whether the president of the high court will even be nominated to the People's Congress at all. In addition, courts typically receive a large portion of their budgets from the government and are therefore financially beholden to the executive branch. As a result, a court at a given level typically is not independent

240 *Governing System*

of the executive branch at that level, even though on paper they should be. It is not unusual for someone who holds a high position in the executive branch to call, write, or pass along instructions to court judges in his district to influence case outcomes. Often, the court becomes another tool to protect the personal interests of powerful individuals.

In addition, the legal system is designed so that its three components, the police, the prosecution, and the courts, are tasked with monitoring each other, but sometimes it can go too far. In China, anyone who is responsible for a case in which a person is wrongly accused or penalized must be held responsible. Although well-intentioned, this policy can have disastrous implications. A seasoned partner at a law firm told us, "When dealing with such a case, the police shoulder responsibility if the case is not sued in the procuratorate. The police officers in question are punished or removed. Even worse, they may be punished falsely for charges they've brought upon others. If the court doesn't give a verdict after a case has been brought up [in the procuratorate], then the procurator is to blame. If a not guilty verdict is given during the second trial, then the [judge from the] first trial is to take the blame. As a result, it leads to the practice that if one step [in the legal system] is wrong, then the rest of the legal system will keep it that way [wrong]. Nobody wants to try to correct that wrong during the process, otherwise you will destroy [a peer in the legal system's] career or even life."

As described earlier, all three components of the legal system effectively report to the CPLC within the party system. A common practice of the CPLC is to coordinate the activities of the three components. Again, this is well-intended but completely hinders the independence of each component of the legal system. One of our informants lamented, "There are various good existing systems, but they seem distorted when put together. It is said that bad guys will change their ways under good systems while an inappropriate system will make one go awry."

The second challenge is organizational. The courts are run almost like firms in that lower ranking judges report to higher ranking judges. The higher ranking judges often supervise the work of lower ranking judges and make case decisions even when they have not been involved in, or present for, the actual litigation. This organization structure leads to a phenomenon often criticized within the Chinese legal ranks: the one who presides over courtroom litigation does not judge and the one who judges does not preside over courtroom litigation. This makes the actual courtroom litigation a sideshow instead of the mechanism that determines the outcome of a case. Another result of this "firm-like" organizational structure is that judges at higher levels tend to give orders to those at lower levels, and judges at lower levels have no choice but to execute them to the best of their ability. We once had a conversation with a city police chief in which he disclosed that they have an internal requirement to solve 98% of all death cases. One can only imagine what kinds of behaviors such "hard" objectives would lead to downstream.

The third challenge is behavioral, namely, corruption. Corruption seems to be widespread based on news reports and the fact that the new generation of Chinese leaders has made cleaning up the legal system its top priority. Legal corruption has become a flashpoint in Chinese society. A corrupted senior judge can refuse to accept a case, delay a case, suppress evidence and witnesses, and of course, rule in favor of a particular party. We once had a conversation with a CEO from a coastal province, and he told us about ongoing litigation with another company that refused to pay a debt it owed. To make sure his case went smoothly, he asked friends in his circle to help introduce him to one of the senior judges in the court where the case would be heard. After much wining and dining, the judge eventually came back to him and said, "I would love to help, but unfortunately, I found out that the defendant has connections at higher levels, and I really can't do anything for you now."

Some cases of interference in the courts by senior level government officials (almost certainly related to bribes) are borderline hilarious. We were told by an informant that once a vice governor intervened in a divorce case being processed in a remote area in his province. In another story circulated by insiders, an official in the central government gave contradictory instructions to a court on a particular case, one for the plaintiff and one for the defendant, within 15 days of each other. (The story includes the name of the person, but there is no way for us to verify, and thus we keep it anonymous. However, none of our informants who heard this story doubted its authenticity. Evidently, such things do happen, and with some frequency.)

In addition to these three major challenges, the legal system is also struggling to become an unbiased and law-abiding entity in society. It is still not a rare occurrence for those who are arrested to receive various harsh treatments in order to extract confessions. In addition, the presumption of guilt (discussed in Chapter 4) leads to disregard for defendants' rights. Both practices have been foundational in many dynasties over the last few thousand years, and it will take some time for the Chinese to change both their mindsets and their behaviors.

Road Ahead

A legal system is the foundation of a society, and Chinese society will not function well nor sustain itself unless a just legal system is in place. All Chinese people, from ordinary citizens to the new generation of leaders headed by Xi, understand this. We are very confident that major structural, organizational, and behavioral changes are on the horizon. Behavioral changes will be easiest to see, as they will be a tangible outcome of the current anti-corruption campaign in China. The Chinese will not want to step out of line during such a campaign; of course, it is yet to be seen whether new (hopefully ethical) behavior patterns will persist over the long term.

Structural changes are also being discussed in China. One possible scenario is that the lower tier court system will only report to the court above it, not to the executive branch in the same district. But this, of course will hurt many groups' vested interests. This is a hotly debated topic and a resolution has not yet been found, although some degree of separation is expected in the near future.

The hardest change from our perspective is organizational. It is much more difficult, and against the general practice of the CPC, to allow anyone to have

242 *Governing System*

independent powers. It would be a seismic shift to allow judges to rule on cases without the supervision of a higher ranking person. Thus, we do not expect any substantial organizational changes in the foreseeable future.

Notes

1 Decision of the Standing Committee of the National People's Congress on Improving the People's Jury System (Adopted at the 11th Meeting of the Standing Committee of the 10th National People's Congress, August 28, 2004), retrieved January 2014 from http://www.gov.cn/gongbao/content/2004/content_62980.htm
2 Criminal Procedure Law of the People's Republic of China, Article 147: "Trials of cases of first instance in the primary and intermediate People's Courts shall be conducted by a collegial panel composed of three judges or of judges and people's assessors totaling three. However, cases in which summary procedure is applied in the primary People's Courts may be tried by a single judge alone. When performing their functions in the People's Courts, the people's assessors shall enjoy equal rights with the judges."

38 Corruption

When the Chinese talk about corruption, many cite the following joke: "If you ask all the government officials to stand in a line, and arrest all of them for corruption, you probably will have wrongly accused someone. But if you arrest every other one, you will surely have missed some [corrupt officials]." We have, of course, no way to substantiate this claim, but given the publicly available data, stories from our informants, and the fact that the new leadership headed by President Xi is treating corruption as its utmost priority and an existential threat, we can safely say that corruption is a cancer in the political system in China that both the top leadership and the populace want to remove. A report released by the CPC in December 2013 stated that 108,000 officials were punished during the first 9 months of the year.[1]

In this chapter, we first describe the perfect storm enabling corruption in China. We then discuss the who, what, and why of this corruption. We conclude with a discussion of the national anti-corruption campaign. In the Road Ahead, we make an optimistic prediction that corruption will likely be substantially reduced in China in the coming years.

Perfect Storm

Three factors have contributed to the rampant corruption that currently exists in China: too much power, weak morals, and too little monitoring. Government officials in China have powers that could not be fathomed by an American politician. In China, the government owns many large companies and therefore controls their business relationships. During this stage of astronomic growth, the government has been overseeing many infrastructure development projects and determining who wins construction contracts. The government also purchases large quantities of products for its own use, just like every government in the world—except on a larger scale and with much less transparency. The government also owns all of the land, and officials decide how to divide it, who leases it, and for what purposes. Finally, government officials create economic policies that are either favorable or unfavorable to specific parties and decide whether particular projects will be supported in their jurisdictions. All of these powers can be potentially used to create or destroy wealth.

The second factor facilitating corruption in China is weak morals. As discussed in Chapter 20, the pursuit of wealth has become the dominant life objective of the Chinese people. Thus, the environment is perfect for those who have power

244 *Governing System*

because it may be exchanged for money. We once heard people in their thirties discussing the power–money exchange in society as if it were enshrined in the constitution, which is quite a scary thought. One senior executive stated to us, "Corruption cannot be avoided when power can be traded for money. Why do so many people want to become public servants? It is because of the abuse of power. I think the year of 2013 can be best described by the word 'corruption' based on the current status and the heated anti-corruption campaign."

Finally, there is not enough monitoring. As a matter of fact, the monitoring is so weak and perfunctory that accepting bribes in some government branches has become an open secret among all government officials. In 2007, Wang Chengming, former party secretary and CEO of Shanghai Electric Group, was sentenced to death with a 2-year reprieve for accepting enormous bribes in the form of public assets worth over RMB 300 million. Wang wrote a letter of remorse behind bars, stating, "My personal value lies in the power in my hand!" He concluded, "Since I was rarely monitored on my power, I finally became unscrupulous and took bribes for myself, relatives, and friends, which turns out to be undisputable proof that unsupervised power will definitely go awry."

Who

There are two major types of corruption: bribery among government officials at different levels and bribery between businessmen and government officials. Government officials who serve at lower levels of government may bribe officials above them in the political hierarchy in order to obtain personnel and project approvals. In many cases, a government official who wants to be promoted to a higher level or more powerful position must bribe the senior officials who have control or influence over who gets promoted. In these situations, bribes may be offered through third parties, usually business owners. In general, one will not promote an incompetent subordinate, even if that person is willing to bribe. Bribery only works when someone is on the borderline or is one among many qualified candidates for promotion. Sometimes lower level officials bribe higher officials to benefit the people they serve, not for personal gain. On August 8, 2013, Liu Tienan, former deputy director of the National Development and Reform Commission (NDRC), was reported to have abused his approval authority for major energy projects to yield profits for himself and his business-owner relatives totaling nearly RMB 150 million.[2] In addition, Hong Jinzhou, a deputy governor of Southeast Guizhou and mayor of Kaili City, offered over RMB 1 million in bribes to Liu Tienan for approval of a RMB 10 billion power plant project on December 3, 2012.[3]

The list of corruption cases between politicians and businessmen seems endless. For example, businessman Lai Hongzhong offered huge bribes to two consecutive heads of the Environmental Protection Administration. In 2003, Lai wanted to win a contract to manage the industrial waste treatment station affiliated with the Environmental Protection Bureau in the city of Dongguan. The well-connected Lai got to know Wu Zhanhui, head of the bureau who acquiesced after Lai promised to share half of the profit, totaling RMB 49.7 million. In addition, Yuan

Shaodong, who succeeded Wu as head of the bureau in March 2007, accepted bribes from Lai worth approximately RMB 7.5 million.[4]

In order to bribe an official, one needs to "find the right door." An official will never accept anything from someone he does not know well, and definitely not from a stranger. Officials first and foremost must protect themselves, and second, ensure that they actually want to help because they do not want to help incompetent people. The majority of corrupt officials want to strike a balance between taking bribes and fulfilling their official duties. In their minds, they can justify taking bribes if they believe the quality of the work will not be compromised (for example, when they allocate a piece of land to a specific developer). In most cases, each official is surrounded by one or a few trusted intermediaries who serve as a firewall of sorts by screening people who want to offer bribes.

What

In the early 1990s, people did not have the same access to material goods as they do today; therefore, bribes at that time were the likes of tobacco, alcohol, and electrical appliances. Toward the end of the 20th century, as the soaring economy vastly improved the quality of life in China, officials began to set their sights on cash rather than on real goods. In 2002, real estate was added to the list of highly sought after items along with watches, bags, antiques, and other small luxury items. Currently, real estate remains an important bribery mechanism. It is estimated that between 2000 and 2013, about 100 officials at the provincial and ministerial levels were removed from their positions for accepting bribes in the form of real estate.[5] Li Chuncheng, former deputy secretary of Sichuan province and alternate member of the Central Committee of the CPC, was the first provincial-level official to be ousted after the 18th National Congress of the CPC. He was implicated in the land sale for a large-scale real estate development project in Chengdu.

We heard several stories about real estate bribes. In one scheme, a government official may bring one or more business owners along on a trip to the United States (often on official government business), and he will take them to tour some residential developments. The government official may casually mention, "Oh, this house looks very nice," and one of the business owners will buy the house later, often registering it under a different person's name. Other times, bribes can take a very innocent form. One of our informants told us that a businessman once found out that the child of a government official was attending a university in the United States. The businessman told the official that he had a friend in that city who had a house and cars that were essentially going unused. So he said he would ask his friend if the official's child could live in that house and drive one of the cars. This provided a way for the official to accept the bribe, yet justify to himself (and others if need be) that no bribe was exchanged. In reality, the businessman had no such friend, but he found someone in the United States to buy a house and a nice car in that city.

Last but not least, sexual bribery is frequently exposed by the media or on the internet. This may take the form of paying for prostitution, philandering with

246 *Governing System*

willing young women, and as discussed in Chapter 17, paying for the expenses of supporting an affair. Sometimes sexual bribery can backfire badly. Lei Zhengfu, Secretary of Beibei District in Chongqing, was removed from his post on November 23, 2012, after his sex video clip went viral. In an alleged elaborate extortion scheme, an 18-year-old mistress hired by real estate developer Xiao Ye secretly filmed herself having sex with Lei, and Xiao used it to blackmail him for RMB 3 million and approval of a renovation and reconstruction project.

Why

There are many reasons why a public official may decide to accept bribes. First, the official may be seeking personal comfort. One official who was removed from his position confessed that he was trying to enjoy his life to make up for tough years in the past. Wang Yuexi, when serving as municipal party secretary, received bribes worth RMB 2.36 million and embezzled public funds worth over RMB 400,000 in exchange for favors granted by his authority. An intermediate court sentenced Wang to 12 years in prison. Wang offered an explanation for his behavior: "The city I served these years is in a period of rapid economic development, therefore it is home to lots of SOEs [state-owned enterprises] and private enterprises. Hoping to get the most out of my senior position, I finally accepted the bribes before my power expired. Especially when I underwent an operation in Beijing and then studied at the Party School of the CPC Central Committee during 2001 and 2002, these people found any chance possible to visit me and to offer bribes in return for promotions or good job opportunities for their children. The amount I took began snowballing from RMB 30,000 to RMB 100,000 with my growing appetite. Gradually I became addicted to the gains, which led me down into the abyss."[6]

In addition, peer pressure from higher level officials is intense. As taking bribes has become an open secret, if you do not follow suit, then you will probably become marginalized, as was the experience of Peng Yinbin. Peng's boss, the former head of the Beijing Local Taxation Bureau, asked him to help a friend whose decorating company was being prequalified for a bid. As requested, Peng recommended this company to the expert on the evaluation panel and thus led the company smoothly through the process. Later, the businessman gave Peng's boss RMB 490,000 in return for several projects the company received from the Bureau. According to Peng, he accepted the bribes because the businessman was a good friend of his boss, and he did not want to jeopardize his promotion.[7]

One of our informants felt similar pressure from his superior: "I served as an assistant to a project leader who came to Beijing to bid for a construction project. He thrust an envelope of money at me during lunch. I was dumbfounded and tried to turn it down. Unexpectedly, the leader patted me on the shoulder and said, 'Just relax, you newcomer. It is taken for granted here to leave an envelope. You don't want to be the exception, do you?'"

Bribes are also used to fund children's education. Education has always been a major concern among Chinese parents, especially government officials, who have high expectations for their kids and like to "keep up with the Joneses." In recent

Corruption   247

years, studying abroad has become a major trend, which imposes an additional financial burden that is impossible to cover on a normal average income. Liu Ketian, former vice governor of Liaoning province, took bribes worth over RMB 1.31 million for this purpose: "I just hate to lag behind when other children have been sent abroad to those famous universities. I always hoped to do better or the best for my children."[8]

A desire to live a comfortable life after retirement is another factor driving corruption. Dong Yongan, a senior official of the Transportation Department of Henan province, was accused of taking bribes worth RMB 25.83 million, EUR 40,000, HKD 100,000, and USD 10,000. He finally confessed, "I was very tempted by the benefits of a comfortable life after retirement and thus agreed. However, I cannot regret more of it now, for I can lead a happy life with my own pension, given the administrative level I hold."[9] Likewise, Yan Shunjun, deputy head of the Bureau of Environmental Protection, accepted RMB 864,000, USD 20,000, and EUR 4,000 in bribes just before his retirement in April 2008. He was sentenced to 11 years in prison.[10]

Another major driving force for corruption is immigration. "Naked officials" (discussed in Chapter 27), whose spouses and children all live abroad with foreign citizenship or permanent residency, try to amass great wealth (often illegally) before fleeing the country. A representative of the NPC angrily said, "When the time is ripe, they will take the huge wealth and join their families abroad. In fact, 'naked officials' are none other than fugitives. It was reported that from 1995 to 2005, 1.18 million spouses and children of officials settled abroad." Some of the most notorious include: Lan Pu, former vice mayor of Xiamen, who immigrated to Australia; Xu Guojun, former Kaiping sub-branch manager of Bank of China who escaped overseas with RMB 483 million; Luo Qingchang, former CEO of Yunnan Travel Group, who escaped abroad in August 1999; and Li Huabo, former official of the Bureau of Finance in Poyang county, suspected of embezzling RMB 94 million in public funds, who immigrated to Singapore with his family and acquired permanent residency.[11] According to research conducted by Chinese Academy of Social Sciences, about 18,000 corrupt officials have fled the country with RMB 800 billion since the late 1990s. Among them are officials and senior executives from SOEs or public institutions. The most popular destinations for corrupt officials are North America, Australia, and Southeast Asia.[12]

Keeping mistresses or concubines is another factor facilitating corruption. It is very expensive to support concubines or mistresses in China today. In some cases, concubines or mistresses even become partners in corruption. According to an ancient Chinese saying, "most corrupt officials are horny." This has never been truer (discussed in Chapter 17). Interestingly, concubines and mistresses have now been dubbed "the most effective anti-corruption force" by people on social media. Many have decided to go public with their lovers' secrets after being dumped. As part of the governmental crackdown on corruption, having an extramarital affair is now sufficient grounds for dismissal from a government post.

Finally, some corruption is driven by jealousy. Traditionally, businessmen comprised the lowest class of Chinese society. Based on our research, it is clear that

248   *Governing System*

many government officials still do not see people in private businesses (versus those working for government-owned businesses) as equals. When government officials see businesspeople making so much money so quickly and enjoying a lifestyle that they cannot afford, they naturally feel jealous. They think it is perfectly acceptable to get a cut from these businesspeople as long as they do not compromise their work.

Anti-Corruption Campaign

As President Xi stated on many occasions, corruption has now become an existential threat to the CPC and the government. According to a report from the Supreme People's Procuratorate on anti-corruption (its first since 1989), between January 2008 and August 2013, 151,350 cases of embezzlement and bribery had been filed for investigation and 198,781 people had been punished nationwide. Among the cases that had been tried in the people's court, 148,931 people (99.9%) were found guilty, including 13,368 who held positions above the county level, 1,029 at the prefecture level, and 32 above the provincial level. Losses of RMB 37.7 billion were recovered in the process.[13] From January to August 2013 alone, procuratorate branches nationwide investigated 22,617 cases of corruption and bribery involving 30,938 people, increases of 3.6% and 3.8% respectively, among which 18,283 (80.8%) were major crimes, up 5.7% from the previous year.[14]

Since the 18th National Congress of the CPC, the anti-corruption campaign has been gaining momentum. Qiu Xueqiang, the deputy procurator general, said that 2,569 national staff members above the county or division level were punished in 2012, including 179 at the prefecture level, and 5 above the provincial level. During the plenary session of the CPC's Central Commission for Discipline Inspection, President Xi Jinping said, "Corruption in any form must be eradicated regardless of the official post of the offenders." He emphasized, "Power should be restricted by a cage of regulations," and reiterated that "anti-corruption is a long term process." In June 2013, he once again expressed his disdain for ostentation, hedonism, and extravagance. Some notable disgraced officials above the provincial level include: Li Chuncheng, former deputy secretary of Sichuan Province; Liu Tienan, former deputy director of National Development and Reform Commission; Ji Jianye, former mayor of Nanjing; Ni Fake, former deputy governor of Anhui province; Jiang Jieming, former director of State-Owned Assets Supervision and Administration Commission; Yi Junqing, former director of Compilation and Translation Bureau of the CPC Central Committee; Guo Yongxiang, former chairman of Literature and Arts Association of Sichuan province; Wang Suyi, former member of the Standing Committee of the Inner Mongolia Autonomous Region and former minister of the United Front Work Department; Wang Yongchun & Li Hualin, former vice general managers of China National Petroleum Corporation; Liao Shaohua, former member of the Standing Committee of Guizhou province and municipal former party secretary of Zunyi; Chen Bokui, former chairman of Hubei Provincial Committee of the CPPCC; Zhou Zhenghong, former member of the Standing Committee of Guangdong and former minister of United Front

Work Department; and Li Daqiu, former vice chairman of CPPCC of the Guangxi Zhuang Autonomous Region.

Road Ahead

Despite current widespread corruption in China, we have a rather positive outlook for the future. There will always be officials who will accept bribes (including officials in the United States), but we see the scale of corruption in China decreasing substantially in the coming decade. The motivation is clear: the new leadership recognizes corruption as an existential threat, and unlike the two generations of leaders before him, Xi has absolute authority over all interest groups, including the military, because of his family's involvement in the founding of the PRC and his status as a member of the Red Second Generation. In a plan released in December 2013, the Communist Party of China (CPC) has vowed to eradicate corruption, or at least reduce it to a level eliciting public satisfaction within five years.

We also feel comfortable predicting that this goal can be accomplished. The Chinese often point to Hong Kong and Taiwan, which were previously corrupt and are now shining examples of clean governments. Achieving this may be a process of trial and error, and putting people in prison may not be sufficient. Punishment efforts may need to be coupled with substantial increases in compensation and benefits packages for government officials, including a way for government officials to accumulate wealth after they leave their posts (as in the United States) and potentially an amnesty program to remove some of the resistance.

Notes

1 Jiang Jie (2013, November 30), "108,000 officials were punished during the first 9 months of the year," *People's Daily*, retrieved January 2014 from http://fanfu.people.com.cn/n/2013/1130/c64371-23702284.html
2 Wang Xiuqiang (2013, August 15), "Liu Tienan gained over RMB 150 million in illegal income," *The 21st Century Business Herald*, retrieved January 2014 from http://www.21cbh.com/2013/8-15/2MNjUxXzc0MjM2MA.html
3 Jinghua.cn (2013, August 14), "Former mayor of Kaili under investigation on suspicion of involvement in Liu Tienan's case," *Jinghua Times*, retrieved January 2014 from http://epaper.jinghua.cn/html/2013-08/14/content_18328.htm
4 Liu Guannan (2013, December 11), "Giving RMB 57 million as bribes for two heads of the Environmental Protection Bureau," *Southern Daily*, retrieved January 2014 from http://epaper.nfdaily.cn/html/2013-12/11/content_7253968.htm
5 Liu Debing (2013, October 9), "Half of the downfall of about 100 officials since 2000 was related to real estate," *China Economic Weekly*, retrieved January 2014 from http://www.ceweekly.cn/2013/1008/65361.shtml
6 Guo Fengqing & Gao Shan (2008, January 19), "The downfall of Wang Yuexi: From a secretary selling red dates to one selling his pride as official," *China Youth Daily*, retrieved January 2014 from http://zqb.cyol.com/content/2008-01/19/content_2039146.htm
7 Li Haixia (2011, May 25), "Former vice director of Beijing Local Tax Bureau exposed the bidding and tendering scandals," *Beijing Evening News*, retrieved January 2014 from www.chinanews.com/fz/2011/05-25/3066778.shtml

250   *Governing System*

8 Li Mingyao, Tang Ying, & Fan Jifang (2006, December), "Corrupt officials receiving bribes to send children to study abroad," *Procuratorial Daily*, retrieved January 2014 from http://www.jcrb.com/n1/jcrb1151/ca570912.htm

9 Dahe.cn (2013, July 11), "Former Minister of Transportation talked about corruption—to lead a more comfortable life after retirement," *Dahe Daily*, retrieved January 2014 from http://newpaper.dahe.cn/hnsb/images/2013-07/12/A04/04.pdf

10 Chen Yijun (2009, August 28), "Deputy head of the Bureau of Environmental Protection stood trial," *Youth Daily*, retrieved January 2014 from http://www.why.com.cn/epublish/node4/node25760/node25764/userobject7ai191488.html

11 Zhang Yuan (2013, April 3), "Corrupt official fled to Singapore where he was sentenced to 15 months in prison," *Sina.com*, retrieved January 2014 from http://finance.sina.com.cn/column/international/20130403/122815043663.shtml

12 21cbh.com (2011, December 2), "Corrupt officials fled overseas with trillions of Chinese capital," *21st Century Online*, retrieved January 2014 from http://www.21cbh.com/HTML/2011-12-2/5MMTQ3XzM4NTI5MA.html

13 Cao Jianming (2013, October 23), "Report on Supreme People's Procuratorate," retrieved January 2014 from http://news.xinhuanet.com/politics/2013-10/23/c_125584259.htm?prolongation=1

14 Zhao Yang (2013, October 17), "18,283 cases of corruption under investigation by the procuratorate organs during the first 8 months this year," *Legal Daily*, retrieved January 2014 from http://www.legaldaily.com.cn/zfzz/content/2013-10/17/content_4941822.htm?node=53450

39 Social Thoughts

During the Cultural Revolution and until 1976, all Chinese citizens pinned decorative buttons to their outerwear exactly like political campaign buttons in the United States, typically with Chairman Mao's picture on them. Some buttons were made of ceramic, and some unfortunate souls went to prison after accidently dropping them on hard surfaces and breaking them. The political environment was, as some of our informants reflected, exactly like North Korea today.

China has come a long way since then. It is true that China still has a one party political system; however, criticizing and making fun of top leaders, and even spreading damaging unverified stories about their private lives are now popular activities on social media and around the dinner table, among both close friends and new acquaintances. Conversations about the governance of the CPC can also be very candid. Based on our observations, the Chinese feel comfortable talking about anything related to the political system with one exception: They do not talk about how one should go about actually replacing CPC as the governing party in China. This topic is taboo.

Unbeknownst to most people outside China, some conversations about the political system are not just outlets for complaining and venting but actually reflect several different political philosophies that are hotly debated in public, among both intellectuals and the general citizenry. The existence of distinct schools of political thought and public debate among them may come as a big surprise to many. In China, these schools of political thought are called social thoughts.

In this chapter, we provide a brief background on social thoughts, their unique characteristics, and examples of both "inside the system" and "outside the system" social thoughts in China. We conclude in the Road Ahead section by discussing where this will lead the Chinese.

A Brief History of Social Thoughts

To understand current social thoughts, one must go back in history to 1919, to the so-called May 4th Movement that began when college students protested against the Treaty of Versailles that gave Germans in Shandong province formal rights to Japan, even though China was on the winning side of the war. This was one of the most important events in China's contemporary history, as it marked a shift in the New Culture Movement (which began after the collapse of the feudal system in 1911 and lasted until the early 1920s) from the realm of culture to the realm of

252 *Governing System*

politics. Many different political ideas were introduced, revisited, discussed, and debated. Some people held on to Confucianism and variations of traditional Chinese thoughts on governance, and others adopted all types of Western political philosophies. Some advocated drastic change and the wholesale adoption of Western ideas (i.e., abandonment of all traditional Chinese ideas), and others preferred moderate adaptation to the outside world. The intellectuals of the time promoted the idea that the Chinese should only respect two "people," Mr. D. (democracy) and Mr. S. (science).

Today's social and political thoughts can all be traced back to that period, and these debates continue today in academic publications, blogs and social media, and around dinner tables. It is said that the Chinese began to think about how to transition from the feudal system to a world-class nation during the May 4th Movement. Nearly 100 years later, almost all Chinese agree they are still seeking the right way to make this transition. An observer must keep this in mind when she tries to understand China.

Overview and Characteristics of Social Thoughts in China

We describe three main characteristics of social thoughts in China: detachment from politics, problem orientation, and agreement on foreign political issues. Of course, other characteristics exist, but these three are rather salient points of comparison with the rest of the world.

First, social thoughts are not attached to specific political parties or movements. The fact that these schools of thought are called social thoughts in China instead of political philosophies or ideologies is indicative of their status in China. Unlike in other countries, there are no corresponding political movements or parties that espouse particular social thoughts. (The government imposes this constraint.) This does not mean that individual government officials do not lean towards particular social thoughts and even implement policies consistent with those ideas—they just do not openly claim to do so. Chinese citizens even label top leaders based on their leanings.

The second characteristic is that social thoughts are all oriented toward solving the most urgent social problems faced by the current members of Chinese society. As discussed in the previous section, this tendency likely originated from the "transition mindset" that has dominated China's political landscape since the May 4th Movement. The goal is to search for the best solution for China, while taking into consideration thousands years of Chinese culture. In Western nations, the transition to modern society was accomplished primarily by shifting governance responsibility from a few people (monarchs and religious leaders) to groups of people (publicly elected officials). However, for 2,000 years in China, the feudal system was governed by a philosophy: Confucianism. This makes the transition to modernity much more complex, and as a result, many Chinese still reject the idea of transplanting the Western political system into China. We suspect this is partially why social thoughts in China reflect more of a prescriptive approach to finding solutions to social challenges instead of a normative approach. (Of course, one may argue that communism is a normative approach, but few people in China discuss communism at all; at most, the Chinese debate variations of socialism, discussed in the next section.)

The third characteristic is that the Chinese tend to agree on many important political topics outside China. There is essentially no debate on topics that are important in most other countries, such as foreign policy (especially those related to territory disputes), gay rights, racism, or taxation.

An abundance of social thoughts currently exist in China, and we do not even attempt to mention all of them here. The purpose of this section is to show that they do exist and are characterized by stark differences covering the entire political spectrum of ideologies found in the United States or Europe.

Contemporary social thoughts in China can be traced back to three origins: socialism, capitalism, and Confucianism. The first two come from the West (many Chinese thinkers in the early 20th century admired France for being the birthplace of modern democratic ideologies) and the third is obviously homegrown. Social thoughts of Western origin can be further classified as liberal, socialist, and conservative. Since the Chinese have now effectively adopted many capitalistic ideas and rules, all are fair game in the current debate. The question is: What is the optimal mix for China?

To help readers better understand social thoughts, we classify them into two groups: those "inside the system" and those "outside the system." The Chinese use the phrase "inside the system" to refer to people who are either CPC members or government officials, or cadres in government-owned entities such as state-owned enterprises (SOEs) or even universities.[1]

"Inside the System" Social Thoughts

Social thoughts that are "inside the system" constitute topics of internal debate within the CPC. The dominant social thoughts that have been guiding major policies since 1978 were proposed by Deng Xiaoping: the so-called Socialist Market Economy with Chinese Characteristics, or the Deng Theory. (We use the term Deng Doctrine here, as the word "doctrine" is more indicative of his ideas.) The Deng Doctrine has three core components, often nicknamed the Cat Theory, the Stone Theory, and the No Quarrelling Theory. The Cat Theory refers to Deng's adoption of a well-known saying among farmers: "It doesn't matter whether it's a white cat or a black cat, whichever can catch the mouse is the good cat." The Cat Theory laid the foundation for China to open up to a market based economy after 1978 and ended the debate on whether adopting a market economy would equate to abandoning socialism. The Stone Theory is based on another popular saying in China: "You wade through an unfamiliar river by feeling where the river stones are." In essence, it means that one should dare to experiment and learn what works and what does not work as one goes, but without rushing. The No Quarrelling Theory is based on a speech Deng gave in 1992 in which he asked people to stop quarrelling about who is right, who is wrong, and who is more efficient; quarrelling complicates matters and wastes valuable time. The 30 years of modernization in China have been based largely on the Deng Doctrine. Many people, however, are now arguing about some of the negative ramifications of the doctrine, including the deterioration of the environment and destruction of traditional cultural sites.

Figure 39.1 Tourists outside Mausoleum of Mao Zedong.

While the Deng Doctrine is the official version of CPC ideology, there are at least two additional types of social thoughts in government these days: the Old Leftwing and the New Leftwing. Old Leftwing social thoughts are left over from the Mao era; proponents want to get rid of the market economy and insist on a pure socialistic society in which everything is black or white. New Leftwing social thoughts have their roots in both socialism and other left-leaning ideologies. Proponents oppose the market economy, capitalism, and globalization and generally regard the Cultural Revolution as positive. But unlike the Old Leftwing, the New Leftwing arguments are based on political philosophies often seen in the West as well. Some Chinese politicians are closet New Leftwingers and implement certain local policies that reflect their beliefs. However, in China, they must maintain superficial consistency with the party's overall philosophy, which is the Deng Doctrine. Before his meteoric fall in 2013, for example, Bo Xilai, a member of the Politburo and party secretary of the metropolis of Chongqing, had launched a "Sing Red" campaign requiring school children and business and government employees to sing songs from the Cultural Revolution era (mostly idolizing Mao). The fact that many citizens voluntarily and enthusiastically participated in the campaign is indicative that New Leftwing social thoughts are alive and well in China.

"Outside the System" Social Thoughts

The key representation of "outside the system" social thoughts is liberalism. People with liberal social thoughts in China support a constitution-based system and universal rights, among others. (Note that the term "liberalism" in China may not correspond exactly to the term used outside China.) The debate between New Leftwing

Social Thoughts   255

and liberal social thoughts dominated intellectual circles in the 1990s and repercussions are still being felt. The key differences between the two types of social thoughts are their attitudes toward globalization, the Cultural Revolution, and universal rights.

Social thoughts based on populism and nationalism also have emerged in China. Proponents of nationalism see the West as evil; they oppose globalization, and typically support a more militarily aggressive stance. Some have even suggested that nationalism in China has now acquired characteristics of statism. Populism has gained greater influence recently, largely due to easy access to various communication tools (discussed in the part of communication system). In China, populist social thoughts are based on opposing a substantial wealth gap in society and believing that commoners are the most important and smartest members of society. Interestingly, we have observed numerous examples of attacks on elites from populists on social media; many jokes are made at the elites' expense, although some observers note that populist opinions often are based on limited knowledge. Because of the power of masses, many elites do not dare to get into arguments with the populists. Social media and the internet have made it easier to sensationalize a popular topic and generalize based on an isolated incident.

Finally, we want to mention New Confucianism. Based on the doctrines of Confucianism, proponents of New Confucianism advocate for a society that is governed based on principles; some also advocate for democracy. New Confucianism has emerged against the backdrop of the re-emergence of GuoXue. "Guo" is the Chinese word for nation, but in this context, it refers to China only, and "Xue" refers to systematic knowledge. Narrowly interpreted, GuoXue refers to Confucianism; broadly interpreted, it refers to all knowledge developed throughout Chinese history. GuoXue is the hottest topic now in China among the wealthy, intellectuals, and government officials—basically all societal trendsetters. It is no surprise that New Confucianism is gaining traction.

Road Ahead

Looking into the future, we see the national policies being influenced by some of the sentiments underpinning these social thoughts, especially nationalism and populism. Both nationalist and populist social thoughts advocate more radical policies and actions, and this trend must be followed carefully by policy makers, both in Beijing and elsewhere.

We also see a trend that intellectuals are spending less time developing and debating social thoughts, and fewer are doing so. Interestingly, our informants told us that some intellectuals now are busy making money because they or their families need it, and they can easily monetize their elite status. After all, there are only 24 hours in a day. Of course, many other reasons have probably contributed to this ebb in social debate as well.

Note

1 Notably, university professors are generally not considered to be inside the system even though universities are owned by the government, but the deans and above are considered to be inside the system.

Part IX
Economic System

40   The Three Types of Chinese Companies

Like most countries, China has laws and regulations governing how one can set up, run, and dissolve a company. In almost all cases, these laws and regulations are similar if not identical to those in the United States. When we talk to executives and government officials in China, however, they typically differentiate companies based on their ownership: state-owned enterprises (SOEs), people-managed companies (PMCs), and foreign capital companies (FCCs). In this chapter, we first provide an overview of these three company types, including the sectors in which they operate. We then discuss the culture and management of each company type, followed by their unique opportunities and challenges. We conclude in the Road Ahead section that we see a convergence of SOEs and PMCs, and a diminished role of FCCs in the future.

Overview

An SOE is a company owned or controlled by either the central government or another level of government (e.g., provincial). During the 1950s, 1960s, and 1970s, all Chinese companies were SOEs and their operations were dictated by governmental objectives, typically to preserve and increase the value of government-owned assets, produce tax income for the government, and contribute a percentage of their net profit to the government. In addition to paying 8% of their profits in taxes, SOEs must hand over a portion of their post-tax profits to the state in the form of dividends. Dividends-to-earnings ratios generally range from 5% to 15%, depending on how profitable an industry is (10% for common industries, 15% for natural resource companies, 5% for military industries and research enterprises). Some are exempt from paying dividends to the government. However, this dividend rate is projected to increase based on current legislation drafts (i.e., by 2020, 30%). Taxes and dividends are used by the government to increase efficiency and control certain sectors that are critical to society.

The use of the term PMC is actually quite intriguing and telling. In fact, there is no legal definition for PMC in the official laws and regulations in China (e.g., *Company Law of the PRC, Sole Proprietorship Enterprise Law of the PRC, Partnership Enterprise Law of the PRC*, etc.). Nevertheless, PMC is the term popularly used by the general public, business executives, and government representatives, in both official and nonofficial media, to refer to anything that is not an SOE or FCC.

260   *Economic System*

Broadly interpreted, some Chinese scholars believe the term PMC includes all companies that are not owned by the government. In this sense, it includes both privately held companies and publicly traded companies. For privately held companies, it includes both those controlled and/or owned by an individual/family, called privately owned companies (POCs) in China, or those controlled by people from the same town, called a collective. It is mostly used, however, as a euphemism for POCs. In China, due to historical reasons, the term POC conveys negative connotations. As a result, investors, owners, managers, and employees of POCs, and policy makers who want to help bolster their development, prefer to use the term PMC instead. To move away from the sensitive issue of ownership, one should also note that PMC is a term based on how the companies are managed, not who owns the companies (unlike SOEs and FCCs).

All of the business owners we interacted with referred to themselves and their colleagues as "PMC entrepreneurs," even though they owned their companies. Nobody ever refers to himself as a privately-owned company entrepreneur. In their pursuit of respect and equality, some business owners are now asking for more (or less, in this case). One business owner told us, "I think it is discrimination to call us PMC entrepreneurs. Why can't others just call us entrepreneurs? Why do we have to differentiate the PMC entrepreneurs from the SOE entrepreneurs?" His point is well taken. This is not just a syntactical difference. Our informants told us PMC entrepreneurs are treated like the government's stepchildren.

Foreign capital companies (FCCs) are joint ventures between Chinese and foreign investors or foreign-owned companies established in China. (Note that this does not include foreign companies incorporated outside China with offices or operations in China.) There are three different forms of FCCs: Sino-foreign equity joint ventures (formed as limited liability companies, foreign partners must invest a minimum of 25%), Sino-foreign contractual joint ventures (flexible form, contract based), and wholly foreign-owned enterprises (all investments are made by foreign companies/individuals).

According to the *China Statistical Yearbook (2013),*[1] in 2012, there were a total of 343,769 enterprises nationwide, including 17,851 SOEs, 189,289 private enterprises, and 30,973 companies funded by foreign investors, among others. Though small in number, SOEs were large in scale. The SOEs accounted for 40.61% of total corporate assets, despite the fact that SOEs constituted just 5.19% of the total number of companies in China. In contrast, assets registered to FCCs accounted for 13.81% of the total but they constituted 9.01% of all companies. Although 55.06% of all companies were PMCs (which are generally small), the total assets registered to them stood at 19.85% of total corporate assets in China.

Sectors

SOEs are concentrated in sectors deemed to be important to the government, either exclusively or in competition against PMCs and FCCs. Based on the total assets reported in the *China Statistical Yearbook (2013),* the government's main focus lies on industries related to energy and manufacturing, such as the production and supply of electricity and heat, coal mining and washing, smelting and pressing of ferrous metals, automobile manufacturing, petroleum and natural gas extraction, raw chemical materials and chemical products manufacturing, etc.

In a narrow sense, central SOEs are non-financial sector companies, supervised and administered by the State-Owned Assets Supervision and Administration Commission of the State Council. By July 2013, there were 114 central SOEs in a variety of industries, including: electricity (10; e.g., State Grid Corporation of China, China Southern Power Grid), civil aviation (6; e.g., China National Aviation Holding Company, China Eastern Air Holding Company, China Southern Air Holding Company), energy (12; e.g., China National Nuclear Corporation, China Nuclear Engineering Corporation, China National Petroleum Corporation, China Petrochemical Corporation), iron and steel (4; e.g., ANSTEEL GROUP, Baosteel Group Corporation, Wuhan Iron & Steel Group Corp., Sinosteel Corporation), railways (7; e.g., China Railway Signal & Communication Corporation, China Railway Engineering Corporation), and telecommunications (3; China Telecommunications Corporation, China United Network Communications Group Co., Ltd., China Mobile Communications Corporation). In 2012, according to the State-Owned Assets Supervision and Administration Commission, total revenue generated by central SOEs was RMB 22.5 trillion, contributing a profit of RMB 130 million, a year-over-year increase of 2.7%.

According to statistics from the *2013 Report of the All-China Federation of Industry and Commerce on the Top 500 Private Enterprises,* 75% were distributed in eastern China while the remaining 25% were located in mid-western China. According to the *China Statistical Yearbook (2013),* a substantial number of PMCs are in the manufacturing sector and produce non-metallic mineral products, raw chemical materials and chemical products, electrical machinery and apparatuses, textiles, and food products, among others.

By law, there are sector restrictions for FCCs. Traditionally, they are prohibited from operating in the press, publishing, radio, television, and film; insurance; and mail and telecommunications. In addition, FCC operations are limited in public services, transportation, real estate, trust investment, and leases. However, the current generation of leaders is considering relaxing some of these restrictions. As described in the decisions[2] made during the 3rd Plenary Session of the 18th CPC Central Committee in 2013, "We will have the same laws and regulations on Chinese and foreign investment, and keep foreign investment policies stable, transparent and predictable. We will promote the orderly opening up of finance, education, culture, healthcare and other service sectors, lift limits on access for foreign investment in childcare, care for the elderly, architectural design, accounting and auditing, trade and logistics, electronic commerce and other such service sectors, and further liberalize general manufacturing."

Company Culture and Management

The culture and management styles of these three types of companies are very different. We were told by our informants who are senior executives or business

262   *Economic System*

owners (in the terminology used here, PMC entrepreneurs) that they can easily tell which type of company an executive is working for just by observing how he or she interacts with other people.

SOE executives behave as if they were government officials, and in a sense, they are. Given that the performance of a central SOE has no direct bearing on the appointment, promotion, or removal of managers, the leaders can rest easy as long as the enterprises do not break the law. So their behavior is quite similar to the behavior of government officials. On the positive side, SOEs are essentially part of a huge conglomerate in which managers and executives can acquire vast experience and learn from the best. They also have developed an institutionalized evaluation and promotion system, and executives all have experience on the frontlines. In addition, a formal rotation system is in place; one may be rotated not just within a large SOE but also across SOEs, as they are all owned by the government. SOEs also are able to attract the best talent from outside, even overseas. Almost all senior executives in SOEs tend to have strong technical backgrounds and at least a college degree. While a civil servant position in China is called an "iron rice bowl" because the income is stable and generous, a post in a central SOE is lauded as a "golden rice bowl" because the income is so high. NetEase, a leading Chinese internet technology company, conducted a survey of central SOEs and their listed subsidiaries which showed that annual average salary among 287 enterprises was RMB 111,357, up by 8.2% over the previous year, and 3.8 times that of private enterprises. Central SOEs in the financial industry topped the list, with an average salary of RMB 327,479, and Shanghai was the location with the highest average salary of RMB 179,992.[3] This is an extremely high average salary, considering a typical college graduate earns about RMB 6,000 per month.

PMC executives are different. The traditional Chinese focus is on creating personal wealth, bringing glory to ancestors, and passing that wealth and glory on to one's own children and ideally, the generations to come. Therefore, PMC executives typically focus on implementing whatever the owners want. It is also very difficult for an outsider to effectively manage such a company, as the family's interests always win out. (The phrase "blood is thicker than water" is very much believed and practiced.) After prompting, one business owner even told us that if his brother cheated him of money, he would be mad, but not that mad; after all, the money would have stayed in the family. Most PMCs are still run by people, not by an institutionalized system. Truly professional management is hard to achieve in such an environment. The best talent normally does not want to work for a PMC. Many PMC entrepreneurs do not have college degrees, yet they are also the most diligent students we have seen. They always are pursuing new knowledge, ideas, and ways to create wealth. In China, EMBA programs have become popular among many successful PMC entrepreneurs.

The company culture of an FCC generally reflects the culture of its respective foreign investors. FCCs can attract the best talent much more easily than PMCs. Most senior executives have acquired a high educational level and experience abroad. However, the "glass ceiling" for Chinese employees in FCC enterprises prohibits them from climbing the social ladder. Chinese employees typically find it difficult to get promoted once they reach the senior management level, which is usually headed by a foreign executive who may have been promoted directly from corporate headquarters. This trend, however, is changing. When we spoke to the CEOs of a few American companies (in the range of USD 5 billion in revenue), they seemed to be very adamant about promoting local people to run their operations in China.

Challenges

Each type of firm is now facing key challenges; we discuss a few major ones in this section. However, before we do, we want to highlight two common challenges for every firm in China. The first is navigating the gradual transition from low tech to imitation and finally to innovation in every sector. The second is figuring out how to sustain business operations without harming the environment.

For SOEs, one challenge is determining how to compete successfully in the market if the government decides to open a tightly controlled sector to PMCs and/or FCCs. Such a shift would require SOEs to operate in a manner more similar to for-profit entities (including raising dividends and reducing subsidies). The second challenge is how to integrate into the global economy. A third challenge centers on the motivation of the C-suite executives. As one of our informants put it, "High level SOE leaders feel less motivated, for they are usually appointed, promoted, and dismissed by the government, regardless of the SOE's performance." In general, given their dominant positions in each sector, they currently do not face substantial existential threats.

Many PMCs, on the other hand, face numerous existential threats. The most urgent challenge lies in diversifying away from manufacturing because labor costs are increasing in China (making the current model less competitive), and the post-90 generation is no longer willing to endure high intensity assembly line type jobs for long hours each day. The second challenge is associated with adopting a professional management style. Family-style management limits how large a PMC can become. The third challenge is figuring out how to address the less favorable business environment; however, this will require governmental intervention. Citing a survey of enterprise financial costs in Zhejiang province in 2012, the Chairman of the All-China Federation of Industry and Commerce said, "The average interest rate for small loans stood at 20%. In fact, private enterprises of a larger scale would have been wild for joy when loans were available at an interest rate of around 10%. But what about central SOEs? The average interest rate is a staggering 5.3%!"[4] Our informant further commented, "Banks are more likely to make loans to SOEs for the following reasons. First of all, abundant capital in SOEs ensures their ability-to-repay. Even if they fail to stay solvent, the lenders will not shoulder much responsibility, for SOEs are backed by the government and the money will remain under the government's control. However, that is not the case for private enterprises." Fourth, they need to wean themselves off the government market (i.e., purchases from the government). We have personally witnessed this mental model in action among some PMC entrepreneurs. In one visit to a PMC in

264   Economic System

Shanghai, the CEO asked the visiting group (us and several other successful PMC entrepreneurs) for suggestions to quickly increase the company's market share. The consensus from the visiting PMC entrepreneurs was to sell to the government. Finally, PMCs need to build credibility in the eyes of the government, consumers, and society in general. As we discuss in detail in Chapter 42, PMCs are the least trustworthy firms from the people's perspective by a huge margin. This needs to be remedied.

FCCs are currently faced with both challenges and opportunities. The first challenge is avoiding grey (or even illegal) operational practices in China. Such behavior will hurt not only their business in China but also their brands and operations globally. In July 2013, for example, GlaxoSmithKline senior executives in China were investigated for bribery. The second challenge is a waning advantage in China because favorable policies are expiring and domestic competitors are becoming more sophisticated. The *Law on Corporate Income Tax* was implemented in 2007, which unified the tax code for domestic companies and FCCs. Previous preferential tax treatment was gradually phased out over a five-year period, with the exception of high-tech enterprises or service enterprises with advanced technology. This move marked an end to 30 years of preferential tax policies in China for FCCs, which spurred enterprises such as Nestle & Bosch to establish R&D centers in China. Before, domestic enterprises were subject to a 33% tax, while their foreign counterparts paid only 15%. As of 2013, all enterprises were charged the same income tax of 25%. Domestic companies (SOEs and PMCs) also have gradually acquired both technology and management knowledge over the last 30 years, and they are now becoming formidable competitors to FCCs. Even more challenging, the Chinese government now has moved to protect and facilitate the growth of domestic companies, sometimes by restricting FCCs. Third, FCCs must now treat China as a sophisticated and major market, and conduct their business accordingly. Finally, FCCs now have an opportunity to enter new sectors, as indicated by the 2013 decisions of the 3rd Plenary Session of the 18th CPC Central Committee, and most importantly, the China (Shanghai) Pilot Free Trade Zone has been established, which is a major step toward foreign investment and cooperation.

Road Ahead

Chinese entrepreneurs, especially PMC entrepreneurs, are among the most driven entrepreneurs in the world. There is no doubt in our minds that they will play an increasingly larger role in China's economy in the near future. The negative perceptions associated with PMC entrepreneurs will gradually disappear as more PMCs move into innovation and technology (instead of manufacturing), and a new generation of PMCs is founded by people who are highly educated or have other high social status (e.g., senior executives from SOEs). As a result, the entire concept of PMC will likely disappear as well.

We also foresee a convergence of SOEs and PMCs as the government pushes SOEs to become more market-oriented and PMCs become larger and more professional. We also see FCCs treating China as a major innovation center because of talent, market, and favorable policies towards innovation. This trend has already begun and will only become bigger. Overall, however, we see FCCs playing a relatively smaller role in the future economy of China as the indigenous firms (SOEs and PMCs) mature. Foreign investment will continue, and even increase, but most likely will be from shareholders.

There is also a trend that everyone should note. SOEs and PMCs are on the brink of expanding to overseas markets on a scale that few people can imagine now. According to the Ministry of Commerce, in 2012, non-financial FDI made by Chinese investors amounted to USD 77.22 billion, covering 4,425 overseas enterprises in 141 nations and regions.[5] Some of these investments were made to acquire new technologies to better serve domestic markets in China; others were made to compete in attractive markets. In the coming years, North American consumers (especially those in the United States) will be exposed to many Chinese branded products (not just made-in-China products). In our view, it is a question of when—not whether—Chinese cars and smart phones, for example, will become legitimate options considered by American consumers.

Notes

1 *China Statistical Yearbook 2013*, compiled by the National Bureau of Statistics, retrieved January 2014, http://www.stats.gov.cn/tjsj/ndsj/2013/indexch.htm
2 For more information on "Building a New Open Economic System," see the English version of *Decision of the Central Committee of the Communist Party of China on Some Major Issues Concerning Comprehensively Deepening the Reform,* retrieved January 2014 from http://www.china.org.cn/china/third_plenary_session/2014-01/16/content_31212602_7.htm
3 Netease Financial (2012), "The 2012 report on the incomes of employees in central SOEs," retrieved January 2014 from http://money.163.com/special/wage_report2012/
4 SouthCn.com (2013, January 3), "Chairman of the National Federation: Profits of SOEs lower than interest on loans," *Southern Weekly,* retrieved January 2014 from http://finance.southcn.com/f/2013-01/04/content_61332753.htm
5 Ministry of Commerce (2012, January 31), Brief on the non-financial FDI of China in the Year of 2011, retrieved January 2014, http://www.mofcom.gov.cn/article/i/jyjl/m/201201/20120107943151.shtml

41   Business to Business

"B2B is one of the most important strategic focuses in expanding our market share in China," said Park JaeChun, director of Samsung Electronics China, to the Chinese media in January 2014. Samsung's B2B vision for China is based on the fact that the Chinese B2B market is the second largest in the world, accounting for 13% market share and maintaining an annual growth rate of 15%, compared to the 1.8% average growth rate for the rest of world. In this chapter, we first briefly describe the B2B market in China. We follow with discussions on two important types of B2B transactions: no-bid and open-bid. We conclude in the Road Ahead with predictions about how the B2B market will evolve.

Overview of the B2B Market

The B2B market in China looks very much like the B2B market in the United States. During the last 30 years, the B2B market in China has matured, the purchasing process has become much more professional, and most government purchasing activities have evolved to an open-bid format. E-commerce is booming, and with support from both the central and provincial governments, it will likely account for an even bigger share of the B2B market in China in the coming years. The central government even has a dedicated website[1] called the Central Government Procurement Center.

Unlike the United States, however, government purchases comprise a much larger proportion of the B2B market in China. As discussed in several places in this book, the Chinese government owns many large state-owned enterprises (SOEs). Currently, government agencies also are managing a nationwide construction boom, much of it centered on building complex infrastructure (e.g., high-speed rail) with the goal of matching (and even surpassing) the capacity of highly developed countries. Based on its sheer size, power, and assets, the Chinese government therefore generates huge demand for products and services.

On November 27, 2013, Liu Kun, deputy minister of the Ministry of Finance, summarized changes in government purchasing patterns over the previous decade: "The scope of procurement changes … expanded from general goods and services to specified and professional goods and services, and developed from meeting the needs of the government to [meeting the needs of] the public. The size of government procurement reached RMB 1.40 trillion in 2012, compared to RMB 100.9 billion in 2002." Thus, government purchases increased from 4.6%

268   *Economic System*

of annual expenditures to 11.1% over a single decade. A company that is serious about implementing a B2B strategy in China cannot ignore the government as a key target; in 2014, Samsung was planning to do just that. We focus the rest of our discussion in this chapter on the Chinese government as a key B2B market player.

No-Bid Business

Successful no-bid business deals in China center almost solely on relationships. A CEO of a large construction company told us he teaches his employees to remember that success depends on technical knowledge (20%), communication skills (40%), and the ability to seize opportunities (40%). He classified the second and third components as being part of emotional intelligence (EI) (also known as emotional quotient, or EQ). He added, "Doing business will be difficult if you don't become friends during the first interaction."

The concept of EQ is so popular in China these days that we heard people use it to evaluate (and in some cases compliment) others countless times. For example, one person made a comment about a recent college graduate who was very smart but not experienced in handling working relationships as having "high IQ, but low EQ." We also heard people introduce themselves by saying, "I don't have high IQ, but I have high EQ," as a subtle way to promote themselves without sounding like they were bragging. In China, it is no exaggeration to say that EQ is much more important than IQ, especially in the business world. We have met many informants whose secret to success is their EQ; they can anticipate a client's needs without explicitly being told. Our experiences in different contexts revealed that EQ/EI in China actually overlaps substantially with the concept of empathy.

As stated by the successful CEO, EQ is critical in no-bid business deals. (IQ, or business capability, is important as well, but to a lesser extent.) EQ can help a person fulfill two critical needs of a potential business customer: (1) the need to build and deepen relationships in circles; and (2) the need for interest exchange.

The need to build and deepen relationships in circles is essential and must be addressed. People prefer to deal with others who are (or could potentially be) in their circles instead of with abstract entities (i.e., companies). A dean at a major business school in China told us that he was engaged in a collaborative initiative with another business school simply because he trusts the dean at that school. Understanding this need is a perfectly legal (and even optimal) strategy in a society characterized by the presumption of untrustworthiness (discussed in Chapter 4).

Based on our research, there seem to be at least two important reasons for why building personal relationships is supremely important in the B2B context. First, dealing with a person who is either already in one's circle or has been introduced by a trusted person in one's circle reduces the chance of being cheated in the deal. After all, many informants told us that they often cannot trust their existing partners to pay on time or deliver the product after payment has been made. Many even sadly joked that they have to exchange money for products simultaneously. In a tightly connected circle, however, the cost of breaking a commitment is too high and thus substantially reduces such occurrences. At a dinner we once attended, one of the senior executives received a phone call, and he later told us that a friend had asked him whether he would be willing to vouch for another party in a business deal whom the senior executive also knew. Although all three men belonged to different circles, the friend told him, "If you tell me I can do a deal with him, I will." This is an example of how circles can be used in deal making.

Second, business deals are seen as opportunities to expand and solidify one's own circles. Typically, building relationships does not involve explicit business transactions. Rather, it is achieved through drinking and dinner parties, evening activities, and gifting (but not kickbacks in this context, and not linked to a deal), all of which are discussed elsewhere in the book The objective here is to increase one's personal value by strengthening connections in circles, which can be helpful in both personal and business activities later. One of our informants said, "The relationship between companies is actually the relationship between people. Doing business in China in many cases means establishing friendships before deals. Even if a deal fails, the friendship will assure potential chance of cooperation in the future. The worst outcome is failing to develop friendships before business deals." However, he did point out that as China has developed, capabilities have begun to matter more: "Though relationship still matters quite a lot more than other factors, things cannot work out without strong capabilities, which I think, is an improvement. It will be a win-win game when business is done with the person in your circle or introduced by your trusted friends."

The need for interest exchange can seem less innocent, but some requests that may seem unethical to Americans are perfectly legal in China because getting almost anything done requires favors in Chinese society. One type of interest exchange is to solve an (often personal) problem for one party in exchange for the deal. Here is one quite typical example we heard. A manager of an SOE was negotiating a financing loan business with a bank. Before signing the final contract, the bank executive proposed a dinner during which he asked the manager to find a position for his child in the SOE. Requests such as this are quite common in the business context.

However, such requests often cross the line into corruption. Requests for illegal kickbacks are quite common. One informant said, "We are the largest company in the field of semiconductor devices with a high reputation for high product quality and reasonable price. But for some reason our company could not get onto one company's designated supplier list. After careful research, we found out about kickbacks to the customer's personnel in key positions, which turned out to be why their prices were higher than ours! We are a publicly traded company and cannot provide illegal kickbacks, so eventually we found a distributor who got us onto their designated supplier list." Our research revealed that this company's strategy of finding an intermediary to circumvent the conflict between a "need" for kickbacks and strong corporate ethics is quite common. In extreme cases, a publicly traded company may even set up a separate small company for the explicit purpose of handling these types of transactions without involving the publicly traded company.

270 *Economic System*

Open-Bid Business

As economic and social development has progressed in China, many best practices from other countries have been adopted. Open-bidding for government projects (including SOEs) is one such example, and this practice has been used by non-SOE businesses in some situations as well. On January 1, 2000, the *Law of the People's Republic of China on Tenders and Bids* was introduced to increase efficiency, reduce cost, and eliminate corruption. A newer version of the law came into effect on February 1, 2012, *Implementing Regulations of Law on Tenders and Bids*. The law states that any project must have three more or bidders to be valid, and bids will be judged by a randomly selected panel from an expert database set up by relevant government agencies. It states that all major construction projects at the national or provincial levels must adopt the open-bid format. The open-bid format also must be used if the capital for the project comes from the government or from an SOE. There are three types of bids: project based (typically used for construction projects), service based, and material based (including both materials and equipment).

While open-bid is a great system in theory (and in practice elsewhere), participants must be aware that many open-bid projects in China are rigged. We discuss several typical (and illegal) collusion methods companies use to circumvent the original purpose of the open-bid system. There are two types of collusion in open-bidding: among bidders, and between a bidder and a buyer. Note that all of the behaviors described below are explicitly prohibited by Rule 39-41 in the 2012 law.

Collusion among bidders may take one or more of the following forms (which are not mutually exclusive): complementary bidding, bid suppression, and bid rotation. In complementary bidding, some bidders will coordinate bids so that one "real" bidder can win. The complementary bidders may, for example, all agree to bid substantially higher than the real bidder. In its simple form, others participate just to satisfy the requirement that an open-bid must have three bidders (in this case, the buyer may even be part of this collusion). In bid suppression, a bidder may entice other bidders to drop out of the bidding process. For example, as our informants explained to us, a bidder may arrive a few days early at a bidding city when the bids require personal presence, then they will seek out those other bidders and try to persuade them to drop out by offering them cash (or other benefits in the future). Given the competitive landscape, many potential bidders will take such offers and walk away, although typically only for small to medium projects. Finally, bid rotation is a more organized form of collusion, where different bidders take turns acting as complementary bidders in different open bids, or a winner agrees to share the project with others later.

Widespread collusion also exists between bidders and buyers. Sometimes collusion is motivated by personal gain (i.e., the buyer will receive a kickback from the bidder), but other times it is simply because the bidder and the buyer have other mutual business interests and they would like to keep the money in the "family." Since the buyer has access to all relevant information and makes the final decision, collusion in this format can take many forms. One commonly used format is to estimate the expected bid (called the baseline bid) in the open-bid specifications and decide internally that whoever bids closest will win. (Note that Chinese law encourages, but does not require, buyers to include an expected bid estimate and stipulates that buyers use the expected bid as a guideline, not as the only evaluation criterion.) Once this is set up, all the buyer needs to do is leak the expected bid to the bidder.[2]

In some cases, so-called white-black contracts (also called yin-yang contracts), are executed between the buyer and the bid winner. The white contract is public and legally binding. However, the buyer and the bidder also sign a secret black contract dictating how the project actually will be executed. This practice is especially common in construction projects.

There are also instances in which a bidder works with a buyer to set the parameters for a successful bid, thereby customizing the specifications so that his company is the only one that can win the bid. Sometimes a buyer must collude with a bidder because a bidder finds a senior government official (or agency) to back him whose request cannot be ignored by the buyer. Almost comically, sometimes bidders will compete to see who can find a bigger backer in the government. The worse sector for this type of collusion is land auction and construction. In one offhand comment, an informant told us that sometimes developers who are competing for a nice piece of land in the capital of his province must go and find a backer in Beijing (a senior official in the central government), otherwise they will not stand a chance. Sometimes a buyer will collude with a bidder by influencing the bid evaluation process, by either manipulating the evaluator selection process so that only those favoring a particular bid from the pool will be selected (even though the law dictates it must be randomly selected) or by requesting/bribing experts directly once they are selected.

Winning a bid is not the end of the process, however. Once a project is won, a company must continue to build relationships with the various government agencies that will issue relevant permits. Thus, the cycle continues.

Road Ahead

While we discussed many hidden obstacles in the B2B market in China, this by no means is meant to diminish its importance and attractiveness. Looking forward, we are fully confident that collusion in bidding will be substantially reduced. EQ, relationships, and circles, however, will continue to play a fundamental role in the B2B market. As one informant stated, although relationships alone are no longer enough, they will continue to be a required element of successful B2B deals.

Notes

1 www.zycg.gov.cn
2 Ren Xue & Zhao Chenxi (2011, June 3), "Unspoken rules in construction projects," *Legal Daily*, retrieved January 2014 from http://news.xinhuanet.com/politics/2011-06/03/c_121491893.htm

42 The Business to Consumer Market

With a consumer market of 1.4 billion people, China is a dream come true for many companies. As one business owner told us, "There are so many people out there, even if some of them just try [your product] once, you will do really well." Maybe precisely because of this mentality, many firms do not take consumers' long-term interests seriously and are solely interested in turning a profit as quickly as possible. This has created an environment in which firms employ any tactics imaginable (even unethical ones) to persuade consumers to buy their products while consumers constantly try to defend themselves against being cheated. This confrontational relationship based on mistrust is probably the most salient characteristic of the B2C market in China.

In this chapter, we first discuss how typical Chinese firms segment the B2C market in China. We then present two sections describing corporate and consumer perspectives on the market. We conclude in the Road Ahead section that we expect to see a resolution to this issue of mistrust in the coming years.

Segmenting the B2C Market by City

It would be futile to try to comprehensively describe every possible segmentation scheme for the Chinese B2C market in one section of a short chapter. The goal here is to introduce readers to one popular market segmentation scheme used by Chinese companies: a tier system based on city population. Rural populations are not classified as a separate segment since they have relatively low disposable incomes; in addition, the current central government is trying to incent the majority of rural residents to move to new and/or expanded towns and cities, and migration from rural to urban and suburban areas continues to increase.

Cities are important in China because there are so many, and each has a tremendous number of residents. The number of residents in a medium-sized city in China is similar to those of the largest cities in the United States or Europe. Based on statistics from the *Sixth National Population Census (2010)*, there are 87 cites in China with populations of more than 1 million. To put this in perspective, we provide a comparison with the populations of several major North American and European countries. The entire population of Canada (35 million) equals the combined populations of the two largest cities in China (Shanghai and Beijing). The populations of the United Kingdom and France, each between 63 and 65 million, are equivalent to the total population of the four largest cities in China.

274   *Economic System*

Even Germany's population of 80 million is only equivalent to the combined population of the six largest Chinese cities. The United States, with its population of 318 million, is the third most populous country in the world; yet the population equals the combined population of just the 100 largest cities in China.

This is a dream geographic distribution for any business interested in developing new markets and solidifying existing ones. The concentration of potential consumers in these cities facilitates efficient operations across all firm functions. Unlike other countries, in China, earning power and disposable incomes are highly correlated to city size; residents who live in larger cities (not just some, but almost all official residents) have the highest disposable incomes. In addition, preferences within the same city tend to be more similar than between different cities, due to subcultural differences and a desire to maintain parity with peers (both are issues discussed elsewhere in the book). This perfect combination of factors enables companies to develop sophisticated market segmentation and targeting strategies.

While people frequently discuss city tiers, classification schemes vary. The main differences are two-fold: the number of tiers (four or more) and which cities belong to which tier outside Tier 1 (almost all classification schemes agree on Tier 1 cities). In terms of criteria, some focus on administrative status (e.g., provincial capital) while others focus on economic dimensions (e.g., type of sector, ease of attracting talent). We describe a five-tier system here. Tier 1 generally includes four cities: Beijing, Shanghai, Guangzhou, and Shenzhen. Due to the proximity of Guangzhou and Shenzhen, sometimes they are combined, and Tier 1 is referred to the BSG. Tier 2 includes major cities not on par with BSG but clearly one step above the rest. Typically, Tier 2 includes capitals of some of the most well-developed provinces (e.g., Nanjing, Wuhan, Xi'an, Hangzhou, etc.) or large cities reporting directly to the central government instead of to provinces (e.g., Chongqing, Tianjin). Tier 3 includes most of the remaining provincial capitals and some large non-capital cities in well-developed provinces (e.g., Suzhou and Wuxi in Jiangsu province). Tier 4 includes well-developed cities below Tier 3, and Tier 5 includes the rest.

The central government is now embarking on an ambitious plan to incent the rural population to move to towns and cities by building and expanding existing cities. There are also discussions in policy circles about building a city-group model in China. In this sense, China already has 11 established city-groups, such as the Yangtze River Delta city-group around Shanghai, referring to over 30 cities in Shanghai, southern Jiangsu, eastern and northern Zhejiang. Currently, there are 14 de facto city-groups under development, such as those around Wuhan, and there are potentially 7 more city-groups to be developed in the future. It is said that by 2030 there will be 32 city-groups with 800 million residents (1.2 billion if people living around these city-groups are included).

Businesses in the B2C Market

The Analects of Confucius includes teachings about the relationship between money and morality: "Wealth and honors that one possesses in the midst of injustice are like floating clouds" (meaning that the pursuit of money itself is no reason for blame if morality is kept in mind; however, money can never be made through improper or unethical means). In today's market, however, many companies do not take this teaching seriously. Profit is the most important (and often only) metric. From this perspective, the best choices are those that lead to the highest profits in the shortest period of time. Countless unspoken trade practices exist that are meant to trick, cheat, exploit, and dupe customers. For instance, in the frozen seafood market in Beijing, each pack contains 20% seafood and 80% water.[1] Although exploitation is easily discovered and repels customers, large profits can still be made because there is a steady flow of new customers, and with them, revenue.

Meanwhile, honest companies are having a hard time. Cheating merchants defeat honest companies by charging lower prices and thus seduce more companies into cheating. One example is the use of melamine in milk powder. In order to cut costs and increase protein levels measured during quality tests, milk powder producers added melamine, an industrial raw material. As more and more companies got away with it, this practice became ubiquitous in the industry.

It is hard to imagine that the delicacies served in many restaurants are made with disgusting gutter oil, the production and distribution of which has now been industrialized. Refining one ton of gutter oil reclaimed from restaurant kitchen waste only costs about RMB 300. Producing a small barrel of gutter oil yields a profit of around RMB 80. One person can collect four barrels of gutter oil every day. After refinement, the oil can be sold for half the price of regular oil in the market, yielding over RMB 10,000 in profit per month, equal to the salary of a white-collar employee.[2] Lured by such high profits, many merchants have set up industrialized chains dedicated to gutter oil production. For example, between March 2010 and July 2011, Huikang Oil Co., Ltd., in Henan province sold 8,000 tons of gutter oil, valued at over RMB 64 million. It should be noted that while there are a handful of producers (eight major cases recently), the number of restaurants that buy gutter oil are numerous and widespread, and almost all know exactly what they are buying.

In order to prolong the freshness of enokitake (a type of mushroom), merchants in Fujian province brew them with industrial citric acid. When asked by a law enforcement official whether he would eat such a product, the owner of the company replied, "We never dare to eat our own products."[3] Similarly, vegetable producers also say they never eat vegetables from their greenhouses because of the excessive pesticide residues. Instead, they reserve a patch of ground to plant and grow vegetables for their own families. Furthermore, makers of quick-frozen dumplings do not care that they produce their food in an extremely unsanitary environment (i.e., they make dumplings while smoking) because they never eat the food.

Based on our research, it appears that many companies completely (and deliberately) disregard the welfare of their consumers. We even heard people in the food industry say, "As long as they don't die after eating my products, I am okay." A sad joke we heard from consumers is, "We cannot always go to the same restaurant to eat; we need to rotate our poison." The idea is that although no restaurant

276   *Economic System*

can be trusted, at least different restaurants will use different unsanitary (or toxic) materials, so by rotating among the restaurants, one will not be seriously poisoned by a specific toxic material.

Having said this, we also want to point out that many companies feel that Chinese consumers are unreasonably demanding. They want the best possible products at the lowest possible prices (ideally free), and they disregard corporate needs to stay profitable, which is unfair to companies. Some informants did not see the point of trying to treat consumers fairly because they will leave at the first sign of lower price from a competitor and will not trust that a business has done right by them anyway. Based on our own observations (some discussed below), this perception does have some truth to it.

How Consumers See Business

Historically, there is an ingrained bias against merchants. In ancient China, there were for four major social classes based on societal contributions (namely, scholars, farmers, artisans, and merchants, in descending order). Even during the Tang Dynasty, the most open-minded and prosperous age in Chinese history, merchants were treated with disdain. The low status of merchants is portrayed in a famous poem that every school child can recite, *A Lute of Jade,* by Po Chu-I, which laments the fact that when she became old, a popular singer, her face faded, and her life in decline, had to marry a merchant.

In today's China, people firmly believe the old saying, "If you do not have the ability to deceive, you cannot became a businessman, and vice versa." This means that honest men cannot afford to be businessmen, and thus all successful and thriving merchants must be shifty. Clearly, all the negative media coverage on unethical corporate practices further solidifies this impression.

From the consumers' perspective, companies are generally unethical and are making an obscene amount of money on everything they sell. While some companies may indeed engage in questionable practices and others may make a lot of profit, generalizing these characteristics to all businesses is, of course, erroneous. But perceptions are what count. As a result, consumers' general attitudes toward companies can be summarized as: (1) do not trust, and if one must buy, watch out for all possible ways that the firm can cheat you; and (2) get as much as possible for as little money as possible.

From a consumer perspective, merchants usually cheat, contaminate, bid up, or engage in false advertising. Never believe signs that say "Sale! Three days only!" because after three days, the prices will be the same and the signs will still be there. According to statistics from the China Consumers Association, 256,713 complaints were received during the first half of 2012 related to product quality (52.2%), after-sale service (11.1%), marketing contracts (10.9%), price disagreements (6.4%), false promotion (2.2%), safety (2.0%), contamination (1.4%), measurement (1.4%), and offenses to personal dignity (0.3%).[4] Food safety problems are the most alarming. A Google search for "food safety" on February 7, 2013, yielded 22.8 million results; that number increased to 32.5 million on July 11, 2013, just five months later.

Consumer attitudes have contributed to two phenomena. First, consumers do not believe that companies set fair prices, so they negotiate the price in every transaction. Knowing this, firms tend to price products at a much higher level, which further exacerbates consumers' suspicions. This self-fulfilling cycle contributes to some ridiculous prices in China. Second, customer service expectations are unrealistic in China. As a matter of fact, a real estate agent in the United States told us that her most demanding customers are originally from China. Such unruly customers are even more difficult to satisfy in the service industry, and Chinese servers are often reproached for negligence. In one example, a young man and two ladies dined for about 30 minutes and the young man called waiters for various services as many as 22 times for all types of requests.[5] Interestingly, during a dinner with a group of friends at a restaurant in Shanghai in 2013, we accidently overheard the manager commenting about us to her colleagues; she said, "These people are really polite." All we did was say thank you after they brought food to the table!

Extreme consumer suspicion about companies has led to a very unique purchasing habit: buy only from people you know. Instead of shopping in malls, Chinese people prefer to purchase commodities, especially big or valuable goods, through acquaintances or familiar channels, because such purchasing methods seem safer and more cost-effective. When quality problems are encountered, it is much easier to ask acquaintances for help than to deal with the frustration of terrible post-sale customer service provided by an anonymous merchant.

Road Ahead

As described above, there is a fundamental lack of trust between companies and consumers in China. Sadly, a negative and self-fulfilling cycle has been created. We, however, see this as a great market opportunity for firms that are willing to take the extra steps to demonstrate to their consumers that they are fair and trustworthy. We think this will happen in the coming years and that it will be facilitated by the government's current push to eliminate corruption and enforce business rules and regulations. China is a huge B2C market, and it is attractive not only because of its size and purchasing power but also because of the geographic concentrations of customers (who likely have similar preferences) that makes promoting and delivering products and services to them very efficient endeavors.

Notes

1 CCTV News (2013, November 13), "Sina Microblog," retrieved January 2014 from http://weibo.com/2656274875/AiuGNhqPz
2 Chongqing Electronic Evening News (2010, March 18), "Three million tons of gutter oil eaten in China every year: Ten years to completely prohibit," retrieved January 2014 from http://www.cqwb.com.cn/cqwb/html/2010-03/18/content_202272.htm
3 Shenzhen Evening News (2012, June 7), "35 tons of carcinogenic enokitake uncovered: Producers dare not eat their own products," retrieved January 2014 from http://shipin.people.com.cn/GB/18102639.html

4 China Consumers Association (2012, July 26), "Analysis on the customer associations' acceptances of complaints in the first half of year 2012," retrieved January 2014 from http://www.cca.org.cn/web/xfts/newsShow.jsp?id=58157

5 Chen Yinfeng & Peng Weiwei (2012, July 25), "Waiters encounter demanding customers: 22 times called for service in 30 minutes," *Changsha Evening News,* retrieved January 2014 from http://cswb.changsha.cn/html/2012-07/25/content_3_7.htm

43 Brands

To say brands are important in China is an understatement. Chinese consumers not only are willing to pay very high prices for products with high brand recognition but also are willing to pay only nominal prices for non-branded products. In this chapter, we discuss three reasons why the Chinese care so much about brand, which we follow with an illustrative analysis of preferred brands from different countries. We conclude by observing two issues related to the pricing of branded products. We discuss how the brand landscape will evolve in China in the coming years in the Road Ahead section.

Why the Chinese Care About Brand

In addition to conventional reasons why consumers buy branded products in general, the three most salient reasons why the Chinese buy branded products are: to show off, quality, and safety. According to published research, many people buy a particular brand because the brand reflects an aspect of their personality (e.g., honesty, competence, ruggedness, sophistication, sincerity). However, many Chinese consumers do not care about these aspects of brands; instead, they want brands to project wealth, or at least success in life. We discuss this in more detail in Chapter 44 on the growing obsession with owning expensive products in China.

The second reason is quality. While brands may indeed be used as quality indicators, this is not a critical factor influencing non-Chinese consumers' purchasing decisions. Product quality in the United States, for example, is generally quite good, making it less impactful as a point of differentiation. In China, however, product quality is generally much lower overall. Therefore, using brand recognition as a proxy for decent quality is an effective way for consumers to ensure that they are not wasting their money on subpar products (see our discussion about consumer mistrust in the previous chapter). This is important because companies now use quite sophisticated techniques to produce inferior products that typically look just as good as high quality products. We once bought a nice decorative jewelry box from a store in Shanghai that was labeled as solid redwood. It looked and felt like solid wood—until it was accidently dropped on a granite floor and we discovered it was made from composite wood. An umbrella we bought in Shanghai literally disintegrated during its first day of use. Such examples are the norm instead of the exception in many categories. However, branded products have a much better reputation in terms of quality.

280   *Economic System*

The third reason is safety. Food is the most critical (discussed elsewhere), but Chinese consumers also have safety concerns about other products. During a casual chat, one informant who had just finished building a house in a Shanghai suburb told us that they had to let the house sit empty for six months so all of the harmful elements in the construction and decorating materials could dissipate. A known brand gives consumers more confidence that the products will at least have no serious safety issues associated with them.

Brands by Country

In this section, we want to help our readers understand the role of brand by framing our discussion around manufacturing location. The Chinese are very conscious of the country origin of each brand and their purchasing decisions reflect this knowledge. Organizing brands in this way (rather than by product category) thus provides a more intuitive and informative way to discuss brands in China. Product brands and even stores are marketed based on where products are manufactured. We have come across stores that simply position all of their products as "Made in Australia." In extreme cases, some retail chains position themselves as selling only imported products.

According to the *Survey of Foreign Brand Favorability in 2012*[1] conducted by Global Network, 67.2% of Chinese respondents had favorable impressions of foreign brands. We first briefly discuss domestic brands before discussing foreign brands from the United States, Europe (i.e., Germany and France), and Asia (i.e., Japan and Korea) that have a significant presence in China and are highly valued by the Chinese.

Domestic brands in China have come a long way over the last 30 years; they do very well in capturing the middle market, somewhere between international brands and generic goods. Domestic brands are particularly successful in expanding markets in the Tier 3 or Tier 4 cities. Domestic manufacturers are also more attuned to government policies and Chinese customers' shifting preferences. Some of these brands are now able to command substantial prices. When we visited a sporting goods manufacturer, the owner told us that their athletic shoes retail for more than USD 50 a pair, more than what an American would pay for a typical pair of Nike shoes. Even in the durable product categories, some Chinese brands are doing well. In the LCD television industry, for example, domestic brands have increasingly shown potential and even advantages over foreign brands. During the first three quarters of 2012, the domestic LED television brands clearly had competitive advantages. Among them, Skyworth continued to rank first in sales with a market share of 17.4%; TCL ranked second with a market share of 16.9%; Hisense ranked third with a market share of 16.4%; and Changhong ranked fourth with a market share of 13.3%.[2] But Chinese car manufacturers still have a lot of catching up to do. In July 2012, 63% of Chinese car buyers chose foreign brands. As the EFE news agency reported, in January 2010, the domestic market share for Chinese branded cars was 49.2%; in 2012, that figure had dropped to 37%.[3]

American brands are doing very well in China. The most talked about international brand in China, for example, is Apple. In the eyes of Chinese consumers,

Figure 43.1 KFC.

brands from the United States are unique. According to statistics published by the *Wall Street Journal*, four of the top nine favorite American brands (i.e., Starbucks, KFC, Gillette, and Coca-Cola) are associated with fast moving consumption goods (FMCG); the rest are associated with durable goods (i.e., General Motors, Apple, Microsoft, Intel, and Nike).[4] American brands have also had substantial impact on Chinese culture, especially fast food brands such as KFC and McDonald's.

Demand for European brands is also high among Chinese consumers. To the Chinese, German brands represent superior engineering and high quality. Germany's rigorous work style assures Chinese consumers that German products will be high quality. An image of refinement and high quality is associated especially with German cars and appliances. According to the *Survey of Foreign Brand Favorability in 2012*, the top five favorite foreign car brands of respondents were BMW, Audi, Mercedes-Benz, Volkswagen, and Porsche; the ranking remained unchanged in 2013. Other well-known German brands that are popular with Chinese consumers include Siemens, Bosch, and Bayer. Given the recent contamination scandal in the domestic milk powder industry, many Chinese consumers have chosen to buy German brands instead. One person posted on the Tianya internet forum: "Milk powder in Germany, regardless of whether it is high-end, mid-range, or low-end, is tested by the EU and the German Drug Department, so we do not need to worry about safety and quality." In China, French products are famous for high quality, luxury, fashion, and elegance, especially the top luxury brands. Young people especially covet Chanel, Hermès, Chloé, Céline, Dior, Cartier, and

282 Economic System

LVMH products. In addition, French wine (e.g., Pernod Picard, Petrus, Lafite) and restaurants are well regarded.

Brands from Asian manufacturers also sell well in the Chinese market. However, preferences for Japanese brands are highly influenced by Sino-Japanese political relations. For instance, during the second half of 2012, after the dispute over Diaoyu Island escalated, Japanese brands suffered immediately. Interestingly (and quite unthinkable to Americans), top-selling Japanese cars (i.e., Toyota, Honda, Hyundai, Nissan, and Mitsubishi) do not sell well in China, according to the *Survey of Foreign Brand Favorability in 2012*. However, Japanese cosmetic brands such as Kosé, Shiseido, DHC, and Shu Uemura have been generally well received by Chinese consumers (except during the second half of 2012). Data on cosmetic imports in China from January to April 2013 showed that the total value of cosmetic imports from Japan fell 17.4% compared with the same period in 2012, while imports from the European Union, the United States, and South Korea showed steady growth.[5] Korean brands, especially Samsung, are also ubiquitous in China. Many Chinese see Korean brands as innovative and stylish. Korean sitcoms and movies are also widely popular.

Chinese consumers differentiate products based on where they are manufactured, even within a brand. When the Chinese buy clothes, for example, many will check garment labels to see where pieces were manufactured, unlike most of their American counterparts. This is due to the fact that many international companies have built factories in China specifically to produce inferior products for the domestic market. On October 24, 2012, Nike, Inc., received a fine of RMB 4.87 million due to this double standard towards Chinese customers, the first ever fine levied against a corporation by China's Ministry of Commerce and Industry. Nike Zoom Hyperdunk 2011 basketball shoes were produced in China and sold for RMB 1,299 (approximately USD 215), while in the United States, a higher quality version of the same product sold for USD 125.[6]

Prices

Taking a closer look at branded products in China, we can make two major observations. First, branded products, both domestic and foreign, are very expensive in both absolute and relative terms (compared to non-branded products). Second, the same international brands are much more expensive in China than outside China.

For many Chinese people, price is the most critical measure of the quality of a commodity. The Chinese know that manufacturing high quality products costs more; therefore, it is hard to convince a Chinese consumer that a product with a low price has high quality. Thus, top brands are "forced" to price their products higher, as few people will buy the products if they are priced reasonably. Take, for example, a domestic brand product: the Erdos cashmere sweater. The market price for a typical crew neck sweater made of 100% cashmere costs over RMB 1,000 after a 50% discount. For many, it would be unthinkable that a sweater made from 100% cashmere could cost less. In addition, a dress by the Chinese brand Elegant

Prosper costs more than RMB 1,000. Although such a dress (fabric composition: 95.8% viscose fiber plus 4.2% spandex; inside material component: 100% polyester) is well designed and the brand has a good reputation, the price is exorbitant for a single piece of clothing. According to China's National Bureau of Statistics, the per capita income of all urban residents in 2012 was RMB 26,969, and per capita disposable income was RMB 24,565.[7] In other words, the per capita monthly disposable income of an urban resident is about RMB 2,000. Therefore, if a Chinese consumer wants to buy a branded cashmere sweater or dress, it will cost half of her monthly income. On the other hand, non-branded, but otherwise similar pieces of clothing can be purchased for RMB 200 to 300.

The second observation is that prices for the same product are almost always substantially more expensive in China than elsewhere. This is as true for luxury products as it is for ordinary product categories like jeans. Levi's jeans produced in Dongguan, Guangdong province cost about USD 30 on Amazon.com, but in China, they sell for the equivalent of USD 150. Products in China (which are often inferior in quality) cost about five times more than the same products in the United States. This discrepancy in prices has motivated many Chinese citizens to embark on global shopping trips, a phenomenon we discuss in the next chapter.

Road Ahead

We make two predictions related to brands in China. First, we believe domestic brands will be more competitive relative to international brands, and some of them will even break out of the middle market into the upper market. Relatedly, we also foresee Chinese brands gradually entering the North American and European markets. When a Chinese brand becomes successful elsewhere (e.g., in the United States), Chinese consumers will begin to treat it as an elite brand. The second prediction is related to price. As the mistrust between consumers and companies decreases and the government enforces minimum quality and safety standards, we expect the prices of branded products to decrease and the prices of non-branded products to increase.

Notes

1 Global Times (2012, March 15), "Survey of Foreign Brand Favorability in 2012," retrieved January 2014 from http://world.huanqiu.com/roll/2012-03/2525881.html

2 Ma Weiyi (2013, February 17), "Analysis of China TV market in 2012," *CCID Consulting, China Business Network*, retrieved January 2014 from http://www.cb.com.cn/info/2013_0217/446684.html

3 XinhuaNet.com (2012, August 28), "Dispatches from foreign news agency: Foreign car brands that Chinese consumers increasingly prefer," retrieved January 2014 from http://news.xinhuanet.com/cankao/2012-08/28/c_131813211.html

4 Wall Street Journal Online (2013, May 28), "Chinese people's favorite nine American brands," retrieved January 2014 from http://cn.wsj.com/gb/20130528/PHO103255.asp?source=UpFeature

284   *Economic System*

5 Zhao Xinxing (2013, June 21), "Market share of Japanese cosmetics decreased drastically," *Southern Daily,* retrieved January 2014 from http://epaper.nfdaily.cn/html/2013-06/21/content_7199726.htm

6 Xiao Dan (2012, October 25), "Double standard of Nike," *Beijing Morning Post*, retrieved January 2014 from http://bjcb.morningpost.com.cn/html/2012-10/25/content_190712.htm

7 National Bureau of Statistics (2013, February 22), "The People's Republic of China national economic and social development statistical bulletin in 2012," retrieved January 2014 from http://news.xinhuanet.com/politics/2013-02/23/c_114772758.htm

44 Pursuit of Expensive Products

During a trip to Urumqi, the capital of the Xinjiang Uyghur Autonomous Region, we bought a painting by a local artist. Upon seeing the painting, the first sentence out of the mouth of a business owner who was part of our group was, "How much was it?" When we told him the price we paid, he instantly lost interest in the painting; evidently, it was too cheap to catch his interest. Asking how much people have paid for a product they own, either directly or indirectly, is a common practice in China. The more expensive it is, the more impressive it is. While the Chinese are often characterized as being obsessed with luxury products, we feel it is more appropriate to say that they engage in the relentless pursuit of *expensive* products.

In this chapter, we briefly discuss why Chinese consumers are much more interested in purchasing expensive products than people from other countries, such as Americans. We then discuss how the Chinese can afford these expensive products when their average income is much lower than that of Americans. Finally, we discuss two ramifications associated with this pursuit: overseas shopping and fake products. In the Road Ahead, we predict this trend will continue, however, probably with more emphasis on personal tastes.

Why

The Chinese surround themselves with expensive products both because they want to and because they feel they have to. As we discussed in Chapter 20, the pursuit of wealth has become the life objective of the majority in Chinese society. How can others tell whether a person has succeeded? Often, people manifest their financial success by purchasing expensive products. Expensive material goods may be purchased to create a sense of self-satisfaction or to earn the respect of others. Most people do not directly derive pleasure from owning and using some of the most expensive products; rather, tremendous satisfaction and pleasure are derived indirectly, when other people are envious. In one story circulated on the internet, a group of netizens uploaded photos to an online forum to flaunt their wealth. The one who initiated the competition posted photos of expensive watches such as Rolexes. Many followed with pictures of themselves sitting in expensive cars manufactured by Mercedes-Benz, BMW, Ferrari, Audi, Lamborghini, and Bentley. Others showed off diamonds, bank balances, and "proof of power," in the form of, for example, a mining license. Before long, some "big gun" laid out two dozen house property ownership certificates as well as use permits and

286   *Economic System*

records for state-owned land. All of the other netizens were instantly humbled and acknowledged that this guy was undoubtedly the wealthiest and most powerful. The contest thus came to an end.

Chinese consumers also buy and use expensive products because they feel they have to. For instance, in China, one's outfit makes all the difference. People make judgments about social status and wealth based on a person's clothes, handbag, and car. For instance, a real estate salesperson would evaluate your outfit to determine whether you can afford a residence. If his conclusion is negative, you are likely to be disregarded. Even in regular social interactions, people pay close attention to such things. Some professional women are secretly competing with one another over financial status rather than work performance. Many are well-versed in various luxury brands and strive to own the most expensive leather handbag among colleagues.

The CEO of a medium-sized American company told us a story that highlights an interesting difference between the Chinese and Americans in terms of what they infer about people who own expensive goods. The CEO had contracted with a Chinese company to offshore product manufacturing and visited the company's owner during a trip to China. He was surprised to find that the owner of the company drove a very expensive BMW that costs at least 60% more than the same model in the United States. He asked, "How could someone who is constantly trying to negotiate with me down to the penny and always claims he is not making much money possibly drive a car like this?" From an American's perspective, anyone who is trying to negotiate should drive a beat-up car to make it seem as if he does not have a lot of money. However, to a Chinese person, driving such a car is a way of proving to his American partner that he is worthy of the collaboration. We would not be surprised if this person had borrowed the BMW just to impress his American partner.

Affordability

In January 2012, it was reported that China had surpassed both Japan and the United States as the world's largest consumer market for luxury goods with a total consumption of USD 12.6 billion (excluding private jets, yachts, and luxury cars) in 2011, accounting for 28% of the global luxury market. How could a country with a per capita GDP of USD 6,091 in 2012[1] capture such a large share of the market for expensive products?

First and most importantly, China has 1.4 billion people. While the average income is relatively low in China, similar to the "99%" in the United States, a small percentage of Chinese citizens earn substantially more. Among such a large population, even a small percentage represents a lot of wealthy people in absolute numbers. In addition to the uber-wealthy members of Chinese society discussed in Chapter 23, there are a substantial number of working people who can afford very expensive products if they so desire. People who work for major state-owned enterprises (SOEs) earn an average income of RMB 111,357; considering many of them do not have to pay mortgages and have only one child, they have large disposable incomes (especially if they are married and their spouses work).

The second reason is that the Chinese are willing to allocate a large percentage of their incomes or wealth to buying expensive products. This mentality is very different from that of Americans. For example, someone who makes USD 80,000 per year in the United States would be unlikely to buy a handbag worth USD 2,000 or more. For most, such a handbag would be a frivolous expenditure when the money could be used for something more practical. The opposite is true in China. A person who makes half that amount would feel completely justified spending USD 2,000 on a handbag. It would not only be meaningful, but necessary. They derive a lot more pleasure from owning that USD 2,000 bag than from other things in life. It is not uncommon for a college graduate to use her first (or two) month's salary to buy an expensive handbag as a "reward" for finally making it.

The third reason is the collective purchasing power of the 4-2-1 family. It is considered perfectly normal for parents and grandparents to make extravagant purchases for their children, and now with a 4-2-1 structure, there are typically more earners than pure spenders. Interestingly, the older generation in China, while very frugal in purchases for themselves, do not want their children to have less than others (i.e., they want their children to "keep up with the Joneses"). So, they will purchase USD 2,000 handbags for their adult children, even though they personally consider using a bag worth more than USD 50 to be extravagant.

Fourth, the Chinese are willing to work extra hard and extremely long hours so that they can afford to buy expensive goods. They will take on extra work so that they can save enough money to buy a USD 2,000 Louis Vuitton bag, a USD 5,000 Rolex, or a USD 120,000 BMW. In other countries, most people are not willing sacrifice family and leisure time in order to be able to afford such purchases.

Fifth, demand for expensive goods is high due to the gifting culture in China discussed in Chapter 3. Gifting, either to maintain social relationships or in exchange for favors (corruption), is a societal norm in China. Expensive handbags and watches make perfect gifts in some circles, when one wants to leave an impression. They also make great "thank you" items when others have helped a person with a need.

Overseas Shopping

Because of the demand for expensive products, and since almost all expensive products are foreign brands that can be purchased for substantially less money outside China, many Chinese citizens have become globe-trotting shoppers. Such shopping "generosity" stands in great contrast to the consumption habits of 10 or 20 years ago, when the Chinese liked nothing more than making money in America and spending it in China. But now, the situation has reversed. According to statistics issued by the China National Tourism Administration, in 2012, the number of Chinese tourists traveling overseas reached 83.18 million. Furthermore, Morgan Stanley estimated that in 2015, there will be 100 million Chinese tourists traveling overseas, with overseas luxury consumption reaching USD 194 billion. These tourist shoppers prefer luxuries such as handbags, clothes, and cosmetics.

After observing shoppers on les Champs-Elysées in Paris and on 5th Avenue in New York, one would understand the comment, "The world is neither flat nor

288 *Economic System*

round; it is Chinese."[2] Department stores on les Champs-Elysées, including Printemps Paris and Lafayette, are crowded with Chinese consumers who purchase luxury goods as if they were buying discounted products in a supermarket. Many boutique stores such as Prada & Louis Vuitton hire shopping guides who can speak Mandarin specifically to meet the needs of Chinese customers.

In a recent trend, Chinese businesses are now trying to form foreign alliances and buy ownership stakes in luxury brands. This remains a nascent strategy at the moment, but we expect the scale and scope of such "wholesale" purchases to become much more common in the coming years.

Fake Products

For many, luxury products are not necessities, but merely demonstrations of social status and personal taste. As a result, many people who cannot (or will not) spend that much money on real luxury products have resorted to buying fake products. This has now become big business in China. Fake products are even ranked into classes: A, B, and C. A-class products use exactly the same materials and manufacturing processes, and even the packaging is the same. Sometimes they actually come from the same factories that make the real products. B-class products tend to have minor differences from their real counterparts and can be identified by person with a trained eye. C-class fakes are the lowest class; typically it is easy to tell the difference between C-class products and real luxury products.

High-quality knockoffs are much more reasonably priced. Many Chinese consumers, from high school students to wealthy people, buy and use A-class fake products. An informant told us that once a friend's husband bought a Louis Vuitton leather handbag for her while on a business trip in France. Her colleagues had bought counterfeits of the same design on Silk Street.[3] They carefully compared the real bag with the fake bags to try to identify differences, but their efforts were in vain.

Those who aspire to acquire luxury products even resort to using shopping bags with expensive product logos to pretend they can afford them. One can even now buy such shopping bags without buying the actual products. These second-hand paper bags from the counter normally sell for USD 8 to 10 on shopping websites in China. There are even businesses specializing in manufacturing and wholesaling paper shopping bags with designer logos for almost all famous brands, each priced around USD 3.

Of course, sometimes people may use the similarities between fake and real products to become less noticeable for various reasons, especially when such expenses cannot be justified. An informant told us about a woman who rides her shabby bicycle to markets while wearing Burberry clothing and carrying an Hermès bag. Both she and her husband work in government and could not possibly afford such expensive products on their salaries. Naturally, these expensive goods raised suspicions. When asked by her friends, the answer always was that they were merely counterfeits. Because fake goods are ubiquitous, not a single person ever doubted her words.

Road Ahead

Given the pervasive pursuit of expensive products in Chinese culture, we do not see this phenomenon changing substantially anytime soon. We, however, do expect there will be a subtle evolution. First, the market will segment into different groups, each with distinct preferences. Second, the phenomenon of overseas shopping may change, partially due to enforcement of the General Administration of Customs decree No. 54 issued in 2010, levying a partial tax on overseas purchases over a value limit of RMB 5,000 and levying a full tax on 20 categories of goods, including tobacco and alcohol products. Third, the market for fake products will shrink as the government clamps down on copyright and trademark infringement. Finally, we also believe that more domestic brands will begin manufacturing expensive luxury products; this will take some time, but it will happen eventually. That said, at least for the next few years, China is a market that no luxury product company can afford to ignore.

Notes

1 Data from World Bank, retrieved January 2014 from http://data.worldbank.org/indicator/NY.GDP.PCAP.CD
2 Pan Xiaoling, Yuan Duanduan, & Ding Jie (2010, June 3), "The Chinese carrying LVs," *Southern Weekly*, retrieved January 2014 from http://www.infzm.com/content/45882
3 Silk Street is in Beijing. It initially became famous for its silk merchants and later for merchants who sell premium knockoffs. It underwent a major overhaul in 2005.

Part X
Education System

45 K–12 and Beyond

The Chinese education system is effectively a dichotomous system: K–12 and college. During K–12, students do whatever they can to score as high as possible on the college entrance exam so they can get into the best colleges possible. During college, students enjoy life a bit before doing whatever they can (typically beginning in junior year) to find good jobs upon graduation. In this chapter, we focus our discussion on the K–12 stage from the perspectives of children, parents, and teachers. This is followed by a discussion on unequal educational resources in China. We then briefly discuss college education and the halo effect of the exam system. In the Road Ahead section, we predict a gradual shift away from a sole focus on exam scores. However, this change can only be successful if ethical standards in Chinese society are substantially improved and corruption is reduced.

K–12 Education

The Imperial Examination (similar to the Chinese civil service exam discussed in Chapter 36) was used in China for 1,300 years (until 1905) and was considered to be a fair and efficient way to enable the best talent, regardless of their family background, to assume major responsibilities in managing the country. Although the imperial examination system was abolished long ago, the National College Entrance Examination (NCEE) plays a similarly critical role in the context of public education and individual development. In 1952, China established this transparent and fair national mechanism for determining university enrollment, and it has been used ever since except during the Cultural Revolution (1966–1976).

To its credit, the NCEE system has been associated with very little corruption or cheating. In a society that highly values "relationship," the NCEE is unique in that every student is treated impartially, regardless of personal connections; test scores determine all outcomes. Because it is one of the few areas of Chinese society in which there is zero tolerance for unfairness, students, parents, schools, and society at large all place extreme importance on the NCEE, nicknamed the "single-plank bridge" because it often determines a person's destiny. As with the Imperial Examination, if a student distinguishes herself among the throngs of examinees, her life will be filled with opportunities. For example, a student from a remote mountainous region in Sichuan who scores well on the exam might be admitted to an elite university and eventually settle in a first-tier city like Beijing or Shanghai where there are more opportunities for advancement and prosperity.

294 Education System

To prepare for the NCEE, Chinese students are subjected to severe competition from a very young age. Beginning in elementary school, students take exams every term, month, and even every week, and the evaluation system is based solely on grades. Exam-based education is not only executable on a massive scale but also relatively fair to students. On the negative side, students are classified as being "good" or "bad" based on their test scores. Thus, many students, parents, and teachers are under extreme pressure to perform.

Such pressure generally originates with parents. From the moment their children are born, parents begin to prepare for their futures. They do everything they can to help ensure that their children do not "lose at the starting line." In a country with a large population but limited and unbalanced education resources, fierce competition is inevitable. Thus, most parents feel that it is their responsibility to provide their children with any possible advantage. One informant expressed, "My 8-year-old child has entered the second grade this year. Every night, she has to spend two hours doing homework, though not very much compared to pupils in higher grades. Although I am doubtful about the so-called winning at the starting line, to be honest, we have no better choice, given the overall environment in China."

Students are under constant pressure from their parents. Even if a student achieves a high grade in a class, his relative performance compared to his peers is much more important since a one-point difference can place a student behind dozens of others in the class, let alone the whole province. Therefore, students strive to achieve the highest grades among their peers. A sixth grade student who earned 98 points on a mock examination hated learning because she only ranked tenth in the class and her grade prohibited her from being enrolled in the best school.[1] So even top students bear considerable pressure because they are worried about being outperformed by others. In their eyes, nothing but first place matters; a score of 98 points generates only feelings of failure. The only way to alleviate this intense pressure is to study harder.

A 2010 report on the personality health of Chinese juveniles released by the China Population Communication Center revealed that over 80% of pupils suffer from exam anxiety, for fear of being scolded by parents because of poor grades. In addition, a 2005 joint survey of five domestic cities on juvenile development found that the top three types of pressure relate to the college entrance examination, homework, and unrealistic parental expectations.[2]

Teachers are also under tremendous pressure. Teachers' promotions (academic ranks) and incomes are determined by student performance. Thus, special attention is paid to average class grades, or, in some better schools, the grades of top students. The ratio of enrollment in key universities usually directly or indirectly determines how a teacher is evaluated. Consequently, teachers feel they have no choice other than to cram excessive exercises into the school day. *Oriental Education Times*, together with Fudan Journalism School, conducted a survey on the happiness of Shanghai pre-college educators (teachers in elementary, junior high, and senior high schools). The survey showed that 86.6% of teachers expressed feelings of high work pressure, among which 26.2% felt it gravely, while 60.4% only slightly. Only 5.8% of educators expressed no special concern over high work pressure. In addition, teachers felt pressure over students' grades (57.7%), educational research (36.1%), classroom management (34.3%), and providing exemplary public lessons (33.8%).[3]

An educator's income is mainly comprised of a base salary and a performance-based bonus. According to the 2012 Annual Statistics of Chinese Labor, the 2011 average annual income of educators nationwide was USD 7,365, with large regional discrepancies. Usually, educators in cities such as Beijing, Shanghai, Tianjin, and Zhejiang are paid more than those in provinces such as Hebei, Guangxi, and Gansu. Under such great teaching and economic pressure, pre-college educators often tutor students to earn extra income. In some cases, income from tutoring can be substantially higher than a teacher's regular salary.

On the positive side, this system has created generations of Chinese who are extremely well trained to solve quantitative problems. Even a street vendor in China can do sophisticated mental calculations much faster and more accurately than college students in the United States. It is said if a street vendor in China "accidentally" quotes a higher total price to a buyer, the buyer can almost be certain that the vendor is trying to cheat him because the chance that the vendor calculated it wrong, even without a calculator or paper and pencil, is slim to none!

Unequal Distribution of K–12 Education Resources

While in theory every child in China can change his or her life by performing well on the NCEE, the reality is that K–12 education resources are not distributed evenly in China. Developed regions and metropolitan areas like Shanghai have facilities that rival those in the United States, as well as the best teachers. In less developed places, however, educational facilities are barely sufficient. In some poor regions, usually in remote hard-to-access mountains, even the bare minimum is not available. While China now offers free education through grade 9, families in these regions can barely make a living and often pull their children out of schools early. This is particularly an issue with girls in these regions because of the ingrained perspective of unequal status of men and women in rural areas.

One puzzling observation is that the government is actually capable of building much better facilities in poor regions, but these conditions persist. For example, the semi-official China Youth Development Foundation sponsor *Project Hope* was created so private citizens and companies can donate money to help children in poor regions. By 2012, it was reported that *Project Hope* had raised RMB 8.73 billion (the equivalent of USD 1.46 billion) to subsidize more than 4.5 million students from poor families in rural areas (including primary, secondary, and university students) and to build 18,002 new elementary schools, the cost of which is RMB 500,000. This is all well and good, until one compares this figure with the amount of money various local governments spend on their administrative buildings alone. For example, in a case widely reported in 2012, the county of Minggang, the lowest government level in Henan Province, spent RMB 30 million (USD 5 million) on a new luxury office building.

College Education

Once in college, life suddenly changes dramatically for young people. There is no long exam at the end of the education process on which they must successfully perform. (That is, unless they want to enter civil service or pursue graduate school; but all those are nothing compared to the college entrance exam.) After years of hard work and countless exams, many Chinese students lack discipline and purpose when they enter college, as they are told many times by parents and teachers that they should enjoy the fruits of the hard work they put in during the K–12 period. It is not uncommon for them to just enjoy life until their junior or even senior years, when they are faced with the prospect of finding a job.

College degrees these days are also worth less than they were a decade or two ago, as the Chinese government has substantially increased the number of students who enter college each year. According to statistics provided by Ministry of Education, the number of national college graduates reached 6.99 million in 2013, an increase of 190,000 people compared to 2012. In addition, the number of people with postgraduate degrees is rapidly increasing. In the *2013 Evaluation of Chinese Universities*[4] report, the three schools with the highest ratios of graduate to undergraduate students are the University of Science and Technology of China (2.38, 4,444 postgraduates and 1,868 undergraduates), Peking University (1.79, 6,334 postgraduates and 2,725 undergraduates), and Beijing Normal University (1.59, 3,389 postgraduates and 2,135 undergraduates).

In order to differentiate themselves, and maybe partially because they have been taking exams for their entire lives, many college students are fond of obtaining certificates. They not only list all earned certificates on their resumes when they are hunting for jobs but also boast about them when they go on blind dates. In

Figure 45.1 Bicycles parked near the teaching building, Fudan University, Shanghai.

fact, many of them have no idea why they want certain certificates; they merely act on impulse, perhaps to differentiate themselves, perhaps out of habit. For example, some people with no plans to become accountants will take CPA exams and obtain CPA (Certified Public Accountant) certificates just to add icing on the cake. In 2010, a Peking University student exposed all of her certificates online; she had passed the CET-6 and Computer Level II as a sophomore and obtained miscellaneous certificates after graduation such as a lawyer certificate, CPA certificate, CCNP (Cisco Career Certification), CCIE (Cisco Certified Internetwork Expert), CFAI (Chartered Financial Analyst, International), and so on.[5]

Road Ahead

Almost all of the Chinese citizens we spoke to complained about the current education system; we could even use the word "hate" without too much exaggeration. Although students must pass numerous tests and exercises in order to score well on the CNEE and meet the expectations of teachers and parents, this strategy ignores the meaning of learning itself. As a result, the consensus among the Chinese is that students trained under this system are not creative and lack maturity as adults (e.g., they do not know what they want for themselves or struggle when expectations are not set externally). From an observer's perspective, we believe Chinese students are actually well trained to solve problems from different angles since this system requires students to solve harder and less intuitive problems so that they can differentiate themselves from others. The particular type of creativity used to solve these problems, however, can be taught. This leads to two types of students: one type will mechanically memorize such "creative" methods, and another type will learn how one can arrive at such creative method and thus be able to come up with a new creative method herself later, if needed. What Chinese students do lack in general is the ability to discover important problems on their own. This ability, unfortunately, is critical in both the social and natural sciences.

Regardless, the Chinese are stuck between a rock and a hard place. While the entire Chinese populace complains about the educational system, there currently is no better alternative. To adopt a college admission system like the United States in which admissions decisions are placed in the hands of a few officers at each college would open the flood gates for corruption. After all, the exam system is one of the few things in China that remains untouched by corruption and unwritten rules. Change will eventually come, but in small doses.

Notes

1 Lin Lu (2011, November 15), "Current education system leads to too much pressure for pupils, further leads to their hate of school," retrieved January 2014 from http://www.china.com.cn/education/xiaoxue/2011-11/15/content_23918079_2.htm

2 Zhang Chengcheng (2013, January 5), "Exam anxiety among over 80% of pupils, conflicts strengthened with parents," *Outlook Weekly*, retrieved January 2014 from http://edu.people.com.cn/n/2013/0105/c1006-20090893.html

298 *Education System*

3 Yang Yuhong & Qian Yu (2011, September 7), "Too much evaluation for high school and elementary school teachers, 90% expressed over-pressure," *Shanghai Evening Post* (Forwarded by *China Education News*), retrieved January 2014 from http://www.jyb.cn/basc/xw/201109/t20110907_452699.html
4 Wu Shulian, ed. (2013), *2013 Evaluation of Chinese Universities*, Beijing: China Statistics Press.
5 Zhong Guang (2010, August 7), "Certificate show-off girl from Beijing University: Rather worship knowledge than money," *Huaxi Metropolis Daily,* retrieved January 2014 from http://www.wccdaily.com.cn/epaper/hxdsb/html/2010-08/07/content_220499.htm

46 Studying Abroad

Since ancient times, the Chinese have been teaching younger generations to "read 10,000 books, and walk 10,000 miles" in their quest for knowledge and experience. As early as the Tang Dynasty, stories circulated widely about Monk Xuan Zang visiting India in pursuit of enlightenment from Buddhist scriptures and Monk Jian Zhen crossing the ocean to Japan. These were perhaps the earliest Chinese pioneers in overseas education.

The first wave of large-scale overseas education occurred in 1847 when 19-year-old Rong Hong became the first student from modern China to attend Yale University. Following in Rong's footsteps, many students began attending schools in the United States, including Zhan Tianyou, a famous railway engineer, and Tang Shaoyi, the first Prime Minister of the Republic of China. Since China reopened its doors to the rest of the world in 1978, studying abroad has reached a scale and scope never seen before in human history. In this chapter, we provide an overview of the Chinese study abroad phenomenon and discuss repercussions when students return to China. We predict the study abroad phenomenon to continue in the coming years and discuss possible ramifications in the Road Ahead section.

Going Abroad for Education

According to a survey, between 1872 and 1978, the total number of Chinese students who had studied abroad reached 130,000, and between 1978 and 2000, that figure climbed to 340,000. In the 21st century, since joining the World Trade Organization and developing closer contact with the world, more and more Chinese citizens are regarding overseas education as a way to enhance individual competitiveness. By the end of 2006, a total of 1 million Chinese people had studied abroad.[1] In 2012 alone, 399,600 people went abroad to study, and the number has been increasing steadily every year. From 1978 through 2012, China exported 2.6447 million students abroad.[2]

According to UNESCO statistics, in 2006, 14% of all students worldwide who were studying abroad were Chinese—the most from any country.[3] Now, that figure has risen to 17%, with India and South Korea ranking second and third, respectively. (The UN statistics refer to students studying abroad who have yet to obtain citizenship or permanent residency in their host nation.)

A report published by the UNESCO Institute for Statistics, *Global Flow of Tertiary-Level Students*, revealed the distribution of Chinese students abroad,

300 *Education System*

with the United States (28.87%), Australia (15.56%), and Japan (15.38%) ranking first, second, and third, respectively.[4] While most young people (or their parents) choose studying abroad as a way to become better prepared and more competitive in future careers, many parents also choose to send their children abroad to expand their worldview. As more Chinese students are going abroad, they are also becoming more discerning about where they go and which schools they attend. If they have a choice, North American schools tend to be the most valued destinations. At the Smeal College of Business at the Pennsylvania State University, up to a third of the students in advanced finance or accounting undergraduate classes are from mainland China. It is quite common these days while walking on campuses of major universities in Australia, Canada, and the United States to hear passersby speaking Chinese.

Almost all of those who studied abroad in the 1980s and 1990s were supported by either scholarships from the Chinese government or scholarships or assistantships from the universities they attended. During that period, the U.S. consulate rarely issued a visa to a prospective student who claimed she was going to financially support her studies personally. Back then, the Chinese were not wealthy enough to convince the American visa officers that they could pay for their own expenses. This is no longer the case. The educations of more than 90% of Chinese students studying abroad are self-funded. More and more families can afford to pay for their children's tuition fees and daily expenses. Thus, overseas education has expanded from the elite to the masses.

Another recent trend is that students are going abroad at an increasingly younger age. Many high school students are foregoing the National College Entrance Exam (NCEE, regarded as an important life milestone) and instead are attending overseas high schools so they have more options when they graduate. According to the *Annual Report on the Development of China's Study Abroad (2012)*, the number of students with a high-school degree or below who were studying abroad reached 76,400, accounting for 19.8% of the total number of students studying abroad in 2010. These figures increased to 76,800 and 22.6%, respectively, in 2011.

According to statistics published by the Ministry of Education in 2010, among the 1 million students who chose not to take the NCEE, 21.1% chose overseas education. In the past, high school students who performed poorly on the NCEE chose to go abroad for education. They usually took a one-year preparation course and then applied to overseas universities. However, many have discovered that attending high schools abroad increases their chances of being admitted to the best universities in the world. For instance, one student who had performed at a mediocre level in China successfully received an offer from Cambridge University after receiving a high school education overseas. Examples like this have inspired more and more parents to follow this path. According to statistics from United States Immigration and Customs Enforcement, in 2012, the number of Chinese students in American high schools reached 15,074.[5]

Shanghai is a case in point. Four famous high schools (i.e., Fudan University High School, Shanghai High School, Shanghai Jiaotong University High School, and East Normal University High School No. 2) have departments dedicated to students who want to study at overseas universities. Among 400 graduates of Fudan University High School in 2012, 103 (25.75%) received offers from overseas universities, 162 (40.50%) enrolled at famous universities in China, and only 135 (34%) participated in the NCEE. At the Shanghai International Studies University High School, less than 20 students (4.56% of the student body) sat for the NCEE.[6]

Based on our research and personal observations, Chinese students who are studying abroad may fall into four traps. First, they do not study hard. They grow up in an environment filled with constant external pressure to work harder and perform better. Once they arrive in a culture like the one in the United States, where individuals decide for themselves how much work they want to do, many students lose the discipline and/or motivation to study. In rare cases, they may even resort to cheating. For instance, Virgin Immigration, a company founded by four young Chinese men in London, sold fake diplomas to students (the majority of whom were Chinese) who had failed to meet the requirements for graduation. In March 2009, the police shut down the business and confiscated around GBP 3 million in cash.[7]

The second challenge is that Chinese students must adjust quickly to different ethical standards. University administrators across the United States struggle to help international students learn which behaviors are acceptable and which are unacceptable, and the meaning of academic integrity. Some Chinese students who do not make this mental adjustment end up failing courses or being kicked out of school.

The third challenge is that Chinese students tend not to mix with the locals. Since there are so many Chinese students studying at foreign universities now, most Chinese students share apartments/houses and only socialize with each other. There are even "Chinese classes" at some universities, in which 90% of the students are Chinese. Students in these classes seldom integrate into Western society. In the end, the only interactions they have with native students are related to classroom activities. Unfortunately, this makes their study abroad experience incomplete, as there is a lot more to learn outside the classroom. Although many Chinese students do speak English (or another local language) well, those who truly understand their local cultures are still few and far between.

The fourth challenge is avoiding being corrupted by bad examples. Once they are away from their families and established social networks, many young Chinese students succumb to peer pressure and engage in non-edifying and even dangerous activities. This is particularly critical as more and more Chinese are going abroad during high school, or even earlier. This complication did not exist during 1980s and 1990s, when almost all Chinese students who studied abroad were adults pursuing graduate degrees.

Returning to China

Many Chinese students are studying abroad, and more and more of them are choosing to return to China rather than immigrate. According to statistics compiled by the Ministry of Education, since 1978, more than 1.09 million students

302 *Education System*

have returned to China, comprising 41.26% of the people who went abroad during the same period. In recent years, the percentage of Chinese students returning from abroad has increased dramatically. China has finally begun to strike a balance between "brain drain" and "brain gain." In a survey of students in Beijing and Tianjing who wanted to study abroad, *China Youth Daily* found that only 9.33% hoped to work in or immigrate to a foreign country.[8] Why are so many students returning to China?

The first reason is family. Current students seeking overseas education were born during the 1980s or 1990s—the first generation born under the one-child policy. The thoughts expressed by a female Chinese student who is studying at Kaplan Financial, Singapore are quite representative: "As the only child in the family, I am really attached to my parents. They raised me, and it is time I paid their reward. One should learn to be grateful. I don't want to leave my mother alone in China."[9] Relatedly, Chinese people typically prefer to marry other Chinese people; it is rare for a Chinese student to meet and marry a non-Chinese person while studying abroad. Sometimes students return to China at least partly due to parental pressure (or desire) for them to marry fellow Chinese citizens.

The second reason is career. Recently, due to the financial crisis in the United States and the European debt crisis, career opportunities abroad have become quite scarce. Those who do receive job offers abroad often encounter visa issues and are forced to return to China. In 2013, U.S. Immigration Services received 124,000 H-1B visa applications,[10] a number vastly exceeding the annual limit of 65,000 H-1B visas. Companies that are willing to sponsor international students who hold only B.S. degrees are extremely rare in the current economic environment.

In contrast, the domestic job market is much better. China has aggressively engaged in policy efforts related to residency, entrepreneurship, and life in general to entice successful Chinese citizens who are living abroad to return. For example, the Ministry of Education established The Scientific Research Foundation for the Returned Overseas Chinese Scholar, The Trans-Century Training Program Foundation for the Talented, Yangtze River Scholar Bonus Schemes, etc. Many Chinese citizens who have not fully achieved their career objectives overseas have decided to move back. We personally know of numerous examples, both academic and nonacademic, of Chinese citizens who, after living and working in the United States for 10 or even 20 years, packed their bags and returned to China (but almost always kept their U.S. passports).

Last but not least, the China of today is not the China of 20 or even 10 years ago. The quality of life is very high now, especially for those who have money. There is no longer a huge contrast between living abroad and living in China. As a matter of fact, a person who has found success abroad would probably enjoy a life filled with even more convenience and luxury in China. A senior executive of even a medium-sized company typically has a driver and a company car. It is even very affordable to have a full-time maid. One person who recently returned to Shanghai from the United States for a management position hired two full-time maids plus a driver, something unthinkable in the United States. Young Chinese people also enjoy a much richer life outside work (discussed elsewhere in the book) once they return, especially if they chose not to integrate into the local culture when they studied aboard.

Those returning to China also face two major challenges. The first challenge is cultural. Upon returning, they need to readjust to the Chinese culture and the Chinese way of doing things (as discussed in this book). This is something we call "reverse culture shock." When students decide to study abroad, they are mentally prepared to enter a different culture and change their behaviors. After spending years outside China adjusting to a different culture, they return to find that they have become foreigners in their own land. They find that they are no longer capable, at least initially, of arguing with strangers, cutting in line, or driving with complete disregard for other drivers. Some people revert back to their old habits, but others refuse to change again.

The second challenge is career. The few who studied abroad during the 1980s and 1990s were among the best of their generation and attended the best universities abroad. Today, however, so many more Chinese students of all calibers are studying abroad, and those who return to China are finding that they are not necessarily hot commodities on the job market. Three things can make a potential employee more attractive these days. First, obtain an M.S. degree after earning a B.S. degree abroad. Second, graduate from a well-known and respected university. Third, gain work experience abroad after graduation.

Road Ahead

The trend of Chinese students studying abroad and returning to China will continue, but several changes are on the horizon. First, more Chinese students will study abroad for high school and probably bring one of their parents (typically the mother) with them. Second, there will be a much greater demand for M.S. degrees, especially those that can offer real-world experience to Chinese students. As a matter of fact, several universities in the United States (and elsewhere in the world) recently launched new M.S. degree programs catered primarily to Chinese students as a way to generate more revenue. Third, the influx of Chinese students at some universities has started to have impact on local economies; businesses (and local governments) who understand this may do well by catering to their needs.

Notes

1 Center for China and Globalization (2012, September 18), "China becomes largest export country of international students and 90% self-funded," retrieved January 2014 from http://www.ccg.org.cn/_d275915016.htm

2 Data based on statistics from the Ministry of Education and the *Annual Reports on the Development of China's Study Abroad.*

3 UNESCO (2006, May 31), "UNESCO: The number of international students from China ranks first in the world," *UN News Centre*, retrieved January 2014, http://www.un.org/chinese/News/story.asp?NewsID=5759

304 *Education System*

4 UNESCO (2012, October 26), "Global flow of tertiary-level students," retrieved January 2014 from http://www.uis.unesco.org/Education/Pages/international-student-flow-viz.aspx

5 U.S. Immigration and Customs Enforcement (2012, May 3), "Student and exchange visitor program, U.S. Immigration and Customs Enforcement: FOIA 12-11907," retrieved October 24, 2013, from http://www.ice.gov/doclib/foia/sevis/mainland-china-hong-kong-students-studying-in-us.pdf

6 Li Aiming (2012, June 19), "Only half of the students in famous high schools take the College Entrance Exam," *Peninsula City Newspaper*, retrieved January 2014 from http://news.bandao.cn/news_html/201206/20120619/news_20120619_1927210.shtml?i|162198:1

7 Guangzhou Daily (2010, December 5), "Illegal intermediary agent," retrieved January 2014 from http://gzdaily.dayoo.com/html/2010-12/05/content_1205675.htm

8 Zhang Guo (2013, January 24), "Survey suggests that university students prefer overseas education rather than immigration," *China Youth Daily*, retrieved January 2014 from http://www.chinanews.com/edu/2013/01-24/4515292.shtml

9 Peng Yanping (2012, October 12), "More than 70% of overseas students return to China; a new round of brain gain?" *People's Daily*, retrieved January 2014 from http://www.sn.xinhuanet.com/2012-10/12/c_113349533.htm

10 U.S. Citizenship and Immigration Services (2013, April 15), "H-1B fiscal year 2014 cap season," retrieved January 2014 from http://www.uscis.gov/portal/site/uscis/menuitem.5af9bb95919f35e66f614176543f6d1a/?vgnextoid=4b7cdd1d5fd37210VgnVCM100000082ca60aRCRD&vgnextchannel=73566811264a3210VgnVCM100000b92ca60aRCRD

47 Executive Master of Business Administration (EMBA)

In a society that has historically valued knowledge and learned individuals, even the most successful people can never have too many degrees and certifications, especially if a degree brings prestige. In China, the EMBA degree is one such degree that is a category of its own. It is not uncommon to find billionaires (in USD) in Chinese EMBA classrooms, not as speakers, but as students. It is quite common for both successful business owners and senior executives across all sectors to enroll in EMBA programs, which have become a microcosm of society representing the elite of the Chinese business world. We first provide an overview of EMBA programs in China, which we follow with a discussion on who attends these programs and why. We then discuss student experiences in Chinese EMBA programs. In the Road Ahead section, we make a few predictions about EMBA education in China.

Overview

Figure 47.1 A business owner at his desk, with the lecture notes from the EMBA program he attended prominently displayed on the shelf.

306   *Education System*

In July 2002, the Office of Academic Degrees Committee of the State Council approved EMBA education programs at 30 institutions. By 2013, more than 60 universities had been approved to offer EMBA degrees. In China, the central government decides which universities can offer EMBA degrees. Therefore, unlike other degrees, EMBA programs vary substantially because schools are given much more freedom to determine their content and structure.

Existing programs can be classified into three distinct types, analogous to the types of business in China (discussed in details in Chapter 40). The majority of programs are the first type, which can be thought of as "state-owned enterprises (SOEs)" offered by existing government-run universities (e.g., Peking University, Tsinghua University, Fudan University, Shanghai Jiaotong University) to business owners, senior executives from private companies and SOEs, and government officials. The second type, analogous to people-managed companies (PMCs), tends to be offered by independent, private (or at least not under direct governmental supervision) business schools such as Cheung Kong Graduate School of Business (CKGSB); students tend to be business owners. The third type is analogous to foreign capital companies (FCC) in terms of management style and students, who typically are senior executives from FCCs, such as the program offered by China Europe International Business School (CEIBS). Tensions among affiliates of these programs are so great, they border on animosity. We once heard a dean at an elite university forcefully tell staff members that he does not want his EMBA program even to be compared to FCC or PMC types, as he does not consider them "real" universities.

In each program, students must take a certain number of courses, some required and some optional, and write a thesis. Each program usually determines the specific courses. The normal length of the program is two years, and students typically meet once a month for four days, typically Thursday through Sunday, during which time an entire course is typically taught. The faculty who teach in Chinese EMBA programs, especially the best ones, are a mix of professors with appointments at those university programs and professors from overseas who come to teach a specific four-day course.

The scale of these programs has expanded substantially, not just in terms of the number of programs, but also the size of each program. Some of the best programs are now allowed by the government to recruit up to 700 students each year. Strikingly, although tuition has increased substantially during the last 10 years, the number of applications has not decreased. As one admissions officer told us, it almost seems like the higher the tuition, the more people apply. At present, the top EMBA programs are charging around USD 100,000 for the two-year program; thus the cost is very similar to many American EMBA programs.

Who Enrolls in EMBA Programs and Why

Different programs attract different students, sometimes because of a particular program's focus, reputation, and alumni, and other times simply because of location. For example, the programs in Beijing tend to have a lot more students who are government officials. In general, there are four types of students: business owners, professional managers (executives at various levels and different types of companies), government officials, and freelance professionals (lawyers, doctors, reporters, actors, etc.). Over the last 10 years, the student mix has been evolving. The percentage of business owners is decreasing because the number of business owners who do not have EMBAs is decreasing; the percentage of government officials is also decreasing as many government agencies have cut back on expenses. (Interestingly, the tuition for government officials is usually steeply discounted by as much as 50%.) The percentage of professional managers is increasing, and they now comprise the majority of each EMBA class. Many successful business owners who completed EMBA programs earlier and found it useful have now started to send their senior executives to the same programs. In addition, more mid-level executives from large corporations are now enrolled in these programs than senior executives. Freelance professionals represent a small proportion.

Compared to the composition of EMBA students elsewhere, EMBA students in China are unique in several ways. First, some are very wealthy; although not every class has a billionaire, multi-millionaires (worth at least USD 100 million) typically are enrolled in each class. Second, some students are very senior corporate executives, including board chairmen and CEOs of some of the largest companies in China. The airline China Eastern, an SOE with a size rivaling Delta, sends almost all of its executives, including those in the C-suite, to Fudan University EMBA programs. Third, some students are powerful government officials, typically those in charge of branches related to economic development, but also people at the mayor or vice mayor levels. The enrollment of government officials actually has turned out to be quite valuable in attracting others to attend EMBA programs due to the major role government plays in business in China (discussed elsewhere). Finally, there are huge variations across the EMBA students, even in the same classes and programs. Differences not only relate to wealth and/or status but also to maturity, intelligence, and purpose for attending the program. There is also a wide age range in each class. The average age is late 30s to early 40s, but some students are in their late 50s; a few are even in their late 20s, many of whom are so-called Rich Second Generation students.

EMBA degrees are the envy of many ordinary Chinese and have thus become the subject of scrutiny and sometimes unfair and unfavorable generalizations. For example, some media even portray enrolling in EMBA programs as a way for single attractive women to find rich husbands. This is not true based on our personal interactions with EMBA students. However, as reported by the media, many EMBA students do choose to attend such programs to establish and expand their higher level circles. As a matter of fact, this is one of the major reasons why some people enroll in EMBA programs. Many students also harbor ambitions to find potential business partners in such programs.

The second reason why people enroll in EMBA programs is because they feel they have to—either for future career advancement, or to gain respect (or credibility) from business partners. Of the 25 members of the current Politburo of the CPC Central Committee, 10 (40%) have Master's degrees, and 5 (20%) have Ph.D. degrees (including 2 out of the 7 Standing Committee Members).[1] According to

308　*Education System*

statistics, in 2013, 85% of 87 provincial officials had obtained Master's degrees or above, and 22% of them had doctorates.[2] With such emphasis on the top of pyramid, it is no wonder that many government officials (and the business owners and senior executives who interact with them) feel obligated to obtain graduate degrees, especially from elite schools. EMBA programs perfectly match this demand.

One cannot underestimate the importance of degrees in the careers and lives of the Chinese. Several very successful Chinese citizens have resorted to essentially buying graduate degrees from sham universities outside China. Tang Jun, a top professional manager in China, the "king of Chinese employees" and former president of Microsoft Corporation (China), was once embroiled in a degree-faking scandal. He claimed to have earned a doctoral degree from Pacific Western University in the United States, which was later discovered to be an unaccredited institution that essentially had been selling fake diplomas. As the incident escalated, it was discovered that many politicians and businessmen also had "graduated" from this university, which generated great controversy.

The third reason, of course, is to gain knowledge. The popular media and general public often characterize EMBA students as those who have little interest in learning, but this is not true. They do tend to be picky, however, and are not easy to teach. This, of course, is no surprise, given that most EMBA students are already very successful in life and have substantial experience and knowledge in many areas. If a concept is too technical or detailed, many simply do not want to learn it because they have subordinates (or subordinates' subordinates) who handle those types of issues. Likewise, if a concept is too general, they feel they already know how to handle strategic issues and often have their own opinions. The most welcomed courses in EMBA programs are, therefore, those that can introduce new concepts (i.e., theory, business models, or future trends) or those that can help students synthesize their partial knowledge and situate it in a larger context. Regardless, it is rare to see a student who has absolutely no interest in learning. Perhaps because of the culture, the people we have seen in these programs almost always want to improve themselves, both in their own eyes and in other people's eyes.

Possibly unique to China, the fourth reason why some students enroll in EMBA programs at elite schools is to fulfill their childhood dreams. Many students told us that the universities where they decided to pursue their EMBAs were the universities they had wanted to attend for their undergraduate degrees, but for one reason or another, did not. Enrolling in an EMBA program at a particular university can be seen as a way to compensate for regret. For students with this motivation, the program is less important; having a degree from a particular university is what matters.

The EMBA Experience

In EMBA programs, incoming students typically take a set of required courses first. In addition to ensuring that all students understand a core set of concepts, required courses help build cohesion among students in the same class and year. (Major programs typically enroll three or more classes every six months.) Each class is normally assigned a dedicated administrative staff member (not a professor) who functions almost like a homeroom teacher in a middle school in the United States. The staff member helps the class organize events and addresses any issues they might have during the course of their education. If a student has an issue, he or she would talk to the staff member first.

Each EMBA class also has a cadre system, where they elect a class president and five to eight other students who serve as the management team. Typically, the class president is a business owner who is able and willing to use his or her own resources to support the activities of the class. It is quite common for the class president to pay for expenses related to class gatherings from time to time, although the EMBA classes normally do not lack classmates who are willing (and sometimes competing) to pick up tabs ranging from USD 5,000 to 10,000 for class dinners with 60 to 70 students. This is seen as a way for students to build a good reputation among their classmates.

In addition to resident courses, which are normally taught on the university's campus, each class attends three or more off-site courses during the two years. These are the same courses that they would otherwise take, but they are taught in hotels in different cities, almost always the home base of one of the students in the class. During offsite courses, teaching is often combined with visits to local companies.

The classroom experience is very dynamic and can go in many different directions depending on the course material, the professor, and students. We have heard stories about students who were dissatisfied with a particular professor and walked out of the classroom and demanded that the professor be replaced, or had an open argument with a professor in the classroom, or had heated arguments with each other in the classroom. However, when students are impressed with a professor, they can be very attentive, eager to learn, and extremely polite. Different classes also have different class cultures. In one class we taught, the students would stand up before each class and bow to the professor together, something the Chinese do during K–12 but not at the college level.

A major component of the EMBA experience is interacting with classmates and alumni. In one top EMBA program, an unwritten rule among the students is if a fellow student comes to your hometown for whatever reason, you must go pick up that person at the airport, treat that person to at least one nice dinner, and make arrangements for a hotel, etc., if needed. In order to save face in front of their classmates, some students in this program would go and buy expensive luxury cars (in the USD 100,000 range) when they heard a classmate would be visiting their hometown, just to maintain the image. The last thing any student wanted was for her classmate to go back and tell the others that she was not doing that well. (The Chinese judge a person's status based on her car.)

During the monthly four-day course, the entire class almost always meets for dinner at least once, and the other two nights are small group meetings. While the drinking culture has evolved, some students still drink a lot during each dinner. We are always captivated by the sincerity of these students during these occasions; they often act as if they were living in college dorms and attending frat parties.

310   *Education System*

They also engage in other activities outside the classroom and form clubs, often with current students from different cohorts and alumni. The most popular clubs are related to various forms of exercise, such as golfing, biking, climbing, etc. Every May, there is also a joint EMBA event for students and alumni from several universities called "Walk the Gobi Desert." Many EMBA students participate in this event, not only to test their physical and mental abilities, but also to form bonds with other EMBA students.

EMBA students and alumni also engage in business collaborations. Sometimes one or more students will go to work for another student (typically a wealthy business owner). Sometimes a few people will decide to form partnerships and start new ventures. Sometimes they strike deals between their existing businesses. Students may even form and contribute to class funds that are used to invest in various ventures. Some collaborations are successful, but others fail miserably and cause bad blood among classmates.

Road Ahead

Despite their popularity, in our view, the golden age of the EMBA program in China may have already passed. By this, we mean we will never again see EMBA classes where students on average have so much rich experience and high net worth. The number of EMBA students and applicants will continue to increase, but EMBA programs will gradually become more like those in the United States and Europe, which are comprised almost exclusively of middle level managers.

Competition among EMBA programs will continue to heat up. The best will survive and even expand, but the rest may struggle to maintain their current enrollments. On the other hand, such market pressure will help further increase the quality of the programs, and also push some programs to develop specializations and unique strengths.

Regardless of what transpires in the future, EMBA alumni comprise the elite of both the Chinese business world and society. What they think and do will influence China beyond its economic development. As discussed in Chapter 23, many people now see these people as their aspiration group, and those who earn EMBA degrees eventually become the trendsetters themselves.

Notes

1 Data based on profiles of the Politburo of the CPC Central Committee, retrieved January 2014 from http://www.xinhuanet.com/politics/leaders/

2 Zhang Ran (2013, March 22), "85% of 87 provincial officials have Master's level degrees or above, over 20% have Doctoral degrees," *Beijing Times*, retrieved January 2014 from http://politics.people.com.cn/n/2013/0322/c1001-20874263-2.html

48 Professors and Scholarship

In May 1998, Chinese leader Jiang Zemin announced that China needed to build a set of world-class institutions and universities. The initial group of nine universities—Peking University, Tsinghua University, Nanjing University, Fudan University, Zhejiang University, Harbin Institute of Technology, Shanghai Jiaotong University, University of Science and Technology of China, and Xi'an Jiaotong University—received substantial investments from the central government and benefitted from favorable policies. The so-called 985 Project ("98" referring to 1998 and "5" referring to May) later expanded to include 39 institutions. Fudan University, for example, received RMB 1.33 billion during the first phase (2001–2003), RMB 1.30 billion during the second phase (2004–2008), and over RMB 2.60 billion during the third phase (2010–2020), amounts totaling close to half of the investments from the local government (in this case, Shanghai).[1]

Great institutions, of course, are not defined by the number of impressive buildings they have. They are defined by their faculty—specifically, the scholarship of their faculty. In this chapter, we discuss the hiring and promotion of university faculty in China. We then discuss the three dimensions of scholarship: research, teaching, and service. We conclude in the Road Ahead section that the dream of the Chinese universities to be world class is not only tangible but is becoming a reality sooner than anyone (including the Chinese) would expect.

Hiring and Promotion

The entire Chinese university system is transitioning from a focus on teaching to a mission that combines both research and teaching, with the elite schools placing a lot more emphasis on research. To strike a balance between the old and new missions, universities (especially elite schools) have adopted two-track systems, either explicitly or implicitly. As in the United States, many departments now include both tenure (research) track faculty and teaching track faculty. Existing faculty members normally remain on the teaching track. They have low base salaries, and most incomes are determined by teaching and service workloads, which often are mapped to a point system for compensation purposes. As a result, most faculty members must assume a lot of teaching and service obligations in order to earn a decent income, which leaves little time left for research. There are three ranks for teaching faculty—lecturer (equivalent to assistant professor), associate professor, and professor—although people are rarely promoted to the next level without

312 Education System

significant research output these days. So, many people in the teaching track are now frozen in whatever position they were in before the system changed. Although all faculty members technically sign employment contracts with their universities (professors renew every five years, lecturers and associate professors renew every three years), scholars are rarely fired. If a professor cannot handle his teaching responsibilities, he is typically moved into a supporting role at the university.

The newer research track is quite similar to the tenure track in the United States, although no schools in China currently have the equivalent of lifetime tenure. To fill research track positions, quite a few renowned universities only hire graduates from prestigious universities abroad. The starting salary for a new faculty member at an elite business school is now around USD 50,000–60,000 (other disciplines such as the biological sciences are paying similar starting salaries to returning scholars). Although these faculty have fixed salaries and teach much fewer courses (four courses per year in business schools), the pressure to publish high quality research is enormous. They also sign fixed-term contracts with their universities; however, unlike the teaching faculty, new faculty in the research track explicitly understand that their contracts will not be renewed at the end of six years if they cannot deliver the research output specified in the contract. If they are successful and get promoted to associate professor, their jobs tend to be secure.

The promotion criteria for research track professors at Chinese universities primarily relate to research productivity, but requirements vary from university to university as in other parts of the world. The elite schools' standards for promotion to associate professor after six years are raised almost yearly. Typically, a faculty member at an elite business school must publish at least one academic paper in her discipline's best journal in the world in order to be promoted. Going from 0 to 1 is a significant hurdle, and it will only be a matter of time until the elite schools in China adopt standards similar to the top 40 universities in the United States (typically, six publications in top disciplinary journals in six years). Elite schools can now afford to do this for two reasons: (1) they can afford to pay their top researchers very well; and (2) many Chinese citizens who earned their doctoral degrees from the best universities abroad have started to return to China, including tenured faculty from schools in the United States.

In China, however, a faculty member does not reach the pinnacle of her career by attaining the rank of full professor. As a matter of fact, there are four levels within the full professor rank. Normally, only a top-ranking Class 1 professor can be granted the title of academician. As discussed elsewhere in the book, higher positions are associated with more power in China. In a society in which power can be monetized, scholars never stop climbing the academic ladder until they achieve the academician title. Being an academician yields personal benefits as well. One Class 2 professor explained to us that academician is a lifetime appointment. Academicians are not required to retire (otherwise professors must retire by age 65) and enjoy healthcare, transportation (government car), and other benefits enjoyed by officials at the vice-governor level in the Chinese administrative hierarchy.

Sadly, it has been reported that the academician election process has almost become a political campaign that sometimes involves corruption. Zhang Shuguang, former deputy chief engineer of the Ministry of Railways, pleaded guilty to accepting RMB 23 million (around USD 3.8 million) in bribes in 2007 and 2009 to apply for an academician post. He confessed that these bribes were related to the academician election. It was also revealed that a technical book on basic theory and engineering technology applications in the high-speed railway context authored by him in 2007, a cornerstone of his scholarship included in his application, was actually written by a team of 30 professors and associate professors from many disciplines and universities. The fact that he felt a need to offer that much money in his failed bid to get elected (he lost by one vote), and the fact that 30 well-established scholars were willing to write a scholarly book and attribute sole credit to him, is quite indicative of the backdoor dealings in the promotion process.

Unlike professors in the United States, many university faculty in China compete for administrative positions such as dean, associate dean, and even department chair; some even accept positions in university support functions (e.g., director of human resources, etc.). In a society that values power, one senior professor at an elite university told us, an administrative title allows a professor to obtain more resources and command more respect from others, both within and outside academia.

Research

Research is the most important component of scholarship everywhere, and this is now an accepted criterion in China as well. A positive aspect of striving to be world class is that it forces Chinese universities to adopt the same research criteria used by other world-class universities. For example, in basic science disciplines, the elite Chinese universities want their faculty to publish in journals like *Science* or *Nature*. Similarly, Chinese business schools want their faculty to publish in the top 30 academic journals compiled by UT Dallas, or the slightly bigger set of 40 journals listed by Financial Times as the most influential.

The overwhelming majority of Chinese professors are not publishing at this level—yet. Most are under pressure to publish as many papers as possible in journals listed in the *Science Citation Index* or *Social Science Citation Index*. From 2001 to November 1, 2011, Chinese scientific researchers published a total of 836,000 papers, ranking second in the world.[2] Likely influenced by engineering disciplines, Chinese professors are also under tremendous pressure to win research grants and work on industrial projects. Many projects are applied in nature and have little academic value; nevertheless, a faculty member will not be promoted unless he or she has a substantial number of grants and/or projects. Grants and projects are also attractive because they provide supplementary income, as well as support for research, travel, and other expenses. The blind pursuit of these grants and projects, however, has distracted professors from scholarly work in many cases.

One interesting and puzzling phenomenon in China is that administrators are also expected to do research. The dean of an elite business school in China told us that he is expected to win a grant and publish papers, in addition to all the work he is doing as the dean. In the United States, some excellent scholars decided to move

314   *Education System*

into administrative positions later in their careers, but to our knowledge, none continued to work on research while serving as deans or university presidents. They would be derelict in their duties if they continued working on research while serving in such time consuming, stressful, and responsibility-laden roles.

Teaching

Teachers have earned a special place in the hearts of the Chinese people. Not simply bearers of knowledge, they are, historically and culturally, the people who help children become adults. Under Confucianism, the Chinese have been taught to show respect for five things in life: heaven, earth, the emperor, parents, and teachers. Even now, the Chinese use the phrase "Teach me one day, forever, my father" to compliment teachers who have positively impacted their lives.

Things have changed, however, in recent decades. People put professors on par with other professionals such as lawyers or doctors or engineers now. Although professors are still treated with courtesy, the public now has a much lower opinion of them than they once did. One reason is because many professors have focused on income-generating activities in order to make a decent living; thus their careers have become less about the noble pursuit of knowledge and more about the pursuit of wealth. Furthermore, in a society focused on the pursuit of wealth, professors have diminished status because they are not among the top earners in society.

Another part of professors' teaching component is training doctoral students, the next generation of scholars. We have noticed, however, that this relationship has become an exchange of sorts in China. Doctoral students often work on projects for their advisors, and in return, their advisors will help them find good jobs once they graduate. In one instance, we heard a doctoral student complaining so vehemently about his advisor behind his back, we could not help but ask, "If he is so bad and you cannot learn anything from him and have no respect for him, why do you continue to be his student?"

Service

A third component of scholarship, as typically defined in the United States, is service to the institution and to the discipline. Compared to service activities elsewhere, professors in China tend to engage too much in service, and for utilitarian purposes. Given the administrative structure in China, a faculty member is normally not in a position to decline requests from department chairs or deans to help with school-related activities or even requests to work on projects led by senior faculty. As a result, they are spending way too much time on activities that are unrelated to their own research, or even teaching. In addition, service activities are too utilitarian in that they are monetized. As mentioned earlier, everything a faculty member does, regardless of how small, is converted into points which are used to determine his or her compensation at the end of the month. Most service activities (e.g., supervising a Master's thesis) in the United States are considered part of the job and are not directly linked to income. While such points systems help incent professors to engage in service and provide additional income, they also monetize everything a professor does.

Road Ahead

The Chinese can be quite self-critical at times, especially when it comes to scholarship. Many Chinese citizens believe Chinese universities will not achieve world-class status for many years and even claim that there are no first-rate scholars in China. However, we feel that Chinese universities will be among the leading institutions in the world within the next 10 years for two simple reasons: (1) they are now willing to pay a lot of money to attract top scholars to their institutions, and (2) they have now learned to give scholars the discretion and autonomy required to produce impactful work. With this combination, and urban living standards matching those of Hong Kong, Singapore, and even New York, many top scholars (including non-Chinese natives) will join the elite Chinese universities.

Notes

1 Ministry of Education (2012, December 27), "Introduction to a new round of joint building of '985 Project,'" *Reform and Development of Higher Education in China*, retrieved November 2013 from http://www.hie.edu.cn/zcfg_detail.php?id=890

2 Chen Lei (2012, August 13), "Experts responding to SCI questioning: The quality of domestic papers improves faster than the quantity," *Science and Technology Daily*, retrieved November 2013 from http://digitalpaper.stdaily.com/

Part XI
Communication System

49 Unidirectional Communication

We use a four-type classification scheme to describe the different types of Chinese communication: unidirectional, bidirectional, open circle, and closed circle. In this final section of the book, we devote one chapter to each type of communication.

In this chapter, we describe unidirectional communication, which we define as any communication in which a sender conveys information, but there is no easy way for the receivers to share their own information, with either the sender or other receivers. We first provide an overview of unidirectional forms of communication in China, which we follow with a discussion about how unidirectional communication forms are used, by whom, and for what purposes. We then discuss challenges associated with unidirectional communication. In the Road Ahead, we discuss the future of unidirectional communication in China.

Forms

The so-called traditional media are forms of unidirectional communication, and some online and mobile communication forms also belong to this category. Traditional media include newspapers, magazines, books, television, and radio. Unlike other places in the world, however, all of these communication formats in China are considered to be governmental tools for communicating to the masses. As a result, it is quite rare for messages conveyed by traditional media to deviate significantly from official governmental positions. One exception is that some newspapers are allowed to publish investigative pieces on issues such as corruption, as long as content does not contradict overall policies.

An essential traditional print media, newspapers still have a large readership in China. However, along with the rise of digital media and the internet, the popularity of newspapers among the younger generations is declining. According to data on Chinese newspapers in the *China Copyright Yearbook 2012*, a total of 1,928 newspapers are published in China; 217 are affiliated with the central government and 1,711 are local publications. Content-wise, newspapers are either comprehensive or specialized. Comprehensive newspapers, such as *People's Daily* and *Wen Hui Bao*, publish content for the general public, including a variety of news stories and comments. In 2009, 806 different comprehensive newspapers were published, accounting for 41.61% of all newspapers and 68.65% of total print media. Specialized newspapers are targeted to a certain field or age level. For example, *China Health Daily* closely follows healthcare issues, and *China Teenager Daily* is

Figure 49.1 A news stall.

targeted to teenage readers. In 2009, 1,131 specialized newspapers were published, accounting for 58.39% of all newspapers and 31.35% of total print media.

Newspapers are distributed either nationally or locally. In 2009, 225 different national newspapers (e.g., *People's Daily*, *Global Times*) were published, accounting for 11.61% of all newspapers. Local newspapers focus on local news. In 2009, 825 different provincial-level newspapers were published, accounting for 42.59% of all newspapers; 871 different prefecture-level and municipal-level newspapers were published, accounting for 44.97% of all newspapers; and 16 different county-level newspapers were published, accounting for 0.83% of all newspapers.

Magazines and books are two other print-based unidirectional communication formats. It is very difficult to publish a new magazine, but very easy to publish a book. There is tight control over the number and type of new magazines (including academic journals) approved, so someone who wants to start a new magazine typically will try to buy an existing magazine to obtain its publication permit, and then shut it down and publish the new one. This is very similar to the way liquor licenses are handled in many states in the United States. New books are not subject to such quota control, although book contents are reviewed by publishers for any sensitive information.

Television is the most significant traditional media used by the Chinese to maintain contact with society and the outside world. Basically, every household has a television; some even have two or three. All family members typically gather together to watch certain shows. For example, *The Voice of China*, a Chinese reality show based on *The Voice* franchise, is popular across all age groups. Many popular television shows are heatedly discussed on the internet. According to *China Radio and TV Yearbook (2012)*, in 2011, China had 2,607 radio and television broadcasting institutions. Of the 16,753,029 hours of public programing nationwide, 44% were allocated to films and television series, 13.5% to news reports, and 8.5% to variety shows, among others. Programs produced by different television stations (e.g., Hunan sat-TV, Zhejiang sat-TV, Jiangsu sat-TV) are quite varied. In addition to local stations, CCTV-1 is a national comprehensive channel that broadcasts richer content in various formats, including series (33%), news (17%), and variety (10%) programs, among others.[1]

The role of radio broadcasts pales in comparison to press and television. Radio is gradually fading as a communication medium. The Chinese do not often listen to radio nowadays, except some older citizens who have maintained their listening habits, teenagers who listen to music, or drivers who listen to news or traffic information programs. One of our informants who lived in Beijing told us that due to the traffic congestion, radio stations are beginning to gain more listeners and many companies have now increased their spending on radio advertisements. According to *China Radio and TV Yearbook (2012)*, in 2011, there were 197 radio stations nationwide that broadcasted variety programs (27.4%), news (20.3%), and feature programs (23.2%), among others.

As in other parts of the world, many traditional media outlets in China now have a presence on the internet, even on mobile platforms. New online media outlets also have emerged, mostly in the form of news and entertainment websites. As shown in *The 33rd Statistical Report on the Development of China's Internet*, China has 618 million internet users and internet penetration has reached 45.8%. Currently, about 69.7% of Chinese internet users (approximately 410 million people), use desktop computers to surf the internet.[2] Some official government news outlets include xinhuanet.com, china.com.cn, and people.com.cn. In addition, there are four portal websites in China: Netease (163.com), Sina (sina.com.cn), Sohu (sohu.com), and Tencent (qq.com). Netease, for example, provides news, entertainment, sports, finance, and economics information, as well as email services. In addition, Netease provides detailed reports on specific topics.

Video websites also are very popular. Many people watch on their computers, but netizens also watch videos on mobile phones and tablets (either pre-downloaded or via Wi-Fi) to kill time while waiting in line or waiting for the metro or bus. Youku is the equivalent of YouTube, which cannot be accessed in mainland China. Youku is a comprehensive video website focused on news, life, and entertainment, including videos related to sports, automobiles, science and technology, finance and economics, fashion, and humor, as well as movies, television series, and variety shows. Youku is the only commercial website with both broadcasting and television certificates and thus is a legal platform for distributing, transmitting, and marketing copyrighted video programs. More than 60 media outlets, such as Zhejiang TV, Beijing TV, and Guangdong TV, are Youku partners. As of January 2012, the total number of television series on Youku surpassed 60,000. In March 2013, Youku merged with Tudou (Tudou.com), bringing the combined total number of users to more than 305 million. iQiyi (iqiyi.com) is another popular video website. After iQiyi merged with PPS, another video

322 *Communication System*

website, total users hit close to 300 million, ranking it second in the industry based on number of users.[3]

Usage

Unidirectional communication is mostly used to convey news and entertainment content. Here, we describe some of the most popular news and entertainment television programs. *Network News Broadcast* on CCTV (China's Central Television) can be regarded as the exemplary national news program in China, reflecting official governmental positions on a wide range of issues. It has aired from 7 to 7:30 pm every day since September 1, 1982. The program has become an important platform for broadcasting official news with a focus on important events in China and abroad. The news report begins with stories about conferences and visits made by national leaders, followed by brief coverage of important events all over the country, and concludes with approximately five minutes of international news reports. *Network News Broadcast* follows a consistent and strict programming form and style. As in the United States, local sat-TV stations air their local news reports just before the national news broadcast.

Two of the most popular entertainment program types in China are reality shows and historical sitcoms. Reality shows often relate to topics most Chinese people care about these days. One of the most popular is *If You Are the One*, a large dating show open to the public and produced by Jiangsu sat-TV, which first aired on January 15, 2010. As of July 2013, *If You Are the One* was the most watched variety show in mainland China and was being followed by over 4,090,000 netizens on Sina Weibo. On the show, 24 female guests get to know a male guest through three rounds ("feel first," "then assess," "now decide") and indicate their decisions by turning a light on or off. After three rounds, if there are any lights on, it is the male guest's turn to make his choice. *If You Are the One* has sparked major public discussion and debate on values related to love and family life, including money worship and relationships with in-laws.

Historical sitcoms typically highlight contemporary issues in the context of a particular historical event/person/period. For example, the 76-episode series *The Legend of Concubine Zhen Huan* follows the complex relationships among the members of Emperor Yong Zheng's harem during the Qing Dynasty. It unfolds as the heroine Zhen Huan transforms from an innocent girl into a scheming woman. Although the story is set over 300 years ago, the issues confronted by the characters are not dissimilar to issues confronted by employees in the current job market. Sun Li, the actress who plays Zhen Huan, advised white-collar employees to ruminate on the plot of the series: "The philosophy behind all the success and failure of those concubines is easy to understand, and I think it can also be applied to current career life." The plot of another 46-episode series, *Ming Dynasty 1566*, set during the reign of Jiajing, centers on how officials strategize against each other while trying to gain the support of the emperor. Most members of the Chinese audience love watching shows about political struggles and intrigue in the royal court with complicated interpersonal relationships and gripping conflicts.

In addition, Chinese viewers enjoy South Korean and American television programs. Many well educated Chinese especially enjoy American shows such as *The Good Wife*, *The Big Bang Theory*, and *Homeland*.

Challenges

There are three challenges associated with unidirectional communication in China: perceived and/or real information bias, online competition, and competition from open and closed circle communications. Several explicit laws and regulations control the establishment of unidirectional media outlets and the publication of specific content in China. For example, according to Article 11(3) of the *Teleplay Censorship Administrative Regulations* released by the State Administration of Radio Film and Television (SARFT) in 2010, "Teleplays involving serious issues or any issue related to sensitive materials such as politics, the military, diplomacy, national safety, portraying a united front, nationality, religion, the judiciary or public security (hereinafter referred to as special issue), shall present comments in written form from the concerned authorities in the provincial government, autonomous district government, municipal government or superiors." According to Article 15, "The censorship and licensing system is adopted for domestic teleplays, co-produced teleplays, and imported teleplays. No teleplay shall be allowed to distribute or broadcast without a distribution license." In Article 48 of the *Newspaper Publication Administrative Regulations* released by the General Administration of Press and Publication (GAPP) in 2005: "GAPP is responsible for the examination of national newspapers. Local press and publication administrations at different levels are responsible for examining the newspapers published within their administrative regions. Press and publication administrations at lower levels shall submit examination reports to the administrations at higher levels on regular basis. Competent departments shall examine their newspapers and submit examination reports to the local press and publication administrations on a regular basis." In addition, the publishers of unidirectional communications often self-censor their content. As a result, news from unidirectional outlets often is seen as incomplete or even biased, and thus citizens tend to seek alternate information channels.

The second challenge, online competitors, is faced by all traditional media. Like people in other countries, modern Chinese citizens are more likely to seek information online rather than turn to traditional media. In order to survive, unidirectional publishers must now seek a balance between online and offline outlets.

The third challenge is the threat posed by open and closed circle communications (e.g., Weibo, WeChat), which we discuss in two separate chapters. Given the widespread addiction to mobile phones in China, information is normally delivered much faster via open and closed circle communication formats than via unidirectional communication. This threat is especially serious in China, as the Chinese tend to trust information generated by users in their circles more than information generated by the government and conveyed via unidirectional communication channels.

324 *Communication System*

Road Ahead

We do not see unidirectional communication changing substantially in the future. In China, unidirectional communication is considered to be the voice of the government, which must be regulated and, if necessary, financially supported. While current forms of unidirectional communication will persist, we suspect their relevance will further decrease in the lives of ordinary Chinese citizens.

Notes

1 Data based on CCTV's programs from July 29, 2013, to August 4, 2013, retrieved January 2014 from http://www.tvmao.com/program/CCTV-CCTV1-w6.html
2 China Internet Network Information Center (CNNIC) (2014, January), "The 33rd statistical report on the development of China's internet," retrieved January 2014 from http://www.cnnic.net.cn/hlwfzyj/hlwxzbg/hlwtjbg/201301/P020140116509848228756.pdf
3 Yan Huawen (2013, May 10), "Comments on Baidu's purchase of PPS and the messy pattern of the video industry," *iResearch*, retrieved January 2014 from http://www.iresearch.com.cn/View/199387.html

50 Bidirectional Communication

The second type of communication in our classification scheme is bidirectional communication. We define bidirectional communication as any communication in which a sender can share information and the receivers (one or many) can share their own information with the sender, but not with other receivers. We first review how bidirectional communication has been used historically in China and for what purpose, and then we discuss how such communication is used today. Finally, we discuss challenges associated with bidirectional communication. In the Road Ahead, we discuss the future of bidirectional communication in China.

Traditional Bidirectional Communication

Bidirectional communication serves at least two important purposes: to convey messages and feedback between two parties, and to deepen understanding and build a stronger relationship between two parties. The first role is straightforward and has fewer social ramifications. The second role, however, substantially influences how people build relationships and how deep their relationships will be.

Friendship is critical in China. The first paragraph in *The Analects of Confucius* (one of the *Four Books and Five Classics* that serve as the foundation of Confucianism) speaks to the importance friendship: "Having a faraway friend coming to visit, how happy that would be." Indeed, during the 2,000 years since, the Chinese have placed paramount importance on receiving and treating a friend properly.

In the old days, although people wrote (sometimes elaborate) letters to each other, the most important form of bidirectional communication was face-to-face interaction. Based on the teachings of Confucius, many protocols must be followed during such interactions. When one wants to introduce himself to another person for the first time, he must go and visit that person at his house. Going to another person's home for a meeting shows humility. It is also important to bring a gift to show respect and sincerity. The one being visited should come all the way outside of the house to receive the guest in order to show graciousness. They then walk into the house together, normally with the host on the right and the guest on the left. Once the visit is over, the host must walk the guest outside of the house to say goodbye. However, this is not the end of the encounter because the host now must pay the guest a visit. The literal translation of a Chinese teaching is: "[Guest] coming but without [you] going, not a polite behavior." The proper time for a return visit is the next day. Now, very importantly, the original host

326 *Communication System*

should bring the gift received the previously day back to the former guest and current host. So in essence, no gifts are exchanged, emphasizing that the friendship is based on virtue, not on material gain. Of course, if the statuses of the two people are not equal, the lower status person should go visit the higher status person with a gift, but the higher status person will refuse to accept the gift, and will not need to pay the guest a return visit. Over thousands of years of history, the practice of returning gifts gradually disappeared, even though such visits and return visits are still being honored. When two people are of similar status, it is important to bring a gift of similar value or importance during a return visit.

In the past, when a friend came to visit from afar or was going away (often one would not see each other for years, or forever), it was important to treat her with extreme generosity. Some of the most famous poems throughout Chinese history were written for going away parties, which also involved playing music, singing, and (heavy) drinking. One would typically accompany the friend to the starting point of his trip, for example, to the boat if the person was traveling by water, or to the town border. Even in 2013 when we visited Henan province, the cradle of Chinese culture, our local hosts got into another car when we left and followed us until we reached the entrance to the national highway, where we stopped and got out of our cars to say goodbye before we parted ways.

Current Bidirectional Communication

Face-to-face interaction in the form of visiting someone else's home is still an important component of bidirectional communication. It is colloquially called "going from door to door" which essentially means paying visits or simply dropping in, quite often unannounced. It is very common to pay these types of visits to relatives, friends, and colleagues (especially superiors) during the holidays, particularly during Chinese New Year. It is quite common for a government official's home to have a continuous stream of guests during the holidays, all unscheduled. Drop-in visits are also a common form of personal interaction, especially among those who live slower paced lives (i.e., rural residents, retired people), but now people tend to call before they come. It is also common for the leader of an organization (e.g., government branch or business) to visit the homes of the key subordinates who have made substantial contributions or who need support during the holidays, which is a great honor for those who are visited.

This form of communication, however, is quickly being replaced by virtual forms of communication in the fast-paced society of modern China. Regardless, if one pays another person a visit, a return visit is expected, and on both occasions, the visitors must bring gifts. These customs are still alive and well. As a matter of fact, many American professors are puzzled as to why their Chinese Ph.D. students always bring gifts for them when they first come to the United States. Well, it would be rude if they did not, based on Chinese culture.

Unlike in the United States and Europe, there was a relatively short period in China when telephones (fixed line or mobile) were widely available but the internet was not. Even in the late 1980s, only senior government officials had phones at their homes. The telephone was the dominant virtual bidirectional communication tool for just 10 to 15 years, from the early 1990s to the early 2000s.

Another leapfrogging phenomenon also has impacted bidirectional communication in Chinese society. Email was the dominant form of bilateral communication in the United States for a long time after the dawn of the internet age because connection speeds and bandwidth were limited, and text was the only thing that computers and the internet could handle. However, by the time the Chinese widely adopted the internet, computation power had evolved to the point where audio and video could be realistically transmitted. As a result, email has never been a mainstream bidirectional communication tool in China. According to *The 33rd Statistical Report on the Development of China's Internet*,[1] just 42% (about 259 million) of Chinese internet users use email, and typically they are highly educated. One can register and use a Gmail account, but access to Gmail can be slow and inconsistent in China (although there are ways to get around this problem). Therefore, when communicating with a Chinese person, email should not be the primary bidirectional communication tool. Most people who do have email accounts do not check their messages, nor do they reply in a timely manner, as it is not the social norm. Those who interface with non-Chinese colleagues (e.g., academics, business executives) are more likely to use email and reply in a timely fashion, however.

What is much more widely used is something called QQ. Tencent QQ is an internet-based instant messaging (IM) software. Launched in February 1999, it provides online chat, video (similar to Skype), voice, file transfer, etc., and it is one of the most widely used messaging tools in China presently. During the second quarter of 2013, monthly active QQ user accounts reached 818.5 million; in addition, there were 626.4 million monthly active QQ space accounts and 840 million online QQ game accounts.[2] Tencent QQ game is a platform launched in August 2003 that now has more than 70 online games. Students use QQ most frequently. QQ video chat enables users to see people who are far away, so students who are studying elsewhere in China or in foreign countries prefer to chat by QQ with their parents. QQ also is used as an important office tool. Early in 2008, Tencent reported that the number of simultaneous online QQ users in offices hit more than 12 million, four times the number of MSN users during the same period. In corporate settings, most people use QQ to transfer files and exchange information.

The mobile phone is now becoming an increasingly important channel for bidirectional communication. Most people who want mobile phones now have them. In addition to voice communication, text messaging (SMS) is very popular on the mobile phone platform. However, costs for these two traditional services on mobile phones are high in China, so demand has been decreasing recently. The standard price for SMS is 1.67 cents per message (containing about 70 Chinese characters), while a 1 KB message (containing 512 Chinese characters) costs only 0.5 cent on network platforms such as WeChat, discussed in detail in the chapter on closed circle communication. So it is not surprising that SMS experienced negative growth for more than 12 consecutive months in 2013, when the number of point-to-point short messages fell to merely 431.34 billion, a decline of

328   *Communication System*

13.7% from the previous year.[3] The same challenges are associated with traditional voice service. According to the *Telecommunications Industry Statistical Bulletin of the First Half of 2013*, from January 2011 to February 2013, use of voice services dropped sharply from 27.5% to 5%, a 22.5% reduction.

Instead, WeChat has become the preferred bidirectional communication format in China. In addition to its primary function as a social media outlet, it offers text, audio, and video communication, often at a very low cost. We discuss this format of communication in depth in the closed circle communication chapter, as most Chinese value it for its closed circle communication capability.

Challenges

Bidirectional communication is moving to the virtual world on the internet and mobile platforms. This is already fundamentally influencing how people form friendships in China. Circles have been important in China throughout history, but friendship between two people has been the bedrock of Chinese culture since the time of Confucius. Despite their dominant role in modern society, the Chinese have never been taught to develop circles of acquaintances. Instead, the Chinese are taught from a young age to make a few good friends. There is a saying that one could die without regret if he has one friend who truly understands him. Such deep connection becomes much harder in virtual bidirectional communication. The ease of connecting to many more circles at a higher frequency in today's China has come at a cost of decreased emphasis on deeper friendship with a few people. Nearly all interactions are group-based, and one-on-one interactions are out of fashion (or people simply lack the time). Even in the drinking culture, almost all drinking happens during group gatherings. Rarely do two people (friends or not) get together and drink until they are drunk, which is how the Chinese used to connect on a personal level. Because of this shift away from one-on-one bidirectional communication, the content of such communication has become much more superficial in general. Often, our informants told us, the purpose of bidirectional communication today is to remind people you still exist and/or you have not completely forgotten about them.

Road Ahead

Current changes in bidirectional communication in China are consistent with what is happening in other developed countries. The unfortunate aspect is that such changes have torn the fundamental fabric of Chinese society—namely, how one makes friends and maintains friendships. Confucius said in the *Analects*, "One can benefit from three types of friends: those who have honor, those who are honest, and those who are knowledgeable. It will be detrimental if one has three other types of friends: those who kiss up, those who badmouth you behind your back while complimenting you to your face, and those who are glib-tongued." Today's bidirectional communication methods are much more conducive to expressing compliments than honest opinions. There is a danger that people may end up making a lot of the last three types of friends instead of the first three, without even knowing it.

Notes

1 China Internet Network Information Center (2014, January), "The 33rd statistical report on the development of China's internet," retrieved January 2014 from http://www.cnnic.net.cn/hlwfzyj/hlwxzbg/hlwtjbg/201301/P020140116509848228756.pdf

2 Tencent (2013, July), "The performance announcement of the second quarter and the first half year of 2013," retrieved January 2014 from http://tech.qq.com/a/20130814/015686.htm

3 Ministry of Industry and Information Technology (MIIT) (2014, January), "Telecommunications industry statistical bulletin 2013," retrieved January 2014 from http://www.miit.gov.cn/n11293472/n11293832/n11294132/n12858447/15861120.html

51 Open Circle Communication

The third type of communication in our classification scheme is open circle communication. We define open circle communication as any communication among a group of people where a sender can send information, receivers can share their own information with the sender and other receivers, and anyone in the circle can function as a sender. Anyone can join the circle, and people in the same circle typically do not know each other. Such circles may have no, one, or a few people who play central roles. After a brief overview, we focus on Weibo, the most popular form of open circle communication in China. We follow with a discussion on how Weibo is used, by whom, and for what purposes. We then discuss challenges associated with communication on Weibo. In the Road Ahead, we discuss the future of open circle communication in China.

Figure 51.1 Residents in Shanghai show off their pet birds in an early morning.

332 *Communication System*

Form

Historically, open circle communication in China took place in teahouses. People would go to a teahouse, have tea, chitchat with both friends and strangers, share some rumors, and comment on current events or argue about historical events. Anyone could go to a teahouse and join such discussions, but their physical presence was required. There may have been one or more dominant opinion leaders in a given teahouse, but not always. Often, the teahouse owner or longtime waiters effectively functioned as communication facilitators. In some teahouses, various forms of entertainment were offered. In modern China, teahouses have evolved into private gathering places for friends. In its place, Weibo, a microblogging site, has taken open circle communication to a whole new level and become a true phenomenon in China.

Weibo is the Chinese version of Twitter, which is inaccessible in mainland China. Since Sina Corp launched Weibo in 2009, Tencent, Netease, Sohu, People's Network, and others have followed suit and set up their own microblogging platforms. The number of Weibo users surpassed 300 million in 2012, dramatically outnumbering Twitter users, but decreased to 281 million by the end of 2013.[1] Many users have accounts on more than one microblogging platform. On Weibo, users can not only edit their own microblogs with pictures and statements of less than 140 words but also repost others' microblog entries. It is also possible to include a link to a longer post or multimedia content. According to *The 33rd Statistical Report (2014) on the Development of China's Internet*, as of January 2014, the rate of Weibo usage among Chinese netizens was 45.5%. However, the number of Weibo users on mobile platforms had decreased by 5.96 million since the end of 2012 to 196 million, representing 39.3% of users. There are many ways for netizens to access Weibo, including personal computers, smartphones, and tablets. More than 100 million microblog posts are issued every day, a large percentage of which are reposts. Most users access Sina Weibo on mobile devices between 8 am and 11 pm, with an activity peak around 10 pm.

Anyone can open a Weibo account anonymously, although there is also an option to have your identity verified by submitting your national ID or passport. Once verified, a Weibo account is designated with a "V." Both individuals and companies can open Weibo accounts, and even some government agencies have opened official Weibo accounts. While Twitter is prohibited in China, foreigners can open Weibo accounts; many have done so, and their posts tend to be in English.

One can become a fan of another Weibo account without asking for permission from the account holder, thus the open circle nature. Fans can post comments and follow any posts of the account owner. Comments can be seen by all other fans of the same account holder, which essentially establishes information exchange among the fans of the same account holder. The account holder can decide to delete a comment or a fan if she wishes, but it happens quite rarely.

Since the number of fans a person has is public on the Weibo platform, in order to create a perception of popularity, shadow operations exist where a person can purchase more "fans" (thousands or tens of thousands) to make his account look very popular. This increases the probability that a real Weibo user will join, playing on the following-the-masses mentality among many Chinese. While some of these fans are real people, others are so-called zombie fans. Zombies are Weibo accounts that do not correspond to real people. These zombie fans are very cheap to buy; supposedly 4 yuan (67 cents) can buy 1,000 zombie fans.

Usage

Like teahouses, Weibo serves multiple purposes. One can obtain news, spread rumors, access entertainment, express opinions, and simply talk to other people. However, like other internet content in China, the content on Weibo is monitored by the government, and material deemed inappropriate is quickly deleted. (The format used for closed circle communication, WeChat, has not been censored by the government thus far.) We discuss various usages based on the type of account owner—individual, company, or government agency.

Among the 300 million Weibo users, individuals constitute the majority. Just 7% of users have only one account; the per capita number of accounts is 1.45. On each account, an average of 2.13 microblog posts are issued and an average of 3.12 are shared and reposted every day. Users between the ages of 26 and 35 constitute 50.6% of all users, and 87.7% have undergraduate degrees or higher, according to the *2012 Blue Book of China Weibo*.[2] These days, Weibo has developed from a simple platform for receiving news into a public platform that combines social discourse, entertainment, news, public welfare, and marketing.

In addition to posting pictures and statements of less than 140 words, Weibo users can repost and comment on others' microblogs. Original microblogs come in many forms, including organizational press releases, personal remarks about current affairs, humorous anecdotes, or sales promotions. According to the *2012 Blue Book of China Weibo*, many reposted microblogs contain: information and activities related to personal interests or hobbies (50%), amusing duanzi (49.15%), videos (45.93%), inspirational or comforting pieces known as "chicken soup" (45.33%), leisure/gossip/travel information (44.42%), and health/medical treatment/cosmetology information (40%).

Most enterprises and governmental administrations are real registered users. As of September 2012, more than 160,000 companies had registered on Sina Weibo. These companies were distributed among 22 fields; catering services was the most common with 50,000 registrants, followed by automobile/transportation, commercial services, electronics, and IT companies, each with more than 5,000 registrants. According to the *2012 Blue Book of China Weibo*, the top five things Weibo users pay attention to in company posts are discount information (54.01%), the latest information about known brands (53.31%), commodity/product information (47.77%), activities (46.79%), and company/brand activities (42.83%). Since Weibo allows a company to reach its customers instantly, it has also become a battleground for competitive promotion and price matching promises.

Government and party organizations as well as their officials all have verified accounts. According to a 2013 report released by Sina, through the end of October 2013, the total number of government-related Weibo accounts was

334 *Communication System*

100,151, including 66,830 accounts for party and government organizations, and 33,321 accounts for officials. Guangdong, Jiangsu, and Sichuan are the top three provinces with the most government-related Weibo accounts. The three most influential accounts belong to public security offices (30.0%), government administrations (21.5%), and judicial entities (5.0%).The Weibo accounts of judicial entities are quite impressive. Since the Supreme People's Court opened its account in November 2013, the High People's Courts in all 31 provinces and more than 150 Intermediate People's Courts established a presence on Weibo. Prefecture level agencies have the most influence among the netizens. Here is a post from the mayor of Kunmin, the capital of Yunnan province, who had 249,895 followers as of August 1, 2013: "In July, fellow netizens filled me in on many issues, as well as many opinions and suggestions. For the 275 items with clear-cut appeal and suggestions, I have already arranged functional departments to deal with them seriously. As of now, I have replied to 218 items, while the rest are being dealt with." [3]

Challenges

Weibo communication is associated with several challenges stemming largely from its open circle communication format. Here, we briefly discuss three of them: infringement on privacy, rumor spreading, and addiction.

The Chinese generally have less respect for others' privacy than members of other cultures. In addition, Chinese people traditionally like to seek out the opinions of the masses when they get into disputes. Whether their disagreement is with a stranger or a spouse, they typically will get third-party opinions to determine who is right. Weibo has adapted this practice to a much larger scale, often at the expense of other people's privacy and sometimes with dire consequences. In a recent case, a bystander snapped a photo of a taxi driver spitting on a handicapped person that included a partial license plate number. After spreading through Weibo, many users engaged in a so-called human flesh search. Before long, all of the personal information of the taxi driver had been found and revealed on Weibo in retaliation, and he was openly harassed and seriously threatened. The taxi driver made a heartfelt plea to the Weibo community that he was not the person captured on the photo and begged everyone to leave him alone. The Chinese are now becoming more aware that they too could be victims of this kind of privacy infringement and are taking steps to protect themselves. For example, in May 2010 in Hangzhou, a 75-year-old man took photos of a young girl who refused to give him her seat on a bus, and planned to post them online. The girl and her boyfriend asked the man to delete the photos but he refused and the couple called the police.[4]

The second challenge is the spreading of rumors. Compared to users of open circle communication platforms in other cultures, the Chinese are more likely to believe and spread a piece of news without judging whether it is true or false. Unfortunately, one reason for this behavior is their general suspicion of news conveyed through official channels by the government or regular media outlets. In a society that lacks trustworthy information sources, people are more likely to believe and spread something that may not be true. Microblogging sites, with

300 million users and an average of 100 million posts every day, can become cesspools of rumors and false information. It has been reported that 51.7% of rumors in China originate on Weibo.

Why has Weibo become a source of rumors? First, many people share firsthand information about their experiences, feelings, and opinions on Weibo. Although some of the information pertains to real experiences, the fragmented statements can be easily misunderstood by receivers. Thus, widely reposted information may or may not be true. Finally, some people intentionally create fake and sensational news for various reasons, sometimes even just to attract more fans. On September 9, 2013, the Supreme People's Court and the Supreme People's Procuratorate issued penalty guidelines for spreading rumors, lies, and slander on the internet: "Slandering other people by fraud will be affirmed as 'grave' as is stated in the first item of the 246th article of the *Penal Law* once any one circumstance of the following emerges: 1. Very libelous information has been clicked and viewed 5,000 times or more, or reposted 500 times or more; 2. The aggrieved person or his/her close relative develops psychiatric disorders, engages in self-mutilation, commits suicide or experiences other serious consequences."

In February 2010, an earthquake rumor caused millions of Shanxi residents to run into the streets despite the cold early morning temperatures. The Shanxi Earthquake Bureau refuted the rumor afterwards. More often, information is inaccurate or out of date. We once checked the information content of a widely circulated Weibo post asking people to donate clothes and books to children in poor areas. The post[5] included specific information on the schools in need, including contact information, the form of donations, mailing addresses, as well as student photos. After trying to contact all 21 schools included in the post, we were only able to contact one, in Donglan county, Guangxi province, which confirmed their need to us.

The third challenge is addiction. Many Chinese are addicted to Weibo (and WeChat, discussed in the next chapter). To many people, browsing and posting microblogs on Weibo are required daily activities; otherwise, they would feel out of sorts and cut off from the world. There is also an almost compulsory urge to share opinions and daily activities with the world. It is not uncommon for a person who is dining in a restaurant to post opinions about a dish he is eating on Weibo. Even at some dinners we attended, very well educated people put their mobile phones on the table and constantly checked new Weibo posts. (Beginning in 2013, they also spent more and more time checking WeChat.) This behavior would be considered extremely rude in Western countries. In effect, Weibo has replaced much of the actual face-to-face interaction in China and created problems for families, just like any addiction.

Road Ahead

While still the dominant open circle communication tool, Weibo has passed its heyday in China now. It will continue to play an important role in society, but not as *the* communication tool. The communication tool of choice as of 2013

336 *Communication System*

was WeChat, which we discuss in the next chapter on closed circle communication. When we asked people why they are using Weibo less and less in favor of WeChat, they gave us two reasons: Weibo has too much junk now, and the content is censored.

Notes

1 China Internet Network Information Center (2014, January), "The 33rd statistical report on the development of China's internet," retrieved January 2014 from http://www.cnnic. net.cn/hlwfzyj/hlwxzbg/hlwtjbg/201301/P020140116509848228756.pdf

2 DCCI Internet Data Center (2012, December), *2012 Blue Book of China Weibo*, Beijing: DCCI Internet Data Center, retrieved January 2014 from http://vdisk.weibo.com/s/cWAM5

3 The mayor of Kunming, Post on Weibo (23:25, August 1, 2013), retrieved January 2014, http://weibo.com/3258074703/A2MrmwqqR?mod=weibotime

4 Zhu Yan (2010, May 10), "Girl refused to offer her seat and an old man took photos to post online," retrieved January 2014 from http://hznews.hangzhou.com.cn/shehui/content/2010-05/10/content_3263959.htm

5 Retrieved January 2014 from http://mp.weixin.qq.com/mp/appmsg/show?__biz=MzA4 MTA3NTkxOA==&appmsgid=10000136&itemidx=1&sign=4849960f871d205c59216e d5b6bdf0e2&scene=1#wechat_redirect

52 Closed Circle Communication

Recently, a widely circulated duanzi (discussed in Chapter 31) mocked users of WeChat, the dominant form of the fourth type of communication in our classification scheme—closed circle communication. The duanzi goes like this:

> WeChat users marched in the National Day Parade in Tiananmen Square, and the announcer described them as follows: "Ladies and gentlemen, here comes the WeChat group. Look! They are wearing pajamas and shouldering pillows, with iPhones in their left hands and Samsungs in their right hands. Pots of Chicken Soup [for the Soul] are on their backs and Buddhist sutras and secret recipes for health are hanging on their chests. They stride past the stands, looking glassy-eyed and half-dead; meanwhile, they are muttering inspirational classics and duanzi to themselves." Then, President Xi Jinpin said, "Hello comrades! Did you just wake up?" The WeChat group answered loudly, "Hello, Mr. President! What is the Wi-Fi password of Tiananmen Square?"

Anyone who has used (or even seen someone use) WeChat regularly could not help but agree with (and laugh at) the vivid and accurate description of how WeChat has influenced the lives of many Chinese people. When we go to restaurants with friends in China, oftentimes the first thing they say after sitting down is, "What is the Wi-Fi password?"

We define closed circle communication as any communication in which a sender can share information, the receivers can share their own information with the sender and other receivers, and anyone in the circle can function as a sender. Unlike open circle communication, one cannot join a circle unless the circle wants to accept her, and in almost all cases, people in the same circle know each other. Such circles may have no, one, or a few members who play central roles. We first provide a brief overview of closed circle communications in China with a focus on WeChat, which we follow with a discussion about how WeChat is used, by whom, and for what purposes. We then discuss challenges associated with the WeChat communication platform. In the Road Ahead, we discuss the future of WeChat and other forms of closed circle communication in China.

Formats

Closed circles are critical components of Chinese society (as discussed in Chapter 11), so it is only natural that closed circle communication plays an integral part in

338 *Communication System*

Chinese life. A real life face-to-face equivalent would be the dinner parties hosted by members of their circles that Chinese people must attend regularly.

In the West, the most prevalent virtual version of closed circle communication is Facebook. In China, Facebook is banned. But there is an equivalent social network website called Renren Network. Founded on December 8, 2005, Renren Network is the oldest SNS community in China and monopolizes the Chinese market. At first it was only open to undergraduates, but later it was made available to middle school students and white collar workers. It does exactly what Facebook does. One post-80 informant told us that when he was in college, he logged into Renren on his phone before getting up every morning and after going to bed every night to check his classmates' new posts, reposts, and messages. One day he was surprised to find that he had been on Renren continuously for more than 600 days. Every time he got on the internet, he would spend a lot of time skimming Renren pages, whether they were meaningful and interesting or not.

Today, the hot social networking platform is WeChat. WeChat is a mobile text, voice, and video messaging communication service developed by Tencent. The application was launched as Weixin in China in January 2011 and re-branded as WeChat in April 2012 after its expansion overseas. It is available on all major platforms and supports many languages other than Chinese. In essence, it is a type of instant messaging (IM) conducted over mobile platform, similar to the popular WhatsApp Messenger outside China.

Like any closed circle communication format, the more users it has, the more others want to use it. As of November 10, 2013, WhatsApp handled more than 10 billion messages each day. In a December 2013 blog post, WhatsApp claimed that it had 400 million active users each month. By comparison, on January 15, 2013, WeChat announced that they had hit the 300 million user mark, and in August 2013, Tencent announced that it had 100 million registered international users. In mid-2013, daily messages sent surpassed 1 billion.[1]

The popularity and lightning fast adoption of the WeChat platform was enabled by widespread adoption of smartphone technology during the same period in China. The proportion of Chinese internet users who surf the web via mobile phone has reached 81%.[2] In February 2012, the number of mobile phone users nationwide officially surpassed 1 billion. According to *Telecommunications Industry Statistical Bulletin 2013 (January 2014)*, Beijing, Liaoning, Shanghai, Guangdong, Jiangsu, Zhejiang, Fujian, and Inner Mongolia all had penetration rates over 100%.[3] At the beginning of 2013, it was reported that over 66% of Chinese citizens used smartphones. Also, 3G users had already reached 400 million with a penetration of 32.7% of total mobile phone users as of January 2014.

In China, WeChat has drastically transformed the way people communicate. While WeChat enables the type of one-to-one communication normally achieved via telephone, more importantly, it translates real life circles into the virtual world and enables two unprecedented types of interaction. First communication can happen 24 hours a day, 7 days a week since one is assumed to have constant access to a mobile phone. (In real life, people do not even have that level of interaction with their families.) Second, real life interaction can be emulated via real-time multimedia. As on Facebook, WeChat members can post messages and pictures or forward articles and news to their circles and friends can comment or "like" content. However, unlike Weibo and Facebook, users can only see the comments of friends they have in common, which better protects user privacy. In 2012, WeChat also started to provide public platform services, providing a convenient way for enterprises, organizations, media, or individuals to send mass texts; this service is similar to Weibo, with the same inherent pros and cons.

Usage

The Chinese use WeChat as a bidirectional communication tool as well, which we discussed in Chapter 50. Here, we focus on the two WeChat modes that are used for closed circle communication: Groups and Moments. Almost all WeChat users spend the majority of their time in these modes, either sending or reading posts.

Groups are purposefully constructed connections among a set of people. They normally are set up by one person, and new people can be added to the Group only by existing members. Most content on Groups is devoted to real life communication as well as sharing topics of common interest to group members. Any member can post to the Group via text, voice, or video, and everyone in the Group instantly receives that message. There are no moderators, and everyone sees what everyone else has sent. A person who is in a Group can also leave anytime she wants simply by dropping her account from that Group. Groups tend to be semipermanent because they are comprised of people who are close friends in the real world. Temporary Groups are also constructed quite often. For example, one will create a Group for people who plan to attend a particular event, so any updates about the event can be instantly communicated. In a given Group, there is typically no leader, although people may have different levels of power based on their power offline. Of course, the amount of information can be overwhelming as the size of a Group increases and/or one joins more Groups. We know of one Group with 400 members, for example, and posts to the group are literally nonstop. An EMBA student told us that after she checks her WeChat account at the end of a 2-hour class, she may see hundreds of new posts across all of her Groups.

Moments are slightly different and more similar to posts on Facebook. The content on Moments is more diverse and includes personal updates, reflections, useful information, and entertaining pieces (e.g., duanzi). Basically, a user can post anything she likes in the Moments section of WeChat, and all of her contacts in WeChat can see it (unless she explicitly excludes certain people in her contact list from receiving her posts). So in a sense, Moments allow a user to share information with all of her friends, even though some may not know each other. On the receiving end, a user can choose to see all of his friends' posts on his Moments feed, but he may also selectively block some contacts' posts. Friends also can comment on each other's posts on Moments. As mentioned before, WeChat will only show your comments to your WeChat connections, while the author of the original post can see all comments. In the Moments mode, the author of the original post is the center of the circle, but people who know each other can comment on each other's comments to the original post as well.

340   *Communication System*

One important trend on WeChat is the desire to monetize richly connected circles. Just before the Chinese New Year, on January 25, 2014, Tencent launched its Red Envelope app. As discussed in Chapter 3, a traditional way to give money to children (or younger people) and employees is in a red envelope. Tencent created a virtual form of this tradition on WeChat by allowing users to electronically link their bank accounts, instantly capturing users' attention. In addition to enabling users to give virtual red envelopes to individuals, they also created an app that specifically targeted WeChat Groups, called Lucky Money for Groups. With this app, users can choose a total amount and the number of red envelopes they want to send. However, the amount of money each individual receives when he opens his red envelope is decided randomly by the application. This has created tremendous interest among WeChat users. According to statistics released by Tencent, during the Chinese New Year season, about 4.82 million used the Red Envelope app, with a peak of 25,000 red envelopes opened per minute at midnight on the actual holiday. Through WeChat Red Envelope, Tencent has now effectively converted WeChat into a popular mobile payment method. It was actually quite amazing to observe how this event unfolded in real time as we were writing this book and is quite telling of how the Chinese view "freebies," luck, and fun.

Challenges

Closed circle communication formats such as WeChat share a few challenges with open circle communication formats (some more serious than others), as well as a few unique challenges. We discuss four major challenges in this section: addiction, rumor, commercialization, and liability.

The combination of WeChat and smartphones creates a perfect context for addiction. People are becoming increasingly addicted to mobile phones as they become more prevalent. Some have even likened smartphones to inseparable lovers. According to the *White-Collar Phones Index Survey 2013* by Zhaopin.com,[4] the top three cities where white collar workers spend the most time on their phones are Beijing, Xi'an, and Shanghai, with average daily usage of 6.72, 6.15, and 5.45 hours, respectively. Most of that time is spent on WeChat, with Weibo coming in second. Moreover, many of these hours are spent in beds, buses/cars, and bathrooms. To be more specific, more than 70% of white collar workers use mobile phones before they go to sleep, while 55.06% and 43.34% are used in vehicles and while using bathrooms.

More than 80% of white collar workers admit that they are addicted to their phones, and 75.84% keep their phones on 24 hours a day. According to the aforementioned survey, 68.56% look for their mobile phones the moment they wake up; 60.39% clearly concede that face-to-face communications with people nearby are reduced; and 63.59% have poor sleep resulting from their mobile phone habits. Since one has only a fixed number of hours each day for social interaction, many WeChat users have become too busy to spend time with friends and family members in real life. During dinner, many do nothing but take photos, send posts, check Moments, etc. As we have personally witnessed, with WeChat on a mobile phone, it is possible to participate in simultaneous virtual conversations with several Groups and close to 10 friends, all while engaging in a conversation with the people who are sitting at the same dinner table.

It is true that while mobile phones decrease the effects of spatial distance, they increase psychological distance. Indulging in the virtual world for long periods of time can alienate family members and create conflict. In a sense, it brings those who are far away closer, but pushes those who are close farther away. Unfortunately, many Chinese people have not yet realized this.

The second challenge is the spreading of rumors, which is a problem in open circle communication as well. While rumors generally do not spread as fast on WeChat as on Weibo, people tend to trust the information passed along via WeChat much more because they know their contacts personally. We have seen posts in Moments that are absolutely false and unscientific just based on common sense and basic scientific facts, but most members of Chinese society would never correct a friend in front of all of her other friends.

The third threat, which we see as a major one, is the desire of WeChat users to monetize the Groups they are in or to establish Groups for the main purpose of commercial activities. It is perfectly fine for a third party to build a commercial presence on WeChat, where members can opt-in or opt-out, but one crosses an important line when he tries to leverage friendships for money. We are aware of large WeChat groups set up for this purpose (many users are actually business owners), who promote their own products on the group's WeChat space, all to people they otherwise call friends. Many business owners also have asked us how to monetize WeChat contacts. One should think very carefully before crossing this line. Circles may disintegrate quickly if members perceive a motive other than friendship. Whether or not WeChat will continue its growth, or even maintain its position, may likely depend on how untouched it can remain by the pursuit of wealth.

Last but not least, in our view, is the potential liability of WeChat posts. Many people let their guards down when they post or comment on WeChat, as they believe they are among friends. But this is an illusion, as anything one says on WeChat can be quickly reposted to groups that a person does not belong to and be seen by a whole new set of people. More importantly, since WeChat is based on real-time interaction, a person normally posts without thinking twice (which is further complicated by multiple simultaneous interactions). However, since WeChat is a written format that can be preserved forever, unlike spoken language in real life, it cannot be taken back or denied. This can lead to serious potential liability and lawsuits. We have identified at least two types of liabilities. The first is a risk of defamation when people call each other names and make accusations during heated exchanges within a group. (Not all group conversations are pleasant, just like any real life circle.) The second is sexual banter that is very close to (or has already crossed) the line of sexual harassment according to standards in the United States. If someone decides to sue, all exchanges are recorded and nobody can claim that they do not remember. Some posts have left us speechless, many of them written by very successful people. It might take a few lawsuits before people

342 *Communication System*

change how they communicate on WeChat. People currently have a false sense of security and informality.

Road Ahead

The future of closed circle communication, especially WeChat, depends on how some of the challenges listed above are addressed. But Chinese society has historically and continuously been built on closed circles in real life. We do not expect the role of closed circle communication to change, and we do not even expect the importance of mobile closed circle communication to subside. But there will be a happier medium. As one informant told us, WeChat is used to maintain the second most important type of circles; the most important circles still require face-to-face gatherings and communication on a regular basis. We will not be surprised if in a few years, a new type of closed circle communication tool emerges that takes China by storm.

Notes

1 Operation Monitoring and Coordination Bureau (2013, July 5), "The field of information consumption develops well from January to May," *Ministry of Industry and Information Technology (MIIT)*, retrieved January 2014 from http://www.miit.gov.cn/n11293472/n11505629/n11506323/n11512423/n11512603/n11930035/15483087.html
2 China Internet Network Information Center (2014, January), "The 33rd statistical report on the development of China's internet," retrieved January 2014 from http://www.cnnic.net.cn/hlwfzyj/hlwxzbg/hlwtjbg/201301/P020140116509848228756.pdf
3 Ministry of Industry and Information Technology (MIIT) (2014, January), "Telecommunications industry statistical bulletin 2013," retrieved January 2014 from http://www.miit.gov.cn/n11293472/n11293832/n11294132/n12858447/15861120.html
4 Zhaopin.com (2013), "White-collar phones index survey 2013," retrieved January 2014 from http://ts.zhaopin.com/whitecollar/white_collar.html

Index

addiction to internet, mobile phones, and social media 197

administrative system 231–5; constituents 234–5; evolution of 235; internal operations 233–4; organizational structure 231–3

affordability of products 286–7

age: equality 72–3; marital, cultural expectations of 114–5

Age Discrimination in Employment Act (ADEA), The 73

All-China Women's Federation 80, 81, 86, 110, 115

America; *see also* United States: brands 280–1; nightlife in, *vs.* China 213; television programs 323

American Volunteer Group (AVG) 153

Analects of Confucius, The 160, 274–5, 325, 329

Anhui (Hui) cuisine 202

animal zodiac, Chinese 182–3

Annual Report on the Development of China's Study Abroad (2012) 300

Annual Statistics of Chinese Labor (2012) 295

anti-corruption campaign 248–9

appearance equality 73–4

arrest Hu 179

Art of War, The (Sun Tzu) 6

arts and entertainment: cuisines and restaurants 199–206; duanzi 193–7; nightlife 207–13; skills in nine traditional areas of culture 187–91

Asian brands 282

assembly line structure 237

attitude, maintaining positive 131

Australia, emigration statistics for 164

bachelorette status of women 118; *see also* leftover women

bars 212–3

baseline bid 271

BBC Country Rating Poll 155

Beijing, subcultures in 59

Beijing TV 321

bidding on government projects, unwritten rules and 27

bidirectional communication 325–9; challenges associated with 328; current 326–8; email 327; face-to-face interaction 326; future of 328–9; mobile phones 327–8; QQ 327; telephones 326–7; text messaging 327–8; traditional 325–6; virtual forms of 326

binding women's feet 78

black duanzi 193

blood-based tribe 2

blood is thicker than water 262

bodily signals, superstition and 180–1

Book of Honor, The 11

Book of Rewards and Punishments, The 160

Book of Rites 16

books 320

Bo Xilai 12

brands 279–83; by country 280–2; future predictions related to 283; prices of 282–3; reasons for buying 279–80

Breeze Teahouse 212

344   *Index*

bribery 244–7; among government officials 244–5; between businessmen and government officials 244–5; for material goods 245; real estate 245; reasons for 246–7; sexual 245–6; unwritten rules and 27
BSG 274
Buddha jumps over the wall 202
Buddhism 160, 171–2, 175, 179, 180
bureau dues 26
business: drinking behaviors and 42, 43–4, 45; PQSIB in, examples of 38–9; promises 33–4
businessmen, bribery and 244–5
business to business (B2B) market 267–71; no-bid business 268–9; open-bid business 270–1; overview of 267–8
business to consumer (B2C) market 273–7; businesses in 274–6; consumers' view of 276–7; future of 277; segmenting, by city 273–4

calendar system 182–3
calligraphy 188, 190
Canada, emigration statistics for 164
Cantonese (Yue) cuisine 199–200
card games 211–2
Catholicism 171, 179
Cat Theory 253
CCTV (China Central Television) 39, 129, 321, 322
Central Commission for Discipline Inspection 221, 248
Central Committee (CPC) 26, 51, 71, 221, 245, 246, 261, 264, 307
Central Committee for Discipline Inspection 239
Central Government Procurement Center 267
Central Military Commission (CMC) 221, 222
Central Politics and Law Commission (CPLC) 238, 240
Century of Humiliation 151–3
Chen Bokui 248
Cheng guan 53
chess 211–2
Cheung Kong Graduate School of Business (CKGSB) 306
children; *see also* families: challenges faced by 94–5; 4-2-1 family structure and 91–2; 4-2-2 family structure and 95; ideal 99–100; one-child policy 91–3, 95;

relationships between grandparents, parents and 93; 2-1-1 family structure and 92
children of migrant workers 86–7
China Central Television (CCTV) 39, 129, 321, 322
china.com.cn 321
China Consumers Association 276
China Copyright Yearbook 2012 319
China Daily 153, 154
China Europe International Business School (CEIBS) 306
China Health Daily 319
China National Nuclear Corporation (CNNC) 146
China National Petroleum Corporation (CNPC) 147
China National Tourism Administration 287
China Radio and TV Yearbook 320–1
"China's Got Talent" 131
China (Shanghai) Pilot Free Trade Zone 264
China Statistical Yearbook 203, 260–1
China Teenager Daily 319–20
China Youth Daily 125, 233, 302
Chinese Academy of Social Sciences 247
Chinese Cities' Development Report No.4 on People's Livelihood 2011 124
Chinese companies, types of 259–65; FCCs 259–65, 306; PMCs 259–65, 306; SOEs 220, 259–65, 306
Chinese Dream 126; cultural identity and 158–9; wealth accumulation and 126
Chinese Great Leap Forward Movement 26
Chinese Marxism 176
Chinese New Year 18, 23, 31, 118, 193, 326, 340
Chinese People's Political Consultative Conference (CPPCC) 219, 222, 227, 232, 248, 249
Chinese People's University Crisis Management Research Center 103
Chinese Poems Association 190
Chinese Way of Life: An Analysis of Chinese Character, The (Lin Yutang) 161
Chinese way of life (CWOF): foundation of, concets that form 1–7
Chinese zodiac 182–3
Chuan (Sichuan) cuisine 200–1
circles 2; *see also* social circles
Citizenship and Immigration Canada 164
City Urban Administrative and Law Enforcement Bureau (CUALEB) 53

Classic of Filial Piety, The 160
classmates, in social circles 64–5
closed circle communication 337–42; challenges associated with 340–2; formats of 337–9; future of 342; usage of 339–40; WeChat and 337–42
clubs 212–3
collective leadership 217–23, 260
college education 296–7
communication system: bidirectional communication 325–9; closed circle communication 337–42; open circle communication 331–6; unidirectional communication 319–24
Communist Party of China (CPC); *see also* National People's Congress (NPC): Central Committee 26, 51, 71, 221, 245, 246, 261, 264, 307; Chinese Great Leap Forward Movement and 26; corruption and 243, 245, 248–9; EMBA degrees and 307–8; employment discrimination and 69, 71; foreign investment policies and 261, 264; gender based discrimination and 71; harmonious society and 51–2; Politburo Standing Committee and 218–9; religious beliefs of members of 175–6; social thoughts and 251, 253–4; structure of 221
companies, POU and 23
concession-seeking 53
concubines 101–3, 106; corruption and 247
Confucianism 172–5; *see also* Confucius; bidirectional communication and 325, 329; canon of 1, 15–6, 232; contradictions and 160; Doctrine of Mean and 1, 51; etiquette and 15–9; feudal system and 252; friendship and 325; Five Constants of 32; harmony and 51–5; New Confucianism 255; respect and, teaching of 314; social thoughts and 252–2; trustworthiness and 32; usefulism and 5
Confucius; *see also* Confucianism: *Analects of Confucius, The* 160, 274–5, 325, 329; equilibrium and 1, 51; *Four Books and Five Classics* and 15–6; rite-focused education and 16; Shandong cuisine and 201; on women 78
Constitution of People's Republic of China (PRC): court system 238; legislative system 225–7; religious believes, protection and restriction of 175
contradictions 159–61

copycatting 39
corruption 243–9; anti-corruption campaign 248–9; bribery 244–7; desire to live comfortable life after retirement and 247; factors contributing to 243–4; future outlook of 249; immigration and 247; jealousy and 247–8; mistresses or concubines 247; types of 244
court system 238–9
Criminal Procedure Law of the People's Republic of China 22
cuisines 199–206; Anhui (Hui) 202; Cantonese (Yue) 199–200; Fujian (Min) 202; Hunan (Xiang) 202; Jiangsu (Su) 202; Shandong (Lu) 201; Sichuan (Chuan) 200–1; Zhejiang (Zhe) 201
cultural identity 157–62; Chinese Dream and 158–9; contradictions 159–61; historical context of 157–8; personal problems 159; public property and, lack of respect for 161–2; rapid changes in 161
Cultural Revolution 79, 124, 133, 251, 254, 255. 293
cultural stereotypes 57–8
culture: geographic location and 4; skills in nine traditional areas of 187–9
customs and traditions: drinking culture 41–7; etiquette 15–9; gifting 15, 17–9; honor, three-tiered Chinese version of 11–4; presumption of untrustworthiness (PCU) 21–4; promises 31–6; pursuit of quick success and instant benefits (PQSIB) 34–5, 37–40; unwritten rules 25–30
cynicism 6–7

Dai Lake Bridge 179
date of birth and eight characters of a horoscope 182–3
Decisions 69, 71
democratic centralism 225–6
Deng Theory (or Deng Doctrine) 176, 253–4
Deng Xiaoping 72, 223, 253
Department of Immigration and Border Protection of the Australian Government 164
dialect, subcultures and 58, 59, 61
dianping.com 207, 209, 212
Diaoyu Islands 155
dignity 11–2
dim sum 199, 203

346   *Index*

dirty duanzi 193
disabled citizens, employment
   opportunities for 71
disasters, rituals for 16
disrespectfulness, in harmonious society
   54
divorce 107–11; divorced women 109–10,
   111; historical equivalent of 107–8; life
   after 109–10; rate of 108–9
Di Zhi 182
Doctrine of Mean (DoM) 1–2
Dong-A Ilbo 153
Dong Zhongshu 37, 77–8
drinking culture 41–7; in developed *vs.*
   less developed regions 45; drinking as
   job requirement 46–7; historical context
   of 41; interactions with Westerners
   and 45–6; reasons why Chinese drink
   alcohol 42–4; rules of drinking 44–5;
   toasts 42, 44–5
drinking vinegar 199
drumming 16
duanzi 193–7; on addiction to internet,
   mobile phones, and social media
   197; categories of 193; defined 193;
   on distorted social norms 195–6; on
   frustrations in life 194–5; grey 193, 194;
   on public officials 196–7
durable goods 281

economic system: brands 279–83; business
   to business (B2B) market 267–71;
   business to consumer (B2C) market
   273–7; challenges 263–4; Chinese
   companies, types of 259–65; company
   culture and management 261–3; future
   of 264–5; overview of 259–60; products,
   pursuit of expensive 285–9; sectors
   260–1
education: bribes to fund children's
   education 246–7; divorce and 109, 110;
   emancipation of women and 78–9;
   faux emigration and 164–5; gender
   discrimination and 72; ideal child and
   99–100; marriage of women and 116,
   118; migrant workers and 84, 86–7; of
   people's jurors 238; post-50 generation
   and 133; post-60 generation and 134;
   post-80 generation and 135, 136;
   reeducation through labor and 239
education system: college education 296–7;
   EMBA 305–10; K-12 education 293–5;
   K-12 education resources, unequal
   distribution of 295; professors and

scholarship 311–5; studying abroad
   299–303
EFE news agency 280
effortlessism 6
elections, challenges associated with
   227–8
Electoral Law 226
email 327
emigration se faux emigration
emotionalism 5
emotional quotient/emotional intelligence
   (EQ/EI) 268
empathy 268
employment equality 69–75; age equality
   and 72–3; appearance equality and
   73–4; future outlook of 74–5; gender
   equality and 71–2; hiring and 73–4; laws
   to ensure 69–71; promotions and 74;
   retirement (mandatory) and 74; state of
   69–71
empty plate movement 205
entertainment television programs 322
environment 143–8; artificial factors
   contributing to concerns 145; citizen's
   environmental movement 145–7; state
   of 143–5
environmental movement cases 145–7;
   *Resisting Chemical Production (PX),
   Kunming, Yunnan Province, 2013* 146–7;
   *Resisting Metal (Alloy) Production,
   Shifang, Sichuan Province, 2012* 147;
   *Resisting Nuclear Fuel Production,
   Jiangmen, Guangdong Province, 2013*
   146
environmental signals, superstition and
   180–1
EQ/EI (emotional quotient/emotional
   intelligence) 268
equilibrium 1, 51
era of lyric poetry *see* Song Dynasty
era of poetry *see* Tang Dynasty
errand commissions 26
ESSEC Business School 123
ethics: in unwritten rules 26; usefulism
   and 4
ethnic groups: employment opportunities
   for 71; in subcultures 58
etiquette 15–9; *see also* Nation of
   Etiquette; components of 16; favors and
   16–7; gifting and 17; importance of 16;
   pervasive nature of 16; types of 16
European brands 281–2
execution of power, challenges associated
   with 228–9

Executive Master of Business Administration (EMBA) 305–10; experience of 308–10; future of 310; students who enroll in 306–8
extramarital relationships 101–6; concubines 101–3, 106; future predictions of 105–6; mistresses 103–4, 106; social acceptance of 104–5, 105–6

face: concept of 11; within couples, giving 14; dignity and 11–2; do no harm and 13–4; gifting and 18; helping others achieve 13; respectability and 12; saving, promises and 34; self and, achieving for 12–3; superiority and 12; as three-tiered honor 11–2
face-to-face interaction 326
fake products 288
families 91–5; children, challenges faced by 94–5; contemporary structure of 91–3; 4-2-1 family structure 91–2; 4-2-2 family structure 95; grandparents, challenges faced by 93–4; historical structure of 91; major changes in 95; of migrant workers, challenges of 85–7; one-child policy 91–3, 95; parents, challenges faced by 94; relationships between grandparents, parents, and children 93; 2-1-1 family structure 92
fast moving consumption goods (FMCG) 281
fatalism 7
faux emigration 163–7; Australia and, emigration statistics for 164; Canada and, emigration statistics for 164; education and 164–5; future of 166–7; overview of 163; purpose of 164–6; quality of life and 165–6; state of 163–4; United States and, emigration statistics for 164; wealth accumulation and 165
favors 16–7
feeding one's mouth 199
Fei Xiaotong 63
Feng shui 181–2
festivities, rules for 16
feudal system: concubines and 101–2; Confucianism and 252; cynicism and 6; emancipation of women and 78–9; hierarchicalism and 3; New Culture Movement and 251–2; women under, role of 77–8
feudal system, role of women under 77–8
finding the happy medium 51
firefighting 52–3

firefighting and 52–3
First Sino-Japanese War 152, 158
fit to be eaten 199
Five Classics 15–6, 232, 325
five constant virtues 77–8
Five Mountains 16
the fives 29
Flying Tigers 153
food sector, unwritten rules and 28–9
food therapy 189
foot baths 209–10
foreign capital companies (FCCs) 259–65, 306
foreign nations, attitudes towards 151–6; Century of Humiliation and 151–3; Japan 154–5; United States 153–4
foreign policy 3
four arts 187–8; calligraphy 188; Go 187–8; guqin 187; painting 188
Four Books 1, 15, 232, 325
four treasures of study 204
4-2-1 family structure 91–2
4-2-2 family structure 95
freebies 6, 340
friendship, circles based on 64
From the Soil (Fei Xiaotong) 63
frustrations in life 194–5
Fujian (Min) cuisine 202
funerals, rituals for 16

Gan-Zhi 182
Gao Shuzhen 130
GDP 26, 144, 286
gender equality 71–2
General Administration of Press and Publication (GAPP) 323
General Office of the State Council 234
generations 133–6; post-50 generation 133–4; post-60 generation 134; post-70 generation 134; post-80 generation 135–6; post-90 generation 134–5
gifting 15, 17–9; etiquette and 17; face and 18; outlook for societal custom of 19; value of 18; what to gift 18; when to gift 17–8
Glass Street 27
GlaxoSmithKline Investment Co. Ltd. (China) 28
Global Flow of Tertiary-Level Students 299–300
Global Times 123
Go 187–8
going from door to door 326
golden age 188–9, 310

348 *Index*

golden lotuses 78
golden rice bowl 262
good Samaritans, behaving like 130–1
governing system: administrative system
231–5; corruption 243–9; legal system
237–42; legislative system 225–9;
political system 217–23; social thoughts
251–6
government: harmonious society and 51–2;
news outlets 321; POU and 23; PQSIB
in, examples of 40; promises 33; women
in highest levels of 79
government officials, bribery among 244–5
grandparents: challenges faced by
93–4; relationships between parents and
children 93
Grant Thornton International 79
Great Depression 133
grey duanzi 193; *see also* duanzi
*GroupM Knowledge–Hurun Wealth Report
2013, The* 139
Guangdong, subcultures in 59
Guangdong TV 321
guests, protocols for receiving 16
GuoXue 255
Guo Yongxiang 248
guqin 187, 190–1
gutter oil 39

Hai style 60
Han Dynasty 37, 59, 77–8, 107, 124
Han Feizi 32
harmonious society 51–5; concession-
seeking and 53; disrespectfulness
and 54; firefighting and 52–3; future
pursuit of 54–5; as governing doctrine
51–2; historical context of 51; in law
enforcement contexts 54; migrant
workers and 87; timidity and 54
healing 189
healing (food therapy) 189
helping those in need, role models and
130
herd effect 38
hierarchicalism 3
hiring, age discrimination in 72–3
historical sitcoms 322
Holy One, The *see* Confucianism
Home Credit 13
Hongda Mo-Cu (Molybdenum-
Copper) Alloy Deep Processing and
Comprehensive Utilization Project 147
Hongda Square 147
Hong Jinzhou 244

honor 11–2; *see also* face; dignity and 11–2;
dishonor and 12; respectability and 12;
superiority and 12
Horizon China 153
"How Many Leftover Women Deserve Our
Sympathy?" 115–6
Huang Kecheng 26
Hui (Anhui) cuisine 202
Hu Jianxue 179
Hu Jingtao 228
Hukou 98
human flesh search 334
Human Resource Development Report 73
Hunan (Xiang) cuisine 202
husband, ideal 97–8

idealism 4
If You Are the One 322
immigration: corruption and 247
individuals, polymorphism across and
within 4
"inside the system" social thoughts 253–4
instant messaging (IM) 147, 327, 338
interaction, circles based on 64
*Interim Provisions on Strengthening the
Supervision of Party and Government
Officials, The* 165
*Interim Provisions on the Accountability of
Party and Government Leading Cadres,
The* 165
internal investigation system for party
members 239
internet: addiction to 197; as unidirectional
communication 321–2
interpersonal attitudes, POU and 23
interpersonal communication, rules for 16
intra-person polymorphism 4
IQ 268
iQiyi 321–2
iron girl 79
iron rice bowl 262

jade, giving 16
Japan, attitudes towards 154–5
jealousy, corruption and 247–8
Jiang Jieming 248
Jiangsu sat-TV 322
Jiangsu (Su) cuisine 202
Jiang Zemin 311
Jian Zhen 299
jiayuan.com 113
Ji Jianye 248
Jin Dynasty 59, 160
jing jiu 42

karaoke (KTV) 207–9
K-12 education 293–5; exam anxiety and 294; income of teachers 295; NCEE and 293–4, 300; pressure endured by students 294; pressure endured by teachers 294–5; resources, unequal distribution of 295
kickbacks, unwritten rules and 27–8
Klingon 11, 12
Kweichow Moutai Company Limited 41

Lai Hongzhong 244
Lan Pu 247
Lao-Tzu 160
law enforcement contexts, in harmonious society 54
Law on Promotion of Employment 69, 71
Leftover Forever 115
Leftover Goddess 115
leftover women 113–8; age, cultural expectations of marital 114–5; concept of 113; materialization of marriage and 113–4; media and 115–6; parents, relatives, and friends 116–8; spouse searching heuristics, unequal 114; 3U Bachelorettes and 118
legal system 237–42; challenges in current 239–41; court system 238–9; future changes in 241–2; internal investigation system for party members 239; overview of 237–8; POU and 22
Legend of Concubine Zhen Huan, The 322
legislative system 225–9; *see also* People's Congresses
Lianghui 227
Liao Shaohua 248
liberalism 254–5
Li Chuncheng 248
Li Daqiu 249
life, frustrations in 194–5
life objectives 123–6; *see also* wealth accumulation
Life of Reason, The (Santayana) 151
Life Times 46
Li Huabo 247
Li Hualin 248
Li Keqiang 218, 219, 221, 222
Lin Huiyin 78–9
Lin Junde 129–30
Lin Yutang 160, 161, 175
liquor 189
Liu Tienan 244, 248
Liu Wei 131
Liu Yunshan 218, 219, 221, 222

Lucky Money for Groups 340
Luo Qingchang 247
Lushan Conference 26
Lu (Shandong) cuisine 201
Lu Xun 157

magazines 320
Maotai 41
Mao Zedong 21, 22, 23–4, 72, 79, 217–8, 223, 254
marriage and family; *see also* migrant workers: child, ideal 99–100; divorce and divorcees 107–11; extramarital relationships 101–6; families 91–5; leftover women 113–8; spouse, ideal 97–8
Marriage and Family Research Council 105
Martian language 134–5
Marxism 176
massage 209–10
material goods, bribes for 245
materialization of marriage 113–4
May 4th Movement 251–2
mean, finding 1
media, leftover women and 115–6
men: hierarchicalism and 3; ideal husband and 97–8
midnight snacks 211
migrant workers 83–7; children of 86–7; family challenges of 85–7; harmonious society and 87; history and overview of 83–4; marriages of 85–6; new generation of 84; social challenges of 84–5
Migrant Workers Report 83, 85
military rituals 16
military servicemen, in social circles 64–5
Min (Fujian) cuisine 202
Ming Dynasty 21, 59, 124, 152, 202
Ming Dynasty 1566 322
Ministry of Civil Affairs 108
Ministry of Commerce and Industry 265, 282
Ministry of Education 113, 135, 190, 233, 296, 300, 301–2
Mintel 99
mistresses 103–4, 106; corruption and 247
mobile phones 197, 327–8
morals, usefulism and 4
Most Inspiring Chinese, The 129
mouth-watering aroma 199
mutton-stuffed fish 201
My Country, My People (Lin Yutang) 160

350   *Index*

naked officials 165, 247
National Bureau of Statistics, 80, 84, 283
National College Entrance Examination (NCEE) 293–4, 300
National Development and Reform Commission (NDRC) 244
National People's Congress (NPC): bills proposed by 228; Chinese Dream doctrine and 158–9; indirect election for selecting representatives 226–7; meetings 227; *Organizational Law of the National People's Congress* 227; overview of 237; power of, execution of 228–9; relationship with other governmental organizations 225; structure of 222
National Swimming Championship for the Disabled 131
Nation of Etiquette; *see also* etiquette: defining concepts of 16–7; historical context of 15–6; restoring original aspects of 19
Netease 321, 332
netizens 285–6, 321–2, 332, 334
Network News Broadcast 322
new generation of migrant workers 84
Newspaper Publication Administrative Regulations 323
newspapers 319–20
news television programs 322
Ni Fake 248
nightlife 207–13; bars 212–3; card games 211–2; chess 211–2; Chinese *vs.* American 213; clubs 212–3; foot baths 209–10; karaoke (KTV) 207–9; massage 209–10; midnight snacks 211; public dancing 210–1; teahouses 211–2; Western influences 212–3
985 Project 311
no-bid business 268–9
Nohain, Jean 193
non-blood-based tribe 2
non-interference 3
No Quarrelling Theory 253
nouveau riche 139–41; behaviors of 140–1; defining 139–40; preferences of 140–1
Number, Structure and Features of the New Generation of Migrant Workers 2012 84

offerings, etiquette and 16
Office of Academic Degrees Committee of the State Council 306
one-child policy 91–3, 95
open-bid business 270–1

open circle communication 331–6; challenges associated with 334–5; forms of 332–3; future of 335–6; usage of 333–4; Weibo and 331–6
Organizational Law of the National People's Congress 227
Oriental Education Times 294
"outside the system" social thoughts 254–5
overseas shopping 287–8

painting 188, 190
paraxylene (PX) 146–7
parent official 234
parents: challenges faced by 94; leftover women and 116–8; relationships between grandparents and children 93; role models devoted to 131
party members, internal investigation system for 239
peasant workers *see* migrant workers
Penal Law 335
Peng Dehuai 26
Peng Yinbin 246
people.com.cn 321
people-managed companies (PMCs) 259–65, 306
People's Congresses 225–9; direct election process 226; elections, challenges associated with 227–8; execution of power, challenges associated with 228–9; overview of 225–7
People's Daily 319
People's Republic of China (PRC) 102, 175, 222; *see also* Constitution of People's Republic of China (PRC)
personal life: drinking behaviors and 43–4; PQSIB in, examples of 38; problems in, privacy and 159; promises and 34; unwritten rules in 29
Pew Research Global Attitudes Project (2013) 153
PISA test 99–100
PM2.5 166
poetry 188–9, 190
Politburo Standing Committee 218–21
political system 217–23; collective leadership at other levels of government 220–1; CPC 221; future changes in structure 222–3; legislative, executive, and judicial branches 222; Politburo Standing Committee 218–9
pollution 162
polymorphism 4
portal websites 321

Index 351

post-50 generation 133–4
post-60 generation 134
post-70 generation 134
post-80 generation 135–6
post-90 generation 134–5
power, challenges associated with execution of 228–9
pragmatism 4
Premier 231–2
presumption of untrustworthiness (POU) 21–4; companies and, attitudes toward 23; governments and, attitudes toward 23; interpersonal attitudes and 23; legal system and 22; origins of 21–2; persistence of 23–4
prices, brands and 282–3
principles: polymorphism and 4; striving for the middle 1, 2
privately owned companies (POCs) 260
private sector, unwritten rules in 27–9
probable crime 21, 22
products: affordability 286–7; expensive, pursuit of 285–9; fake 288; illegal materials and processes to produce 39–40; overseas shopping 287–8; taxes on 289
professors and scholarship 311–5; future of 315; hiring and promotion 311–3; research and 313–4; service and 314–5; teaching and 314
Project Hope 295
promises 31–6; broken 32–5; business 33–4; context of making 35–6; discerning original intention of 35; governmental 33; personal 34; PQSIB and 34–5; reverting back to traditional value system 36; saving face and 34; social norms around 34; trust and 35–6; trustworthiness and, traditional teaching on 32
promotion, age discrimination in 73
Protestantism 171
protocols, etiquette and 16
public dancing 210–1
Public Official Image Crisis Report—2012 103
public officials 196–7
public property, lack of respect for 161–2
public sector, unwritten rules in 27
purpose, circles based on 64
pursuit of quick success and instant benefits (PQSIB) 37–40; in business, examples of 39–40; causes of 38; effects of 37; future of 40; in government,

examples of 40; in personal life, examples of 38; promises and 34–5; in work, examples of 38–9

Qigong 172
Qin Dynasty 59
Qing Dynasty: Beijing and 59; bribery and unwritten rules 27; contradictions and 160; Hunan (Xiang) cuisine and 202; Manchu and 152; POU and 21; red envelopes and unwritten rules 25–6; Yong Zheng and 322
QQ 147, 327
Queen of Leftover 115

radio broadcasts 321
real estate bribes 245
reality shows 322
Records of the Grand Historian 36, 123
red duanzi 193
Red Envelope app. 340
red envelopes 25–6, 28, 29, 340
Red Second Generation 3, 222–3, 249
relationships; *see also* social circles: drinking behaviors and 42, 43–4; extramarital 101–6; hierarchicalism and 3; usefulism and 4
religious beliefs 171–6; *see also* Confucianism; Buddhism 160, 171–2, 175, 179, 180; Catholicism 171, 179; of CPC members 175–6; diverse 171–5; protection and restriction of 175; Protestantism 171; superstition 179–80; Taoism 160, 171–2, 175, 179
Renren Network 338
"Report of Global Commerce" 79
Report on Public Opinions between China and Japan 155
research, scholarship and 313–4
Resisting Chemical Production (PX), Kunming, Yunnan Province, 2013 146–7
Resisting Metal (Alloy) Production, Shifang, Sichuan Province, 2012 147
Resisting Nuclear Fuel Production, Jiangmen, Guangdong Province, 2013 146
respectability 12
restaurant industry: contemporary 203–4; recent changes in 204–6
retirement, corruption and 247
retirement (mandatory), age discrimination in 73
reverse culture shock 303
rice bowl 199

352   *Index*

Rich Second Generation 3, 307
RMB 15, 27, 28, 33, 41, 93, 103, 110, 113, 117, 123, 125, 136, 139–41, 163, 203, 204, 207, 208, 211, 212, 227, 244–8, 261, 262, 267, 275, 282–3, 286, 289, 295, 311, 313
role models, categories of 129–32; behave like good Samaritans 130–1; dedicated to work 129–30; devoted to parents 131; evaluation of 131–2; help those in need 130; maintain positive attitude 131
romantic relationships, hierarchicalism and 3
routine honoraria 26
rules, unwritten *see* unwritten rules
running 141

Sanlu infant milk powder 28, 136
Santayana, George 151
satisfy emotion, satisfy reason 5
scholarship *see* professors and scholarship
Second Sino-Japanese War 152–3, 154, 155, 158
self, achieving for face 12–3
self-interest, unwritten rules and 26
Senkaku Islands 155
service, scholarship and 314–5
seven cans 107–8
sexual bribery 245–6
Shandong (Lu) cuisine 201
Shanghai, subcultures in 60
Shanghai Pilot Free Trade Zone 264
Shang Yang 36
Shenzhen, subcultures in 60–1
Shenzhen Special Economic Zone 61
She Xianglin 22
Shifang Municipal Council 147
shuanggui 221, 239
Sichuan (Chuan) cuisine 200–1
Silent China, The 157
Sina 321, 322, 333–4
single women *see* leftover women
Sino-Japanese War 152–3, 154, 155, 158
Sixth National Population Census 92, 115, 273
skills in nine traditional areas of culture 187–91; calligraphy 188, 190; Go 187–8; guqin 187, 190–1; healing (food therapy) 189; liquor 189; painting 188, 190; poetry 188–9, 190; swordsmanship 189, 191; tea 189
Snowden, Edward 193
social challenges: extramarital relationships, acceptance of 104–5, 105–6; of migrant workers 84–5

social circles 63–7; classmates in 64–5; fellow military servicemen in 64–5; future utility of, predictions about 66–7; maintenance of 66; raison d'être for 63–4; rules within 65; structure of 65–6; types of 64–5
Socialist Market Economy with Chinese Characteristics *see* Deng Theory (or Deng Doctrine)
social media, addiction to 197
social norms, distorted 195–6
social structure: employment equality 69–75; harmonious society 51–5; migrant workers 83–7; social circles 63–7; subcultures 57–62; women, status of 77–81
social thoughts 251–6; characteristics of 252–3; history of 251–2; "inside the system" 253–4; "outside the system" 254–5; overview of 252
Sohu 321, 332
someone who eats well everywhere 199
Song Dynasty 21, 78, 160, 188
southerners 58–9
South Korean television programs 323
Special Rules on the Labor Protection of Female Employees 72
spiritual epic of the contemporary Chinese 129
spouse, ideal 97–8
spouse searching heuristics, unequal 114
Standing Committee of the Party at "X" *see* Politburo Standing Committee
standing out 1
Star Trek 5, 11
State Administration of Radio Film and Television (SARFT) 323
State Bureau for Letters and Calls (SBLC) 234
State Council 222, 234, 261, 306
State of Yan 59
State-Owned Assets Supervision and Administration Commission of the State Council 248, 261
state-owned enterprises (SOEs) 220, 259–65, 306
stereotypes, cultural 57–8
Stone Theory 253
striving for the middle principle 1, 2
strolls 145–6
studying abroad 299–303
subcultures 57–62; in Beijing 59; cultural stereotypes and 57–8; dialect and 58, 59, 61; ethnic distinctions 58; evolution of, factors influencing 61; in Guangdong 59;

historical 58–9; merging of 60–1; northerners 58–9; in Shanghai 60; in Shenzhen 60–1; southerners 58–9; in Wenzhou 59

Sui Dynasty 232, 234

Su (Jiangsu) cuisine 202

Sun Donglin 31

Sun Shuilin 31

superiority 12

superstition 179–83; date of birth and eight characters of a horoscope 182–3; environmental and bodily signals, inferences about 180–1; Feng shui 181–2; future pervasiveness of 183; overview of 179; religious 179–80

Supreme People's Court 222, 237, 238, 334, 335

Supreme People's Procuratorate 222, 237, 248, 335

Survey of Foreign Brand Favorability in 2012 280, 281, 282

swordsmanship 189, 191

Taiping, Princess 78

Tang Dynasty: Buddhism and 172; as era of poetry 188–9; Kaiyuan Era of, teahouses and 211–2; merchants and, status of 276; overseas education and 299; POU and 21; seven cans and 107–8; women and, role of 78; Wu Zetian and 78

Taoism 160, 171–2, 175, 179

taxes on products 289

tea 189

teaching 314

teach me one day, forever, my father 262

teahouses 211–2

Telecommunications Industry Statistical Bulletin of 2013 328, 338

telephones 326–7

Teleplay Censorship Administrative Regulations 323

television 320–1; American programs 323; entertainment programs 322; news programs 322; South Korean programs 323

Tencent 321, 327, 332, 338, 340

10 Heavenly Stems 182

ten thousand yuan family 134

text messaging (SMS) 327–8

Third Survey of the Social Status of Chinese Women 80

33rd Statistical Report on the Development of China's Internet, The 321, 327, 332

three can'ts 107–8

three cardinal guides 77–8

Three for One 171, 172

"Three Obediences and Four Virtues" 77

three religions and nine schools 160

"Three Represents" 176

3U Bachelorettes and 118

Three Years of Great Chinese Famine 133

Tian Gan 182

Tian Gan-Di Zhi 182

tier of face 11–2; dignity 11–2; respectability 12; superiority 12

timidity, in harmonious society 54

toasts: rules of 44–5; types of 42

"Top 10 Shenzhen Concepts" 61

Tractate on the Unseen Judgment by the Great Emperor of Literary Thriving, The 160

Training and Communication Center of National Health and Family Planning Commission 113

transaction, circles based on 64

transfer taxes, unwritten rules and 29

tribalism 2–3

trust: drinking behaviors and 43; promises and 35–6

Tudou 321

Twain, Mark 6

12 Earthly Branches 182

Twenty-One Demands 152

2-1-1 family structure 92

2010 Survey on the Attitudes and Behaviors of China's Urbanites on Dating and Marriage 105

2013 Report of the All-China Federation of Industry and Commerce on the Top 500 Private Enterprises 261

2012 Blue Book of China Weibo 333

UNESCO Institute for Statistics 299–300

unethical unwritten rules 26

unidirectional communication 319–24; books 320; challenges associated with 323; entertainment television programs 322; forms of 319–22; future of 324; historical sitcoms 322; magazines 320; newspapers 319–20; news television programs 322; online media 321–2; radio broadcasts 321; reality shows 322; television 320–1; usage of 322–3; video websites 321–2

United States; *see also* America: attitudes towards 153–4; emigration statistics for 164

United States Immigration and Customs Enforcement 300

unwritten rules 25–30; future changes in 29–30; origins of 25–6; in personal

354   *Index*

life, examples of 29; in private sector, examples of 27–9; in public sector, examples of 27; unethical 26
usefulism 4–5
us *versus* them mentality 2–3
utilitarianism 4

video websites 321–2
Villages of Concubines 102
Vimalakirti sutra 160
vote buying 227, 229

"Walk the Gobi Desert" 310
Wall Street Journal 281
Wang Chengming 244
Wang Qishan 218, 219, 221
Wang Suyi 248
Wang Yongchun 248
Wang Yuexi 246
War of Jiawu 152
wealth accumulation; *see also* nouveau riche: campaigns promoting 124–5; Chinese Dream and 126; cultural identity and 161; diversified life objectives and 125–6; as dominant life objective 123–4; factors contributing to dominant role of 124–5; faux emigration and 165
wealthism 5
Wealth-X 140
websites, video 321–2
WeChat 66, 147, 193, 197, 327–8, 333, 335, 336, 337–42
Weekly Quality Report 39
Weibo 147, 331–6, 339, 340, 341
Wen Hui Bao 319
Wenzhou, subcultures in 59
Western influences on nightlife 212–3
white-black contracts 271
White-Collar Phones Index Survey 2013 340
White Paper on China's High Net Worth Population Consumption Demand, The 164
wife, ideal 98
women; *see also* divorce: children and career 80; Confucius on 78; current status of 79–80; divorced 109–10, 111; emancipation of 78–9; female senior executives, percentage of 79; under feudal system, role of 77–8; future status of 80–1; gender equality and 71–2; in government 79; hierarchicalism and 3; ideal wife and 98; marriage and career 79–80; in 1911 to 1976 78–9; oppression of 77–9; regional differences associated with status of 81;

status of 77–81; stereotyping 80–1; "Three Cardinal Guides and the Five Constant Virtues, The" 77–8; "Three Obediences and Four Virtues" 77
work; *see also* employment equality; migrant workers; women: drinking behaviors and 42, 46–7; PQSIB in, examples of 38–9; role models dedicated to 129–30
World of Go, The 189
world views: cultural identity 157–62; faux emigration 163–7; foreign nations, attitudes towards 151–6
Wuliangye Yibin Company Limited 41
Wu Zetian 78
Wu Zhanhui 244

Xiang (Hunan) cuisine 202
Xi Jinping 133, 158–9, 205, 218, 221, 222, 248
xinhuanet.com 321
Xuan Zang 299
Xu Guojun 247

Yangpu district of Shanghai 110
Yangtze River Delta city-group 274
Yi Junqing 248
yin-yang contracts 271
Yi Ya 201
"You Are the Heavenly April on Earth" (Lin Huiyin) 79
Youku 321
YouTube 321
Yuan Dynasty 59, 152
Yuan Shaodong 244–5
Yue (Cantonese) cuisine 199–200
Yu Zhengsheng 218, 219, 222

Zen Buddhism 172
ZengZi 32
Zhang Baoqing 233
Zhang Dejiang 218, 219, 221, 222
Zhang Gaoli 218, 219, 221, 222
Zhang Shuguang 312–3
Zhang Wentian 26
Zhaopin.com 340
Zhejiang TV 321
Zhejiang (Zhe) cuisine 201
Zhe (Zhejiang) cuisine 201
Zhou Dynasty 59, 77
Zhou Xiaozhou 26
Zhou Zhenghong 248–9
zodiac, Chinese animal 182–3
zombie fans 333